Reinventing Allegory asks how and why allegory has survived as a literary mode from the late Renaissance to the postmodern present. Three chapters on Romanticism, including one on the painter J. M. W. Turner, present this era as the pivotal moment in allegory's modern survival. Other chapters describe larger historical and philosophical contexts, including classical rhetoric and Spenser, Milton and seventeenth-century rhetoric, Neoclassical distrust of allegory, and recent theory and metafiction. By using a series of key historical moments to define the special character of modern allegory, this study offers an important framework for assessing allegory's role in contemporary literary culture.

CAMBRIDGE STUDIES IN ROMANTICISM 22

REINVENTING ALLEGORY

This series aims to foster the best new work in one of the most challenging fields within English literary studies. From the early 1780s to the early 1830s a formidable array of talented men and women took to literary composition, not just in poetry, which some of them famously transformed, but in many modes of writing. The expansion of publishing created new opportunities for writers, and the political stakes of what they wrote were raised again by what Wordsworth called those "great national events" that were "almost daily taking place": the French Revolution, the Napoleonic and American wars, urbanization, industrialization, religious revival, an expanded empire abroad, and the reform movement at home. This was an enormous ambition, even when it pretended otherwise. The relations between science, philosophy, religion, and literature were reworked in texts such as *Frankenstein and Biographia Literaria*; gender relations in *A Vindication of the Rights of Woman* and *Don Juan*; journalism by Cobbett and Hazlitt; poetic form, content, and style by the Lake School and the Cockney School. Outside Shakespeare studies, probably no body of writing has produced such a wealth of response or done so much to shape the responses of modern criticism. This indeed is the period that saw the emergence of those notions of "literature" and of literary history, especially national literary history, on which modern scholarship in English has been founded.

The categories produced by Romanticism have also been challenged by recent historicist arguments. The task of the series is to engage both with a challenging corpus of Romantic writings and with the changing field of criticism they have helped to shape. As with other literary series published by Cambridge, this one represents the work of both younger and more established scholars, on either side of the Atlantic and elsewhere.

For a complete list of titles published see end of book

REINVENTING ALLEGORY

THERESA M. KELLEY

University of Texas at Austin

CAMBRIDGE
UNIVERSITY PRESS

Published by the Press Syndicate of the University of Cambridge
The Pitt Building, Trumpington Street, Cambridge CB2 1RP, United Kingdom

Cambridge University Press
The Edinburgh Building, Cambridge CB2 2RU, United Kingdom
40 West 20th Street, New York, NY 10011–4211, USA
10 Stamford Road, Oakleigh, Melbourne 3166, Australia

First published 1997

Printed in the United Kingdom at the University Press, Cambridge

Typeset in 11 on 12.5 point Baskerville

The University Cooperative Society has generously awarded a subvention
for the publication of this book.

A catalogue record for this book is available from the British Library

Library of Congress cataloguing in publication data
Kelley, Theresa M.
Reinventing allegory / Theresa M. Kelley.
p.   cm. – (Cambridge studies in romanticism: 22)
(Includes bibliographical references and index.)
ISBN 0 521 43207 3 (hardback: alk. paper)
1. Allegory.   2. Literature – history and criticism.
1. Title.   11. Series.
111. Series: includes bibliographical references and index.
PN56.A5K45   1997
809'.915 – dc20   96–44963   CIP

ISBN 0 521 43207 3 hardback

CE

For Thomas and Patrick Baylis

Contents

Illustrations

Acknowledgments

Oh, there's nothing to be hoped for from her! she's as head-
strong as an allegory on the banks of the Nile.
Sheridan, The Rivals 3.3, in Plays 60

Sheridan tells the truth, but there is more. I began this book as a fellow of the Society for the Humanities at Cornell University. I thank its director Jonathan Culler, as well as Mary Jacobus, Reeve Parker, and Cynthia Chase, for conversations then and since. I complete this book in gratitude and homage to Elizabeth Dipple, whose generous intellect and spirit were gifts indeed to her students and friends. I am fortunate to have been both. Other colleagues, far-flung and close at hand, have helped me to think about this project: Leah Marcus, Rita Copeland, Peter Manning, Susan Wolfson, Neil Fraistat, Andrew Cooper, Kurt Heinzelman, Sheila Kearns, Warner Barnes, Richard Sha, Frederick Hoerner, Elizabeth Hedrick, John Farrell, Lance Bertelsen, Frank Whigham, Berndt Lindfors, Michael Simpson, Barbara Goff and Kevin Gilmartin. At Cambridge University Press, Kevin Taylor encouraged this project, as have Marilyn Butler and James Chandler, general editors of Cambridge Studies in Romanticism. Josie Dixon has given this book unwavering support at every stage. Linda Bree, Leigh Mueller, and the production staff at the Press meticulously supervised the last stages. Albert Field kindly gave permission to use the image that appears on the cover. The American Council of Learned Societies, the National Endowment for the Humanities, and the Research Institute of the University of Texas at Austin have generously supported my research and writing of this book. The curatorial staffs at the Harry Ransom Humanities Research Center, the New York Public Library, and the Yale Center for British Art welcomed all research inquiries and made my work much easier. For all kinds of help along the way, I thank other friends and, from first to last, Thomas and Patrick Baylis.

List of Abbreviations

Note to the reader

In addition to the abbreviations listed below, parenthetical and note references follow these conventions: VI:10 (meaning volume and page); 10.2 or 10.2.2, p. 35 (book/canto . line/stanza, followed by page); 5.4.2 (act.scene.line); and 365, *Blake* 45 (meaning line 365 in *Blake*, page 45).

Annals	*Annals of the Fine Arts.*
BL	S. T. Coleridge. *Biographia Literaria.*
Blake	William Blake. *Complete Poetry and Prose.*
Browning	Robert Browning. *Poems.*
CN	S. T. Coleridge. *Notebooks.*
Coleridge	S. T. Coleridge. *Poetical Works.*
CPW	John Milton. *Complete Prose Works.*
FQ	Edmund Spenser. *The Faerie Queene.*
GS	Walter Benjamin. *Gesammelte Schriften.*
Keats	John Keats. *The Poems of John Keats.*
LJK	John Keats. *Letters.*
PL	John Milton. *Paradise Lost.*
PR	John Milton. *Paradise Regained, the Minor Poems, and Samson Agonistes.*
Prelude	William Wordsworth. *The Prelude 1799, 1805, 1850.*
PU	Percy B. Shelley. *The Prometheus Unbound Notebooks.*
PW	Percy B. Shelley. *Complete Poetical Works.*
"*SM*"	S. T. Coleridge. "Statesman's Manual." In *Lay Sermons.*
SPP	Percy B. Shelley. *Selected Poetry and Prose.*
SWorks	Percy B. Shelley. *Complete Works.*
TL	Percy B. Shelley. *The Triumph of Life.*
RB	Robert Browning. *The Ring and the Book.*
WProse	William Wordsworth. *Prose Works.*

CHAPTER I

Introduction

Ariosto and *Spencer* ... are hurried on with a *boundless, impetuous* Fancy over Hill and Dale, till they are both lost in a Wood of Allegories, – Allegories so *wild, unnatural,* and *extravagant,* as greatly displease the Reader. This way of writing mightily offends in this Age; and 'tis a wonder how it came to please in any.

Blackmore, "Preface," Prince Arthur

Blackmore's 1695 complaint snappishly declares what many readers since the Renaissance have disliked about allegory. Evidently unnatural, made-up and extravagant, allegory is an affront to the realist, empiricist bent of early modern and modern English culture from the end of the sixteenth century to the present. Yet whatever else it is, the story of Spenser and Ariosto lost in a "Wood of Allegories" is a brief allegorical vignette. Few readers in Blackmore's time or ours would fail to recognize this allusion to the opening scenes of the *Divine Comedy* and *The Faerie Queene*: much as Dante in the middle of his life finds himself lost in a wood, so do Una and the Red-crosse Knight become lost in the wood of Error.[1] Although Blackmore does not mention Error, it is hard not to imagine this "wild, unnatural, and extravagant" figure as the unindicted co-conspirator of his complaint. Even if this allusion is supposed to be parodic, the resonances it sets in motion work for allegory, not against it. Picture Spenser and Ariosto lost in a wood and you create a persuasive emblem of the allegorical tradition that reminds readers why people read, or once read, allegory.

Scholars have long insisted that similar objections, which become commonplace in English culture by the late seventeenth century, mark the end of allegory as a viable symbolic mode. The reasons given for this cultural event include: the replacement of Platonic "realism" by the nominalist conviction that "Truth" and "Justice" are names, not ideal universals; a sharp decline in literary allusions to myth and biblical typology; the dissolution of the system of aristocratic patronage which had supplied learned readers who knew how to read arcane allegories and emblems; the Protestant and Puritan animus against complex or learned emblems and allegorical interpretations of the Bible; and arguments in favor of verisimilitude and a "plain style." Under the collective pressure of these cultural shifts, it has been claimed, allegory is forced out by the standard-bearers of modernity: empiricism, historiography, realism (in the modern sense), and plain, rational speech.[2]

I agree that these shifts produced the end of allegory as a symbolic mode based on Platonic ideas, Christian theology or syncretic versions of these and other belief systems. My argument in this book concerns rather the allegorical impulse in modernity that persists despite Blackmore's effort to write its epitaph and a chorus of similar objections from the late English Renaissance to the present. If allegory is evidently alive and well in recent critical theory and metafiction, it is so because it has managed to survive in modernity's fundamentally hostile climate.[3] That hostility is especially intransigent in the English literary and philosophical tradition, which rightly supposes that allegory is a key metafigure for the role of abstractions in thought.[4] It assumes a fully canonical shape when English Romanticism casts out allegory in the name of the symbol. Throughout much of the twentieth century, the figure of allegory as a lackluster literary remainder has been a staple of Anglo-American literary criticism. The same figure lives on in the cultural mainstream.[5]

This book asks two related questions: why does allegory survive modernity and what does modernity (still) have against it? The answers I give emphasize English literary culture, whose critique of allegory casts its modern character into sharp relief, and within this tradition, the internal conflicts in Romanticism which allegory dramatizes. I argue that allegory survives after the Renaissance, against pressures that ought to have done it in, by making border raids on the very categories that have been presented as its contraries: realism, mimesis, empiricism, and history. The claim that allegory should be set apart from history and realism has for too long masked the degree to which all three terms are implicated in questions about knowing and representability that permeate modern culture. In opposition, as it were, ever since the Renaissance, allegory maintains a shadow ministry by encroaching on and mimicking those in power. Like the forced "marriages" between different cultural zones in Doris Lessing's *Canopus in Argos*, allegory makes unexpected alliances with historical and realist particulars to insure its status as a resident alien in modern culture. For this reason, it is an important modern site for what W. J. T. Mitchell calls "literary theorizing as an activity scarred by history."[6]

Although the cultural shifts that accompany allegory's passage into modernity occur throughout the West, they are especially marked in English culture after the mid seventeenth century, when theories of knowledge and language – from simple to complex – are used to justify Restoration arguments in favor of a plain rhetorical style that rejects extravagant figures like allegory. Behind this philosophical occasion I believe there is another – the partisan use of allegory before, during, and after the English Civil War to vilify assorted oppositions. Thereafter, the Neoclassical objection to allegorical agents in the epic and the Romantic polemic against allegory register different interpretations of its figural power. Arrayed in opposition to the cult of the particular, the historical, and the phenomenally real, allegory becomes the abjected "other" to be cast out in the name of modernity. At the high end of nineteenth-century French realism, "A Real Allegory" – the key phrase in Courbet's subtitle for *The Painter's Studio*, – limits allegory to the picture space created by this painter and his aesthetic objects.

Though I grant the factitious, provisional character of terms like Renaissance, Neoclassicism, and Romanticism, they are essential to the story I tell about allegory's role in the cultural and political temper of modernity.[7] For if Neoclassicism is not exclusively the age of empiricist epistemologies, it is an era in which a preference for observable phenomena works against allegory. Although not all writers of this era assent to these views, those who do assume that the truth value of empirical evidence is superior to that of fabulous allegorical narratives.

My approach to this topic is selective and textual, not encyclopedic. I emphasize moments in English culture when its resistance to allegory is strongest: the iconoclast critique of allegory in the sixteenth and seventeenth centuries; the Neoclassical attack on allegorical poems and paintings; the Romantic ambivalence toward allegory; Victorian efforts to sustain the division between allegorical and realist narratives; and the return to allegory in twentieth-century critical theory and recent fiction. The philosophical framework I give this argument moves beyond the limits of English culture to assess what is at issue at key moments in allegory's modern survival. Four writers anchor my discussion of those moments.

The first is Spenser, an exemplary allegorist who nonetheless assents to the iconoclastic critique of emblems and allegorical narratives. I contend that this paradox, textually inscribed in *The Faerie Queene*, is an instructive site for recognizing how the theory of allegory becomes in modernity "an activity scarred by history." The second is Milton, an anti-royalist, anti-allegorist who, in *Paradise Lost*, serves up allegorical figures that trouble later efforts to separate allegory from particularity and history. The last two are Hegel and Benjamin, who specify allegory's conflicted appeal in Romantic and post-Romantic English culture. Hegel assumes that allegory is what Neoclassical writers had said it was – excessively fantastic, not very interesting, rigidly abstract, or by turns all of these. In practice however, he imagines allegory in two ways: as a rigid system of figural reference and as an unstable, prolific circulation of external, "sensuous shapes" that overpower or diversify inner, ideal content. Different versions of this hidden ambivalence infiltrate the Romantic preference for symbol over allegory and extend the logic of Romantic experiments with visual and verbal figures.

For Benjamin, who inaugurates the modern critical return to allegory, it occupies a world where Hegel's hoped-for alliance between inner spirit and outward form has given way. In its place are melancholy or exuberant allegorical figures that are brilliantly reinventive. Whereas Hegel's analysis of Persian and Indian poly-theist art dramatizes the lure and danger of allegory, Benjamin's theory of allegory looks backward, then forward to a post-industrial understanding of material forms in a feverish pursuit of receding spirit or essence.

The weight of this study falls on the Romantic era, when early modern and modern thinking about allegory enters a new, more explicitly theoretical phase whose effects are still being felt in contemporary criticism. Romantic writers give a definite (and at times indefinite) shape to apprehensions about allegory that had been brewing in England since the Renaissance. Though they insist on the priority of the symbol over allegory, they nonetheless make remarkable use of allegorical figures. Until recent decades, this Romantic ambivalence went unrecognized, probably because it existed below the threshold of the critical discourse Coleridge inaugurates concerning the symbol as the capable figure for the containment of meaning in a translucent form. Twentieth-century critics who have been persuaded by Coleridge's preference for the symbol conclude that allegory has no significant role to play in the modernist aesthetic, whether realist or symbolist.[8] I argue to the contrary that allegory does play such a role, for reasons that follow from its modern character as a mode of figured speech with compelling narrative interests.

As this description suggests, I situate modern allegory's differences from its predecessors within the domain of rhetoric, in part because Greek and Romantic rhetoricians were among the first in the West to theorize about allegory but more essentially because allegory's rhetorical nature persists throughout its long history. Even its modern detractors imply as much. Thus when Coleridge asserts that allegory is alien because it is so evidently made up, he recognizes a fundamental truth about allegory as a figure of rhetoric. Allegory *is* alien; its ancient rhetorical status as "other speech" survives all other adjustments. There is always an irreducible difference between allegorical representation and its referent, whether that referent is a Platonic idea or a prelapsarian world to which Christian allegorists harken back. Either way, allegory is "a genre of the fallen world."[9]

In modernity, allegory looks even more alien and monstrous because the lack of a stable referent for its "other speech" invites exaggeration of its extremes. At one extreme are its material agents – whether texts or images or real referents or all of these – on which allegory depends to convey what lies at its other extreme – the provisional, transcendent idea to which those agents putatively refer. For De Man, irony and deferral are figural markers for the distance between these two extremes. Both occur in earlier allegorical theory and practice. Quintilian defines allegory as a figure of irony and, as Freccero's readings of Dante's *Inferno* make stunningly clear, ironic deferral is a narrative constant in this medieval pilgrimage to eternity.[10]

As allegory enters modernity, its relation to rhetoric shifts ground in two ways: its figures and visual imagery become identified as the effective, because material, agents of allegorical meaning; and as its abstractions seem to become more material, they also become strategically linked to pathos, the rhetorical figure that accords human feeling to strong figures. Whereas the first reworks an ancient

rhetorical alliance between allegory and images, the second tempers
its more emphatic and at times mechanical abstraction by returning
to Longinus, who had argued that pathos justifies the use of hyperbolic figures, including allegory.

Whether it is a personified figure who acts, an emblematic scene
or tableau, or a guiding figural impulse within a narrative, modern
allegory reimagines its ancient philosophical proximity to *phantasia*,
variously defined since Plato as image, imagination, phantasm,
illusion, and fancy. Quintilian advises orators to become skilled in
phantasia (literally "image-making") because this figure depicts absent
things as though they were present (*Institutio* 6.2.29). This advice,
which later rhetoricians echo, specifies the logic of allegory's reliance
on images, whether imagined or visual. Medieval allegorists and
commentators assumed that because words were imperfect guides to
meaning, images might "at some ideal level of visual form" be
transparent to higher truths.[11] For Protestant iconoclasts whose
arguments against images, especially allegorical ones, are differently
at work in Spenser and Milton, the medieval concept of ideal visual
form seems to have dropped away. Since the Renaissance, allegory
has been "beset by images" in the sense that its pictorialism is often
taken to be a material agent in the production of allegorical
meaning.[12] Thus Neoclassical writers who object to the hermeneutic
complexity of traditional allegory argue that allegory ought instead
to use highly simplified visual images or verbal imagery.[13] So much
for the medieval and neo-Platonic argument that allegories and
emblems help readers imagine the ideal visual form or idea of their
"other speech."

The compressed visual wit of the allegorical emblem survives in
modernity nonetheless, like the return of the repressed. It turns up,
for example, in Freudian and post-Freudian accounts of the figurative logic of the dreamwork. Echoing Quintilian and Freud on
phantasia, Ricoeur suggests that dream images work like words
because "a figured language ... gives a contour or a visibility to
discourse."[14] Like Freud's dreamwork, allegory's punning verbal
(and visual) wit invites readers to work out its meaning by piecing it
together from the figures and images at hand. In recent metafiction,
including magical realism, science fiction, and cyberpunk, this
allegorical disposition sponsors a near-riot of combinatorial possibilities in figures and in plots.[15]

This critical understanding of allegorical language and imagery rejects earlier assertions that the literal text of an allegory is merely a "veil" which conceals its hidden, allegorical meaning from all but the initiated. Quilligan blames medieval exegesis or *allegoresis* for manufacturing this split, which Renaissance neo-Platonists also assert when they creatively misread Egyptian hieroglyphics as models for how the allegorical emblem hides philosophical secrets.[16] Yet among late classical and medieval writers, the operative term seems not to have been "veil" but *integumentum*. Allegoresis, which "delivers up" the allegorical meaning, is that integument. As its skin or husk, the work of allegorical interpretation is to specify the outward shape for allegory's "other speech."[17] Few recognitions are as prescient for modern allegory, where putative distinctions between narrators, readers or theorists, and allegory tend to dissolve. Thus, for example, Benjamin's readings of late nineteenth-century Paris, Baudelaire's poetry, or Baroque German tragedy are themselves allegorical, as are readings supplied by the narrators of Browning's *The Ring and the Book*, Hoban's *Riddley Walker*, or Murdoch's *The Sea, the Sea*.

Beginning with Neoclassical writers, modern critics of allegory have repeatedly objected to its abstraction or, conversely, to its presentation of abstractions that come to life. Among recent critics, Fletcher has noted the demonic agency of medieval and Renaissance allegorical figures that move compulsively toward reified abstractions. Mitchell wryly notes the loss of a reliable allegory with the demise of Communism in the old USSR: "the United States ... has emerged as the undisputed heir to the crown of imperial dominatrix, when there is no longer an 'Evil Empire' to provide a kind of global moral allegory." Hollander suggests that a deft poetic ekphrasis might "rescue the very personhood of allegory from captivity by the reductive language of its own inscriptions."[18] As these assessments and Spenser's story of Malbecco make clear, allegorical abstractions have a tremendous undertow: they drag human particularity toward a fixed form and idea.

If, as Hagstrum argues, "a powerful, allegorizing strain *can* drain a conception of all visual and palpable reality,"[19] modern allegory more typically uses images that reify abstraction. Confronted by such figures, readers become restive and testy. In Texas, tanned youthfulness (as a reality or faded vision) and Southwestern summers define a highly visible subculture. In the heat of one Texas summer, as I waited for a traffic light to change, I saw this sticker on a white convertible whose male driver was tanned, blond, and middle-aged:

"the occupants of this car may seem larger than life." With all the *brevitas* of a Renaissance emblem,[20] this composite text of message, car, and driver suggests why allegory has a bad name in all but the most rarefied critical circles. Self-conscious and extravagantly fictitious in its appropriations of real objects and people, allegory may zoom into view then veer away into its own atmosphere, leaving ordinary mortals behind in the heat and dust.

Critical theory is hardly immune to this implicit tyranny of readers and texts. Consider this passage from a recent article in an academic journal: "Most of the famous modern agendas for history are allegorical – historiographic allegories, literary allegories. Hayden White's tropological encoding of history slips into allegory ... The Hegelian–Marxist agenda is perhaps the purest allegory ... Equally allegorical ... is the most optimistic of all models for conceptualizing history, the program of literary realism."[21] I have exaggerated the schematic vicegrip of this statement by omitting its descriptions of each theorist's particular concerns. So reconfigured, the statement is both victim and perpetrator. Because this ironic self-consciousness matches the present critical climate, we are disposed either to find allegory everywhere or to pick up allegorical moves that earlier generations of readers missed. This disposition risks, though, grinding all texts into the mill of fixed, unyielding abstractions.

Whether it is identified with the German Baroque, nineteenth-century industrialism, or a Nietszchean will-to-power shared by critics and figures, this implied figural violence haunts modern theories of allegory. As Hertz observes, de Man's "lurid figures" convey a violence that looks as though it might be real and material, not figural. Teskey argues that this violence is a metaphysical necessity inasmuch as allegorical abstractions are fundamentally hostile to human particularity.[22] As a figure that both names and abstracts, allegory is prone to "forms of violence" akin to those imposed by a tribe or community on a victim who is punished in the name of, or instead of, everyone else.[23] In contemporary theory this violence takes the form of a temptation to invent abstract schemas.

The role of pathos in modern allegory is one warrant for taking this risk. For without pathos, allegory might otherwise constantly reproduce the mechanization that Neoclassical critics hoped for (a mechanical allegory is at least safely dead), but which Romantic and post-Romantic readers have despised. A recent children's film about appliances that come to life suggests how pathos redirects modern allegory such that its abstractive powers are checked by feeling and particulars. Titled *The Brave Little Toaster*, the film puts pathos on show with a story about several home appliances, including the toaster-hero of the title, who leave an abandoned summer cabin to search for the boy who used to come to visit them. Once the appliances come to life, as it were, they look like a demented parody of Neoclassical complaints about allegorical abstractions that walk and talk. When the built-in air conditioner, whose grillwork looks like a real mouth and eyebrows, learns that the other appliances are about to leave the cabin as it cannot, it explodes with rage, its "mouth" and "eyebrows" violently contorted. After cracking the walls, it freezes over in an apoplectic fit. As a mechanical "face" that freezes in an expression of fury (and freon), the air conditioner dramatizes the compulsive rigidity of allegories that are so demonically propelled by the logic of the abstraction they represent that they become rigid, mechanical figures.[24] Like allegory's will-to-power, visibly at issue when the abstraction represented is fury or rage, this appliance will brook no opposition.

Yet the pathos of the air conditioner's predicament also disrupts this figure of mechanical anonymity. Left alone and trapped in the walls of an abandoned cabin, what else could it be expected to do but explode in a fit of impotent rage? When the other appliances are later rescued from a garbage dump by a warm, friendly man who takes them to his appliance repair shop, they barely escape vivisection. In the film's last scene, the boy (*their* boy) finds the appliances just in time to save them from being crushed on a conveyor belt and thrown onto the scrap heap. *The Brave Little Toaster* dramatizes the internal contradiction within modern allegory. For if the film's characters are on the one hand just appliances with interchangeable parts, they feel passionately and struggle heroically. Modern allegory gains its characteristic purchase by shuttling at least as awkwardly between human attributes and abstract ideas, as Neoclassical writers repeatedly complain. To make this shuttle work, to be believable as the appliances are believable, allegory needs what ancient rhetoricians call pathos, the strong feeling that justifies exaggerated, even monstrous, figures.[25] With its carefully sustained relay between feeling and mechanization, *The Brave Little Toaster* shows how modern allegory works along the border between pathos and abstraction.

In recent theories of allegory, pathos is more sharply at issue with the loss of a secure transcendent referent for allegory's "other

speech." As a narrative figure whose subject is technically absent
because not literally represented in allegorical texts and images,
allegory has long been a figure of desire, hence the erotic plots
(sublunary and divine) of medieval and Renaissance allegories like
The Romance of the Rose, Dante's *Commedia*, and Spenser's *Faerie Queene*.
Although it is differently marked in the work of Benjamin and de
Man, their unrelenting critical desire for a lost or alien referent
invites a strong readerly pathos for what allegorical figures do not or
cannot contain, and even for the personhoods of these critics.[26]

Modern allegory requires an enlivening, particular shape to get
our attention. For if we still read it, we do so because of this
unexpected convergence between particularity, strong feeling, and
abstract ideas. In this sense allegory offers one way to reimagine the
ancient debate between Plato and Aristotle about the relative
importance of particulars and abstractions. Whereas Plato asserts the
priority of universal ideas or abstractions over particulars, Aristotle
argues that particulars direct our understanding of abstract principles. Nussbaum finds confirmation of Aristotle's position in Plato's
teacher Socrates, whose unreformed desire for Alcibiades shows how
a particular person animates eros, whereas the argument that all love
objects are equally valuable does not.[27] Or, as Nussbaum argues
concerning Sophocles' *Antigone*, "it was one thing to *ask* Creon to
describe his views about the family; it was another to confront him
with the death of a son." For Creon, the moment of tragic recognition is his son's suicide, after which he can no longer take refuge in
abstraction, generalities, or ideas as the work of the state. Such
examples urge Aristotle's claim that the adherence to principle must
go through, not above, particulars.[28] In modernity, the force of
allegory similarly depends on its capacity to animate and thereby
particularize its figures, even when it careens toward the spiritual,
the other-worldly and away from representations that seem so real
you could touch them.

My argument here works in counterpoint to de Man's theory of
allegory. For though he insists that allegorical figures are forged in
time and subject to decay, the cumulative effect of his readings is
surprisingly transhistorical: allegory becomes the property of language in general, a plot of figures redone and undone that is
"modernist" insofar as it echoes twentieth-century modernism's
sense that it is cut off from the past and thus outside history.[29] For
this reason, the "rhetoric of temporality" he ascribes to allegory does

not include asking how it might change over time to register variable pressures on its figural speech. de Man thereby assents, though for different reasons, to the Neoclassical demand that allegory be held apart from particular human actions and historical events. Nor is it always possible to claim, as de Man does, that allegory is an adequate defense against the "aesthetic formalization" of the Romantic symbol and self-referential philosophical systems.[30] Allegory is at least as capable of reifying its abstract or material referents, although it does so openly by wearing its factitiousness on its sleeve (so to speak), whereas the symbol presents itself as an organic form that is indivisible from its transcendent ground.

I argue in this book for an ethical and rational potential in modern allegory that de Man very nearly refuses when he critically aligns rationality with the formal closure of the symbol and the philosophical claims of Kant's third *Critique*.[31] Because it is wayward, provisional, and openly factitious, modern allegory can assist a line of reasoning that breaks open self-enclosed symbols or systems and thus break out of the "habitus" of culture, whose patterns of received knowledge would otherwise close off inquiry.[32] Thus, if it is always possible to end up with an allegory like Spenser's Malbecco, in the end no longer a man but a beast named Jealousy, allegory may also sustain the assorted claims of particularity, feeling, and abstract idea that Spenser's narrative teaches Britomart to become. As such, modern allegory is a metafigure for the rule of abstractions over particulars (or the reverse) and the presence or absence of knowable referents.[33] This book assesses when and how allegory moves either toward abstraction or toward particulars from the Renaissance to the present.

Readers who are wary of grand narratives will recognize the extent to which this argument posits such a narrative. Some will also recall Jameson's charge that master narratives are allegorical insofar as they manifest a "political unconscious" with a strong desire for hegemonic control.[34] I have written this book with these cautionary tales in mind. I offer here warrants for risking this argument nonetheless, beginning with its implications for theories of genre.

The improvisational character of modern allegory encourages forms and patterns that do not always resemble traditional medieval or Renaissance allegories. Longxi complains, with some justice, that the postmodern enthusiasm for allegory, which tends to find it everywhere, needs to be more stringent about what is and is not allegory.[35] Others have objected that what emerges after Spenser is not allegory, but something else – *allegoresis* or interpretation writ large. In some measure, these complaints assume what Derrida rather provocatively calls "the law of genre," which supposes that a genre is largely defined by a set of traits. For those who imagine that genre works in this way, transgressions lead to "impurity, anomaly or monstrosity."[36] Throughout its long history, allegory is guilty as charged: it has been (and still is) a rhetorical figure, a carefully patterned narrative or dramatic form or genre (more strictly defined),[37] and a method of interpretation. Because allegory after the Renaissance often looks like a transgressive mutant of earlier forms, it is more useful to approach its modern history with a different premise about how genres work. As Rosmarin observes, the real power of genre may be its resistance to strict notions of what a given genre can include.[38] Much as Renaissance theories of genre emphasize the "resources of kind" in generic hybrids and mixed modes, so does allegory gain new strength by being impure, anomalous, and monstrous.[39] What interests me about modern allegory is less its accommodation to a transhistorical idea of allegory than the way its social, cultural, and aesthetic differences interfere with the reiteration of traditional formulae. For this reason, my argument is alert to works that challenge what Jauss calls "the authoritative generic norm" to keep "the historical process of the genre moving."[40] Jauss's formulation conveys the tension between generic authority and radical change that is written all over modern allegory, which makes sustained but quirky use of precedents from classical rhetoric to Spenser.

A second warrant for my argument derives from its claim to be a literary history. Post-structuralist critics have objected that history, particularly literary history, is theoretically and practically impossible because it can never be complete, accurate or fully objective.[41] So what passes for history is necessarily makeshift, an "inelegant bird's nest" of bits and pieces that catch the eye of scholars who feather their nests with what lies at hand. No reader of Lévi-Strauss could fail to see how this figure demotes the structuralist's *bricolage*.[42] Other liabilities are logically consequent: explanatory models used to justify haphazard collections of evidence are tediously evolutionary (rise, fall, or rise and fall), "too much inclined toward watersheds and convulsive turning points," or impatient with enlivening particulars because they disturb a masterplot.[43]

This critique is at once unyieldingly perfectionist and resistant to the need for synecdoche, for positing a whole of which one's work is part, to do the work of criticism. For if all such backward glances are partial, so is all intellectual work, subject as it is – and as modern allegory repeatedly shows – to exigencies of time, place, and subject. Yet precisely because any retrospective discussion of modern allegory is partial, circumstanced by its own time and place, it offers a critical advantage. Like all explanatory models, my argument gives access to details that might otherwise escape notice. From where we stand now, we can see how the work of reinventing allegory is not alien, but intrinsic, to modernity.

The analogy Nietzsche uses to argue that we need to forget the past suggests that it may be worse not to do history, including literary history. Because those who look at present culture from an imagined vantage point in the past may decide that the future can offer nothing better (those were the good old days), it is better, Nietzsche suggests, to confine our understanding to the "closed and whole" horizon of the present, like a herd of animals mindlessly but contentedly chewing its cud.[44] If ever a simile cut against the grain of an assertion, this one does. Reading the same figure, Barker charges that it represents the disaster of postmodern theory and consumption.[45]

This book argues rather that allegory is a historically contingent genre and idea whose survival in modernity retrospectively conveys the cultural and literary interest of its earlier forms and historical moments. With each "return call" on its past, modern allegory makes one of many "uncertain and incremental return[s] to a starting point" that Hobson uses to describe the post-structuralist understanding of history. To explain how this process works, she compares it to the game of *fort-da* which Freud noticed his young grandson invent after seeing his mother go out of the room and then come back. Freud concludes that the boy initially repeats these words to reassure himself that she will return as before and, with each subsequent reiteration, he becomes more confidently aware of his separateness from his mother. As Derrida notes, Freud himself returns on several occasions to his grandson's game. Because these returns – like the boy's repetition of the words *fort-da* – are each different from the last, they are incremental, not identical. Hobson makes yet another return to the boy's game and what these two psychoanalysts have made of it to argue that, as each "return call" builds incrementally on the last, it produces not one but several different sets of claims about the meaning of the game.[46] Even so do I understand the history of allegory's modern reinvention. With each return to its earlier moments and forms, allegory becomes incrementally different, yet strangely familiar.

CHAPTER 2

Allegory, phantasia, *and Spenser*

There are certain experiences which the Greeks call φαντασίας,
and the Romans *visions* [*visiones*], whereby things absent are
presented to our imagination with such extreme vividness that
they seem actually to be before our very eyes.

Quintilian, Institutio 6.2.29

> All those were idle thoughts and fantasies,
> Devices, dreames, opinions unsound,
> Shews, visions, sooth-sayes, and prophesies;
> And all that fained is, as leasings, tales, and lies.
> Emongst them all sate he, which wonned there,
> That hight *Phantastes* by his nature trew.

Spenser, FQ 2.9.50–52[1]

Quintilian's praise for *phantasia* (literally "a making visible") is a
virtual set piece in the history of rhetorical theory and practice.[2] It
asserts that a rhetorical style that mimics those "certain experiences
which the Greeks call *phantasia*" is likely to be more forceful, hence
more persuasive. I want to read this praise against the grain of its
familiarity, as a statement about how early philosophical and
rhetorical interest in *phantasia* exposes questions about representation
that haunt allegory's modern reinvention. For it is allegory's principal game to bring ideas to life and thereby make absent things
seem present. In early rhetoric and philosophy, the alliance I identify
between *phantasia* and allegory is implicit and to some degree
conjectural, but crucially at issue in a long dispute about whether
phantasia is the basis of representation or merely a rhetorical tool. In
late classical and medieval literary culture and hermeneutics, *phantasia* and allegory repeatedly intersect on the terrain of the dream
vision. In the Renaissance, those who advocate a vivid rhetorical
style and emblematic allegory are also suspicious about *phantasia* by
way of its English cognates – "fantasy" or "phantasy," "fancy,"

"feigning," "outlandish appearance" (Shakespeare's Lucio is "a fantastic"), "phantasm," "image," and "imagination."

When allegorical figures are so vivid that they seem to come to life, they dramatize the resources and hazards of fictions whose meaning is suspended somewhere between human particulars and abstractions. The alliance between *phantasia* and allegory thereby refuses the logic of a well-policed division between the allegorical text and its meaning or "other speech." In the *Purgatorio*, argues Freccero, Dante's *fantasia* bodies forth meaning (and bodies) in ways that are modelled on Statius' theory of conception.[3] As fertile invention, *phantasia* exemplifies one of allegory's career paths from the classical era to the Renaissance. Along another, more familiar path, allegorical figures and images are the veil or obscuring curtain flung over a meaning that is hidden and made available only to readers whose philosophical or theological preparation is sufficient for the task of deciphering difficult signs. Renaissance writers mistakenly (albeit fruitfully) compared this task to reading Egyptian hieroglyphics. So understood, the literal events and figures in an allegory are an impervious cover for meaning hidden beneath, or behind, the surface of the text.[4] Under the sign of *phantasia*, the more "fantastic" or "phantasmatic" an allegory's visual and lexical surface is, the more it challenges the topos of allegorical darkness and impenetrability simply by calling attention to that surface. At the same time, and precisely because they exceed verisimilar norms, its figures resist the desire for allegories whose meaning is fully declared on the surface of text and image.

Spenser's allegorical practice tacks between these two paths in ways that are brilliantly informative about the direction of allegory's modern reinvention. Thus if *The Faerie Queene* is a cornucopia of emblematic scenes and actions,[5] what those scenes and actions mean is more likely to be obscure than apparent and thus easily misread. It is hardly surprising that the poem warns against the lure of *phantasia* by allying most of its English cognates ("image," "dream," "prophecy," "insatiable desire," "vanity," "fancy" – meaning "unreasoned interest or attraction" – and, above all, "delusion") with some degree of moral or interpretive failure. For although Spenser admits elsewhere that "fantasie is strong,"[6] in *The Faerie Queene* he projects the liabilities of imagination and vision onto forms of vice that are unforgettable because they are so pictorial, beginning with the monstrous figure of Error (*FQ* 1.1.14–15). When these ideas cluster near the figure of Archimago, they specify the degree of moral hazard Spenser locates at the heart of his allegorical method.[7] By these turns of argument and figure, his divided engagement with *phantasia* anticipates later doubts about allegory, including those expressed by theorists who scapegoat this poem and allegorist for making allegory's inherent difficulties visible.

Protestant iconoclasm informs Spenser's persistent relay between allegorical tableaux and scenes in which those tableaux are destroyed.[8] For the poem is *phantasia* writ large, a fertile, poetic invention with visions false and true. Everybody makes mistakes and errs along its allegorical paths. The Red-crosse Knight begins with a simple-minded equation of truth or essence with visibilia that causes no end of trouble. Britomart cannot read aright her dream-vision in Isis Church. Even readers of the poem are, like Spenser's characters, sublunary wanderers at work and play (or simply lost) in an allegorical terrain, reading cues as best we can. Because it is a narrative and not simply a series of fixed emblems, Spenser's poem looks like the dreamwork of a vast Renaissance emblem on the move. Its allegorical wit, like that of dreams, is the interplay of image, text, and the reader who is prepared both to play the game and to acknowledge the allegorical seriousness thus put in play.[9] To read *The Faerie Queene*, readers must experience the lesson of its "alienation effects" – those scenes whose phantasmal or delusory images bring readers (and characters) up short by reminding them that what they see may not be real virtue but its "false semblance."[10] Within the poem, "semblance" is the term often used to describe visions that turn out to be false. By echoing Puttenham's contemporary definition of allegory as "false semblance" in this way, Spenser emphasizes the limitations of his allegorical pictorialism.[11] Collectively these difficulties make the poem a critical text for thinking about the modern reinvention of allegory, where diverse engagements with images and curious fictions look back to Spenser through mirrors fissured with differences and glimpsed similarities.

When it first appears in late classical Greek sources, the term *allegory* (ἀλληγορία) is used more or less synonymously with ὑπόναια, a classical Greek word that means "conjecture," with a hint of "doubt" or "suspicion." As Jean Pépin explains, "conjecture" (literally ὑπο-νοεῖν or "under-thought") describes the epistemological relation between a sensible given – whether an object of perception, a narrative, or a work of art – and its "intellectual representation."[12]

It is in this sense that allegory is a metafigure for broader questions about the relation between texts and their referents or, more precisely, how it is that texts refer (or whether they refer). To explain how allegory conveys its meaning and works on an audience, the Greek rhetorician Demetrius declares: "In the phrase actually used the speaker has shrouded his words, as it were, in allegory (ἀλληγορία). Any darkly-hinting expression is more terror striking, and its import is variously conjectured (ὑπονοούμενον) by different hearers. On the other hand, things that are clear and plain are apt to be despised, just like men when stripped of their garments" (*On Style* 365). Here Demetrius uses etymological evidence to argue that allegory entails conjecture about its meaning – precisely what readers do to make sense of ideas.

Whereas allegory is etymologically linked to doubt, obscurity, and conjecture, *phantasia* designates what is visible or made visible. Plato is resolutely committed to a bare and thoroughly dismissive construal of this etymology. In *The Republic* and other dialogues, he assigns *phantasia* (usually translated as "imagination") to those false "visions" which the god will not fabricate.[13] Aristotle's subsequent and much more equivocal use of the term provokes an inquiry that continues into the late classical era, particularly in Stoic logic, where the term signifies the fundamental "presentation" on which arguments depend. In *On the Soul, phantasia* means variously "sense impressions," "weakened sensation," the memory of an absent sense experience or emotion (here synonymous with *energeia* [ἐνέργεια]), "imagination," and, with an air of unwilling admission, the mental process in reasoning beings called "deliberative imagination."[14] In his *Rhetoric*, Aristotle uses *energeia* as a near-relative to *phantasia* to specify the forcefulness of metaphor in general as the act or actualization of something a person is capable of doing or habitually does; in the *Poetics*, he argues that if an action is to appear "life-like," it must seem to be actually carried on before us.[15] Thus identified with rhetorically persuasive figures and an epistemological range of meaning that extends from simple sense experience to the cognitive activity required to invent images, *phantasia* looks like trouble.

This early disagreement about whether to grant *phantasia* epistemological status forecasts its split personality in English, where it is usually translated as "imagination." Its less desirable affiliation to false visions or hallucinations is foisted off on "phantasy" (or "fantasy" or "fancy"). In the nineteenth century, Coleridge "desynonymizes" the terms so that he can claim "imagination" for Romantic poetry by sequestering "fancy" as a lesser, derivative mental operation.[16] The long, intervening history of affiliations between *phantasia*, allegory, and the rhetorical forcefulness of certain figures actively resists Coleridge's subsequent claim that they belong to distinct semantic fields.

That history begins with the Stoic reply to Plato and Aristotle. Unlike Plato, the Stoics preferred to reify "acts of knowledge" instead of forms or universals, in part because they recognized no essential difference between divine or physical reason and human reason. They may well have been intrigued by the range of meanings Aristotle assigns to *phantasia*. For in Stoic logic the term is a critical anchor for mental operations. Writing in the second century AD, Longinus briefly defines *phantasia* along lines developed by the Stoics and taken up by Greek and Roman rhetoricians:

Weight, grandeur, and energy in writing are very largely produced, dear pupil, by the use of "images." (That at least is what some people call the actual mental pictures [φαντασίας].) For the term Imagination [φαντασία] is applied in general to an idea which enters the mind from any source and engenders speech, but the word has now come to be used predominantly of passages where, inspired by strong emotion, you seem to see what you describe and bring it vividly before the eyes of your audience.[17]

Longinus here joins ideas or forms to pathos, then places these terms under the sign of *phantasia*, a conjunction that reemerges with instructive force in Romantic poetics. Especially striking is his assertion that *phantasia* "engenders" language. Stoic philosophers imagined the relation between these terms as a two-way street: "language makes *phantasiai* explicit, and *phantasiai* bring language into existence."[18] To distinguish the kinds of *phantasia* available to animals and humankind, they argued that only the human mind experiences *phantasia logike* – impressions or presentations that are accessible to different levels of rational inquiry. By a process of rational, comparative inquiry, Stoics supposed, the mind is able to determine whether a *phantasia* is true or false.[19]

Modern scholars emphasize the deictic character of Stoic *phantasia* as that which points to or indicates "not merely itself but also that which is supposed to have brought it into existence." The Stoics themselves compare this aspect of *phantasia* to *ekphrasis*, the verbal description of works of art that are absent from the lexical terrain of such descriptions, and made available only by means of *deixis*.[20] So defined, *phantasia* subtends allegory's identification with the pictorial and the ekphrastic as deictic signs that point elsewhere. It also specifies the mental activity that allegorical presentations require. Finally, because *phantasia* is aligned with what is visible or can be made visible, it works in productive opposition to allegorical abstraction. The Stoic claim that *phantasia* is heuristically more valuable than abstraction forecasts the special relationship between sensible particulars (imagined or perceived) and abstraction in modern allegory.[21]

The classical and medieval impulse to ally allegory with expressive, visible figures is similarly at work in the early history of *figura*. In his survey of that history, beginning with Latin and Hellenized Roman sources, Auerbach notes that *figura* means "plastic form," something living and dynamic. Not surprisingly, this usage is prominent in Ovid. It is also well represented by Pliny the Elder's observation that the *figurae* of a portrait are "extremely life-like." Tertullian and Augustine distinguish "figural" interpretation from what Auerbach calls a "purely abstract" notion of allegory. The kind of allegory these and later writers willingly identify with *figura* is grounded in historical events. Hence the use of figural interpretation to mean the study of Old Testament events as prophetic types or signs later fulfilled by events in the life of Christ and His disciples.[22] It is in this sense that the figural is living, dynamic, even historical. So allied to allegory, *phantasia*, like *figura*, insists on the attachment of allegorical meaning to a visible or imagined form and, more broadly, on the necessary proximity of abstractions to real particulars.

In one sense Roman rhetoricians seem not to have been interested in the relation between allegory and conjecture, although they too present allegory at its most extreme as riddle or enigma, hence deliberately obscure and mysterious. Quintilian's caution on this point is instructive (and meant to be so): "when, however, an allegory is too obscure, we call it a riddle: such riddles are, in my opinion, to be regarded as blemishes, in view of the fact that lucidity is a virtue" (*Institutio* 8.6.52). This description implicitly discounts the earlier Greek notice of an alliance between allegory and conjecture. Yet Quintilian also makes use of arguments derived from Cicero and the Stoics to situate allegory in a contestable middle ground between the evidence of the senses and the lack of such evidence. He does this by offering *inversio, illusio, ironia* as synonyms, and by presenting a number of figures and terms that collectively specify the figural work allegory can be expected to do: *prosopopoeia* (personification), *visiones* (*phantasia* or φαντασία), *illustratio,* and *evidentia* (*enargeia* or ἐνάργεια; sometimes confused with *energeia* or ἐνέργεια).[23]

By transliterating the Greek term *enargeia* or ἐνάργεια as "vividness," Quintilian confuses terms that more often than not remain confused in the ensuing rhetorical tradition, which frequently presents *enargeia,* usually translated "vigour" or "clearness," as a variant or approximate term for *energeia,* the vivid or lifelike quality conveyed by dynamic imagery.[24] This shift from Aristotle's definition of *energeia* as a philosophical idea of action or actualization to a style that counterfeits it repeats the slippage in the meaning of *phantasia,* which throughout its long history has been understood to mean "false visions," "phantoms," and "apparitions," as well as "sense impression," "imagination," or (in Stoic logic) "presentation." Quintilian actually secures the double identification of *enargeia* and *energeia* with *phantasia* by suggesting that *energeia,* translated as "vigour" in the modern Loeb edition (whose translator does not correct Quintilian), is a "near relative" to other aspects of style, among them *phantasia* or imagination, "which assists us to form mental pictures of things" (*Institutio* 8.3.88–89).

As Quintilian becomes more expansive about what *phantasia* accommodates and how it arises, he forecasts its role in medieval discussions of dreaming as an occasion for allegorical narrative or interpretation:

When the mind is unoccupied or absorbed by fantastic hopes or daydreams, we are haunted by these visions of which I am speaking to such an extent that we imagine that we are travelling abroad, crossing the sea, fighting, addressing the people, or enjoying the use of wealth that we do not actually possess, and seem to ourselves not to be dreaming but acting. (*Institutio* 6.2.30)

Cicero had been far less circumspect about why orators must make-believe to establish their believability. Complaining that among his generation only actors display eloquence, he bluntly defends rhetorical pretense:

There can be no doubt that reality beats imitation in everything; and if reality unaided were sufficiently effective in presentation, we should have no need at all for art. But because emotion, which mostly has to be displayed or else counterfeited by action, is often so confused as to be obscured and almost smothered out of sight, we have to dispel the things that obscure it and take up its prominent and striking points. (*De Oratore* 3.56.215)

This statement models the rhetorical practice Cicero advises. By mining the resources of *phantasia* and *energeia*, he conveys the rhetorical advantages of "clarity," arguing that the emotion elicited by a speaker conveys what "reality unaided" cannot. For it is, Cicero insists, real emotion rather than rhetoric that confuses, obscures or otherwise "smother[s] out of sight" those feigned emotions the orator summons to move his audience.

In ways that the medieval and Renaissance preference for allegorical images was to make more compelling, Cicero's argument about the reality-effect of a speaker's make-believe serves as a warrant for the special power of allegory as a factitious narrative. When Quintilian identifies allegory as an extended figure or metaphor, he implies its categorical authority over metaphor. One modern definition captures the synecdochic relation between these terms: "Die Allegorie ist für den Gedanken, was die Metapher für das Einzelwort ist" – (Allegory is to thought what metaphor is to the single word).[25]

Quintilian's synonyms for allegory, in part derived from Cicero, signal what is potentially troublesome about its narrative extension. As a vehicle for *ironia*, *illusio*, and *inversio*, allegory extends in narrative time the edge of doubt and suspicion conveyed by the Greek word for "conjecture." Indeed, all three Latin synonyms mark a duplicity of aspect that goes beyond the claim that allegory is or can be obscure (*Institutio* 8.6.52). Whether it inverts meanings or otherwise ironizes the narrative it offers, allegory disturbs ordinary expectations that outward appearances might accurately convey meaning. As *illusio*, allegory makes the effects of duplicity felt in ways that are especially compelling for the versions of allegory that obtain after the Renaissance. For the allegorical use of visual images may convey several, quite different, views of their relation to allegorical ideas. Images may be all illusion, all make-believe or they may be so obscurely related to allegorical ideas that readers are left with the task of making explicit what seems obscure. Thus when allegory becomes enigma or riddle, it follows its logical angle of repose as a figure of irony or illusion. Quintilian puts a less quizzical face on the task of identifying a speaker's ironical intention by asserting that it is "made evident to the understanding either by the delivery, the character of the speaker, or the nature of the subject" (*Institutio*

8.6.54).[26] His earlier warning, however, that allegories may be obscure and, as such, riddles or enigmas (*Institutio* 8.6.52) puts this claim in some doubt.

Quintilian's discussion thereby suggests how allegory acts as a lightning rod for the liabilities of metaphor in general. For whereas metaphor makes some demands on its audience, allegory imperiously makes more and greater demands. Its potential tyranny is suggested by discussions, beginning with Aristotle, of metaphor in general as "forceful," or irresistible, because it relies on images or, more precisely, because it helps hearers imagine or see in their mind's eye a metaphorical "tenor." Quintilian's claim that *phantasia* or *visiones* can make things that are absent seem present "before our eyes" implies the coerciveness of vivid rhetorical figures. Such figures compel assent, on quasi-empiricist grounds. For if we think we have good visual evidence, we believe what we see. This visual forcefulness or irresistibility is a model or figure for the coercion (pleasurable or not) that vision-based theories of metaphor imply.[27] This point is especially pertinent for allegory as the figure whose narrative extension invites us to imagine it alive and moving as well as visible. As metaphor does not, allegory makes present to the imagination figures categorically alien to human experience, such as Satan flailing his vast windmill arms at the bottom of Dante's *Inferno,* the very embodiment of "the exhalation of all evil," or Spenser's Errour, with her error-whelps clinging to body and tail. As figures animated within and by a narrative, both are grotesque, fabulous, yet surprisingly life-like.

The persuasiveness of allegory in fact depends on the degree to which its figures *seem* life-like: if Spenser's beast Error works well allegorically, it is because her massive, grotesquely visual presence and actions very nearly compel us to believe in Errour as a palpable, endlessly fecund presence in human life. When eighteenth-century and Romantic writers dismiss allegory as mere imagery or when they avoid it on the grounds that it is rigid or mechanical, they offer a mixed recognition of its potential tyranny as a metafigure for the special, coercive power often attributed to metaphor in general. Wordsworth and Coleridge imply their partial recognition of this difficulty when they name sight (or, in their oddly concrete figurative reduction, the "eye") the "most despotic" of the senses, a Romanticized echo of the Enlightenment preference for deriving ideas from evidence said to be offered by the senses. Now the intended object of the eye's despotic control is only nominally nature; the real object is poetic speech, always complexly implicated in Romantic discussions of knowledge and the senses.

Allegory's relation to *phantasia* specifies its ambiguous, ironic deployment of visual images that may be cognitive, imaginative, illusory, nightmarish or, worse, all of the above. Hans Kellner's suggestion that irony is a "master trope"[28] might be applied to allegory as well, as the figure that draws to itself the collective strengths and liabilities of figurative speech. Quintilian's and Cicero's definition of allegory as an extended figure or metaphor conveys its potentially *endless* emplotment of figure such that its interpretation might go on, turn back, and go up in all the registers made available by medieval (and Blakean) fourfold vision. This possibility makes allegory both attractive and risky. Its fictions can be absorptive of readers as well as of figures when it binds both to its hermeneutic plot. Both possibilities reappear in medieval and Renaissance considerations of allegory, *phantasia*, and rhetorical *energeia*.

Macrobius, the fourth-century commentator on Cicero's "Dream of Scipio" who set the medieval standard for reading dream visions as allegories, distinguishes bad dreams (*phantasma* or *visum*) from prophetic dreams (*visio*) that merit an allegorical commentary like the one Macrobius attaches to Cicero's account of Scipio's dream.[29] In the dream Scipio is transported to a heavenly vantage point from which to consider (and thus put in appropriate perspective) his future career and civic responsibility in Carthage. In Macrobius's taxonomy, *phantasia* devolves into *phantasma*, hence a dream not worth remembering or reading allegorically because it deals merely in "apparition," those low forms of dreaming life that occupy the bottom of this sliding scale, along with "nightmares." Dreams worth remembering and reading allegorically are either enigmatic, prophetic (Latin: *visio*), or oracular. Macrobius finds examples of all three categories in Cicero's meditation on Scipio's dream. As a synonym for *visio*, *phantasia* inhabits the unsettled ground of allegory and dream vision in the medieval tradition.

This influential distinction between *phantasia* (by way of *phantasm*) and the allegorical dream vision is lost on Chaucer, despite his honorific description of Macrobius as "interpreter of dreams." In the proem to the dream vision of *The House of Fame*, Chaucer's narrator offers a pseudo-taxonomy of dream types that undermines Macrobius's confidently hierarchical presentation of five types of dreams and further subdivision of enigmatic dreams into five sub-types. Instead of Macrobius's categorical assurance, Chaucer offers a prayer or, more accurately, a petition:

> God turne us every drem to goode!
> For hyt is wonder, be the roode,
> To my wyt, what causeth swevenes
> Eyther on morwes or on evenes;
> And why th'effect folweth of somme,
> And of sommon hit shal never come;
> Why that is an avisioun
> And this a revelacioun,
> Why this a dream, why that a sweven,
> And noght to every man lyche even;
> Why this a fantome, why these oracles,
> I not.[30]

More or less haphazardly, this list manages to include most of the terms that appear in Macrobius's commentary. Some of them seem slyly misremembered, however, like "avisioun" instead of "visio," which suggests that a bad dream is "a-visio" – the negation of a good one. Indeed, the narrator may by such means imply that the distinction between *visum* (phantasma or apparition, not worth remembering) and *visio* (prophetic and eminently worth remembering) is itself hard to remember since both terms derive from the same Latin root. In this textual environment, a "fantome" is worth about as much as an "oracle" to the interpreter of dreams.

Chaucer's air of confusion deftly plots lexical ambiguities in classical and medieval discussions of *phantasia* or imagination. Scholastic philosophers defined *phantasia* as "the mental apprehension of an object of perception." This definition and its Aristotelian synonym, "faculty or power of imagination," are the least equivocal of the available definitions. Others elaborate the liabilities Macrobius implies. Thus *phantasia* is first (and equivocally) "vision, dream, nightmare"; then follow "illusion, delusion, phantasmagoria, mirage"; Macrobius's demons, "phantom, ghost, apparition," are next. Later usage goes further afield but retains the edge of fakery or perceptual error: now *phantasia* has to do with magic, with "fancy" in the sense of the French "bon plaisir" or caprice, with "finery, pomp, or state." *Phantasma* summarizes the ambiguity that haunts all these cognates: it is either an "image of the mind," an "idea," "imagination," or "delusion." In its adjectival form, its

Aristotelian meanings dissolve entirely, leaving only "imaginary, unreal, abstract."[31]

The widespread medieval use of the term *integumentum* suggests the covert presence of *phantasia* in allegorical exegesis or commentary, a scholarly activity that evidently had much invested in the claim that allegory is obscure and thus in need of interpretation. In medieval hermeneutic theory, allegorical commentary or exegesis – *allegoresis* – is the "veil" or *integumentum*. As such, it is a covering text that is paradoxically both container and contained. Instead of being a belated textual event that occurs after-the-fact-of-the-allegory, the integument supplies the meaning without which the work is no allegory.[32] This reversal of priority might seem dismissable when the "base" text is, for example, Homeric epic and, as such, not self-evidently allegorical. But the same claim might be made about works that are evidently allegories in the sense that, as Teskey puts it, they "are written to encourage readers to interpret in a particular way."[33] For knowing what such works mean as allegories requires the attentive reader–exegete whose hermeneutic task produces the *integumentum*, the veil of allegory whose critical participation in the production of allegorical meaning (always the end and focus of allegory) makes its apparent secondariness less so. This recognition leads to another: that allegory is other to all forms of its representation, whether these are described as allegory or *allegoresis*. Thus the apparent secondariness of an *allegoresis* veils the extent to which it may actually breach that mystery in the name of the allegory.

As the visible or rhetorically vizualizable "making show" of allegory, *phantasia* draws our attention toward the hermeneutic necessity of its rhetorical and pictorial contribution as image and figure, whether perceived, delusory, or (neutrally put) imagined. In all these guises, what is visible and verbal in an allegory is critical to its meaning. We engage allegorical texts and images in the rigorous, combinatorial, and semiotic play Quilligan and Teskey urge because this is the task of allegory, urged on readers as allegoresis, but bound to allegory itself. The word *integumentum* conveys this point. So construed, the "veil" or "integument" of allegory cannot be satisfactorily imagined as something we strip away to get at an allegorical body or essence. Rather allegorical texts and commentaries are oddly porous linguistic skins, figurally bound to each other and, by such means, doubly bound to their absent referents. As such, they map the special negative logic of Quintilian's praise for a speaker whose vivid style seems to make something absent present to listeners, even as it acknowledges that the referent for such meaning is elsewhere, literally absent but vividly figured in and by the text.

During and after the English Renaissance, the mixed status of *phantasia* registers a sharpened account of allegory's double path, in large measure because the influence of emblematic literature more explicitly identified allegory with images – the "making show" of Aristotle's *phantasia* – than before. The emblem for *phantasia* in Alciati nonetheless suggests just how dubious its status is even here. The Greek for *phantasia* is presented above a visual image of Narcissus in love with his own reflection.[34] In Renaissance rhetoric, discussions of *phantasia* and *energeia* forecast the slide between observable truth and falsehood implied by Puttenham's definition and Spenser's allegorical practice."[35] Allegory is also a player in Renaissance efforts to consolidate and defend the role of ancient rhetorical figures in the Christian grand style. Tracking a line of theological argument that extends back through Thomas Aquinas and Augustine to Aristotle, Debora Shugar notes repeated echoes of Quintilian's remarks about *phantasia* in Renaissance claims for such a style, which encouraged a passionate, expressive rhetoric of prayer. Even as rhetoric, says John Donne, makes "absent and remote things present to your understanding," so do religious practices bring the idea of Christ "nearer visible and sensible things." The rhetorician Geraldus Vossius and other writers echo Quintilian when they praise what Edward Reynolds calls "vivid, circumstantial images." Vossius and other Renaissance writers frequently conflate *phantasia* with *energeia* or *enargeia,* and both with the Latin *praesentia* and its equivalent Greek term *hypotyposis.* By these turns of figure, *phantasia* and *energeia/enargeia* signify the dramatic power of image-making figures and even, as Shugar notes, the rhetorical necessity of acting and make-believe: "*enargeia* is less like a painting than a play. Abstractions, inanimate objects, the dead all come alive; they become vivid through personification and *somatopeia* (personifying abstractions), and *idolopoeia* (attributing speech to the dead)."[36] On the edge between dramatic tableau (*hypotyposis* is occasionally identified with something like "filmed action which is stopped on a chosen image"[37]) and a moving representation, allegory enacts what *enargeia* makes possible.

As arguments about the tyranny of visual images take shape during the late sixteenth and seventeenth centuries, these rhetorical affiliations specify what Protestant and later Puritan iconoclasts feared about strong visual images and figures – that they might come to life in the minds of readers and viewers who found them persuasive and thus worthy of further conjecture. In the Renaissance, as Spenser's poetics makes clear, the relation between allegory and visual images retrospectively declares the cumulative weight that had by then accrued to arguments about images, conjecture, and allegory.

The Renaissance alliance between rhetorical vividness and images that move kinetically even as they move readers creates enormous, if productive, difficulties for Spenser's allegorical theory and practice in *The Faerie Queene*. His reservations about *phantasia* are openly declared by the figure of Phantastes, whose purported ability to see into the future looks less and less reliable as the narrator catalogues his other traits. Berger notes that Phantastes's foresight is impelled by "a kind of irritability, a restlessness impelling him to premature judgment"[38] – a state of mind that makes him susceptible to delusory visions, "idle fantasies" of fabulous monsters, an unhappy parade of deluded human beings, and "all that fained is," including tales, lies, dreams. Although I agree that the poem as a whole defends "poetic fiction and the imagination producing it," that defense does not urge a distinction between phantasy and imagination. Like Puttenham, Spenser uses these terms and their cognates interchangeably: either can be good or bad.[39]

Spenser does more here than merely anticipate the Restoration complaint against the waywardness of his allegorical fantasy or, as Blackmore would put it, "fancy."[40] Whatever his shortcomings, and they are many, Phantastes's prophetic vision, even when it is wildly off-course and delusory, is critical to the momentum and direction of allegorical speech, which throws off image after image as it invites readers to read prospectively, with an eye toward the "other speech" to which those images imperfectly refer. In the Castle of Temperance, Phantastes's excesses are tempered by Alma's other two counsellors, a wise old man of "goodly reason," and a blind old man whose "infinite remembrance" preserves the past as "ensample" to the present. As *The Faerie Queene* proceeds, Spenser offers sterner and more intricate assessments of the perils that await characters and readers who believe everything they see and hear, without appealing to reason or memory. The last and sternest of these may be the book VI figure of Calidore, the knight of "courtesy" whose speech and actions add up to something less than unalloyed virtue.

In his "Letter to Raleigh," published in 1590 with the first three books of the poem, Spenser grants "how doubtfully all Allegorie may be construed," but defends his invention of "a continued Allegorie, or darke conceit" because it teaches "doctrine by ensample, then [than] by rule" (*FQ* 15–16). He then lists the "ensamples" provided in the first three books: "the first of the knight of the Redcrosse, in whome I expresse Holynes: The second of Sir Guyon, in whome I sette forth Temperaunce: The third of Britomartis a Lady knight, in whome I picture Chastity" (*FQ* 16). Here the three virtues look like tidy emblematic packages and allegorical persons, each fully representative of the truths embedded in the "continued allegorie" of the poem. Yet in telling the allegorical stories about these figures, Spenser soon parts company with this unconditional rhetoric of visual and allegorical clarity. As Teskey wryly observes, Spenser does not confine himself to the scheme he offered readers as an interpretive guide.[41] On the contrary, his narrative development of their stories works as much against as within seductive images and vignettes, those "shaping fantasies" of his allegorical imagination. What emerges in the poem is an allegory whose truths are neither fixed and fully visible nor easily at hand. Instead the poem entertains multiple, shifting representations so that it might glimpse, however transiently, some aspect of those truths. So construed, Spenser's allegory must risk its fantasies, as a visual and mental inventory of available resources.

For a poet and poem whose declared task is to depict allegorical characters in search of the truth of their being, stumbling at the edge of delusion by, for example, mistaking Duessa for Una, is an enormous risk, yet it is also one written into the poem's understanding of the usefulness of error. The punning on *error* and *erring* in the opening canto of the poem is a neon sign, a well-lit advertisement, by way of Dante's use of the same figure, for what goes by the name of allegory in *The Faerie Queene*. As readers of the poem have long recognized, its characters perennially make mistakes about what they see, usually because desire blinds them in some way. And so should they err, given the subtly anti-iconoclastic edge of Spenser's argument. Allegorically speaking, full presence would be "idolatry" since the truth is elsewhere, its "other speech" beyond the limits of pictures and forms. What Gregerson has called the "conspicuous friability and slippage" of *The Faerie Queene* cannot be dismissed, in short, as though it belonged to a category of "minor, and reparable,

flaws in a grand scheme of cosmic closure."[42] For this reason,
Spenser's allegorical plots and characters tack back and forth,
threading their way through arenas of conflict, erring on their way to
truth (or its dissimulation). They take from materiality what they
need to perform or read the allegory, then discard (as best they can
and when they can) those seductive material shapes that are distrac-
tions. Spenser's pictorialism is from this vantage point a narrative
problem – the reader's problem – not the easy solution neo-
Spenserian poets would later imagine it to be.

If Spenser's pictorialism does not suffice for an allegorical
narrative, his allegory and his readers cannot do without it. This
dilemma permeates modern allegorical theory and practice. Its
semiotic ground is a theory of signs drenched with an ethos of
longing and ineluctable absence which Gregerson traces to Augustine. In a dialogue between himself and his dead son, Augustine
invents a syllogism, "Adeodatus is not a man," to figure semiotically
the absence of the boy – from the father and from the state of
manhood. Gregerson argues that Augustine counters the absolute
break between presence and absence figured by his son's death in a
system of signs that refer only to other signs. The figure of this
"discontinuous method" is error, here understood as running back
and forth in dialogue between Augustine and the imagined speech
of his son. Applied to *The Faerie Queene*, this method asserts that the
longing for signs that are adequate to meaning is "a necessary,
enabling, and unaccommodated mistake."[43] The pathos of Augustine's text reemerges in Spenser's poem via *eros*, the longing that
leads characters to mistake themselves and those they desire in
amorous intrigues which redouble as the story of Britomart takes
center stage.

The figural practices Spenser uses to make this argument offer a
virtual taxonomy of the strange, hybrid forms allegory increasingly
assumes after the Renaissance. Gregerson's distinction between
"exemplary" and "catalytic" allegorical figures provides a useful
point of departure for that taxonomy. An exemplary allegorical
figure embodies the "psychic or material condition for which it is
named," like Spenser's House of Pride and trial of Mutability, or
medieval allegorical parades of the seven deadly sins.[44] Exemplary
figures are less threatening because they do little except take their
places in allegorical tableaux. They thus display the pictorial fixity
writers after Spenser either praise or deplore in allegory, as if

exemplary figures were or ought to be the only figures that could be classified as allegorical.

Catalytic figures, which Gregerson defines as the "precipitating cause or occasion of the condition for which [they are] named," are more troublesome because readers can never be quite sure that an exemplary figure will not end up being catalytic as well, or vice versa. Thus Spenser's Malbecco is his own allegorical catalyst; his jealousy impels him toward his eventual (and final) emergence as an exemplary figure of Jealousy. The bitter irony of this transformation is locked inside its own mirror stage. The possessive husband finally becomes a beast whose "absolute coincidence with meaning is a kind of possession."[45] Eighteenth-century writers are apprehensive about the catalytic potential of personifications that seem at one moment dead abstractions but at another disturbingly lifelike.[46] What Berger calls Malbecco's "*condensation* into human form of a set of conventional notions and psychological forces" is a sign of allegory's exceedingly odd traverse between what is human and what is abstract.[47] For Malbecco, this condensation ends in dehumanized abstraction:

> he through privy griefe, and horrour vaine,
> Is woxen so deform'd, that he has quight
> Forgot he was a man, and *Geolousie* is hight.
> (Spenser, *FQ* 3.10.57–60)

The various distortions of apparently real or material details which Berger finds in *The Faerie Queene* – "stereotypes, exaggerated, fantastic or literary characters" and "outlandish pageants of monsters, mishaps, and perversions"[48] – are marks of its allegorical nature. Fletcher suggests further that the process of learning to read Spenser's allegory is itself marked by similar distortions: "On our first encounter the figures are miniature, like the knights Proust imagined on his bed, jousting in the playful light of a magic lantern. But as we read our way *into* Spenser, his figures grow large with another size, of dull reverberations, by alluding to other cultures, other religions, other philosophies than our own."[49] Fletcher's next subheading, "Forms of infinite magnitude and detail," shows how distortions of realist norms become allegorical cues. To so read or so imagine Spenser's characters is to reify them, to abstract meaning from them as indeed allegory requires us to do even when it inhabits particulars.

The figural means available for marking allegorical reification can be, as they are for Spenser and Dante, curiously weighted with materiality. Thus for Freccero the "infernal irony" of Dante's *Inferno* proceeds by way of compressed or distorted figures. Each sinner's punishment is a synecdoche that expresses itself as a "concretized form of the sin itself, a literary conceit, an etymology," "an emblem travestied," or "an hyperbole."[50] Such figures advertise their deviations from verisimilitude, either by contraction (the conceit and the emblem), by a self-evidently literary appeal to the history of words (the etymology of *Mal-becco*: "bad/evil billy-goat/cuckold"), or by way of exaggeration, monstrosity or simply fixation. As Hagstrum's discussion of emblematic caricature in Swift also makes clear, any of these techniques can be combined.[51] At one extreme, allegorical figures display primitive, calcified identities. In the *Purgatorio* of Dante's *Divine Comedy*, Beatrice chastizes Dante, calling him "stone-like, such in hue that the light of my word / dazes you."[52] Berger notes that Spenser's comparison of the entwined Amoret and Scudamor to a marble statue of Hermaphrodite signals their primitive, alienated vision of *eros*, which desires to remain fixed at a single moment, in a close embrace,[53] much like the "happy, happy lovers" of Keats's *Ode on a Grecian Urn* whose eternal stasis soon wears on the speaker of that poem.

These techniques disturb the expected allegorical relation between tenor and vehicle (or spirit and letter) because they move restlessly from materiality to figure and back again. Spenser's Malbecco makes curious work of this shuttle. First a man who is jealous and finally a bestial embodiment of Jealousy, the allegorical Malbecco will not let go of materiality. The more allegorical he becomes, the more grossly material in body than before, until he figures avaricious jealousy more thoroughly as an old goat than he did as a man. Malbecco exemplifies what happens when an allegory works at the extreme edge of abstraction. Possessed by and obsessed with his allegorical identity, Malbecco is consumed and deformed by abstraction. This process, which Fletcher has brilliantly characterized as the demonization of allegory, represents one extreme in Spenser.[54]

The other is suggested by Britomart, whose identity as Chastity is crosshatched with indications of a developing inner psychological reality. Whereas Wofford understands this development as the sign of a widening gap between the narrative of the poem and its allegory,[55] I argue that Britomart's allegorical nature emerges in these narrative adjustments. To read them instead as evidence that Spenser's representation exceeds the limits of allegory is to constrict the range of allegory unnecessarily, as though only Malbecco and his kind could be called allegorical on the grounds that they submit to this kind of allegorical reduction. Within the repertory of allegorical techniques, in other words, reduction articulates one extreme. Against this technique Spenser arrays another in Britomart, whose allegorical identity and narrative function emerge via an efficacious relay between compression and expansion.

Readers have productively linked two episodes to talk about the kind of allegory Britomart exemplifies as a character who expresses inner life or self-consciousness as, for example, Malbecco does not. The first is Britomart's seaside lament in book 3 and the second is her invasion of Busirane's castle at the end of the book. When Britomart, who has searched everywhere for Artegall, arrives at the sea-coast to lament her state of mind and body by comparing it to a ship tossed at sea (*FQ* 3.2.8–10), the Petrarchan and emblematic tradition which subtends this lament compresses her identity within the iconic space of image and text. As Wofford notes, here and elsewhere in book III the risk of such moments in and for the allegory is idolatry, a risk writ large in the tapestries and Mask of Cupid which Britomart later finds in Busirane's castle.[56] But when Spenser diffuses Britomart's image by refracting it through the stories of Florimell, Hellenore, and Malbecco, he indicates how a compressed iconic moment in the poem can be made to expand as the narrative plot thickens the figural texture (or vice versa) to take in other allegorical figures and stories that are also concerned with chastity (whether keeping it, losing it, or seeking to enforce it). The question raised by this expansion is whether or not Britomart remains an allegorical figure.

Britomart's erotic lament makes patent and sustained use of external signs to figure her inner distress.[57] The narrator offers a slight syntactic doubling which makes this point inescapable even before she speaks: "to the sea-coast at length she her addrest" (*FQ* 3.4.6). Calling the sea a "huge sea of sorrow, and tempestuous griefe" and herself a "feeble barke," she soon troubles the figural waters by moving the sea inside: "stint thy stormy strife, / Which in these troubled bowels raigns, and rageth rife" (3.4.8). The bodily female trouble indicated here recalls Britomart's "bloody bowels" in canto 2 as she suffers for lack of Artegall 3.2.39). In both instances, Britomart's body is evidently a figure for and of erotic desire. As such, it is also a strangely material vehicle for expressing interiority. Still, the pathos of her lament is secured by her use of the sea and her body to figure inner turmoil and thus to offer evidence of the kind of interiority modern readers identify with psychological realism. The narrator cinches the matter by concluding: "Then sighing softly sore, and inly deepe, / She shut up all her plaint in privy griefe" (3.4.11).[58]

What complicates arguments about Britomart's psychologically real character as it emerges in this passage is the initiating figure of a ship tossed at sea. The image is taken from one of Petrarch's *canzone*, where it exemplifies a radical, erotic subjectivity which "reduces all externality to a mirror of the self."[59] So understood, her lament is an icon of erotic self-absorption. In the castle of Busirane, the dangers of erotic self-absorption and idolatry are likewise represented by icons, first in the tapestries of gods and humans transformed, often bestialized, by eros, in the Mask of Cupid, and in the final scene as Busirane tries to make his way into Amoret's heart with a dagger. The ship image of Britomart's earlier lament also appears in Puttenham's emblem for "allegoria."[60] Thus if Spenser offers readers an interiorized Britomart who eventually achieves her mature identity, he does so by beginning with a conventional emblem which he then appropriates to instruct Britomart about the limitations of her mirror stage.

For Wofford, who reads these passages with an astute critical notice of Spenser's metafigural logic, Britomart occupies a liminal space or border (this image is indebted to Fletcher as well as Geoffrey Hartman on Wordsworth) between narrative and allegory, where narrative stands for an inner psychological development in time and allegory for icon, conceit, lyric lament and thus narrative delay. This opposition between narrative delay and iconic presence mirrors the disjunction between the real and ideal worlds which allegory negotiates.[61] The view of allegory that anchors this reading is productively caught between two ways of defining allegory. The first is represented by Fletcher, who recognizes the compulsions that drive allegorical figures toward abstraction and emblematic stasis. So understood, allegory exists within narrative to frustrate its momentum by inventing characters whose psychological reality is well displayed by frozen, static, neurotic, self-authorizing figures who always double back, who halt narrative to repeat compulsively what they have been before. The exemplary vehicle for such figures is the emblem, particularly the woodcut emblem of the Renaissance,

whose four-square visual solidity is itself a figure of an allegorical
fixity of temperament.

A second definition is suggested by the role Freccero assigns
allegory in the Augustinian theory of signs and by de Man's reading
of allegory as a figure of narrative (and reading) in the rhetorical
tradition inaugurated by Quintilian and Cicero. This allegory is ever
and shiftily narrative in its compulsions as it urges readers to read a
figure one way and then the other, but always figurally, with the
conviction that figural narratives never stop, but always succeed each
other. De Man's contention that referring elsewhere (or deferring to
somewhere else) is itself a narrative, temporal or temporizing gesture
reiterates in a modern key the definition offered by classical rhetoricians, for whom allegory is an ironic, extended figure that refers
elsewhere.

For Spenser and indeed for the versions of allegory that survive
after Spenser, allegory's narrative impulse recasts the allegorical
desire at the center of Augustine's theory of signs. As Freccero
explains, the difference between the sense of desire projected by
Petrarch and that projected by Dante after Augustine has precisely
to do with reference. For whereas Augustine's understanding of
desire (semiotic and otherwise) is that the soul and human speech
always long for God, that *eros* is the name for that longing, and that
this longing places individual speech within and in relation to a
salvation history that begins and ends in Christ, the lyric wordplay
that exemplifies Petrarch's eros for Laura begins and ends in the
figure of the laurel/Laura. The auto-reflexive character of the
Petrarchan love lyric thus stands outside history, against which it
arrays a "counterfeit *durée*," a lyric time which by design stops the
passage of time and inhibits the placement of individual speech
within the salvation history of the New Testament. Against this
counterfeit time, Freccero places allegory as a theory of signs that
refers beyond itself and thus rejects the "idolatry" of signs and
objects that refer only to themselves.[62]

In allegorical theory and practice after Spenser, a similar path
joins allegory to history and narrative, albeit with an edge of doubt
about the precise referent for the "other speech" of allegory. Even if
de Man's exaggeration of this doubt and irony as the undoing of
reference pushes allegory into a figural self-reflexivity on the Petrarchan model, the doubt is unquestionably there. In Spenser's
poem, it emerges most clearly in narrative engagements with visual/

verbal icons and in the poem's various flirtations with iconoclasm. The narrative paths taken and retaken by Spenser's Britomart in books 3 and 4 suggest that she dramatizes this kind of allegory or, more precisely, that she shows how allegory as a figure of extended irony confronts the fixation of images like those Busirane devises. The Busirane episode suggests further how and why both allegorical impulses – one toward fixity, the other toward narrative extension – remain at issue and in conflict in allegory after Spenser.

The possibility of narrative extension is already implicit in Britomart's earlier lament, which moves backward in the allegorical plot when she reiterates her earlier sexual longing by mapping it bodily onto her bowels. She indicates this prospective extension of the allegorical plot when she describes her two guides, "my lewd Pilot" and "fortune Boteswaine," as "bold" and "blind" (*FQ* 3.4.9). The first adjective forecasts the commands she reads on the walls of Busirane's castle, "be bold" and, when she gets to the room where Busirane tortures Amoret, "be not too bold" (3.11.54). The second is an ironic constant enjoined by the tapestries whose mythological allegories of love Britomart examines: just as Cupid is blind, so are his victims blind to the monstrous consequences of submitting to eros. In the stanza that ends the story of her rash wounding of Marinell, the narrator implies the logic of this complicity between mostly fixed iconic messages and the ensuing narrative, which shows how Britomart eventually sorts out what it means to be chaste:

> The martiall Mayd stayd not him to lament,
> But forward rode, and kept her readie way
> Along the strond, which as she ower-went,
> She saw bestrowed all with rich aray
> Of pearles and pretious stones of great assay,
> And all the grauell mixt with golden owre;
> Whereat she wondred much, but would not stay
> For gold, or perles, or pretious stones an howre,
> But them despised all; for all was in her powre.   (*FQ* 3.4.18)

Not lamenting means not stopping – no more lyric delay in and by an emblematic set-piece; but it also means that Britomart does not pay attention to the difference between what is valuable and what can be discarded as she knocks over errant knights in an arrogant, rash display of power. Looking and interpreting what she sees with an eye for differences is one allegorical task she learns after fighting her way into the castle of Busirane.

Busirane's entertainments raise the stakes in the poem's various arguments about acts of imagining, which usually fall under the category of phantasy or fancy. Like Britomart's "feigning [erotic] fancy" for her best knight, Busirane's tapestries and mask of Cupid are "phantasies" like those women invent (*FQ* 3.12.26). Yet these masked figures, which disappear in the room where Busirane tortures the captive Amoret, thereby conduct us to a more dangerous male phantasy. Not able to win Amoret's heart, he digs his way in with a knife, using it as a bloody pen to "figure [ ] straunge characters of his art."

Fortunately for Amoret (and eventually for Britomart herself), this material fantasy of erotic possession and torture is easy to read. Britomart gets the point and forces Amoret's release. As feminist readings of this episode note, Busirane's graphic art looks uncomfortably like Archimago's, Merlin's, the poet's, and perhaps women's erotic, delusory fantasies.[63] Although the narrator attributes destructive "phantasie" to "wauering wemens wit" here and in book 5, where Britomart tries but fails to read her prophetic dream in Isis church as "a thousand thoughts feed [ ] her fantasy" (*FQ* 5.7.12, 17), the *narrative* applies the same criticism to male enchanters. Like other allegorical tableaux and pageants in the poem, this one is full of what Hegel would later call "sensuous shapes," icons that tangibly represent desire or, as Spenser's scandalized narrator puts it, the "thousand monstrous formes" of "false love" (*FQ* 3.11.51).

Yet Busirane's iconic fantasy also serves a purpose. Its visual and narrative complexity slows Britomart down so that her penchant for running knights through (more or less what Busirane threatens to do to Amoret) is held in abeyance as she reads what she sees. Berger astutely notes how Spenser matches the rhetorical pattern of the episode to the way that icons and emblems convey information: "From tapestries to icon to reliefs to masque, and from the beginning to the end of the masque, there is increasing inwardness, compression, and complication, correlated with increasing activity and motion, and, above all, with increasing proximity to the present moment of narrative."[64] For readers like us (and like Britomart), the net effect of this display is dazzling but opaque, inviting interpretation but also reluctant to give information.

Britomart's movement through the castle implies that the way through enchantment and fantasy is not simply to destroy them as Guyon destroys the Bower of Bliss (*FQ* 2.12.83), but to read them. As a reader of allegory, Britomart begins to assume an inwardness or depth of character we identify with our activity as readers of allegory. Or so *we* imagine. The fantasy of reading Britomart as a character whose psychological depth is like ours can itself be read two ways. One is to argue, as some readers have argued or implied, that Britomart ceases to be allegorical or becomes less so when her drive toward inwardness makes her a reader of allegory just like us. We can, however, turn this argument on its head: inwardness and psychological realism are enabling (and shaping) fantasies that allow us to recognize the allegorical task Britomart dramatizes when she tries to read the fixed, iconic images that proliferate, as it were, from the bestialized figure of Malbecco, whose brutality and possessiveness Busirane extends.[65] At the end of book 3, she stands apart from the hermaphroditic embrace of Amoret and Scudamor because her allegorical identity cannot be so encased, nor can it be kept safe from the reality of sexual difference and the passage of time – a reality Amoret and Scudamor try to ignore. When Britomart misreads the dream-prophecy of her own future and royal lineage, that "wondrous [and true] vision," she stumbles as all readers must.

Whereas Malbecco presents the kind of allegorical and iconic rigidity that gave allegory a bad name after Spenser *and* made it safe, Britomart's allegorical nature is embedded in narrative expansion as much as narrative delay. That nature changes, and it changes in ways that make her seem psychologically verisimilar. As such, Britomart signals a critical moment in the history and theory of allegory. For after Spenser the difference between allegorical fictions and what moderns variously understand as real events and characters or a style that is realistic is less an absolute barrier than it is a border for mutual raids. If one end point of allegory is a demonic fixation of form and meaning, a giving over to abstraction, the other is a mutable, temporal allegorical character whose raids on the real or the verisimilar bring its abstractions half-way home, as it were, without impaling the heart on its fantasies.

The Faerie Queene is wary of the first kind of allegory because it may lead to idolatry. This scenario erupts more than once in the poem, beginning with the destruction of the Bower of Bliss, and finally in book 6, when Calidore bursts in on the ideal pastoral world and allegorical dance of the Graces on Mount Acidale. For Berger, this moment figures Spenser's recognition that the self-enclosed and thus self-sufficient ideal vision of pastoral allegory necessarily yields to reality.[66] For Gross, it forces Colin to abandon an erotic, idolatrous relation to the ideal vision to become more like a "discursive, secular allegorist, a cultural historian and glosser of emblems."[67] Both readers astutely recognize the fragility of an ideal pastoral vision and the limited range of a Colin, who can admire the vision on Mount Acidale yet be unable to take the truth of that vision back to the world.

Yet neither reading pays enough skeptical attention to Calidore's behavior and strategic use of courteous speech to ingratiate himself with Meliboe, to court the daughter Pastorella, to keep the jealous Coridon at bay, and to excuse himself for disrupting Calepine and Serena in their love-making and for making the vision of the Graces disappear by stepping into the clearing. Neuse argues that Calidore, the social, public man known for his consummate ease, reveals the inner moral bankruptcy of Courtesy.[68] In a poem whose imagined spiritual goal is the court of Gloriana, Calidore serves as the very pattern of knightly courtesy. He also embodies Puttenham's definition of allegory as "the courtly figure" of "*false semblaunt or dissimulation.*"[69]

The first sign of trouble is the narrator, whose glib introduction of Calidore is as slippery about telling the truth as the knight is:

> For his fair usage and conditions sound,
> The which in all mens liking gayned place,
> And with the greatest purchast greatest grace:
> Which he could wisely use, and well apply,
> To please the best, and th'euill to embase.
> For he loathd leasing, and base flattery,
> And loved simple truth and stedfast honesty.   (*FQ* 6.1.3)

The knight who knows how to purchase grace, then "wisely use, and well apply" also lies when it suits his purpose. He invents a story about saving Priscilla from a monstrous knight (with severed head as proof) so that she can return from her lover to her father (who had commanded she marry someone else) in the guise of a lady "most perfect pure, and guiltlesse innocent / Of blame" (*FQ* 6.3.16–19). The deception, carried out with the air of easy friendship that is Calidore's strong suit, is deception nonetheless. As Nohrnberg puts it, "his allegorically veiled truth is the polite white lie: indirection, the disguise of ulterior motives, the studied use of misrepresentation, and the hermeneutical virtues of subtlety and finesse all serve his cause."[70]

Among the shepherds, Calidore flatters Meliboe, Pastorella's pastoral shepherd / adopted father, to gain access to the maiden. He then woos her assiduously, all the while making sure that the jealous Coridon looks a poor match by comparison. Toward Coridon, Calidore is consistently duplicitous, pretending friendship to defuse their rivalry by means of public shows. Toward Pastorella, he is oddly inconsistent. He woos her passionately, wins her, and, then, by a species of inattention in which the narrator is complicit, woos and wins her favor again after destroying the pastoral vision, then seems to lose interest, off in pursuit of the Blatant Beast.

Calidore's actions exaggerate narrative errancy to the point of truancy. In one sense, of course, this possibility has been at hand since the beginning of book 3. Episodes interrupt others; damsels like Florimell and Amoret are left in the clutches of evil men until such time as the narrator chooses to retrieve them. For some readers, the image of Justice in book 5 only suppresses, and temporarily at that, the ambivalences that increasingly govern the poem's production of moral truths by allegorical means. In book 6 and in the person of Calidore, narrative errancy is pushed to a worrisome extreme, particularly in the concluding canto. There he captures the Beast, puts him through obedience school, only to have him break his iron chain to harass the world again and, pointedly, to "rend [ ] the Poets rime" (6.12.40). The narrator repeatedly finesses these difficulties, much as Calidore or Courtesy smooths over his various disruptions and intrusions with an easy, courtly speech. Neuse concludes that courtesy is inadequate to the demands placed on it by social reality, figured as the Blatant Beast, and by the allegorical ideal vision on Mount Acidale.[71] What makes this line of reasoning at once disturbing and compelling is the unnerving symmetry of knight and Beast.

Both are wilful iconoclasts whose destruction (courteously masked or not) of idylls and idols is monstrously refigured by the Beast, whose Puritan rampage is the subject of the last canto. The knight's disruptions only seem less violent because they are so courteously managed. Having "rudely" disturbed Calepine and Serena, Calidore excuses the intrusion to himself as "his fortune, not his fault" (*FQ* 6.3.21) and proceeds to "acquit [ ]" and seek "pardon" for himself so skilfully that Calipine finally asks him to sit down. The courtesy at issue in the scene seems at best skin-deep. It is a breach of eros as well as etiquette to disturb the pair; Calidore heals the breach with courteous words. There seems no good reason, allegorical or otherwise, for this disruption: he saw the pair "approaching nye, / Ere they were well aware of living wight" (*FO* 6.3.21) and could have turned from the scene. A similar pattern of greedy eyes and wilful disruption marks his relation to the pastoral vision and dance of the Graces. He could have simply looked, idolatrously, like Colin Clout and much as Calidore himself had first looked at Pastorella with "hungry eye" (*FQ* 6.9.26). Advancing to find out whether the vision is a delusion, Calidore makes the entire scene vanish. To Colin's act of idolatry, in effect, Calidore inadvertently acts like an iconoclast, one who begins by doubting images and then destroys them.

The exaggerated form of iconoclasm in the book is evidently the Blatant Beast, whose predations in and out of church Calidore briefly halts by capturing it and putting it on an iron chain. The allegorical interest of this gesture is suggested by Plato's comparison of the soul to

one of those many fabulous monsters said to have existed long ago. Imagine to begin with, the figure of a multifarious and many-headed beast ... Now add two other forms, a lion and a man ... Then join them in such a way that the three somehow grow together into one ... all our words and actions should tend towards giving the man within us complete mastery over the whole human creature ... letting him take the many-headed beast under his care and tame his wildness.[72]

The Renaissance emblem for Plato's visual analogy is "Self-Restraint," a man who restrains a lion or dog on a leash. Spenser's fidelity to this idea is obvious and instructive.[73] Calidore turns the Beast, who has raged lion-like, into the likeness of "a fearefull dog" that is chained with an iron chain. As does the emblem, Spenser's image makes this beast a visual projection of the man who restrains him, then does not. Like Britomart's earlier comparison of herself to a ship tossed at sea, this allusion is "conspicuous,"[74] a deliberate appeal to a familiar emblem and, perhaps more significantly, to the kind of reading or interpretation emblems invite.

With this appeal, Spenser's image of a chained Blatant Beast turns a potentially idolatrous moment when the image suffices into allegorical practice as readers of Spenser, like readers of emblems, work from a verbal image and its visual source to its embedded significance in a larger narrative. The ludicrous and dangerous character of Puritan iconoclasm is, in Spenser's designation, the Blatant Beast, but so is the world of courtesy, whose preoccupation with verbal surfaces separates images and figures of speech from necessary referents. The fact that Calidore does not *look* like a villain or a beast is part of the allegorical point. Like the Blatant Beast and like Archimago – whose transformations of subordinates into perfect simulacra of Una, Florimel, and the Red-crosse Knight cast a long shadow over the poem's allegorical imagery – Calidore is a figure of Spenser's recoil from allegory. That recoil is instructive about the power of polite as well as coercive allegorical figures, but not absolute. For allegory's liabilities are those of all figures writ large. The modern reinvention of allegory begins with this recognition. It then proceeds, as best it can, against the grain of iconoclastic, then empiricist, warnings about the use of figures, particularly those that seem to cross the divide between abstraction and real life.

CHAPTER 3

"Material phantasms" and "Allegorical fancies"

quaint Emblems and devices begg'd from the old Pageantry of some Twelf-nights entertainment at *Whitehall,* will doe but ill to make a Saint or a Martyr.   Milton, *Eikonoklastes, CPW* III: 343

these are the Images which are originally and most properly called *Ideas* and Idols, and derived from the language of the Graecians, with whom the word *Ειδω* signifieth to see. They are also called *Phantasmes,* which is in the same language, *Apparitions* . . . a man can fancy Shapes he never saw; making up a Figure out of the parts of divers creatures; as the Poets make their Centaurs, Chimaeras, and other Monsters never seen: so can he also give Matter to those shapes . . . these are also called images, not for the resemblance of any corporeal thing, but for the resemblance of some phantastical inhabitants of the brain of the maker.   Hobbes, *Leviathan* 358–59

we cannot perceive the manner of any of Natures operations, but by proportion to our *senses,* and a return to *material phantasms.*   Glanvill, *Vanity of Dogmatizing* 67

Joel Fineman's remark that "allegory seems regularly to surface in critical or polemical atmospheres, when for political or metaphysical reasons there is something that cannot be said"[1] succinctly identifies the reason seventeenth-century English culture despised allegory yet could hardly get enough of it. At a time when England was, as Stephen Zwicker puts it, "entangled by polemic, splintered by religious dissent, riven by partisanship," a great deal that could not be said directly was conveyed by allegorical figures, emblems, or exegesis.[2] The best-known examples of this practice are royalist and conformist, such as John Denham's *Coopers Hill,* revised after the death of Charles I to include an "allegory of the stag" which patently alludes to the dead king, and *Eikon Basilike* or *The King's Image,* the royalist pamphlet published just after Charles's death, to which Milton responds in *Eikonoklastes.*[3] Milton's animus against "quaint

43

Emblems and devices" reminiscent of court masques at Whitehall half-disguises (by seeming to trivialize those emblems and devices) a wariness about allegory and rhetorical figures that extends well beyond the fact of their use as royalist propaganda.

Milton and his contemporaries had good reason to be wary. Despite Luther and the Reformation effort to wipe allegory and exegesis off the map of religious faith and scriptural understanding, allegory is on all sides of seventeenth-century culture – royalist and parliamentarian, conformist Anglican, and nearly every permutation of nonconformist from Presbyterian or Independent to radical Puritans, Ranters, early Quakers, Familiasts, and Perfectionists. To be sure, the evidence is complicated by significant adjustments within these factions and sects from one decade to the next. Much as a Presbyterian of the 1630s might hold quite different political convictions from a Presbyterian of the 1650s or even 1640s, so do attitudes toward allegory shift from one decade to another. In the 1640s, royalists often used allegorical emblems and codes to broadcast political secrets and strategems. Echoing Renaissance allegorical practices that imagined Egyptian hieroglyphics were mysterious codes whose meaning would be legible only to those initiated into sacred, elite sects, seventeenth-century royalists conveyed secrets to compatriots via printed allegorical texts and images.[4] After the Restoration, royalist and conformist writers deplored the nonconformist and radical use of allegory and other figures on political as well as linguistic grounds. Fierce political realities evidently govern these shifting polemics, but they also point to something else that cannot be said or is at least not openly declared about allegory itself during this period.

Milton's invective against the *Eikon Basilike* is a case in point. The famous emblematic frontispiece of this royalist pamphlet situates Charles I typologically: he is a beleaguered David who recalls the martyred Christ (a crown of thorns lies near where Charles prays) and Mary at the Annunciation (Charles kneels much as Mary does in that well-rehearsed iconographic tradition). Milton's scorn for the "Image-doting rabble" (*CPW* III: 601) taken in by the king's image conveys a fundamental anxiety about the persuasiveness of a work whose "moment of solidity" (339) extends to the dead king, presented "as in his Book alive" (330).[5] At once pathetic, seemingly alive, and the apparent model of the divine right of kings, the figure of Charles in the *Eikon Basilike* is seductive and persuasive. Milton counters this rhetorical effect by aligning the allegorical imagery of the pamphlet and its frontispiece with court masques, those expensive but ephemeral royal entertainments whose actors were courtiers and, in the case of Charles I, the king himself.

Material shapes and referents like the king's image exert remarkable pressure on seventeenth-century figural practice, but particularly on allegory as a figure whose narrative extension (whether implied or discursively presented) requires the fiction of lifelike movement and being. What is everywhere at issue in the century and cannot be said is just this uneasy mix of materiality, pathos, and abstraction. When Milton attacks this mix in *Eikonoklastes*, he does so because it serves a royalist polemic and long-term strategy that is successfully concluded with the restoration of Charles II to the English throne in 1661. The apparent clarity of Milton's rhetorical purpose obscures its self-reflexive energy. In the anti-prelatical tracts of the early 1640s and, with less insistence and no small caution, in later writing as well, Milton deploys a similar and equally potent mix of materiality and abstraction.

For Milton and other seventeenth-century writers, the material, even visceral, aspect of their allegorical practice helps to make its ontological status undecidable, split along a fault line that is visible in definitions of *phantasm* as either a potentially deluded imagination, like the "phantasy" to which Robert Burton attributes bad dreams, or something akin to material shape. Echoing Bacon's critique of idols of the mind in the *Novum Organum*, Hobbes's *Leviathan* insists on the first definition at mid-century.[6] His fellow conformist Joseph Glanvill promotes the second when he explains that "material" (as opposed to merely notional or delusory) "phantasms" convey to our minds what the senses "being scant and limited" cannot convey.

By an ironic twist of circumstance and history, the Protestant and early Puritan rejection of allegory lent critical support to the seventeenth-century compulsion (at times unwilling) to make the material shapes of allegorical figures declare the solidity, even the corporeality, of the ideas to which they refer. Kibbey has argued that the logic of this materialist turn derives from the Puritan reinterpretation of the classical idea of *figura* as a "dynamic material shape" or even a "living corporeal shape." When William Franklin and Mary Gadbury proclaimed themselves spiritual incarnations of Christ, his spouse, and their divine offspring *in utero*, the fierce prosecution of these "Allegorical fancies" exposes Puritan antipathy to the material incarnation of spirit and thus to the experimental bias at the heart of Puritan doctrine.[7]

In the volatile mix of seventeenth-century English political and sectarian conflict, slippages between the figural and the literal could be intoxicating and potentially lethal insofar as savage verbal rhetoric might invite or echo real violence and born-again Puritans might take the word literally, as Luther had urged them to do. Consider this tidbit of biblical exegesis, which the radical Puritan Richard Coppin presents as an edifying gloss on Isaiah 66:3 ("as if he cut off a dog's neck"):

That by Dogs is meant carnal men, such whose nature is doggish, and dwells in them, as to be alwayes barking, biting, snapping, and snarling, as persecuting, reproaching, slandering and back-biting their fellow-creatures, catching at what they can, either in words or actions, that they might have to accuse them, as the Pharisees did by Christ, and so bring them into bondage or under contempt of the world.[8]

The barely sheathed ferocity of this exegesis may have a local and visceral object in view, the neck and severed head of the dead king. Published in 1649, the year that began with the execution of Charles, *Divine Teachings* walks a narrow path between biblical exegesis and the rhetoric of partisan violence. Allegory is the sign of both.

Although Renaissance writers, not all of them Puritans, certainly recognized the power of rhetorical figures like allegory,[9] seventeenth-century writers of assorted persuasions took special note of what happens when such figures allegedly get up and move. Insofar as such figures look or act like deeds or are by law so judged, they suggest how abstract ideas might be invaded or overtaken by material particulars. From this perspective, allegorical practices have everything to do with a fundamental philosophical concern of early modern culture – the domain shared or divided by abstractions, language, and particulars. Against the possibility that language might not be capable of mediating between abstractions and phenomenal reality, some seventeenth-century writers urge (or hope) that language is or might once again become a transparent and stable medium for ideas. To this hope, skeptical epistemologies reply that language is not a transparent medium, that it instead offers propositional statements about the relation between sensations, matter, and human ideas.[10]

The importation of neo-epicurean theories of matter and cognition from France by English royalists at the time of the Restoration created space within the framework of a skeptical epistemology for empirical data, those "atoms" whose materiality seventeenth-century philosophers imagine and describe. Neo-epicurean writers grant the existence of sensations and matter (as "atoms"), but contend that they could only guarantee "a merely hypothetical or probable knowledge of things."[11] Against claims for a stable epistemology lodged in sense experience, they insisted that the world and its objects could not be so easily known, that knowledge and being are contingent and propositional, and that words are unstable, if essential, guides to knowledge. As such, words articulate relations, not absolute entities.

In seventeenth-century figural practice, the convergence of atomist theories of matter and epistemological skepticism insures a productive antagonism between the extra figural "weight" imposed by the materiality and visuality of figures, especially allegorical figures, and the epistemological claim that conjectures about the world and subjecthood virtually require figural language. This requirement favors synecdoche as the figure for the relation between observed parts and, in the case of neo-epicureanism, intuited or contingent ideas of the whole.[12] As the ancient metafigure for posited, but not certain, analogies between images, words, and transcendent ideas or truths, allegory is itself synecdochic, referring its visible or legible parts to unapprehended but posited abstractions or beliefs. So construed, allegory may be counted among those "material phantasms" which Glanvill says the mind uses to imagine abstract ideas and concepts for which sense experience supplies only bits and pieces.

Operating within an epistemology that is both skeptical and materialist, allegory thus mediates between material, historical particulars and transhistorical and metaphysical truths. Its figures are material and phantasmatic: they are ghosts of something else, somewhere else, but the evidence for this proposition resides in their material shapes and in local and historical conditions which guarantee one shape and not another. Yet this home truth seems to have been less comforting than troublesome in seventeenth-century allegorical practice. Hobbes's theory of knowledge, whose point of departure is shared by epistemological theory from Descartes to Locke and beyond, suggests why.

For if Hobbes begins the *Leviathan* with an emblematic frontispiece that invites an allegorical reading of this image and accompanying text, his argument is nevertheless well furnished with objections to the *visual* power of allegorical figures. Hobbes is caught in the middle, trapped by the visual and material phantasm of allegorical figures whose debts to the pictorial and emblematic character of Renaissance allegory are everywhere apparent. The oxymoronic inversion of Glanvill's conviction that "material phantasms" are needed to convey "immaterial substances" declares what Hobbes leaves unsaid.[13]

My argument begins with three events in seventeenth-century English culture that summarize allegory's career from the midpoint of this tumultuous century, from the factional use of allegorical figures in the 1640s and 1650s to the Restoration dismissal of allegory and rhetorical figures in the name of experimental science, Anglican conformity, and the crown. In January 1640, Charles I and his courtiers performed the last of the Stuart masques, *Salmacida Spolia* by William Davenant and Inigo Jones, at Whitehall. As the royal seat of government for the last three Stuart kings, Whitehall stood on the site of an earlier palace which had been occupied and rebuilt by successive Tudor monarchs and then James I until it was destroyed by fire in 1619. Commissioned by Charles I to provide a series of paintings for the new building, Peter Paul Rubens created nine allegorical canvases that proclaim various Stuart triumphs in this world and the next, among them the union of England and Scotland under Charles's father James I and, in the central oval, the (presumed) apotheosis of James I. All nine were in place by 1635.[14]

In this charged symbolic space,[15] *Salmacida Spolia* works hard to extend the Stuart ideology of peace and political union from father to son. The masque begins, as Jones's elaborate description explains, with the figure of Discord, "a malicious Fury" whose appearance in a storm is an emblem of her effort to put the "world into disorder." Although the Greek Eris was not one of the Furies, she was, like them, a winged creature. In the political and religious strife that characterized Charles I's reign, this resemblance was almost certainly more than simply visual. Among those listed as having acted in the masque were several who later abandoned the king to join the Parliamentary cause.[16] To these erstwhile courtiers, Discord might well have looked like the fate or fury confronting Charles I and England. In *Salmacida Spolia*, the world (and England) are saved in due course by the king in the character of "Philogenes or Lover of his People," whose secret wisdom quells the storm and its agents, turning disorder into calm, and calm into musical harmony.

In *Salmacida Spolia*, the antimasque of Discord and her Furies is dispelled, its "spectacle of strangenesse" put aside so that the virtues of the people-loving monarch might save the day and nation.[17] Because this outcome must have looked unlikely in 1640 as England approached civil war, the staged appearance of Discord and her allegorical crew amplifies the risk the antimasque typically represented as an anarchic, carnivalesque vehicle for disruption from below and, more specifically, the ironic reversal implied in the masque itself in some Jacobean tragedies where kings or tyrants are overthrown under the cover of a masque.[18] To this risk, Jones and Davenant may have responded by sparing no expense to make *Salmacida Spolia* the most elaborate and resplendent of all the Stuart masques, as though its brilliant scenery, machinery, and court costumes could provide ballast to an otherwise "insubstantial pageant" and reign.[19]

In ways that the last Stuart masque both implies and seeks to deny, seventeenth-century allegorical figures and images are made to conduct themselves like real agents. The extent to which this remains the case even after the Restoration is dramatically conveyed by an incident well into the reign of Charles II, who was by 1681 in serious conflict with Parliament over its efforts to exclude his Catholic brother James from the line of succession. Like his father, Charles II managed the controversy by dissolving his last Parliament. Amid public outcry, he claimed in a Public Declaration that he had taken this action because Protestants were plotting to assassinate him. Soon afterward, a now rare broadside cartoon and ballad appeared. Titled *A Ra-ree Show*, it depicted the king as a two-headed (two-faced) pedlar whose pack folds out to reveal the two Houses of Parliament. Charles's two heads call out "A Ra-ree Show" and "Ra-ree Shite's" as he blows bubbles from a tube. As B. J. Rahn explains, "the pedlar is out to 'bubble' his audience with a false show, i.e., the King intends to dupe the people with a delusive scheme regarding the succession." Emblematic details and adjacent figures identify the king as the head of state and the representative of the people. Other figures carry emblems of political power.[20]

The pivotal moment in the action occurs when the royal pedlar arrives in Oxford to peddle his wares, even as Charles II convened Parliament to Oxford, where Stuart and royalist sentiment was strong, to raise (or extort) funds. The broadside declares that this royal strategem for getting more funds backfires when the king is overthrown by members of Parliament, who had been mere puppets until they were released from his pack. More or less in the form of a dialogue between the "Leviathan"-pedlar who hopes to gull those who see and buy his wares, and one Topham who explains the pedlar's game, the ballad insists that the pedlar is half-Catholic and, for this and other habits of statecraft, "like father like son."

Stephen College, a carpenter, Protestant Joiner, and militant Exclusionist, was accused of being the author of *A Ra-ree Show*, charged with having planned to assassinate the king, convicted of treason, and executed. Although he denied having written the broadside at his trial, College never claimed he had not distributed it. This tacit admission, together with the history of his political dissent, assertions that he had plotted regicide, and testimony (without material corroboration) that preliminary drawings for the broadside were found in his rooms, were enough to convict him.[21] In the course of the trial, he repeatedly argued in his own defense that the case against him was, as Rahn puts it, "a matter of words rather than deeds, of allegations rather than facts." The Lord Chief Justice's reply to this objection insisted that the first evidence of such a conspiracy was "your publishing libels, and pictures to make the king odious and contemptible in the eyes of the people." Stephen College fatally underestimated the political power his accusers ascribed to the popular appeal of an emblematic ballad like *A Ra-Ree Show*. In Restoration England, treasonable words embedded in the popular format of an emblematic broadside were as good or bad as deeds.[22]

The extent to which key players in the civil turmoil of the period implicitly acknowledged the power of allegorical words and images is well summarized by their use of Whitehall as a monumental emblem of state power. When Charles I was executed there in 1649, the event was carefully staged so that he would step from an upper window of Whitehall onto the wooden scaffold where he would be beheaded. In *Eikonoklastes*, Milton explained the scaffold's placement allegorically, as the present and material sign of an absent but not forgotten truth, since it was on this spot that Charles's royal troops frequently harassed citizens as they passed by. Using biblical typology against Charles, Milton uses the site of Charles's beheading to confirm a retributive Divine justice: "*In the place where Dogs lick'd the blood of Naboth, shall Dogs lick thy blood, eev'n thine.*"[23] After the interregnum,

Oliver Cromwell made Whitehall the seat of his Protectorate, perhaps because it was too powerfully emblematic to be left empty. There he also refused the crown and there he died in 1658. With Charles II's restoration to the English throne, the Stuarts reoccupied Whitehall. The two-day coronation marked the event with extensive allegorical pageantry that offered this Stuart monarch as the fulfillment of various biblical and mythological types, among them Christ, David, and Neptune (for Charles as the royal commander of the English navy).[24] By such means, Charles II made his reign out of the same allegorical cloth royalists had used in the *Eikon Basilike* of 1649 to sanctify the memory of his father, Charles I. The son died at Whitehall in 1685, succeeded by his brother after all. James II's reign ended in 1688 when he fled Whitehall by the privy stairs, sacrificing kingly dignity to keep his head. In the Glorious Revolution of 1688–89, William and Mary abandoned Whitehall, the (rebuilt) emblematic center stage for the entrances and exits of the Tudor and Stuart kings, for Kensington Palace.

At different times throughout the century and for different ends, Anglican conformists and radical nonconformists (and most degrees in between) use allegorical figures and exegesis or castigate them as an offense against the emergent standards of an English plain style. It is only with benefit of hindsight that the call for plain speech and linguistic reform by members of the newly created Royal Society seems inevitable or natural. It is in fact the contested end point of a sustained cultural debate, with few fixed positions, about language and figure. This confusion of tongues is not what William Tyndale, sometimes called the father of the English Reformation and early Puritanism, would have wished to see. In 1528, he categorically declared: "Tropologicall and anagogicall are termes of [the Catholic church's] awne faynynge and all together vnnecessary. For they are but allegories both two of them and this words allegorie comprehendeth them both and is ynough ... And Allegory is as moch to saye as straunge speakyngne or borowed speach ... the scripture hath but one sence which is ye literall sence."[25] So presented, allegory belongs to the category of inscrutable, mysterious signs and images, the devil's work of Catholic and later Anglican priestcraft. Allegory survived in spite of (or because of) this demonization, with assistance from an expected quarter: nonconformist, radical religionists of the mid seventeenth century whose extensive use of allegory prompted a backlash among conformist English writers of the 1660s and 1670s.

Whereas most seventeenth-century Puritans asserted that the Bible ought to be understood literally, not allegorically, several radical sects openly espoused allegorical readings that drew typological parallels between biblical events and their own times.[26] In *Eikonoklastes*, Milton implies that the royalist analogy between Charles I and the biblical David in the *Eikon Basilike* is an especially degraded form of Stuart royal privilege and a misuse of biblical typology. Yet many nonconformists believed that the distinction between what is literal and figural in the Bible did not obtain. Nonconformist writers frequently assumed that if the people of ancient Israel spoke "in synecdochies and metonymies," so might they.[27]

Nonconformist writing of the 1640s and after constitutes a highly diversified religious culture which, under the millenarian pressure of the times, extends the inwardness and rhetoricity of Puritan theology and writing to read their own and biblical times allegorically, sometimes by reading one as instantiated in the other.[28] At one extreme, some members of sects like the Ranters and the Quakers believed all speech and action to be allegorical. Among the Ranters, a woman identified by her interlocutor only as "Mrs. T. P." reads her dream as though each scene were an allegorical emblem to be carefully interpreted. The Dutch progenitor of the "Family of Love" sect, Hendrik Niclaes, asserted that the route to spiritual understanding is through "Similitudes, Figures, and Parables."[29] Niclaes's tolerant fable of those who are guided to the peaceful land of Christ along many paths that finally converge makes the Bible its referent (by chapter and verse), although the general application of the fable to England in 1649 would have been apparent to English readers.

The point of departure for such allegorical writing is typically biblical rather than learned, but the impulse to read individual spiritual experience as though it contained mysterious, partially decipherable hieroglyphs is surprisingly faithful to Renaissance allegorical practice. More than a century after Tyndale condemned allegorical biblical exegesis, the nonconformist Theophilus Gale asked: "Where can we find more *proper* and *significant Symbols, Metaphors*, and other such like *Rhetorick Shadows*, and *Images*, than in Sacred Scripture?"[30] Although Gale's patently rhetorical question excludes non-biblical sources, it clearly sanctions the allegorical practice of John Bunyan's *Pilgrim's Progress*, published in 1668, the year before Gales's multi-volume work began to appear. This turn toward allegory late in Bunyan's career, after having much earlier objected to allegory on Puritan grounds, is not as remarkable as it seems. Safely identified with the after life toward which Bunyan's hero plods, allegory is finally safe from the bodily, material phantasms that had troubled Puritan faith and politics in the 1640s.[31]

Before and after the execution of Charles I, royalist writing depended on a full repertory of allegorical devices (enigmas, codes, emblems, anagrams, iconography) to broadcast risky state secrets. In 1641, the year before hostilities between Charles and Parliament broke out in open civil war, John Wilkins's *Mercury, or the Secret and Swift Messenger* provided a virtual handbook of methods for encoding secrets in printed works. At the time a supporter of the Parliamentarian cause, he brilliantly forecast the role of "secret" writing in the royalist cause. From the "expans'd hieroglyphicks" of John Denham's *Coopers Hill* to the *Eikon Basilike* and beyond, royalist arguments were often encoded in allegorical texts. To the chagrin of Milton and his compatriots, the royalist machine, driven by the twin engines of allegorical secrecy and illegal printing, managed to sustain the public sentiment that eventually lent support to (or at least did not oppose) the restoration of the Stuart monarchy in 1661.[32]

In the 1660s and 1670s, conformist Anglican writers launched a sustained attack on the nonconformist prose of the preceding two decades.[33] The Restoration polemic that informs this attack is well displayed by Thomas Sprat's and Andrew Cowley's official declarations of the scientific and linguistic program of the new Royal Society. My point is not that earlier English writers like Ben Jonson who had advocated a plainer style made no impression on these conformist polemics (they evidently did).[34] Nor do I suggest that this style is or was nonexistent, although it was not nearly as "plain," i.e. shorn of figures, as Sprat's influential advertisement implied. The Restoration call for a plain style masks a much broader anxiety about the "enthusiasm" of nonconformist writing.[35]

Arguing in 1670 that nonconformists "have effectually turn'd all Religion into unaccountable Fansies and Enthusiasm ... and so embrace a few gaudy Metaphors and Allegories," Samuel Parker urges that for a nation "shattered into infinite factions with senseless and phantastick phrases," what is needed is an "Act of Parliament to abridge Preachers the use of fulsome and luscious Metaphors."[36] This proposal was by no means unique. Hobbes had made a similar point in 1651, writing in exile from Parliamentary England: "metaphors and senseless and ambiguous words are like *ignes fatui*; and reasoning upon them, is wandering amongst innumerable absurdities; and their end, contention, and sedition, or contempt" (*Leviathan* 29–30).

Allegory is not a named co-conspirator here. Indeed, Hobbes never condemns allegory or other figures wholesale. In his *Answer to Davenant*, he applauds "farre-fetch't (but withal apt, instructive, and comely) Similitudes" (65), and the emblematic frontispiece of *Leviathan* declares the allegorical cast of its argument about civil governments. Yet both works are critical of allegorical figures. Among "the indecencies of an Heroick Poem" he includes the practice of "representing in great persons the inhumane vice of Cruelty or the sordid vice of Lust and Drunkenness" (*Answer to Davenant* 64). What troubles Hobbes about this kind of allegorical figure is its "disproportion," whereby an allegorical abstraction like Cruelty or Lust seems to overcome the "great person [ ]" to which it is assigned. This fault does not occur when such abstractions are assigned to "monsters and beastly Giants" because, he implies, the allegorical representation of vice requires monstrous, grotesque shapes, not human forms such as (the example is mine) those that appear in medieval processions of the seven deadly sins. If we put this argument beside Hobbes's adjacent claim for verisimilitude – "truth is the bound of the Historical, so the Resemblance of truth is the utmost limit of Poeticall Liberty" (*Answer to Davenant* 62) – together they suggest that allegorical abstractions belong elsewhere, among the monsters and giants of a fabulous irreality.

In the *Answer to Davenant*, Hobbes compares divines to clumsy magicians who call up "such spirits as they cannot at their pleasure allay again" and presents the outcome of such misadventures in allegorical terms: "For when they [unskilful Divines] call unseasonably for *Zeal* there appears a Spirit of *Cruelty*; and by like error, instead of *Truth* they raise *Discord*; instead of *Wisdom*, *Fraud*; instead of *Reformation*, *Tumult*; and *Controversie* instead of *Religion*" (*Answer to Davenant* 58–59). The abbreviated paratactic style of this sentence sharpens and tightens the "ambling" pace of preceding sentences to convey Hobbes's polemic against the involvement of Puritan and other "divines" in the English civil war and Parliamentary rule.[37] What is more, allegorical abstractions dominate this syntax as indeed Hobbes believes they dominate English political reality. It is also no accident that the figure that replaces Truth in Hobbes's view is "Discord." By such turns of figure, the aesthetic conversation between Hobbes and Davenant as royalists in exile specifies its political occasion.

Thus while it is true that conformist arguments about language target figures which have over time encouraged the decay and abuse of meaning, not figures in general,[38] they also convey a deep-seated antagonism toward the extravagance and passion of figures then in use. Sprat's official *History of the Royal Society* asserts that the only cure for such excesses is "to reject all amplifications, digressions, and swellings of style: to return back to the primitive purity, and short-ness, when men deliver'd so many *things*, almost in an equal number of words" (113). In the service of this proposition, Sprat identifies Egyptian "Hieroglyphicks" as the origin of written language and of allegory, then concludes that those hieroglyphics contributed to the "corruption" of language by concealing ancient knowledge of nature and humankind (5). Like Hobbes, Sprat opposes reason and rational conjecture to the misguided enthusiasm of figures inspired by "*Fancy*," "its slaves, *the Passions*" and (getting down to cases), "specious *Tropes* and *Figures*." It will be the task of the Royal Society, says Sprat, to correct "this vicious abundance of *Phrase*, this trick of *Metaphors*, this volubility of *Tongue*" (112). The present age, he sagely assures (or commands) his audience, has little use for "Phantasms, and Fairies, and venerable Images of Antiquity [as] did long haunt the world" (29). Invoking a chain of resonances that leads back to Quintilian's *visiones* and *phantasia* by way of the Renaissance emblem, Sprat's "Phantasms" specify the visual (and apparitional) nature of allegory as hieroglyphic sign – a visual shape whose excesses remind Sprat of rhetorical excesses – as though these too were shapes, not merely words, with designs on susceptible minds.

The political undertow of Sprat's programmatic rejection of elaborate rhetorical figures and allegory surfaces when he comments on how language changes during "times of war." The particular instance, "our late Civil Wars," brings the argument home. During this time, Sprat says, "fantastical terms ... [were] introduced by our *Religious Sects*, and many outlandish phrases, which several *Writers*, and *Translators*, in that great hurry brought in." To get rid of lexical undesirables, Sprat proposes a more genteel version of Parker's Act of Parliament. A civic patrol of "sober and judicious Men, would take the whole Mass of our Language into their hands, ... would set a mark on ill Words, [then] correct" them (42). This "impartial Court of Eloquence" that could also be expected to write an

adequate history of the "late Civil Wars" turns out to be Sprat and
other fellows of the Royal Society, men whose political engagements
on all sides of those wars were muted under the sign of the
Restoration and Charles II's royal patronage.[39] In the program of
language reform Sprat advances in the name of the Royal Society,
the dismissal of phantasms and allegorical mystery is geared to insure
a new if uneasy peace, when "mens minds are somewhat settled,
their Passions allaid, and the peace of our Country gives us the
opportunity of such diversions" (42). When he charges that "trans-
gression of the Law is idolatry" and proposes experimental knowledge as the "enemy" to "superstitions, to men adoring themselves,
and *their* own fancies" (430), the political edge of his uneasiness about
allegory includes *phantasia*, returned to Restoration England as fancy,
imagination, and phantasm. There is little room for allegory in this
linguistic diet, except insofar as it might or would maintain the "one-
to-one relationship of image and significance" permitted by advo-
cates of a plain style.[40]

Whereas Restoration apologists discredit allegory in part to
suppress the nonconformist use of allegory for political and sectarian
dissent, Milton's allegorical practice suggests a more self-divided
reading of the same cultural moment. If the most prominent
evidence of this concern is the allegory of Sin and Death in *Paradise
Lost*, this episode is both heir and antecedent in a figural itinerary
that extends from his early poems and polemicist prose to the sparse
and problematic figurality of *Paradise Regained* and *Samson Agonistes*.
All along this itinerary, Milton's use of allegorical figures is inventive,
even conjectural, as it calibrates the risks and gains of figures whose
work is phantastical in the sense that it is at once exaggerated and
visually as well as viscerally evocative, such that abstractions assume
a quasi-material and tangible presence. Milton's late monism, which
assumes that "the whole range from the physical, specifically the
senses, to the ultimate Divine [is] *absolutely unbroken*," subtends this
figural practice.[41] Sin and Death are among the most intriguing of
Milton's allegorical figures precisely because each demonically refi-
gures the materialist risk entailed by figures that are doubly attuned
to material referent and abstraction.

In the anti-prelatical tracts of the early 1640s and the allegorical
set-pieces of *Areopagitica* and the *Doctrine and Discipline of Divorce*,
Milton deploys a curious, often grotesque array of material referents
for abstract ideas. By the late 1640s, as royalist writers were making

extensive use of similar allegorical figures, Milton not surprisingly chose to use them less. In his later prose and poems he more sharply addresses the underlying philosophical difficulty which seventeenth-century allegorical figures bring into focus as verbal, visual and suggestively material shapes for abstract ideas.

In the anti-prelatical tracts of the 1640s, Milton invents an array of compound nouns and adjectives that turn Episcopal prelates into allegorical abstractions: "non-resident and plurality-gaping Prelats," "Pulpit-Mountibank," "Sermon-actor," "Church-Maskers," and the widely quoted figure that appears the in tract titled *Church-Maskers*, "what a rich bootie it would be, what a plump endowment to the many-benefice-gaping mouth of a Prelate, what a relish it would give to his canary-sucking, and swan-eating palat, let old Bishop *Mountain* judge for me."[42] These compounds shuttle between abstraction and materiality. In the last example, the quasi-abstraction of "the many-benefice-gaping mouth of a Prelate" is brought uncomfortably near (with a quick assist from internal rhyme) "his canary-sucking, and swan-eating palat." Syntactic echoes and textual proximity invite readers to imagine that the abstract figure of a prelate's mouth stuffed with benefices is a figural inversion of a palate that greedily consumes whole birds as though it were actually a mouth, not simply an appetite. As vivid pictorial representations – of prelates and clergy become abstractions, and of vices given a particular human face and appetite – these epithets work like emblems.

With less syntactic and dramatic flourish, Milton's early allegorical figures variously insist on yoking abstract and material elements. When the figure is commonplace, this strategy tends to slip from critical view, as in "buried Truth" (*Of Reformation, CPW* 1:526). At times he modifies abstractions in ways that suggest animate being: "Admiration" is "glouting," "Indifference" is "a persecuter," "schisme" is a "bolder-lurker," "Falsehood and Neglect" are charged with having "throwne" the Bible into dusty corners, and "vertue that wavers is not vertue, but vice revolted from itself, and after a while returning."[43] On occasion Milton chooses to mortify rather than animate by way of figure. Referring to the (fortunately) hypothetical child whose parents want to rear him in the Anglican church, he exhorts: "rather let them take heed what lesson they instill into that lump of flesh which they are the cause of, lest, thinking to offer him as a present to God, they dish him out for the Devill" (*Animadversions, CPW* 1:722). This passage works hard, even ferociously, to de-animate the child all the way from conception (here "cause") to the Devil's plate.[44] Following the same figural track used to animate abstractions in preceding examples but in the opposite direction, the figure of the child is all matter – a lump of flesh and a tasty dish. The visceral grotesquerie of this figure is not unusual in Milton's prose of the 1640s. In *Colasterion* (the example is admittedly extreme), Milton calls his opponent a "Pork" and "a mongrel" who argues "like a Boar in a Vinyard, doing nought else, but still as hee goes, champing and chewing over, what I could mean by this *Chimera* of a fit conversing Soul, notions and words never made for those chopps."[45] When Milton uses this kind of figure to animate an abstract idea, it begins to look like shock therapy, all the more remarkable because it is often highly compressed.

In these and more extended allegorical figures in the early prose, Milton's strategic mixture of expansiveness and compression secures allegorical interpretation by way of material vehicles. So two-handed a figural engine also makes short work of neat distinctions between allegorical vehicles and tenors. Consider, for example, the phrase "how uneffectual and weak is outward force with all her boistrous tooles" (*Civil Power*, *CPW* vii:259). The brevity of the phrase compresses its allegorical invention, which is not declared until the end with the word "tools." As Milton extends and then recompresses the violent logic of this figure, it works to join opposites much as oxymoron does, but with a critical difference. Whereas oxymorons exhibit a show of force on the level of syntax, the violence implied by Milton's figure is material and local and it is the material vehicle that carries the allegory.[46] This may continue to be so even when the material features of a given vehicle seem to outrun or override the figure: "till the Soule by this means of over-bodying her selfe, given up justly to fleshly delights, bated her wing apace downeward ... forgot her heavenly flight, and left the dull, and droyling carcas to plod on in the old road, and drudging Trade of outward conformity" (*Of Reformation*, *CPW* i:522).[47] Here bodily materiality is everywhere the sign of fallen spirit. As the soul becomes attached to the pleasures of the body or outward form of conformist Anglican ritual, it assumes the material weight of its bodily "carcas," which can then be discarded inasmuch as the soul is now – the irony is bitter – plodding onward, weighed down by bodily functions. Extended or compressed, material referents are in all these examples the real agents of allegorical abstraction.

In the allegorical vignette at the beginning of *Doctrine and Discipline of Divorce*, Milton makes Custom a slick female operator whose rhetoric is so "glib and easy" that a listener may be persuaded to "take and swallow down at pleasure" her "book of implicit knowledge."[48] The unlucky eater inevitably suffers worse than indigestion: he "puffs up unhealthily, a certaine big face of pretended learning, mistaken among credulous men, for the wholsome habit of soundnesse and good constitution; but [ ] indeed no other, then that swoln visage of counterfeit knowledge and literature" (*CPW* II:222–23). When Milton says he will "pursue the Allegory," what he does is sharply limit its agency: "Custome being but a meer face, as Eccho is a meere voice, rests not in her unaccomplishment, untill by secret inclination, shee accorporate her selfe with error, who being a blind and Serpentine body without a head, willing accepts what he wants, and supplies what her incompleatnesse went seeking. Hence it is, that Error supports Custome, Custome count'nances Error" (223). Milton's judicial restraint on Custom, "that daring phantasm, a meer toy of terror" (666–67), forecasts Neoclassical efforts to restrain allegorical figures. Reduced to a "meer face," and capable only of "unaccomplishment," she allies with blind Error by giving it what it lacks, a "face" that, Milton puns, "count'nances" Error.

Areopagitica even-handedly echoes Spenser by including error and temperance among those arrayed on both sides of Truth, who is at once the most frequently invoked allegorical figure in this work and the most endangered of the species. Despite her "ingenuity" (521), Truth's once "perfect shape" (549) has been hacked to pieces and scattered to the winds. Milton continues, "we have not yet found tham all, Lords and Commons, nor ever shall doe, till her Masters second comming; he shall bring together every joynt and member, and shall mould them into an immortall feature of lovelines and perfection" (549–50). A few pages later, however, he allows that in "things indifferent" truth "may have more shapes than one" (563). As Loewenstein understands this admission, it ratifies the myriad "postures and discourses" of the regicide tracts. Yet in *Areopagitica* Milton is subtly cautious about allowing Truth more than a single shape. For here he aligns Truth's different shapes with those Proteus assumes so that he can avoid telling the truth about the future. Only in "things indifferent" – things that are not matters of true Christian doctrine and absolute principle – does Truth take on different shapes "without being unlike her self" (563).[49]

The grotesque viscerality of Milton's disembodied Truth is not, I think, merely rhetorical effect, although it certainly is that. It may recall the quite real bodily mutilations of nonconformists Burton, Bastwick, and Prynne by Archbishop Laud.[50] The relative scarcity of similarly vivid figures in the regicide tracts of the late 1640s suggests further that Milton became uneasy about figures like the mangled, dismembered body of Truth, whose materiality insures that abstractions look more like human bodies and thereby invite a reader's or listener's pathetic response.

The full measure of Milton's reaction against his early allegorical practice appears in *Eikonoklastes*, his polemical reply to *Eikon Basilike*, the royalist pamphlet published soon after the execution of Charles I.[51] To counter the persuasive mix of pathos, emblem, and allegorical figures in this work, his rhetoric is corrosive and predictably anti-allegorical. Less predictably, *Eikonoklastes* introduces allegorical abstractions that are unusual for Milton precisely because they are so resolutely abstract.

Eikonoklastes begins and ends by taking aim at the emblematic frontispiece of *Eikon Basilike*, which depicts Charles kneeling and praying, having put his kingly crown aside to be ready to assume a heavenly crown, but clutching a crown of thorns. Milton scornfully observes, "quaint Emblems and devices begg'd from the old Pageantry of some Twelf-nights entertainment at *Whitehall*, will doe but ill to make a Saint or a Martyr" (*CPW* III:343). By linking the king's image with the illusion and theatricality of court masques staged at Whitehall, Milton draws attention away from the most dramatic and pathetic stage of Charles's reign, the scene of his execution on the scaffold just outside Whitehall.[52] Milton presents the Charles of *Eikon Basilike* as an actor on a royal stage, a figure of empty rhetoric and unreality whose religious devotion is "counterfeit," the "deepest policy of a Tyrant" (361), a "deep dissembler" like Shakespeare's Richard III (362) whose "ill-acted regality" people very nearly hiss "off the Stage" of the Long Parliament (355). So presented, Charles looks less like a tragic protagonist than a usurping, murderous king and a bad actor. The masque Milton invents to describe the *Eikon Basilike* as Charles's histrionic self-justification is more ludicrous than dazzling, thanks in large measure, Milton insists, to the king's fevered imagination, which invents its own "Antimasque of two bugbeares, *Novelitie* and *Perturbation*" (533).[53] Whereas the last Stuart masque *Salmacida Spolia* ended with Charles, in the person of Philogenes, driving out the antimasque of Discord and her compatriots, this one drives out "all endeavors of a Reformation" and allies the dead Charles with the disruptive misrule of the antimasque, not the victorious royal protagonist of the masque itself.

Quoting the printed text of one of the dead king's prayers, Milton presents its allegorical figures as evidence that the king's rage against his own people is unreasoning and hysterical: "instead of praying for his people as a good King should doe, hee prayes to be deliver'd from them, as *from wild Beasts, Inundations, and raging Seas, that had overborn all Loyalty, Modesty, Laws, Justice, and Religion*" (397). In this accumulation of imagined adversaries, Milton implies, allegorical figures are inevitable and wholly imaginary, the "phantasms" other seventeenth-century writers like to identify with allegory. This brief against imagination and "phantasy" as disordered operations of Charles's mind and "a Peece of Poetrie" (406) makes poetry and allegory signs of mental disorder. The problem with this criticism is of course that it comes too close to home, as seventeenth-century critics of his later *Defenses* of the regicide argue when they call him a "fabulist and mere poet" and a "monstrous Polyphemus" whose gigantic proportions are the logical bodily extension of his exaggerated figures.[54] Milton's rhetorical confrontation with the figure of Charles reverberates, in short, with Lacanian irony. Looking into the picture of Charles I, he finds a degraded version of himself as poet. The image he throws back into this picture-become-a-mirror is (called) Charles.

If none of these examples suggests that Milton is a willing allegorist, the cameo appearance of an allegorical Justice in *Eikonoklastes* shows how deft even an unwilling allegorist can be. To counter the humanity and pathos of the king's image in *Eikon Basilike*, he makes Justice highly abstract. In the most telling of its manifestations in this work, Justice here permits an invocation of the image of the beheaded king that is stripped of its usual pathos. To chastize Presbyterian and Parliamentary sympathizers who had never balked at open hostilities against Charles during the civil war but then turned queasy at his beheading, Milton asks why they who thought the king "nothing violated by the Sword of Hostility drawn by them against him, should now in earnest think him violated by the unsparing Sword of Justice" (346). Whereas Milton, in earlier allegorical figures, make pointed use of material referents, even going so far as to imagine Truth mangled and dismembered, here he

assiduously avoids putting the Sword of Justice into explicit contact
with the beheaded king's body. This "clean abstraction," as Corns
pungently observes, avoids the graphic (visual and verbal) descriptions of the scene of death popularized in the English Protestant
tradition and especially Foxe's *Actes and Monuments*.[55] The logic of
Milton's choice is telling: a more material representation of Justice
using her sword to behead the king would have evoked the special
pathos and figural power of allegorical figures that command
material or visual referents.

The viscerality of Truth in *Areopagitica* and the abstraction of
Justice in *Eikonoklastes* convey the difficulty that haunts Milton's
allegorical practice. As modern editors note, the "immortal feature"
lost to Truth until the Last Judgment echoes his use of *factura* in other
works to mean "ideal shape." In *Comus* the Lady exclaims, "Thou
unblemish't form of Chastity! / I see ye visibly," and in *The Reason of
Church-Government* Milton refers to "the very shape and visage of
Truth." Even the fallen Satan of *Paradise Lost* is made to see the
difference between his unfallen "shape" and the one he has now:
"abasht the Devil stood ... and saw / Virtue in her shape how
lovely, saw, and pin'd / His loss" (*PL* 4.846–49, p. 108). Here
Miltonic "shape" subscribes to Cicero's assertion that the visible
"form and shape of Moral Goodness" can direct us to love
wisdom.[56] This conviction guarantees allegory its ontological status
as a visible figure or image, an "ideal shape." Yet Milton's iconoclastic suspicion of outward shape is itself proof against such
guarantees. In *Paradise Lost* Eve becomes a female Narcissus so in
love with her own reflection ("A Shape within the wat'ry gleam
appear'd" *PL* 4.460, p. 97) that she initially refuses to join the mate
for whom she was created. In *Paradise Regained*, when Satan tells
Christ, "thy heart / Contains of good, wise, just, the perfect shape"
(*PR* 4.11, p. 489), this truth is robbed of its moral and allegorical
charge. It is virtual white noise, rhetorical patter Satan uses to veil
his real meaning and purpose. By making Christ's "perfect shape" a
verbal disguise for Satan's real intent, Milton gives the Renaissance
topos of the "veil" of allegory a sharply ironic twist. In *Paradise Lost*,
his repeated use of "shape" to refer to the allegorical figures of Sin
and Death registers all these ironies within a poetic space ill-disposed
to include such figures. For the reappearance of allegory in *Paradise
Lost* is surprising not because Sin and Death are problematic or
anomalous in an epic, as eighteenth-century critics were later to

insist, but because Milton, having long ago assessed the dangers and liabilities of allegorical abstraction, nonetheless invented Sin and Death. This invention is all the more surprising inasmuch as Milton sharply reduced the number of allegorical figures from the list he drew up in an early plan for this epic, which registers his disdain for Spenser's mix of allegorical romance with epic to produce "fabl'd Knights / In Battels Feign'd."[57] Recent accounts of what Milton got or did not get from Spenser affirm a fundamental antagonism between Milton's epic purpose and Spenser's allegory. Quilligan argues that Milton identifies the polysemousness of Spenser's allegorical narrative with fallen language and original sin. Teskey assesses the difference between Spenser and Milton along similar lines.[58] Both critics would thus defend Milton's epic against its eighteenth-century critics by insisting that if *Paradise Lost* is allegorical, as its verbal and structural affinities with Spenser, Dante, and Ariosto invite us to recognize, its commitment to allegory is dubious or at best, guarded.

However guarded his commitment to allegory is, it is also deeply Spenserian in ways that the chorus of eighteenth-century criticism of Milton's Sin and Death inadvertently exposes. Echoing contemporary arguments about Homer's Discord, Addison objects to Milton's use of "some Particulars which do not seem to have probability enough for an Epic Poem, particularly in the Action which he ascribes to Sin and Death" (*Spectator* no. 297, III: 60). For Addison and Dr. Johnson, "particulars" are those parts of a metaphor which I. A. Richards calls the vehicle: literal, material details that carry the figure unless, as Johnson observes, they end up carrying the reader's attention away from the metaphorical idea (*Lives* I:45). He urges a version of this understanding of "the force of metaphor" (one might almost say "the force of particulars") when he insists that once Milton gives Sin and Death "material agency," they are no longer allegorical. Johnson explains that when Death offers to fight Satan and, even more egregiously, when Sin and Death build a road over Chaos of "aggregated Soil" and "*Asphaltic* slime" (10.293–98, p. 243), they perform "work" that is "too bulky for ideal architects" (*Lives* I:186). For "real employment," real labor, you need real men and women.

From Johnson to contemporary readers, the debate about whether Sin and Death are "real" or "allegoric," or whether they can be both, has turned on the same critical wheel. Romantic writers tend

to worry the question much as their immediate predecessors did: if
Sin and Death are material agents, they are at best flawed allegory.
Modern critics have pressed the issue of "material agency" more
closely to ascertain just how much or how little Sin and Death
actually do. Readers who decide that these figures do a lot (Milton's
narrator says "thir Power was great" 10.284) may conclude, as
Teskey says about the allegorical figures of the poem, that we are not
invited to read them "in any sense but the literal."[59] Readers who
argue that Sin and Death have only a very limited agency suggest
that their limitations reflect badly (albeit appropriately for Milton's
allegory) on Satan as their sometime father, consort, and rival. One
recent critic suggests that for Milton Sin and Death are both real and
allegoric, that splitting the two in twain is what Satan does in *Paradise
Regained* when he reads portents in the stars of Christ's future
suffering and remarks that he does not know whether the vision of
the future he sees is "real or allegoric."[60] The mix of hatred and
desire in this rhetoric is transparent: he hopes that Christ will suffer
real and not allegoric "sorrows, and labours, opposition, hate, ...
scorns, reproaches, injuries, / Violence and stripes, and lastly cruel
death" (*PR* 4.386–88, p. 525).

The materialist inclination of Milton's figural practice suggests
that it may well be satanic misprision to insist that Sin and Death be
real *or* allegoric. If Truth is a body in *Areopagitica*, if the angels of
Paradise Lost eat with "Keen dispatch of real hunger,"[61] and if the
"incorporeal Spirits" of the fallen angels "to smallest forms /
Reduc'd thir shapes immense" so that they could fit into the hall
outside the "infernal Court" where Satan and the other fallen
Seraphim and Cherubim meet in secret (PL 1.788–90, p. 29), Milton
can hardly be said to be unwilling to let figures cross between what
is materially real and what is not. The monist theology at work in
these transgressions, which assume that bodies and spirits are not
distinct, virtually entails giving material bodies to abstract ideas.[62]
The triune (and anti-Trinitarian) numerology that Milton uses to
describe the bridge over Chaos certainly suggests that it also
functions as a satanic and ironic impresa, a virtual badge of its
allegorical import, but this fact does not cancel out its real or
material aspect unless readers assume (with Dr. Johnson and the
Satan of *Paradise Regained*) that the bridge must be either real asphalt
and "real employment" by real persons, or an allegorical bridge
built by allegorical figures.[63]

Sin and Death do however present risks for Milton, not so much because they are allegorical figures and material agents but because their agency comes from Satan, who makes them his "substitutes" with "Dominion" over everything below Paradise, but especially humankind (*PL* 10.400–8, p. 246).[64] Moreover, the bridge and "Passage broad" which they construct between Hell and earth give the devils a ready and easy way to tempt humankind; they also create a quick, if one-way, street for humans to go to Hell (*PL* 10.304–5, p. 243). Milton corrects for this satanic power by putting limits on what Sin and Death actually do. Although Sin unlocks the gates of Hell, they apparently fly open "on a sudden" and thus without assistance (*PL* 2.879, p. 38); it is with the "high permission of all ruling Heaven" that Satan escapes the burning lake (*PL* 1.210–12, p. 11–12) ; and the pall which Sin and Death seem to cast over the stars as they pass turns out to have been caused by angels who, Quilligan points out, make astrophysical adjustments under God's orders.[65]

A second and more fundamental risk concerns the way that Sin and Death convey Milton's understanding of the relation between abstraction and visible figure or shape. For if, as Rosamund Tuve observed, theirs is "a very particular relation between concrete detail and philosophical (not just ethical) meaning,"[66] the devil is in those particulars. Here are Sin and Death at the gates of Hell:

> Before the Gates there sat
> On either side a formidable shape;
> The one seem'd Woman to the waist, and fair,
> But ended foul in many a scaly fold
> Voluminous and vast, a Serpent arm'd
> With mortal sting: about her middle round
> A cry of Hell Hounds never ceasing bark'd
> With wide *Cerberean* mouths full loud, and rung
> A hideous Peal: yet, when they list, would creep,
> If aught disturb'd thir noise, into her womb,
> And kennel there, yet there still bark'd and howl'd
> Within unseen. Far less abhorr'd than these
> Vex'd *Scylla* bathing in the Sea . . .
>   The other shape,
> If shape it might be call'd that shape had none
> Distinguishable in member, joint, or limb,
> Or substance might be call'd that shadow seem'd,
> For each seem'd either; black it stood as Night,
> Fierce as ten Furies, terrible as Hell,
> And shook like a dreadful Dart; what seem'd his head
> The likeness of a Kingly Crown had on.
>   (*PL* 2.648–60, 666–73, pp. 48–49)

Sin and Death display the phantasmatic energy that accrues to them as allegorical fictions. Because they are exaggerated, grotesque visual figures, they invite readers to understand their apparent literal truthfulness as evidence of what Ferry calls their "nonvisual, abstract meaning." Moreover, as figures, they are an exceedingly odd couple. Whereas Sin is resolutely all body and concupiscence in the flesh – a figure Ferry argues is thereby reduced to "the physical characteristics of the female shape" or rather Milton's female shape – death is that paradoxically shapeless shape.[67] As such, he is the limit and Blakean negation of Milton's allegorical desire for neo-Platonic shapes that convey an ideal which is whole, not dismembered or evacuated. But ladies first.

As Annabel Patterson has reminded readers of Milton, Sin looks like a picture (horror) show of Milton's fiercest sexual rage against women's bodies – the argument is hers, the analogy mine. The "unspeakable agenda" that Patterson discovers in Milton's turn to allegory "when legal or theological vocabularies failed him"[68] is no less than the problem of allegorical image and figure pushed into the psychic arena and vocabulary where Milton could best grasp that problem (seeing darkly, as do we all). Precisely because Sin is a (fallen) allegory, her materiality is absolutely congruent with her allegorical significance. There can therefore be nothing left over except her offspring, beginning with Death and then Discord, the first of Sin's daughters (*PL* 10.707–8, p. 255). Milton's Discord can be found (in case someone wants to find her) in Chaos "with a thousand various mouths" (*PL* 2.967, p. 52).

Like the figure of Discord in *Salmacida Spolia* and in Hobbes's *Answer to Davenant*, this Discord alludes broadly to the "chaos" of political and religious factionalism and rhetoric in seventeenth-century England and, closer to home, to Milton's enraged view of marriage and female offspring. Calling allegory "perverse" and "unspeakable" because it "tries to give language incarnational force, to provide imaginary bodies for disembodied abstractions"[69] inadvertently registers what is at stake and how pungently Milton's Sin conveys this point. Allegory is unspeakable and perverse not because, in the present instance, it is virulently misogynist, but because Milton's misogyny propels the figure of Sin so absolutely (if appropriately) into unending, fallen materiality. If this is a worst case scenario (or, more precisely, the scenario) for seventeenth-century allegory, matter goes even more downhill when Sin introduces her "Phantasm" consort Death (*PL* 2.743, p. 51).

Although Death's shapeless shape certainly recalls Augustine's theology of evil as the absence of good and therefore without substance,[70] Milton works hard to give bulk and heft to that shape. Death's stride makes Hell tremble (Death is a heavy-footed "Monster"), Satan calls him an "execrable shape," and, after Death challenges Satan, the narrator declares: "So spake the grisly terror, / and in shape, / So speaking and so threat'ning, grew tenfold / More dreadful and deform."[71] All of these details are evidently in the service of the allegory and, as such, rhetorical markers of Death's power over Hell and even over its own shape. But this particular application of a medieval and Renaissance technique for heightening the allegory also means trouble.

In Sin and Death, the shapes of rage, violence, and concupiscence are visibly and gigantically at work in the world as allegorical extensions of Satan's desire for absolute tyranny over the created world. As such, they embody a notion of *shape* that is a demonic inversion of the perfect or ideal form that, for example, Milton's Truth will regain at the Last Judgment. With all the force of the grotesque material figures that appear in polemicist writing on all sides during the 1640s and 1650s, the substantial, visible shapes of Sin and Death expose the unattractive underside of seventeenth-century allegory and its material entanglement with recent English history.

In *Paradise Regained* and *Samson Agonistes* Milton is less ambivalent toward than resistant to the allegorical practices of his earlier writing. In *Samson Agonistes* the logic that governs that resistance is apparent: as idol worshippers that act out another version of the allegorical vignette he had used in *Reason of Church-Government* to present Anglican prelates as Dalila to a seduced English church (in the figure of Samson), the Philistines enact the link between idolatry, emblem, and allegory.[72] The "disappointing failure in metaphor" that Ricks finds in Milton's late poems may well be strategic in a poem that presents the blind Samson, evidently kin to the blind Milton writing after the Restoration, as an iconoclast who destroys the idolatrous Philistines, much as Milton tried to explode royalist figures in *Eikonoklastes*.[73] In *Paradise Regained*, the tenor of Milton's wariness of allegory is almost Neoclassical. Sin and Death return for a cameo appearance as "the two grand foes" to be conquered by

Christ. They are, however, soon conquered by Milton's syntax, which demotes them from allegorical agents to descriptive adjectives: "Satanic strength" and "sinful flesh" (*PR* 159–62, p. 452). In a poem where Satan first appears to Christ disguised as an old man, looking very like Spenser's Archimago, allegorical "false semblaunce" is the problem, not a figural solution (*PR* 314–19, p. 458). Although Milton's Christ makes occasional use of examples derived from Renaissance emblem books (487n.), the poem is punctuated with notice of the idolatrous who have fallen. Thus if, as readers have suggested, one or both poems offer a veiled or allegorized critique of Milton's opponents who were after the Restoration back in favor and government,[74] that critique nonetheless includes a hefty dose of figural reserve, except when Satan talks and his words are usually lies.

Susceptible, even responsive, to the rhetorical demands of different occasions, Milton's allegorical practice witnesses the strategic and necessary function of its material and historical particulars. Aware of the theological and figural hazards of binding materiality and abstraction, he invents allegorical figures when he must, recognizing their power as "serious fictions" with political and metafigural import. What James Clifford has argued about ethnographic identity in the modern world – that the identity of a given culture or of individuals as cultural agents is historically contingent, subject to local reappropriation and therefore at once conjectural and deeply inventive – applies to the seventeenth-century figural practices I have considered here, including Milton's.[75] The implied charge throughout *Eikonoklastes* that the royalist deployment of emblem and allegory in the name of Charles I denies history is an accurate, but partial, representation of relations among allegory, history, and material particulars in the seventeenth century. Other, differently poised relations obtain on all sides of English seventeenth-century culture, and at different moments in Milton's career. For most of that career, he needed the obliquity of allegory and, more significantly, he was well situated to recognize the logic of allegorical displacement, the sense that its "other speech" is always off the chart, always at some critical and semiotic remove from its necessary and representative particulars.

During and after the Restoration, allegory's reputation declines in ways signalled by Blackmore's 1695 complaint about Spenser and Ariosto: allegory is *"wild, unnatural, and extravagant,"* an exercise of "fancy" that registers the disturbing elements of *phantasy* and its cognates.[76] Twenty years earlier, Thomas Rhymer laid out the terrain of eighteenth-century objections, arguing that the "*marvellous* Adventures" of Spenser's allegory (misled by Ariosto) are "fanciful and chimerical" and wholly without "probability" (167). This criticism, not universal but certainly frequent during the Restoration, may have waned slightly around the turn of the century. Blackmore himself praises Milton's Sin and Death in a later essay on epic poetry ("Epick Poetry" 42); in the preface to (in its full title) *The Life and Strange Surprizing Adventures of Robinson Crusoe*, Defoe ambiguously defends the work as either "a just History of Fact" or, should this claim be disputed, something else that will divert and instruct the moral reader ("Preface"). This distinction, which echoes Edward Phillips's 1674 praise for the moral truth of allegory,[77] may invite readers to read the story of Crusoe's "Adventures" (a term Rhymer uses to describe *The Faerie Queene*) allegorically. Michael Seidel notes that the dates of Crusoe's island existence (1659–1687) roughly match those of the Restoration of the Stuarts to the English throne, which Defoe bitterly opposed. Viewed through this political lens and exile, Defoe's novel looks like an allegorical fable of how life might be lived outside Stuart England.[78]

The Neoclassical rejection of allegory emphasizes the problematic linguistic and philosophical status of what Addison calls "allegorical persons" and the challenge of allegorical abstraction to historical truth and verisimilitude. By positing the relation among these terms as a challenge instead of a series of porous, transient boundaries, eighteenth-century writers devised a schema that logically barred the unsteady and unseemly seventeenth-century alliance between allegory and material, historical particulars.

CHAPTER 4

Allegorical persons

Allegorick. After the manner of an allegory; not real; not literal.
A kingdom they portend thee; but what kingdom, Real or
allegorick, I discern not. *Milton's Paradise Lost,* b. iv.
Samuel Johnson, "Allegorick," Dictionary

It is certain *Homer* and *Virgil* are full of imaginary Persons, who
are very beautiful in Poetry when they are just shown, without
being engaged in any Series of Action.
Addison, Spectator no. 357, III:337

There is another sort of Imaginary beings, that we sometimes
meet with among the Poets, when the Author represents any
Passion, Appetite, Virtue, or Vice, under a visible Shape, and
makes it a Person or an Actor in his Poem.
Addison, Spectator no. 419, III:573[1]

The claim that allegory came to an end or was abandoned in the
seventeenth century owes much to those Neoclassical writers who
sought to limit the range of what allegory is and can do.[2] As vitriolic,
partisan rhetoric on all sides of the English civil war had made clear,
allegorical figures give a particular, human shape to abstraction,
convey knowledge to secret sharers, and thereby magnify fractures in
the English body politic. With its strange scattering of attributes
among visual and verbal parts, the allegorical emblem had by the
eighteenth century become an abjected sign of those fractures. Much
as Milton had been chary of the royalist use of allegory and therefore
of his own, Neoclassical critics were similarly uneasy about the
complex response such figures invite. Similarly, much as Restoration
writers had objected to the emotional intensity of nonconformist
allegorical figures, their successors objected to allegories that blend
abstract and pathetic elements in grotesque, that is to say excessive
or fantastical, ways.[3] These reservations produce a curious double
bind and a hamstrung allegorical practice. For if eighteenth-century

writers were, as Bertrand Bronson puts it, "fond" of abstractions,[4] they were not in truth fond of allegory.

I return to the well-known Neoclassical argument against allegory because many still believe it and, more fundamentally, because it has long supplied the historical framework for claims about how allegory came to an end early in the modern era. Thus, for example, one recent critic suggests that the figure of "the female monster" met its demise with "the abandonment of allegory, which began in the seventeenth century with the rise of empiricism."[5] If, as I argue, the "demise of allegory" did not occur then or later, it is nonetheless true that Romantic and modern critics have often wished it dead or thought it safely buried. In an influential account of the decline in the use of mythological and allegorical figures after the Renaissance, D. C. Allen remarked that Tasso's "passion for allegory" increased with his "mental disorder." Later in the essay, Allen specifies the critical judgment implicit in this comment. Whereas Spenser, Drayton, or Jonson offer "mythical figures [that] move like men and women through allegorical episodes," Milton's Sin and Death "can do little more than stand outside what is literal and real."[6] For Allen, the virtue of Renaissance allegory (when it didn't go mad) depends on a putative separation of real or mimetic characters that "move like men and women" from their allegorical function in a narrative. This claim is fundamentally hortative: allegorical abstractions should not be allowed to contaminate "real" people or characters. However modern and historiographic this critical longing – and it is both – it uncannily echoes Neoclassical objections to allegorical "persons" as improbable mixtures of abstract qualities with recognizably human personalities and actions.

Addison's contradictory remarks about whether "imaginary" (i.e. allegorical) persons or beings can act are thus symptomatic of a larger cultural anxiety that Neoclassical and subsequent critics manage by presenting it as a purely literary inquiry with a foregone conclusion. To the question, "What is the appropriate role of allegorical figures as agents in the action of a historical and verisimilar genre like the epic?" Neoclassical writers respond in chorus: "None." Dr. Johnson's mid-century definition gestures toward the larger implications of this policing of generic boundaries. In the *Dictionary* he defines "allegorick" as "not real; not literal." The lines he quotes, then attributes to Milton's *Paradise Lost*, actually come from *Paradise Regained*. As I imagine it, the logic of this misattribution may have been as unassailable for Johnson as it is curious for us. Because the allegory of Sin and Death in *Paradise Lost* is the "imperfection" Johnson lingers over in his life of Milton, he relocates its lexical antidote – a Miltonic text in which *real* and *allegorick* are opposed – where it is most needed. As Johnson's mistake suggests, without a clear (if Satanic) declaration of the difference between the allegorical and the real, early modern writers cannot situate ideas and abstractions apart from, and above the world of shifting particulars, those streaked tulips that prompt Joshua Reynolds's near-visceral disgust with the "accidental deficiencies, excrescences, and deformities of things" that must be subtracted from "general figures" to arrive at "an abstract idea of their forms more perfect than any original" (*Discourses* 44).[7]

This chapter assesses the figural logic of Neoclassical objections to allegory, then considers works written after mid-century that either echo those objections or entertain a less limited view of what allegorical figures might do. Deliberately selective rather than exhaustive, my argument veers away from the platitudes of the neo-Spenserian revival, whose vision of Spenserian allegory as a series of highly pictorial, emblematic, and thus static descriptions made Spenser a safe and easy target for Neoclassical critics. Of the allegorical figures and narratives produced after mid-century – and there were many – some are faithful to Neoclassical criteria, among them Hannah More's pamphlets on edifying topics and works by other writers who encase compromising or controversial political material in allegorical narratives.[8] I am as interested in those eighteenth-century works and writers that end up, at times quite adventitiously, thinking about allegory in ways that Addison, Johnson, and others could not. At least two elements encourage this break with earlier strictures. The first, the use of popular instead of learned allegorical or iconographic materials, is in fact just what Neoclassical critics of Renaissance allegory repeatedly urged. The second is renewed notice of narrative as the figured ground of allegory. Whether that narrative invokes popular fables or adopts a national history to argue for change in the present and future, it necessarily breaks with the claim that allegorical figures should not or cannot act.

Neoclassical critics and some of their descendants insist that allegory is or ought to be open, accessible, and transparent, and should offer a stable, one-to-one correspondence between image and idea. Two allegorical set-pieces of Neoclassicism, Addison's "Vision of Mirzah" and Johnson's "Vision of Theodore," illustrate these principles, which are widely disseminated in late Restoration and eighteenth-century literature. Johnson's "Vision," which is modeled on Addison's as well as classical texts by Prodicus and Cebes is, if anything, quicker to attach allegorical labels, as though unwilling to risk having individual scenes misidentified.[9] This view of what allegory ought to be programmatically excludes the signs of its modern reinvention: polysemousness, the use of fantastical allegorical agents in realistic or historical narrative, and the excess of rhetorical pathos that those agents often bring to verisimilar situations and characters.

One animating figure of this story is Discord, who returns (if indeed she ever left town) safely reincarnated as a figure in Homer's *Iliad*. Finessing the classical evidence, Neoclassical writers agree that this Discord (no mention here of her seventeenth-century counterparts) does not act and, more generally, that allegorical figures cannot move like other epic characters because they are not real. Despite these assertions, Homer's Discord looks and acts like a screen memory for allegory's participation in seventeenth-century discord as real and material as one could hope or fear to find. Perhaps because this reality and history were uncomfortably close, eighteenth-century writers abject the problem of allegorical agency onto a less hazardous aesthetic space whose apparent concerns are epic decorum and verisimilitude.

Addison includes "Discord" among those "Allegorical Persons" who appear in classical epic but do not act (*Spectator* no. 357, III:332). Acting the role of a literary gate-keeper on the lookout for poachers, Lord Kames insists that allegorical agents must be "confined within their own sphere; and never admitted to mix in the principal action, nor to cooperate in retarding or advancing the catastrophe" (*Elements* III:248-49). Dr. Johnson makes Discord the instance that confirms this general principle: "when the phantom is put in motion, it dissolves; thus Discord may raise a mutiny, but Discord cannot conduct a march, nor beseige a town" (*Lives* III:233). Yet in a passage from Homer's *Iliad* that Longinus made famous and Addison considers in earlier *Spectator* essays, Discord does act. She even acts in Pope's translation:

> *Discord*! dire Sister of the slaught'ring Pow'r,
> Small at her Birth, but rising ev're Hour,
> While scarce the Skies her horrid Head can bound,
> She stalks on Earth, and shakes the World around;
> The Nations bleed, where'e're her Steps she turns,
> The Groan still deepens, and the Combate burns.[10]

In a limited sense it is true to say that Discord never fights on the plain of Troy. Yet her allegorical tasks (driving men forward, growing large as the battle begins) make her anything but a static image. As Knapp observes, allegorical agency is troublesome because it "contaminates" real agency.[11] Here that agency is put into the fictive grasp of an allegorical figure that swells in size until her head touches the sky. Even when Discord assumes a fixed position as the figurehead of Ulysses's ship, where she urges the Greeks into battle, she remains an unusually mobile and vocal emblem whose fierce movement through the heavens announces, as it were, the first half of an epic simile the Greeks are supposed to complete: like Eris, so did the Greeks rage toward the Trojan plain.[12]

Arguments to the contrary have a stake in imagining abstractions as lifeless forms, not active, named characters. Consider, for example, Lord Kames's rehearsal of the familiar complaint that Rubens's ceiling fresco of the Luxembourg Palace, which depicts the history of Mary de Medicis, is a "perpetual jumble of real and allegorical personages" (Kames, *Elements* III:248–49). Although other English writers of the period repeat this complaint, none mentions a Rubens much closer to home – the ceiling of the Banquet Hall at Whitehall, where allegorical figures and subjects depict historical events like the Union of England and Scotland. The same critics are also silent about James Thornhill's 1707–8 *Allegory of the Protestant Succession*, painted on the ceiling of the Great Hall of Greenwich Hospital, which mixes historical and allegorical characters as freely as Rubens had done at Whitehall nearly a century earlier.[13] Like Homer's Discord on the loose, the use of allegorical figures to depict English political and constitutional crises may be too volatile to include when the putative subject at hand is epic, not political discord.

This reticence may also explain the eighteenth-century silence about a classical text in which Discord is even more troublesome than she is in Homer – Hesiod's account of Discord's lineage and offspring. The daughter of Night and the sister of War, she is the allegorical birth mother to a nest of disturbing abstractions: Sorrow, Dispute, Slaughter, Lawlessness, Famine, Quarrel, Murder, Forgetfulness, Hunger, Pain, the Oath, and lying stories. For Webster, this genealogy suggests that words or language are quite naturally inclined to become "powerful, independent things which go out to do good or harm beyond the control of their master."[14] Thinking back on the political and sectarian battles of seventeenth-century England, Addison and his contemporaries may well have found this genealogy all too familiar. Through the overlapping lenses of this composite historical perspective, Discord looks like the return of the repressed – a name whose political and historical resonances made her the allegorical figure that would come to mind as writers cast about for examples of why allegory ought to be still.

From classical epic to medieval and Renaissance historical romance, allegorical figures are freely intermingled with realist or historical characters. Special pleading to the contrary about, in particular, Homer's Discord is just that. However dangerous the seepage of allegorical abstraction into the world of verisimilitude or indeed into the world, that seepage is both unavoidable and instructive about the real, human interest of abstractions. The eighteenth-century reluctance to grant this point is in part the residual effect of the preceding century, when allegorical figures and rhetoric were powerful weapons, akin to deeds. To put this conclusion somewhat differently, the appeal to epic decorum required neither the degree of passion nor the near-compulsive repetition that characterize the eighteenth-century polemic against mixing allegory with historical or mimetic genres. The unspoken logic of this appeal is a fear of what might happen if allegorical figures divert the energies of historical or realist narratives into abstract fictions. Whether or not this transformation fully occurs, it destabilizes figures by suggesting that they may become or at least seem "reversible."[15] So imagined and so put to work, allegorical figures act as though the barrier between reality or history and abstraction were a porous membrane instead of a guarded wall that protects what is true from what is not.

For Locke and his intellectual descendants, whether or not they choose to put the matter in these terms, allegory dramatizes the potential risks and anomalies of representation by blowing them up into monstrous, and at times monstrously feminine, figures that look very much like all-too-concrete universals. As such, such figures

make explicit the risks conveyed by the arbitrary or "unnatural"
relation between signs and what they represent.[16] Like the realm of
abstractions and "complex ideas" to which they belong, allegorical
figures are a "mixed mode," born troublemakers to theories of
epistemology because they are so far removed from sense experience.[17] Moreover, as a figure of rhetoric and hermeneutics strongly
identified with medieval scholasticism and biblical exegesis, traditional allegory stands in the way of the plain style and historical
method Locke and earlier Restoration writers advocate.[18] Locke's
theory of language in the *Essay* thus acknowledges that abstraction is
inevitably at issue in acts of naming, including those that appear to
be concerned only with particular things. Even so, allegory remains
for Locke a dramatic figure of the potential waywardness of signs
derived from "mixed modes" (*Essay* 3.2.5, p. 407).[19] In a famous
paragraph late in the *Essay*, he gives Eloquence, whose words are
"perfect cheats," a distinctly female shape and misogynist edge:
"Eloquence, like the fair sex, has too prevailing beauties in it to
suffer itself ever to be spoken against. And it is vain to find fault with
those arts of deceiving, wherein men find pleasure to be deceived"
(*Essay* 3.10.34, p. 508). These sentiments, a virtual setpiece in early
modern commentaries on rhetorical figures,[20] create the verbal
equivalent of an emblematic picture. They also imply a story or fable
in which Eloquence is no longer a manageable abstraction but a
vocal and rebellious female figure who acts and "moves" Locke such
that he produces the very figurative language he wishes to eradicate.
By such means, allegory can be said to blow itself up, to walk and
talk in precisely the ways eighteenth-century writers hoped to
foreclose. As Locke and other writers tell it, the rise and fall of
Credit's fortunes in the eighteenth-century version of a futures
market also lends itself to elaborately misogynist allegories about
how "she" is coy, fickle, unstable, passionate, and mere fantasy.[21]
Whig or Tory, opposed to or in favor of Credit, writers like Locke,
Defoe, Charles Davenant, and Addison exclaim about the ways in
which Credit acts just like a woman.[22]

Eighteenth-century strategies for sequestering the erring potential
of such figures are hardly subtle, nor are they meant to be. They
typically begin by identifying allegory with simple, uncomplicated
visual images or descriptions like the crude woodcuts first included in
Andrea Alciati's *Emblemata*. Modeled on those woodcuts, allegory is
or ought to be unlife-like and static, hence outside narrative and

history. The virtual immobility of many eighteenth-century poetic personifications is one consequence of such claims. Neo-Spenserians rely on an idealized, programmatic image of Spenser's allegory that inevitably runs aground when his allegorical characters do not play by the rules or, indeed, when those characters are put into play.

Neither John Hughes, whose 1715 edition of *The Faerie Queene* consolidated the Spenserian revival begun during the Restoration, nor Addison, who became a friend of Hughes, do much more than report that Spenser's allegory, as Quintilian had written of allegory in general, is a "continued" hence narrative mode.[23] Both writers prefer to identify allegory and Spenser with "poetical picture[s]" and "Emblematical Persons."[24] Shaftesbury's insistence that complex emblematic texts are morally unstable guides to truth conveys the ethical imperative that directs the preference for clear, easily read allegorical images and figures.[25]

Joseph Spence, whose *Polymetis* (1755) repackaged these objections for the next generation, chooses many of the same targets: Rubens, Spenser, and Renaissance emblem books, in particular Cesare Ripa's *Iconologia* (1611), an emblematic and iconographic dictionary widely used from the sixteenth to early nineteenth centuries by artists and writers.[26] Spence's choice of Ripa is directed by Neoclassical assumptions about what constitutes an allegorical emblem. Ripa's *Iconologia* looks very little like earlier Renaissance emblem books, beginning with Alciati's *Emblemata*, which presented witty, oblique verses and mottoes and, in later editions, elaborate commentaries. Early editions of these works, including Ripa's, did not always include a visual image for each figure.[27] Spence assumes to the contrary that allegorical emblems are, above all, visual images. Because Ripan images were by the seventeenth century less encumbered with text, they conformed to what Spence believed allegory to be – a visual or pictorial form. The irony of this misunderstanding is considerable, inasmuch as the interplay of parts in the Renaissance emblem invites and even insures the interpretive relay that subsequent commentators and generations of readers willingly performed but which Spence discredits.

The problem with Ripa, Spence says over and over, is the "busyness" of his visual images, which typically feature a central figure accompanied by various objects and figures that collectively indicate the allegorical idea or ideas. What he wants instead are simpler, less crowded allegories that "speak to the eyes" without demanding reflection on, or arbitration among, competing interpretations. Arguing that Ripa's *Iconologia* is little more than a "book of puzzles," Spence echoes the Abbé Dubos's influential complaint that modern painters and poets are compelled to use ancient riddles for which no key can be found.[28] The real issue for Spence may well be the grotesqueness of such figures, whose meaning is, as it were, dismembered, cast off into components with little if any discernible mimetic correspondence to each other – the globe and compasses of Ripan Beauty or the stag and beehive beside Ripan Flattery.[29]

Spence categorically rejects the metonymic slide on which allegorical figures rely, whereby a hive and bees might represent the production of honey and, by another figural displacement, flattering speech, or a compass and globe the perfect proportion of ideal Beauty. Displacements of this sort are not merely expected in allegory, they are required. As a symbolic mode whose figures and narratives are displaced images of the truth they represent, allegory is necessarily metonymic. Even so common a metonym as flattery by honeyed speech risks exposure of this requirement. Spence implicitly rebuffs this disposition, if he even recognizes it, by arguing for a pictorialist aesthetic of pleasing verisimilitude. Spenser's Discord, whose body manifests her nature, is thus "preposterous" because the poet "makes her hear double, and look two different ways; he splits her tongue, and even her heart, in two: and makes her act contrarily with her two hands; and walk forward with one foot, and backward with the other, at the same time." Alma's Castle of Temperance, because it turns "the human body into a castle; the tongue into the porter, that keeps the gate; and the teeth, into two and thirty warders, dressed in white," is the "grossest" instance of Spenser's erring allegorical ways.[30] Granville works himself up to a similar pitch against poets who invent "Gigantic Forms, and monstrous Births" such as "Vice," who seizes a town yet "varies still her shape" (*Works* 117-18, 172). In this critical climate, the various "shapes" and non-shapes assumed by Milton's Sin and Death could hardly go unchallenged.[31]

Although Addison is not specifically concerned with allegory when he writes about the Polydorus episode in the *Aeneid*, his remarks about this passage suggest the necessarily anti-mimetic relation between the grotesque and allegory. The episode begins as Aeneas tears up a myrtle only to see blood drip from the roots and to hear his dead companion Polydorus explain that he has become that myrtle. Addison recalls the dead man's explanation for "this wonderful Circumstance": "the barbarous Inhabitants of the Country having pierced him with Spears and Arrows, the Wood which was left in his Body took root in his Wounds, and gave Birth to that bleeding Tree" (*Spectator* no. 315, III:144-45). The story is offensive, Addison suggests, because its "marvellous" aspects are not tempered by some degree of probability. For although Polydorus's bleeding proceeds from "Natural Causes" (he is torn so he bleeds), his partial transformation from man to a myrtle that bleeds when uprooted instead of exuding moisture strains the logic of natural causation. The episode would be more believable, Addison implies, if the gods or some enchanter were responsible for this botched transformation. For human beings do not become nursery logs for bleeding plants except in myth, where the verisimilitude required of epic is not in force.

This transformation turns out to be problematic on the same grounds Addison gives for excluding allegorical figures from the epic. Both undermine the clear distinction between natural or probable circumstances and the marvellous. The problem with Polydorus is, I suggest, his instability as a figure. Instead of dying as humans are supposed to die and being transformed in Ovidian fashion into a plant or tree, he is stuck between the human and natural orders, a myrtle tree that nonetheless bleeds from wounds made by spears and arrows that stick and eventually take root. As I read Addison on what is wrong with Virgil's narration, getting stuck and being uprooted are metafigures for the lawlessness of figures like Polydorus who grotesquely refuse to be either a figure or the real thing. In a later *Spectator* essay Addison complains that similar figures violate the fixed, emblematic nature of allegory (no. 273, II:563)

The grotesque allegorical vision of Swift's *Gulliver's Travels* explodes this Neoclassical decorum by engaging in the figural reduction of subjects by "insulting comparisons."[32] Among them is Gulliver's description of the exposed breast of a Brobdingnag nurse: "the nipple was about the bigness of my head, and the hue both of that and the dug so varified with spots, pimples, and freckles, that nothing could appear more nauseous" (*Gulliver's Travels* 130). At close range, he adds, even English women's breasts become as monstrous as a Brobdingnag dug. In the scopic male gaze of this observation, that part of the female body which is a commonplace occasion for the praise of female beauty becomes an alienated allegorical sign of

female ugliness, here raised to a general principle. This misogynist
inversion takes aim at the fashionable use of the microscope by
women during the seventeenth and early eighteenth centuries[33] by
turning female microscopic vision (here demoted to a low-tech
magnifying glass) against itself. Just as women saw enlarged images of
the infinitesimal movements of cell life and reproduction, so does -
Gulliver see apparently small and dainty female breasts for what they
are – surfaces pocked with gross imperfections that are invisible to
the "naked eye." With this parable of naked flesh and male vision
protected by its claim to scientific "experiment," Swift makes the
grotesque female breast the safely isolated material sign of the work
of particulars against abstractions. Great or small, female particulars
breed disgust (the male member seems by contrast a protected
species).[34]

Although Swift's satire may be directed against the fixed allegorical and moral vision of his contemporaries (whose national pride
must suffer the exposure of the ugliness of *English* women's breasts), it
also conveys, in a misogynist key, the Neoclassical distrust of
particulars. Whether the streaks are on a tulip or a female breast,
they may defy or simply draw needed attention from a general idea
of which they are local instances. If the devil is in the particulars, it is
perversely so in the first of these passages, where the unappetizing
particularities of the female breast wreak havoc on general common-
places about female beauty. Swift's allegorical vision thereby displays
the return or survival of the repressed particular, now abjected onto
grotesque bodies. Reynolds's theory of art, nature, and taste would
categorically exclude such particulars, on the grounds that "defor-
mity is not nature, but an accidental deviation from her accustomed
practice" (*Discourses* 124). Pope's Dulness and Swift's tyrannical
abstractions are grotesquely bound, albeit brilliantly, to oppressive,
maniacal, and demonic abstractions akin to the allegorical extreme
represented by Spenser's Malbecco.[35] Grotesqueness and monstrosity are here the negative, terrifying signs of abstractions so
rhetorically effective that they seem to command assent. At the same
time, those abstractions resist material or historical particulars that
exceed and thereby pollute the formal beauty of abstractions. For
Swift, a nursing female breast is the sign of that excess.

More conventional Neoclassical arguments about allegory rever-
berate in poetic theory and practice throughout the second half of
the eighteenth century, particularly in personifications that move

sluggishly, if they move at all, as though weighted down by abstractions and self-reflexive displays of immobilized passions.[36] To cite only one example of a widespread figural practice, Collins's "The Passions: An Ode for Music," describes allegorical "Passions" (Fear, Anger, Despair, Hope, Revenge, Jealousy, Melancholy, Cheerfulness, Joy) who try to play Music's instruments while she remains in her ancient Greek refuge.[37] What Hagstrum has said of Melancholy is generally true of the rest: they are emblematic portraits who act briefly on the stage of the poem in full recognition of their allegorical function.[38] Less obviously but as effectively, they are reflexive images of the abstractions and iconography to which they refer. Although these figures are called "Passions," they lack the intensity of human emotion and response Longinus identifies with sublime figures of "passion." In sharp contrast, allegory's modern reinvention requires extreme passions and shapes, often in contentious array.

Invoking Spenser to argue for a conservative and aristocratic vision of modern England, Thomson's *Castle of Indolence* exaggerates the inertia of such figures. Against the grain of its stated argument, the poem's speaker-poet luxuriates in the pleasures of Indolence at the expense, he admits, of human industry, including his work as a poet. Hoping to sing like a good epic poet of "war and actions fair," he wonders if he can (*Indolence* 1.3, *Works* 263) For the "guests" who are confined inside the Castle, art (but not the labor of the artist) dominates. A favorite theme of the tapestries hung in the castle is the otiose ease of classical pastoral. Indolence himself sings rather cheerfully of the difference between his enervating pleasures and the busyness of human labor, including the work of making war. Other versions of the same contrast supply "great amusement" for the guests of Indolence as they look into a "huge crystal magic globe" to watch "all things that do pass / Upon this anthill earth." The poet himself mocks the passing scenes of work and pleasure, of writers and philosophers, of nations at war (*Indolence* 1.49 and 1.52, *Works* 269–70). The value given to Indolence is only gradually removed in the array of portraits that follows the great philosopher too lazy to think; a fat bard; aimless clerks and bureaucrats; and beautiful women whose "only labour was to kill the time" (*Indolence* 1.72, *Works* 277). The figurative economy of canto 1 says much about the kind of allegory Thomson prefers. Whereas mortal men work, Indolence and his guests limn the frozen self-reflexivity Neoclassical writers prefer for allegorical figures.

In canto II the Knight of Art and Industry acts apace, as if to make up for the poem's imitative indolence thus far. Evidently a hero out of courtly romance, he is also an entrepreneurial genius who harnesses the English agricultural and industrial revolutions for the social good and, not incidentally, for the preservation of a "natural" English aristocracy. His mixed parentage – he is the offspring of a chance union between a forest rustic (allegorically so named) and Poverty – shows that he is the man for the job. The narrator gives the story an air of verisimilitude, though similar couplings are common in medieval romance: the "rough unpolished" Selvaggio "found dame Poverty, nor fair nor coy; / Her he compressed, and filled her with a lusty boy" (*Indolence* 2.6, *Works* 281). The allegorical significance of this coupling is transparent: "natural" parentage and poverty are less likely to spoil the youthful knight-to-be than a life of indolence. Predictably, the knight grows up favored by the gods, who teach him all he needs to know. This narrative, which promotes the economic and political agendas of Tory England by mid-century, is both larger than life and marginally probable. Near the end of the second canto, the narrator remembers Indolence, just as his/its unspecified predations threaten the ideal agrarian retirement the knight has made for himself to rest from his many labors (in characteristically unrestful fashion). He dispatches Indolence in short order and metes out justice to his captives. Because Thomson so thoroughly mythologizes English agrarian and industrial productivity in this poem and in *The Seasons*, the fact that the knight walks and talks seems hardly to matter, as though whatever material or realist presence he might have is, by prior arrangement, indentured to an aristocratic vision of England's past, disguised as its future.

As a personified allegorical figure, Thomson's knight would thus seem to confirm Siskin's definition of personification as a figure that offers "a metonymic affirmation of community."[39] Yet this definition echoes Neoclassical prescriptions about how abstract figures like personification and allegory ought to convey abstractions – prescriptions that covertly seek to preserve political as well as aesthetic decorum. Like those prescriptions, this one categorically rules out the possibility that such figures might precipitate change within discourse, either by using particulars that seem more lively, hence more "human," or by introducing a narrative that disturbs the community to which and of which it speaks. For if it is clear that personification, allegory, and similar figures depend on a degree of generalization or typicality to make their point, the same must be said of all signifying operations. To claim, as Neoclassical critics also argued, that these operations can only occur if figures are or remain static requires that they be transparent mirrors of what Bourdieu calls the "habitus" of culture – the set of values and predispositions that identify a community. Critics may well wish that figures were static, but the history of literature and culture is studded with evidence that the meaning of figures cannot be fixed, and further, that this necessity is bitten deep into their history and etymology as kinds of metaphor.

After the mid eighteenth century, the Neoclassical effort to suppress or rewrite this history partially gives way to two impulses. The first is the adaptation of popular iconography and stories to allegorical figures; the second is a renewed interest in narrative, by which I mean both specific narratives that dissent from Hanoverian and Whig views of English culture and nationhood and a more general, if hedged, notice of the narrative inherent in allegory. Both impulses could be illustrated with more examples and discussion than the representative instances I offer here of a hobbled but intriguing revival of interest in allegorical figures with ambitions that reach beyond Neoclassical strictures.

Hogarth, whose art moves deftly between learned and popular iconographies, uses these two registers such that the difference between particulars and abstractions cannot be fully sustained. In satirical narratives like *The Rake's Progress* and *The Harlot's Progress*, for example, the visual details of individual plates specify the person-hood of this rake, this harlot, and historicize their predicaments such that it is less easy to turn them into abstractions. Hogarth's shift from emblematic portraiture to expressive history, as Paulson has described it,[40] thereby resists even this polarity.

Even in poetry after mid-century, emblematic still-lifes sometimes give way. Smart's *Fables* dramatize the characters of "Fashion," "Old Care," "Generosity," and "Country Squire" in ways that nudge them closer to individual human likenesses. The fact that Smart's Fashion acts and pouts as does Pope's Belinda in *The Rape of the Lock* makes short work of the operative Neoclassical distinction between real characters and abstractions. The more tightly emble-matic story of how Generosity grows old and poor until her late marriage with Old Care insures the welcome offspring Oeconomy, whom the proud parents fondly call "fair Discretion's Queen," makes a swerve away from emblematic decorum when it notes how little return others make to Generosity once she grows old. By disturbing the harmonious moral vision of the fable, in which good virtues are rewarded and the bad get what they deserve, Smart reminds readers of stories that would, if followed, lead back into a more recognizably human moral universe. In "The Country Squire and the Mandrake," the mandrake delivers a sharp moral lesson about Squire Trelooby, who spends his life as a "man of prey" in pursuit of game, fowl, and female. Offended when the squire bends down to look at this "curious vegetable," the mandrake calls the man a "proud member of the rambling race, / That vegetate from place to place." The plant ends the fable by comparing the oddity of a "weed that's like a man" with "a grievous thing indeed, / To see a man so like a weed" (*Poetical Works* 1:41–42, 45–47, 55–57). This odd reversal of Virgil's figure of Polydorus – and perhaps Addison's intervening objection to its grotesqueness – makes grotesqueness the shared burden of a specific class and a particular member of that class. Distantly related to Squire Booby, Trelooby is uncomfortably placed somewhere between vegetable and animal, man in name only. Working in the register of sacred song, Smart's "Song to David" situates this biblical figure between emblem and the particulars of an individual history. The verses that praise David's moral strength, for example, rely on a series of appositions that could each serve as a single emblem, among them "strong is the lion," "the horse," "the whale," and "stronger still ... the man of pray'r." Individually these figures are faithful to the Neoclassical preference for accessible allegories that "speak to the eyes" as a clean-cut emblem ought to do; collectively they celebrate a man and a history.

Without intending this effect, Lowth may have given allegory precisely the point of entry back into narrative and history that it needed at this moment in English culture. For by praising biblical Hebrew for its use of "*Symbols*, and Sacred *Hieroglyphicks*," he resurrects an alliance between allegory, emblem, and hieroglyphics which Neoclassical critics discredited (Lowth, *Commentary* i). Yet even as he vigorously defends the existence of "mystical allegory" in the Hebrew Bible, Lowth dismisses allegory in general as a mode "adopted by nations emerging from barbarism," and thus likely to interest only those "who have made little progress in intellectual pursuits." The usual disclaimer about *The Faerie Queene* is not far behind: despite "some incomparably poetic passages," the poem has "few readers in the present age" (Lowth, *Lectures* 1:214–15n.). Among the generation of writers after mid-century who shared James Macpherson's conviction about the native sublimity of early Celtic cultures and literatures,[41] the Neoclassical cast of Lowth's disapproval loses ground to the conviction that both primitive Celtic and Hebrew cultures produced inspired bards and prophets.

Even in Gray, whose personifications typically favor static, emblematic tableaux over action, as in "Disdainful Anger," "pallid Fear," and "pineing Love," the nationalist impulse occasionally produces allegorical figures who are animated by their role within a historical narrative. Among the horrors "The Bard" foretells is the death by starvation of Richard II. Relishing the image, the Welsh bard explains that this English king unwittingly becomes the main dish in the feast shared by his assassins, Thirst and Famine, who "scowl / A baleful smile" at their victim. The poem closes in "buskin'd measure" with a stately dance of "Pale Grief, and pleasing Pain," but these two are joined by "Horror," by now a well-established guest in a poem whose pro-Welsh and anti-English vision of history requires its services (Gray, *Works* 80–81, 129–30, pp. 60–64). At the end of Gray's "The Triumphs of Owen," a group of figures that includes "Confusion, Terror's Child / Conflict fierce, and Ruin wild, / Agony, that pants for breath, / Despair and honourable Death" (*Works* 33–36, p. 85) looks like a collective emblematic portrait of Owen himself as the tragic hero of Welsh nationalism. Because these figures inhabit a narrative whose argument is fundamentally at odds with the English, Whig interpretation of Welsh history, they recall how an earlier figure of Discord troubled the Stuart monarchy off- as well as on-stage.[42]

I conclude this chapter with G. E. Lessing and Diderot, each of whom imagined allegory in terms of narrative even as they proclaimed allegiance to the Neoclassical definition and critique. Although they write outside the English tradition, both writers have influenced modern theories of allegory and both edge away from Neoclassical principles even as they restate them. Lessing chastises eighteenth-century English poets like Thomson for indulging in allegorical figures borrowed from traditional iconography and the Renaissance emblem. Echoing Neoclassical complaints about the arcane complexity of these traditions, he advises poets to use more accessible figures like "scales in the hand of Justice" instead of figures like "the bridle in the hand of Moderation, the pillar against which

Constancy is leaning." He explains that "poetic" figures (what Coleridge and German Romantic writers would later call "symbols") "signify the thing itself" (scales for Justice), whereas "allegorical" figures signify "only something resembling it" (*Laocoön* 60–61). Lessing's distinction is evidently problematic, for the scales of Justice are hardly more representative (or more literally representative) of the thing itself than the bridle for Moderation or the pillar for Constancy. Scales seem a more natural icon for Justice only because popular iconography has long used them to figure the act of weighing alternatives. Conversely, both pillar and bridle could be made to seem "natural" figures: Moderation reins in impulse even as Constancy is firm, stalwart, a prop in human relations and judgments.

When Lessing meditates in the same essay about the relation between pain and narrative in the *Laocoön* statuary, he implies a view of allegory that is less securely Neoclassical. Against Winckelmann's influential praise for the beauty of the sculpture as an ideal allegory, Lessing presents it as a frozen representation of the excruciating physical pain *Laocoön* and his sons suffer as they succumb to the coils of an enormous serpent.[43] Although the logic of his argument would seem to require that he move on once he has shown that the statuary is a grotesque expression of pain and thus neither ideal nor beautiful, he instead lingers with this example of the limits of "painting." As an intricate, massive sculpture made all the more monumental by Winckelmann's influence, the Laocoön is by Lessing's own account too solid, too material, and too expressive to be so easily put aside or even so easily assimilated as an instance of "painting," even if this term is imagined as a generic for all pictorial art including sculpture.[44] By reminding readers of the poignant narrative that is indicated but not formally contained by the Laocoön statuary, Lessing makes it a virtual emblem of human pain as a temporal event that needs to be read, not simply looked at. In just this way allegory gains a purchase on image, history, and narrative.

This view of allegory may be the unarticulated underside of Lessing's comments about the allegorical difficulty of some emblematic figures. For the metonymic shifts required to represent Moderation as a woman with a bridle in her hand or Constancy as a woman who leans on a pillar are equally needed to represent Justice as a woman who holds up scales. Because all these figures require the labor of interpretation to assemble the dismembered parts of a visual emblem, they encourage recognition of the potential alienation inherent in all figures, even those that seem "poetic" or symbolic. Lessing implies something like this when he compares the limitations of pictorial art with dumbness: "it is as though a man who can and may speak were at the same time using those signs which the mutes in the Turkish seraglio invented among themselves for lack of a voice" (*Laocoön* 59). Because these mutes are eunuchs – what else could they be as male residents in a Turkish seraglio? – castration is here an implied figure for the way visual images cut off and silence narrative.[45] In this extraordinary reversal of Neoclassical and Restoration arguments that hieroglyphs or other visual signs are the origin of language, Lessing makes those signs castrated reductions of words, even as the allegorical details adopted in emblematic images are merely "artistic trimmings" that make the key figure a "puppet." The figure of castrated males works subliminally to circumscribe the potential agency of the emblem; it also implies that the parts of an emblem are like cut-off or dismembered pieces, hence mere puppetry or automata.

Diderot's understanding of allegory as narrative emerges dramatically in his "Salon" of 1765, where he invents a dream vision to critique Fragonard's monumental history painting, *Le Grand-Prêtre Corésus s'immole pour sauver Callirhoe*.[46] In the dream its narrator and others are held captive and forced to watch a series of images projected on the wall of Plato's cave. I quote Diderot's text at some length to call attention to its discursive and theatrical argument about the persuasiveness of allegorical figures that move in lifelike ways:

We all had feet and hands bound, and heads so firmly gripped by wooden vises that it was impossible to turn around. But what astonished me was that most of the others drank, laughed, sang without seeming to be bothered by their chain/... they looked askance (*de mauvais oeil*) at those who tried to free (*récouvrer la liberté*) their feet, hands, or heads – so much so that they called them insulting names and moved away as if those who tried to get free had contracted a contagious disease. Whenever something awful happened in the cave, the rest never failed to accuse them of having done it ... we all had our backs turned away from the entrance to this place and could look only into the recess of the cave, covered by an immense canvas. Behind us were kings, ministers, priests, academics, apostles, prophets, theologians, politicians, conmen, charlatans, craftsmen of illusion, the entire troup of merchants of hopes and fears. Each had a supply of small, transparent, colored images (*figures*) appropriate to his station; and all these images were so well made, so well painted, so numerous, and so various that they could

represent all the comic, tragic, and burlesque scenes of life ... these
charlatans were placed between us and the entrance of the cave; they had
suspended a great lamp behind them which lit up the small images whose
shadows were projected over our heads. The shadows grew larger along the
way until they were stopped by the canvas hung at the back of the cave. On
it they depicted scenes that were so natural, so true that we believed they
were real (*nous les prénions pour réelles*). We laughed out loud as often as we
cried ... the assistants behind the canvas ... were hired to lend those
shadows accents, speech, and voices true to their roles. Despite the
effectiveness of the presentation, there were some among us in the crowd
who were suspicious, who rattled their chains from time to time, and who
wanted most of all to get rid of their vises and turn their heads. But at any
moment, now one, now another of the charlatans would begin to shout in a
strong, terrible voice: "don't turn your heads; evil to him who rattles his
chains." "Don't remove the vises (*respecte les éclisses*)." I will tell you some
other time of what happened to those who ignored this advice, of the risks
they ran, of the persecutions they had to suffer. All this I'll save for when we
do philosophy ... Here I repeat in summary form what I saw happen in
different places, at different times (*à différens intervalles*).[47]

In reply to Diderot's dream vision, a fictive interlocutor named
Grimm, who emphasizes similarities between the scenes projected on
the curtain and those depicted in Fragonard's painting, argues that
both are artful illusions.[48]

Presented under the heading "Fragonard," Diderot's dream is a
patent fiction intended to expose as well as praise Fragonard for his
illusionist use of light, akin to the tricks used by the charlatans in the
dream to make small, colored figures look enormous. Diderot insists
that the scale of Fragonard's monumental painting and its figures is a
stage trick that deliberately boosts the allegorical program indicated
by the figures of Despair and Love, who fly overhead. Fragonard's
painting presents these figures as hovering presences (Despair carries
Love on his back) above the central tableau that includes the priest
and the woman he saves from sacrifice by offering himself instead. In
Diderot's narrative the painting is interpreted as a narrative that
culminates in the priest's suicide. At the point in the narrative just
before Corésus raises the knife to kill himself, Diderot identifies the
supervisory Despair and Love by name (*Salons* ii:194). For modern
readers, these figures may seem subsidiary; but for Diderot and his
contemporaries, they are critical signs of the allegorical and emblematic spin which Fragonard and Diderot put on the historical
subject at hand.

Despite this evidence that the dream is faithful to Fragonard's image, Diderot insists that it is just a dream. I take this as a backhanded critique of Fragonard for having painted a monumental history painting that looks like the hazy cinematic vision of a softporn flick. Diderot insists that he did not see the painting in the Salon exhibition, but dreamed that night of the scenes and captive viewers inside Plato's cave. In the dialogue that follows the dream, Grimm exposes this fiction. A second "Grimm," who soon afterward exposes the first Grimm's fictionality, complains that "Diderot" has been putting words into his mouth or, more precisely, into the mouth of a fictive "Grimm" whom the supposedly real Grimm now displaces. The assistants who lend voices to shadows during the dream are clearly still at work in the text.

Diderot's dream is evidently modelled on allegories whose meaning is accessible and, further, bent on persuading its audience, by force if necessary. Even so, the narrative and political implications of the dream exceed the limits imposed on pictorial allegory for the most telling of reasons: the figures who "move" on the canvas and even those viewers who try to move despite the vises and chains that hold them still are in different ways so persuasive to the captive viewers or to readers of Diderot and Plato that they seem real. This declaration effaces the boundary between personified abstractions that do not move and real persons that do.[49]

Because of its presentation of miniature tableaux that collectively define movements projected onto canvas, as well as attempted movements by those held captive, Diderot's dream has been read as a cautionary (or exhilarating) representation of eighteenth-century theatricality and modern cinematic narrative.[50] For other readers, the visual experience of those held captive in the cave (presumably minus whips, vises, and chains) replicates the ideal relation between the spectator and the theater. Fried argues that for Diderot the spectator "ought to be thought of as before a canvas, on which a series of ... *tableaux* follow one another as if by magic." Indeed, the scenes projected on the canvas illustrate Diderot's definition of *tableau*: "an arrangement of those characters on the stage, so natural and so true to life that, [if] faithfully rendered by a painter, would please me on canvas.[51] Because moving instead of static images (whether their movement is delusory or not) govern this narrative, it also indicates the power allegorical fictions acquire once they are set in motion.

Although Diderot defines *reality* to mean something quite different from Platonic reality, his version of Plato's allegory of the cave is charged with repeated notice of the seeming reality of scenes projected on the canvas at the back of the cave. Especially for Diderot, the scenes are deliberate fakes used by authorities to maintain their hold on the minds and feet of their subjects, compelling them not just to look but to believe. Diderot extends the theme of coercion in Plato's allegory of the cave by adding the illusionist trick that makes small, colored figures seem large when they are projected onto the canvas. Most of all, he dramatizes the coercion of such images as part of a state apparatus. The list of people in charge makes no qualitative distinctions between legitimate authorities (civic, intellectual, or religious) and charlatans. All are hucksters, "merchants of hopes and fears."

Diderot's "Salon" of 1765 marks a critical turn in his semiotics of word and image. In earlier "Salons," he had implied that words might be transparent carriers of meaning. The ancient and still attractive model for such transparency is the hieroglyphic sign, the picture-word or ideograph that displays a natural rather than arbitrary relation between signifier and signified. By 1765, he argues instead that words are arbitrary signs for things, that transparency is not possible. Indeed, his dream of Plato's cave makes transparency the technical means of deception. As Bryson observes of the opening scene where charlatans and their assistants create images that seem real: "transparency materializes as the actual slides the rulers use to distract and manipulate their subjects."[52]

Yet, as a verbal translation of a visual image, Diderot's dream also makes a veiled and hesitant return to the question of transparency by way of the sister arts tradition. In the dream itself, Diderot half-acknowledges the pressure of questions about comparative methodology which Lessing had summarized just a year before, telling Grimm that his account of what he saw on the great canvas summarizes scenes that happened "'in different places, at different times.'" Because the French phrase *à différens intervalles* may refer to place or time, it elides the operative distinction between painting as a spatial art and narratives that unroll a linear sequence. The magic lantern show on the great canvas similarly revokes the static images of Fragonard's representation, where all scenes are depicted simultaneously, and even the narrative sequence in Diderot's account of Fragonard's painting. By these means Diderot manages to appropriate something of the advantages of each medium – the visual display (conveyed by text) of static tableaux and the moving spectacle of narrative as a succession of tableaux. In brief, the images projected inside the cave of Diderot's dream obscure or minimize the difference between painting and poetry. But why?

One answer may be that the visual image seems to offer what linguistic signs cannot, a transparent, natural language. In part, this is the argument Diderot had earlier implied, "our mind is a *tableau mouvant*, after which we are endlessly painting; we take up a great deal of time in rendering it faithfully; but it exists as a whole and all at once: our mind does not move in stages, as does our expression." Bryson suggests that this figure conveys a longing for semiotic transparency in the form of a hieroglyphic sign that might allow "a partial exit from the self-alienating trap of language."[53] Seen against the backdrop of Diderot's comparison of a *tableau mouvant* to a mind that "exists as a whole and all at once," his dream of shifting tableaux that are all illusionist effect is a stunning reversal. Its images are always fragmented, always supplanted by "transparencies" each as illusory as the last.

Diderot's dream echoes earlier eighteenth-century definitions of allegory, but it is patently more interested in allegorical agency than such definitions allow.[54] Like his contemporaries, he prefers to identify allegory with static emblematic figures and tableaux. Yet he abandons this position in his dream of Plato's cave. There allegorical figures that are not confined to static poses make it less easy to distinguish between allegory (where people are or become abstractions) and the real world (where real people exist and real actions occur). Eighteenth-century anxiety on this point implicitly recognizes allegory as a master fiction, coercive insofar as it may urge a specific view of moral or theological truth. The political edge of this recognition is striking in Diderot's dream of authorities who create fictions to insure a complex machinery of mind control. By creating transparent figures that obscure rather than reveal their real means of production, the dream also abandons the ideal of semiotic transparency. It suggests instead that the technology of illusion is part of what allegory is as a narrative figure that insists on its distance from palpable or actual reality. In the language of Diderot's dream, allegorical narratives are projections, not copies, of reality. As the kings and charlatans who are the technocrats of this projection make clear, allegory declares its authority over the meaning of its figures and events. The issue left unresolved by Diderot is whether readers are merely captive viewers, passive before the march of allegorical tableaux or whether they are capable of rebelling against being held to one way of seeing and reading.

Against his own claim that allegory works best as a series of static visual emblems, then, Diderot puts allegorical figures into *tableaux mouvants* that move away from what Bryson calls the "figural" or virtual visual image toward discursive modes.[55] In the 1790s, organizers of French revolutionary festivals reimagine Diderot's *tableaux mouvants* as openly allegorical pageants, while other pro-revolutionary propagandists use similar figures in broadsheets, pamphlets, and playing cards. In each instance, they choose allegorical images because they are visually compelling, even forceful, tools for shaping public opinion that can be blown up or made deceptively small such that their fictitiousness cannot escape notice, however much they refer to real things and events. Projected beyond the wall of the cave and onto the backdrop of the French Revolution, Diderot's dream fantasy forecasts allegory's historical role and shape in Romanticism.

CHAPTER 5

Romantic ambivalences 1

Allegory addressd to the Intellectual Powers while it is alto-
gether hidden from the Corporeal Understanding is My Definition of the Most Sublime Poetry. (1803) ... Fable or Allegory
are a totally distinct & inferior kind of Poetry. (1810)

Blake 730, 554

They look at it [*The Faerie Queene*] as a child looks at a painted
dragon, and think it will strangle them in its shining folds. This
is very idle. If they do not meddle with the allegory, the allegory
will not meddle with them.

Hazlitt "Chaucer and Spenser," *Works* v:38

Shop after shop, with symbols, blazon'd names,
And all the tradesman's honours overhead:
Here, fronts of houses, like a title-page
With letters huge inscribed from top to toe;
Stationed above the door like guardian saints,
There, allegoric shapes, female or male,
Or physiognomies of real men.

Wordsworth, *Prelude* 7. 173–80, p. 234

Romantic writers echo Blake's ambivalence about allegory in different
poetic climates, with different ends in view. Leigh Hunt claims that
Spenser's *Faerie Queene* is "but one part allegory, and nine parts beauty
and enjoyment; sometimes an excess of flesh and blood" ("Spenser"
50). The unaccommodated remainder in this equation registers what
Hazlitt mocks – the specter of allegorical figures alive and on the move
(*Works* v:38). Like Blackmore's earlier rant against Spenser and
Ariosto "lost in the wood" of their allegories, Hazlitt's quip entertains
a slight, but unmistakably allegorical tale. A dragon named Allegory
(or Error) is on the loose, but readers who ignore her may pass
"unalarmed," like Wordsworth before the gates of a Miltonic Hell,
neither bitten nor meddled with (1.988, *Home at Grasmere*, ms. B, 102).

93

As Hunt's formula uncannily predicts, such shapes exceed verisimilar representation by making an issue of their proximity to human
identities and particulars, even as their quirky differences from both
hardly escape notice. Moreover, as Boileau's translation of Longinus's treatise *On the Sublime* had earlier reminded English and
Continental readers, allegorical excess requires exaggerated figures.
Extending this rhetorical tradition, Romantic allegory welds its
abstractions to "flesh and blood," the world of lived particulars and
feeling.

This chapter and the next two investigate allegory's stake in
Romantic spectacles and images. In the midst of a sustained polemic
against allegory, Romantic writers put allegorical emblems to uses
unsanctioned by Neoclassical arguments. The "excess of flesh and
blood" in Spenser's allegory returns in Romantic figures that gain
their characteristic energy and pathos by tacking between abstract
ideas and lived particulars. The present chapter examines allegory's
unsteady fortunes during the French Revolution and among early
Romantic writers. Its topics include Romantic personification as a
measure of what happens when pathos and animation are attributed
to abstract figures; the role of allegory in French revolutionary
spectacles and propaganda; the figure of *phantasia* in Coleridge's
strictures against allegory; and finally the work that "allegoric
shapes" perform in book 7 of Wordsworth's *Prelude*.

My argument begins with Romantic historical consciousness, at
the very least a two-handed engine. Gossman argues that the French
Revolution signals a definitive break with the past that takes two
forms: the Romantic longing and nostalgia for hidden origins for
which Rousseau's *Discourse on Inequality* and later Schiller's *Letters on
Aesthetic Education* so eloquently speak; and Hegel's progressive
histories. In these evolutionary schemas that suture the Romantic
present to the past, Gossman suggests, Romantic nostalgia masks a
deeper anxiety. Whether the object of nostalgia is women, the
Orient, or a hidden, unrecoverable past, its otherness is masked by
the incorporating gesture of Schiller's "sentimental" or Romantic
poet. Without this gesture, the poet and the historian risk a definitive
break with the past that threatens reason and the bourgeois order.[1]
To avoid that break, Romantic historians began prospecting for
ends, preferably better ends, nearly as soon as they began to look
backward. Camouflaged as nostalgia, progressive histories repeat the
organic logic of the Romantic symbol, which authorizes the claim

that present institutions and cultures have evolved from inchoate or imperfectly achieved primitive forms whose vestiges moderns cherish as their "naive" ancestors could not because they lacked (Romantic) self-consciousness.

The other historical engine of Romantic self-consciousness is allegory. Tenacious of particulars, it imagines history as contingent, reinventive, and alert to materials that lie at hand. In a late Romantic recognition of this view of history, Carlyle argues that because "the general sum of human Action is a whole Universe, with all limits of it unknown," history must run "path after path, through the Impassable, in manifold directions and intersections to secure for us some oversight of the Whole" ("On History" 95). Existing in a negotiable middle space between the *Annales* historian and the recognition that history is also a narrative fiction for a chaos of details that necessarily exceed our grasp,[2] this historical consciousness profits from allegory, whose otherness gives the prospective edge needed to imagine and construct a new order.

What English Romantic writers typically called allegory looks more like the Neoclassical model. The personifications of Byron's *Childe Harold's Pilgrimage*, which join abstract names and real tyrants, astutely mark the numbing fixation of such figures.[3] Lady Blessington's "Allegory" in which Pleasure is "the daughter of Virtue and Happiness, and the sister of Innocence and Modesty" suggests the relative safety of such figures. With hardly surprising consequences, Pleasure strays from her family, but is finally reunited with them, although not in this world. Her unsavory double, also called Pleasure, is the child of Extravagance and Idleness. The conventionality of this allegory is the formal sign of its moral cachet: keeping an allegory within acceptable bounds means not being led astray by pleasures and fantasies.[4] Throughout its four-year quarrel with the Royal Academy and some of its members, James Elmes's *Annals of the Fine Arts* echoes Neoclassical strictures and indulges in allegorical satires less searing and scatalogical than Dryden's or Swift's, but otherwise patterned on these models.[5] For Elmes, paintings like Benjamin West's popular *Death on a Pale Horse* were not problematic because they did not use allegorical figures to represent historical subjects. Paintings that did so err risked strong criticism. When James Ward exhibited his monumental canvas (35 by 21 feet) titled *Allegorical Painting of the Triumph of Waterloo*, he attached this explanation: "The Genius of Wellington on the Car of War, supported by

Britannia and attended by the Seven Cardinal Virtues, commanding away the Demons, Anarchy, Rebellion and Discord, with the Horrors of War." The day after the painting went on exhibition, the *Morning Herald* trumpeted: "the most daring violations of nature, consistency, truth and propriety; the most grotesque conceits, the most unbounded extravagances, horror and loathsomeness, are here embodied under the extraordinary name of Allegory."[6] Although Discord's presence in Ward's painting might have triggered this explosion of critical animus, it looks more like a class-action complaint against mixing allegory and history. The manic tone of this complaint haplessly reproduces what it sees – allegory as an excessive, even monstrous, narrative figure and practice.[7]

Largely persuaded that allegory was what Neoclassical critics claimed it was, Romantic writers may assent to this caricature because it speaks to their own uneasy settlement with abstraction. Yet they also invent allegorical figures whose unaccommodated remainder of "flesh and blood" is a striking index of their "otherness," an excess defiant of the law of abstraction and the law of genre. This figural practice bends toward a version of allegory whose differences from the Neoclassical model are emphatic. Temporizing and excessive, it eludes capture much as Proteus tries to avoid capture by adopting different shapes. If gods there be, this one is the household deity of Romantic allegory. Like Proteus, this allegory is bound to successive visible and material shapes that hover over the boundary between idea and material form.[8] The imagined proximity of such shapes to real people and events corrodes the unvarying relation between the general and the particular which Neoclassical critics urged. By way of allegory, Romantic writers investigate a problem that becomes more pressing with the rise of nineteenth-century realism, whose epistemological faith in real particulars William Carlos Williams echoes in a modernist key when he calls for "no ideas but in things."[9]

As an engraver, printmaker, painter, and poet, Blake consistently exercises a formal commitment to emblematic or allegorical structures of meaning. Yet his remarks on allegory are, as Dorothy Wordsworth says of Michael's sheepfold, "in the shape of a heart unevenly divided." In *Europe* Blake identifies allegory with Enitharmon's promise of eternal life "in an allegorical abode where existence hath never come" (5:7, *Blake* 62); in *The Song of Los* with "allegoric [i.e. false] riches" (6:18, Erdman 69); in *Jerusalem*, with

"delusion and woe" (89:45, *Blake* 249); in *The Four Zoas* with the Tree
of Mystery's "Allegoric [i.e. false] fruit" (viii:169, *Blake* 375). In an
1803 letter to Thomas Butts, Blake offers limited praise for "Sublime
Allegory" that is "address'd to the Intellectual Powers," but "hidden
from the Corporeal Understanding" (*Blake* 730). But in the 1810 *A
Vision of Judgment*, where he is principally concerned to distinguish a
lesser "allegory" from greater "Vision," Blake cannot quite decide.
First he ranks allegory below "Vision," then he concedes that "Fable
or Allegory is Seldom without some Vision Pilgrims Progress is full of
it and the Greek poets the same" (*Blake* 555–56). He also very nearly
cancels out this faint praise: "Real Visions ... are lost & clouded in
Fable & Alegory." A devastating syllogism puts an end to this verbal
seesaw: "allegories are things that Relate to Moral Virtues Moral
Virtues do not Exist they are Allegories and dissimulations." The
unstated conclusion – that allegories do not exist – is meant to be
obvious. As if to save Blake from his own waffling, critics have tried
to resolve these contradictions by taking sides. Foster Damon tries to
erase them by assigning Blake's fleeting praise of allegory to "a slip
of the pen."[10] The recent debate about whether Blake executed a
series of drawings of figures identified as "personifications"
("Cruelty," "Pity," etc.) registers the same anxiety.[11] Critics who
defend Blake against allegory have aligned his complex characters
and narratives with "Vision," and consigned rigidly schematic
figures (whether Blake's or some other poet's) to allegory. Northrop
Frye sensibly imagined this difference as one that exists within
allegory.[12]

Blake's vision is allegorical in the sense of the term ratified by the
survival of this mode in modernity. Dangerously split off from a
world of the Imagination identified with "the Eternals" and the
figure of Albion, his prophetic characters objectify the intra-psychic
struggles of Prudentius's late classical *Psychomachia*. The figure of Erin
in *Jerusalem*, where she is identified with Ireland's national consciousness, summarizes Blake's struggle with allegory. In chapter 1 "the
spaces of Erin" preserve the daughters of Beulah. Along with
Scotland, England, and Wales, Ireland is subjected to the urizenic
subdivision into counties that is one of the many signs that the body
of Albion is in imaginative disarray, divided and subdivided as surely
as if it were a complex Renaissance emblem. In chapter 2 Erin is
invaded by an "Aged Virgin Form" from Ulro, also called "Religion." Thereafter the voice of Ireland speaks with religious pity of

the woes begotten by "allegoric generation," by which she means the atomization of the body of Albion into the parts of "creation." Under this regime it is mostly a matter of time (and space) before allegory becomes, as it were, the generic sign for "falsehood" or, as Los now would have us believe, "Divine Analogy." Finally, Blake's narrator takes bitter note of Enitharmon's "little lovely Allegoric Night of Albion's Daughters" (11:10–12, 16:29, 44:27, 50:1, 85:1, 88:31, *Blake* 154–247).

From the obviousness of punning allegorical names like Urizen (Your Reason) to the more subtle and varied allegorical claims he makes for Enitharmon and Los in the prophetic poems, Blake's characters inhabit shifting allegorical frames. As the fallen poet–artist, Los is a minute and yet vast "particular" instance of Blake's allegorical method. Unlike Urizen, whose rigid schematism brilliantly satirizes Enlightenment values and, not incidentally, Neoclassical allegory, Los tests critical preconceptions about what allegory is or can be. Gleckner's statement that Los is an "allegorical anti-allegorist"[13] succinctly declares this equivocal status. Watching what Los does and does not accomplish from poem to poem and even in *Jerusalem* suggests the fragile, if sustained, allegorical enterprise at work in Blake's prophecies.

For these reasons Blake's resistance to allegory warrants attention. Especially in early poems like the 1789 *Tiriel*, whose Hebrew names and puns parody the allegory of Holiness in book 1 of *The Faerie Queene*, Blake takes aim at the rigid allegorical schemas that Spenser's poem soon abandons.[14] Even his description of the now-lost painting *Vision of Judgment* seeks to divide the allegory that speaks to "Intellectual Powers" from that which addresses "Corporeal Understanding." This bifurcation discounts the visual and emblematic disposition of the major prophecies. At worst, the phrase "Corporeal Understanding" is an ironic "negation" – a comparison that cancels both terms. At best, it invites readers to go through, then beyond, what they see, although Blake hardly goes out of his way to announce this option. In part because his illuminated poems make sustained use of the emblematic tradition that supports and complicates allegory's modern survival, we can hardly be expected to read them without making use of our "Corporeal" eyes.

This suspicion of the visual or corporeal aspect of allegory goes well beyond Blake's well-advertised quarrel with Neoclassicism. For although he expects readers to read his illuminated poems as

Renaissance readers read emblems, he is wary of the hermeneutic pratfalls that lie in wait for readers of texts. The compelling hermeneutic invitation of the *Jerusalem* vignettes derives from an "iconic density" that seems very nearly material. So much so, De Luca argues, that readers try to figure out how to repair the narrative whole to which they imagine Blake's vignettes might correspond.[15] Los supplies a real warrant for this effort: "I must Create a System, or be enslav'd by another Mans / I will not Reason & Compare: my business is to Create" (*Jerusalem* 1:20–21, *Blake* 153). The coda to this celebrated statement is, however, chilling: "Obey my voice & never deviate from my will / And I will be merciful to thee" (1:29–30, *Blake* 153).

What worries Blake about allegory is just this lethal mix of absolute control and magisterial pity. Because their suggestions of materiality and arcane mystery threaten to engulf allegory's appeal to the "Intellectual Powers," figures like Vala and Hand are material witnesses for this worry. As Mitchell has argued, Blake resorts to multiple schemas, "abstracts" in the sense that they reduce vast reaches of time and space to linear narrative form, then uses all the material resources of his engraving art to battle against his own creations (Los must needs do likewise). Thus, for example, Blake shuffles the plates in all copies of *The Book of Urizen* (*Blake* 804) such that different readers can align different figures with different fallen or creative tasks. More technical examples of this strategy may include pulls, coloring, or etching of the same plate for different copies. For even if Blake acquiesces to accidental variations in the engraving process, they may yet provide him with unsolicited opportunities for recognizing how hermeneutic differences are allied to material shapes and repeated (but not necessarily repetitive) labor.[16]

These aspects of Blake's poetic activity make the question of form, even allegorical form, literal and immediate as well as abstract. Driven by the Romantic bias toward particularity, Blake works against Neoclassical abstraction by inventing words and images that grapple with the hermeneutic difficulty for which allegory is both a metafigure and a scapegoat in modern culture: how particular forms give shape to ideas beyond their boundaries. The labor required to produce illuminated poems may in this way assist Blake's sometime vision of a "Sublime Allegory." As he solicits a "Corporeal Understanding" of his labor and forms, he imagines an optical relay between the small images presented in his books and the gigantic beings those images represent – Albion, the four fallen Zoas, and the cast of larger-than-life characters who struggle to divide further or reunite.

A vignette from Mary Shelley's *The Last Man* suggests how such inversions advertise an allegorical frame of reference. In Shelley's novel, the referent is the plague – insistently verisimilar, getting closer, but as yet conveyed in newsprint by "diminuitive letters [that] grew gigantic to the bewildered eye of fear: they seemed graven with a pen of iron, impressed by fire, woven in the clouds, stamped on the very front of the universe" (*Last Man* 171). Goldsmith has suggested that the ballooning of these letters in the reader's eye witnesses "the material basis of language ... grotesquely and threateningly fore-grounded."[17] This is surely so; it is also a surprisingly apt image of Blake's process of engraving plates with iron, acid, then (at least in principle and in a Printing House in Hell) broadcasting them across an expansive imagined universe.

The material and iconic character of those letters is not however what makes them expand to that "bewildered eye of fear." Rather it is the referent for those newsprint letters – news of the plague on the Continent and the likelihood that it will soon reach England – that makes them suddenly grow huge. As Romantic allegorical figures often do, the ballooning size of these letters mimics the approach of the plague and point elsewhere – in this case just across the Channel to the plague itself. This moment in Shelley's text is doubly phantasmatic. The explosion in size occurs in a fantastic, not verisimilar, register; it also reduces the figure of the newspaper reader to an abstracted, condensed, and disembodied synecdoche – the "eye of fear" – whose figural reduction mirrors in reverse the effect of the as-yet-absent plague made "present" by newspaper headlines. This strange semiotic cross between iconicity and indexicality is as fundamental to allegory and emblem as it is to Blake's prophetic poems, where the iconic function of engraved images and texts defers to their indexical status as signs for future, imaginative restoration. Indeed, the imaginative sign of this restoration may be, David Clark has suggested, not universal harmony but minutely articulated differences that sheer off one from the next to manifest energies that lie buried or obscured after the Fall and even in *Jerusalem*.[18]

In his earlier designs for the poems of Thomas Gray, Blake specifies the formal and semiotic nature of his allegorical practice. Like Los in the early plates of *Jerusalem*, Blake uses an inverted emblematic structure whose system "imposes" as surely on Gray as the Devil imposes his delighted vision of Hell-fire on the Angel's vision of a scene of perpetual torture in *The Marriage of Heaven and Hell*. In the designs for Gray's *Ode on the Death of a Favourite Cat*, Blake reworks the format of the allegorical emblem to suggest a radically different view of the poem's subject.

The implied premise of Gray's *Ode* – that cats and women are just alike (greedy, vain, impulsive, etc.) – makes short shrift of Dr. Johnson's querulous remark that some lines in this ode could only be suitably applied to the cat Selima and others only to a woman.[19] Even so, his designs for the poem graphically insist on just the difference Gray's casual misogyny elides. In the first few designs Blake offers quite literal interpretations of Gray's cat-woman figure. On the title page, Selima is a cat dressed in a blue vest with a white shawl over her head and shoulders. The goldfishes in the water below look like Fuseli's demons, with webbed wings, strongly masculine bodies, and fish scales. According to Blake's list of designs, these figures correspond to the "angel forms" of Gray's text – a good illustration of how the voice and hand of Blake's "Devil" in *The Marriage of Heaven and Hell* do their work. One of those demon angels welcomes or invites Selima with open arms. The lady is kittenish-coy. The fact that all three figures are at best weirdly verisimilar is made more emphatic by their size: the goldfish are as big as Selima (all the better to mate) and she is no kitten. Even the scale of Blake's setting exceeds that of Gray's poetic invention. This is no "Tub" of goldfish but a vast sea that defines most of the space around Gray's boxed text. Although the verses occupy a small box in the center of each design, they are made subservient to the visual argument that Blake's designs conduct around those boxes (fig. 1). This visual format wittily reverses the ideal relation between an emblematic image and its explanatory text or texts – motto, verse, and commentary. For Blake's "borders" control Gray as surely as extensive commentaries sometimes control the "base" text of Scripture or a Renaissance emblem. This formal irony establishes Blake's designs, not Gray's poem, as the fulcrum of hermeneutic activity.

Figure 1. William Blake. Title Page, Gray, *Ode on the Death of a Favourite Cat*.

The second design features Blake's list of designs (identified by lines from Gray's poem) in the box otherwise reserved for Gray. Now Selima, "demurest of the Tabby kind" is a large, though not excessively large, cat with a very small human female sitting on her

Figure 2 William Blake. List of designs, Gray, *Ode on the Death of a Favourite Cat.*

back. In the water below the goldfishes are just that, with even
smaller human females riding on their backs (fig. 2). Tayler reads
these piggyback figures as "a visual parody of the allegorical method
in which the 'real subject' is made to 'ride' astride the ostensible
one." The target of this parody is the piggyback logic of Gray's
moral at the end of the poem, which makes the story of a cat and
goldfish a cover for the real subject – women greedy for gold or, as
Blake's designs suggest, narcissism.[20]

   Blake's visual argument gradually dissolves these hybrid forms. In
the next design all three figures are mostly human. Selima has cat
ears and a twitching cat tail that coils up behind Gray's boxed text
of the opening one and a half stanzas of the poem. The "goldfishes"
are naked human lovers with gold, fish-like wings. Between water
and land, between life and death, between animal and human,
these figures emphasize their weirdly unreal state. Between the
goldfishes of this design and the gazing Selima are luxuriant
flowering vines (fig. 3). These, together with the Narcissus echo of
the design, suggest that Selima is blind to the lovers below because
she is busy admiring her reflection. In the design that surrounds
Gray's description of how the cat is tempted by the sight of goldfish,
the lady is now cat fore and woman aft and the "angel" fish have
the same human bodies and fish-like gold wings. Instead of Gray's
"Malignant Fate," who stands by like the Greek Atropos, with
scissors that will cut the thread of Selima's life short, in the next
design "Fate" gives Selima a good push. In the water below, an
armed human couple (the female does have scales) flee in horror. In
the last design Selima, now fully a woman, ascends from the deep,
as two large, but not human-sized, goldfish swim by. Blake's visual
allegory asserts not only that Selima lives, whereas Gray's poem
insists she loses all of her nine cat lives "drowned in a Tub of Gold
Fishes," but that she is transformed from a hybrid cat-woman into
a woman.

   As these designs vitiate Gray's line of march toward the concluding
maxim ("all that glisters is not gold"), they also create an interpretive
space needed for Blake's revision of Gray. Whereas the poem
deploys its cat vehicle and woman tenor with a wink and nod at the
wit of it all, Blake's surrounding designs create an allegorical tale
about Selima's ultimate release from this hybrid status. Now Selima's
gold is her uncovered hair, not pilfered goldfish. The grotesque
hybrid figures of the earlier designs and their hints of malignity and

Figure 3 William Blake. Illustration for opening stanzas, Gray, *Ode on the Death of a Favourite Cat.*

violence mark the figural violence of Blake's intervention. To save Selima from a blandly repressive maxim and fate, he deploys figures whose variance from mimetic norms is the visual sign of their allegorical power. The preferences conveyed by this gesture are plain: Selima undergoes a sea-change and becomes a woman, not another emblem, and the fish are still goldfish. Denying the application of Gray's maxim to females who long for gold (presumably, gold baubles), Blake makes gold a natural attributive for Selima as well as the fish.

Blake's visual insistence that Fate is not simply an emblematic rerun of the Greek Atropos but a malignant woman who acts conveys an impatience with Gray's personification that he repeats in other designs, including several that pit eighteenth-century poets against Spenser. In the twelfth design for *The Bard*, Blake puts two small vignettes of scenes from *The Faerie Queene* to the lower left of the text box, and two larger figures to the upper right. The left-hand vignettes position Gray's figures of Grief, Horror, Despair, and Care in Spenserian settings much favored by illustrators and painters – Mammon's Cave and the Cave of Despair.[21] In one scene, Despair offers a knife to a hapless figure; beside the two is a figure of the deed performed – a dead body with a knife in its chest which depicts, Gleckner suggests, Gray's Horror. The other, darker vignette features Mammon, Sir Guyon, and Spenser's "feend." The two right-hand figures are less easy to place. Tayler suggests they are "Truth severe" and "fairy Fiction"; Gleckner believes their theatrical dress fits the "buskin'd measures" of Gray's duo "Pale Grief, and pleasing pain." The small figure cupped in the Bard's hand is probably the fairy Spenser.

The visual iconography Blake uses to revise Gray in this design makes an intriguing case for Spenser. Whereas Gray's Bard and accompanying figures to his right are sketchily presented and not apparently involved in any action, the smaller but well-defined vignettes illustrate well-known Spenserian episodes. The contrast between the "Lilliputian" Spenser – a caricature of the "fairy" Spenser so often invoked by eighteenth-century and Romantic commentators – and the "Brobdingnagian Bard" who plunges to "endless night" in the last plate[22] thus implies that this moment in the line of poetic transmission from Spenser to Blake is clogged with Gray's bulky monumental sculptures.

A similar bias characterizes other designs in which Blake represents Gray's personified abstractions as grotesque shapes, at times just a monstrous head or visage.[23] Monstrous, grotesque, or inert, Gray's personifications may strike a threatening posture, but they do not move like living beings and so cannot be charged with allegorical agency. Blake's designs for Gray suggest that this is precisely what is wrong with his figures, whose vague outlines in *The Bard* pale in the vicinity of the tonal density and clarity of the Spenserian vignettes. As they do in J. M. W. Turner's art, here scalar extremes denote a figural rather than verisimilar argument about, in this instance, the relative values of Spenser's miniature emblematic scenes and the passivity of eighteenth-century personification.

Blake's designs for Gray constitute a highly formal intervention whose goal is, in Giddens's modern phrase, "structuration" – the process by which individuals and groups craft structures within which they live and work, thereby "structuring" them even as they are structured by them.[24] As Blake's subsequent poetic practice shows, the transformation of systemic tyranny into the work of structuration over time requires enormous hermeneutic energy and flexibility. Neither is available in the allegory Neoclassical writers prefer and the personifications Gray offers in receipt of that preference. Both are potentially available in Blake's allegorical narratives, whether the story concerns Gray's Selima the cat-woman or the continuous project of demolition and hard-won formation in *Jerusalem*.

Blake's critique of Gray participates in a Romantic debate about personification that in part concerns the allegorical potential of such figures.[25] Wordsworth's changing view of personification in the "Preface" to Lyrical Ballads conveys a broader Romantic ambivalence about figures whose rhetorical vividness makes them seem animated yet still unlike the human beings whose actions such figures mimic. In 1800 he declares that he has not used personifications of "abstract ideas" in the volume because they do not "make any regular or natural part of" ordinary conversation. Eighteenth-century poets who used a stock lexicon of "poetic" personifications with scant attention to situation and affect are the obvious target of this disclaimer. In later editions he replaces this claim with a Longinian acknowledgment that powerful, even exaggerated figures are appropriate (albeit distinctly not "regular" in the sense of being ordinary or usual) when "prompted by passion." This self-correction makes pathos a double agent: it is both an ancient rhetorical term for what strong, exaggerated figures need in order to be convincing and a thoroughly Romantic point of entry for such figures. Indeed without pathos, those figures gain no entry (*WProse* 11:31–32n.).

So construed, pathos, usually understood to mean passion or strong feeling, looks like safe and familiar Romantic ground. It is not. In her 1798 "Introductory Discourse" for *Plays on the Passions*, Joanna Baillie recommends the dramatic use of "the Passions" to depict tragic protagonists. Although she argues against assigning a master passion such as envy, love, or hatred to protagonists, contending that audiences find such displays unbelievable and therefore unaffecting (35), she implies that strong passions invite abstraction. Whether pathos designates a protagonist's dominant passion and its rhetorical expression or an audience's response, its affinity to abstractions such as "fear," "envy," or "love" is the unresolved contradiction in Baillie's "Discourse." She insists throughout that the protagonist whose character and history are governed by a mixture of passions gains a moral and psychological complexity akin to that of real people. Against the grain of this preference, the plays themselves feature several tragic (or purportedly tragic) male protagonists like De Monfort who are in the grip of a single passion. Her account of the language authorized by the tragic passions suggests the logic that impels this contradiction: "Bold and figurative language belongs peculiarly to [the tragic passions]. Poets, admiring those bold expressions which a mind, labouring with ideas too strong to be conveyed in the ordinary forms of speech, wildly throws out, taking earth, sea, and sky, every thing great and terrible in nature to image for the violence of its feelings, borrowed them gladly" ("Introductory Discourse," *Plays* 1:41). Despite Baillie's objection to the excessive use of this language, her description of protagonists who struggle against passions edges toward allegory: passions are "those great masters of the soul," even "tyrannical masters" whose "irresistable attacks ... it is impossible to repell" (Baillie, "Introductory Discourse," *Plays* 1:39, 43).

Romantic writers trace the origin of this allegorizing impulse in characters to Greek mythology and Roman rhetoric. Writing under the pseudonym Edward Baldwin, William Godwin explained to Romantic schoolchildren that the basis of Greek religion is allegory, which he defines as "the personifying, or giving visible forms to, abstract ideas" (*Pantheon* 9). Campbell's *Philosophy of Rhetoric* notes a similar correspondence: "as metaphor in general hath been termed an allegory in epitome, such metaphors and metonymies as present us with things animate in the room of things lifeless, are prosopo-poeias in miniature" (Campbell, *Rhetoric* II:210). The expanding and contracting semiotic logic of this relay between figures writ small like metaphor and *prosopopoeia*, used here as a synonym for personifica-tion,[26] and allegory as a figured narrative invokes *phantasia* and theatrical spectacles that create the illusion of animation where there are only still images.[27] It also acknowledges that modern allegory is almost wholly confined to personification allegory. Although personi-fication allegory is more commonly used in the early modern period than its medieval counterparts, topical and scriptural allegory,[28] it troubles the distinction between abstractions and persons in ways that Neoclassical writers had already made clear.

Campbell's definition by analogy, which implies that metaphor is a reduced or miniaturized allegory, indicates the visual, at times spectacular, extremes that mark Romantic allegory as it shuttles between the very small and the very large. These extremes mark the distance between real figures and visual images and those whose designs on readers are figural, illusionist, and potentially allegorical. Romantic rhetoricians are by no means easy about this potential. Campbell issues a prior restraint on allegory when he asserts earlier that when *prosopopoeia* or personification uses sensible or concrete things to convey abstract ideas, the outcome is merely rhetorically vivid language (*Rhetoric* 207–8). Notable for its absence here is *phantasia*, "things animate in the room of things lifeless." In Whate-ley's *Elements of Rhetoric, phantasia* makes its way back into Romantic rhetoric by way of Aristotle's *evepyeia* ("the act, or actualization of a potency or habit"), here translated as roughly equivalent to "energy" or "nearly corresponding with what Dr. Campbell calls Vivacity" (*Elements of Rhetoric* 275, 283–84). Whately's subordination of Aristote-lian action to its simulacrum authorizes the slippery slope *phantasia* has travelled from meaning "a making visible" to false vision, "phantoms," fantasy, and fancy. By this path rhetorical *phantasia* comes home to roost.

In Romantic fiction and poetry, reservations about allegory often compete with the depiction of absent things or ideas as though they were present. I offer two instructive instances. In *The Prelude* Words-worth's speaker finesses the contradictions embedded in "fancy" when he characterizes a vision of Druid priests observing the constellations and engaging in human sacrifice as "things viewed, / Or fancied, in the dim obscurities of time" (*Thirteen-Book Prelude*

12:354–55, pp. 312–13). The line break emphatically separates these alternatives. In the 1831 "Preface" to *Frankenstein*, Mary Shelley invokes a string of English cognates for *phantasia*:

My imagination, unbidden, possessed and guided me, gifting the successive images that arose in my mind with a vividness far beyond the usual bounds of reverie. I saw – with shut eyes, but acute mental vision – I saw the pale student of the unhallowed arts kneeling beside the thing he had put together. I saw the hideous phantasm of a man stretched out. (*Frankenstein* 227–28)

From imagination to images in the mind, mental vividness, and phantasm, *phantasia* is the supervising figure of the rhetorical vividness and persuasiveness of this mental image and its unlawfulness. Insofar as his act of creation takes the blame for Shelley's novelistic creation, Victor Frankenstein is the novel's scapegoat (it could not happen to a more deserving fellow).

Shelley's restrospective view of her fictional creation witnesses the resemblance between *phantasia* and figures like the monster that grotesquely exceed norms. My point is not that such exaggerations are necessarily allegorical, but that Romantic allegories use similar distortions of human scale and proportions. By making a spectacle of itself, allegory shows that it cannot be managed by conventional distinctions between what is real and what is abstract. For such spectacles remind us of allegory's ancient link to *phantasia* because they are evidently fictitious, yet oddly persuasive.

The proximity between allegory's palpable shapes and real or material details is especially telling in French revolutionary propaganda. In the early years of the Revolution, writers and festival organizers freely used allegorical images to promote revolutionary ideas. For a brief time Liberty was a woman; cheap pamphlets, broadsides, and jacobin almanacs extolled pro-revolutionary allegorical virtues; and one remarkable deck of playing cards replaced the traditional images of kings, queens, and jacks with allegorical virtues and identities that foster a pro-revolutionary view of culture and class.[29] The advertisement that was sold with the deck explains that it includes no aces because "the law is now supreme." Instead of kings, each of the four suits presents a specific talent and an emblematic figure with props. Each figure has two allegorical names, one across the bottom of the card and another along the upper right border. The king of hearts is now the *Génie* of War (as in Richard the Lion-hearted); the "Genius" of clubs is Peace; the other two are the

Figure 4 Comte de St. Simon. "Nouvelles Cartes à Jouer." Paris: V. Jaume and J. D. Dugourc. 1793–94.

Figure 5 Comte de St.Simon. "Nouvelles Cartes à Jouer." Paris: V. Jaume and
J. D. Dugourc. 1793–94.

Arts and Commerce. Instead of queens, each suit offers an allegorical
dame who represents a designated liberty: the "lady" of hearts stands
for freedom of religion (*Cultes*); she of clubs, freedom of marriage; she
of spades, freedom of the press; she of diamonds, choice of profes-
sions (figs. 4a–d). The jacks, now called "equalities," include the
egalité of rank or power and color or courage (figs. 5a–b). The figure
on this last card is a black man who has been, the advertisement
explains, relieved of his chains and given arms.

Designed by the revolutionary aristocrat the Comte de St. Simon,
hand-colored and published in 1793–94, this deck illustrates the
radically reinventive logic of some revolutionary allegory. At the
same time and for similar ends, allegorical figures also packaged
abstractions for public consumption. Sometime between 1790 and
1792, Helen Maria Williams wrote to an unidentified and probably
fictive English correspondent that she had acted the part of Liberté
in a revolutionary tableau and shouted "Vive la nation!" Writing
and speaking as an early supporter of the Revolution, Williams was
for this moment a living emblem and "speaking picture" whose pro-
revolutionary slogan may well have sent shivers down some
conservative English spines. Lynn Hunt dryly notes that "living
allegories" like this one are effective because their significance is

"transparent," as English Neoclassical critics had urged allegory should be.[30]

Worth a thousand words, as the saying goes, such allegorical figures were intended for members of the Third Estate. Less educated and more likely to believe what they saw, it was assumed, the great, unrepresented majority of the French would be swayed by the power of images.[31] The Neoclassical undertow of this assumption surfaces in the French penchant for adapting the learned iconographic tradition to revolutionary principles. The English Neoclassical argument that allegorical images ought to "speak to the eyes" did not always count for much with the revolutionary French. Even Jacobin almanacs and civic manuals, which were published to enlist support for the Revolution, used some allegorical images that were learned and obscure. Thus the figure of the many-breasted Egyptian Goddess of Nature reappears as multiple spigot of a fountain statuary built early in the revolutionary period on the site of the destroyed Bastille. Only an observer familiar with her iconography would recognize the appropriateness of this design. Soon afterward, the same Nature appears in an emblem titled "Egalité" that was printed in a civic manual titled *L'Ami des Jeunes Patriots, ou Catéchisme républicain*. Here she is placed beside the figure of egalitarianism, who holds a level over the head of the statue in one hand, and a *fasces*, the Roman symbol of authority, in the other (fig. 6).[32]

Yet this *fasces* also implies a troubling consanguinity between revolutionary and Neoclassical allegory. As a symbol of authority, the *fasces* is a reminder of the authoritarian visual code Neoclassical theorists identified with such figures. To the extent that revolutionary leaders assumed they could sway the people with the power of (allegorical) images, they invest the authoritarian principles of the *ancien régime* in a different, more public space. Thus guided by an Enlightenment faith in the truth or at least the persuasiveness of sense experience, they recall the technocrats of Diderot's dream of an illusionist spectacle after Fragonard. Like those technocrats, but without whips and chains, propagandists believed they could convince the French people to join the revolution and assent to its reading of recent history and its ideological program. As the agent of French revolutionary ideology, this emblem objectifies Bourdieu's "hidden violence of objective mechanisms," which work here on the back of the *ancien régime*.

Figure 6 "Egalité." J.-B. Chemin-Dupontes *fils. L'Ami des Jeunes Patriots ou Catéchisme républicain.* 1793–94.

One recent historian who describes the Jacobin use of complex emblematic figures like this in pamphlets directed at a younger, less educated audience notes how counter-intuitive this practice looks to a modern reader: "although they sought to reach the greatest number of readers, they paradoxically resorted to abstract language. Abstraction in a generally allegorical form was, in fact, omnipresent ... Revolutionary engravings also celebrated great feminine figures ... such as Liberty, Justice, Equality, Law ... or France. Around these central figures there developed a series of emblems, red caps, scales, pikes, cockades."[33] The visual argument created by surrounding a central figure with emblematic details is, moreover, patterned on the Renaissance emblem, whose complexity earlier English and Continental critics had rejected. Though Jacobin propagandists introduced more accessible images like pikes and cockades, they incorporated them into a highly traditional emblematic structure.

This practice suggests the contradiction embedded in French revolutionary allegory. For despite evidence that revolutionary propaganda depended on the silently coercive power of allegorical images, revolutionary festivals may have worked both sides of the street. To make this double hermeneutic engine work, Ozouf suggests, festival organizers shuttled between *verismo* and synecdoche:

Reading the official accounts, we should not believe too readily that popes to be whipped, Pitts to be insulted, and Capets to be guillotined were dragged out into the public squares. A more attentive reading tells us that the dummy did not often bear much resemblance to Capet, and that a royal headband, or sometime an even less explicit emblem, served. In short, it was not so much a pope that was being trashed as Fanaticism, and not so much Louis XVI as Monarchy. Fanaticism and Monarchy, but also Abundance, Liberty, Justice – the lesson of the Revolution was conveyed by a swarm of allegorical figures.[34]

By using abstractions to fix moments in a recent and highly volatile history as though they were already "removed" from the real to the abstract and allegorical, those figures could guide revolutionary enthusiasm into safe waters. To effect this outcome, it would be unnecessary and inadvisable to name particular names and events that might produce an anti-revolutionary backlash. Instead, festivals presented the least affecting parts of absent wholes – a royal headband for a headless Louis XVI. Slogans and labels insured that the people would not miss the point.

The difficulty with this model of teaching by allegorical example is the power of *phantasia* as the fictive representation of absent events as though they were happening now. For if the synecdochic details Ozouf lists – "bayonets, rifles, sabers, hatchets, forks and other weapons" – are emblematic, they are also real weapons. The risks of using real props were not lost on festival organizers, who nonetheless hoped that an allegorical framework might contain revolutionary violence. Eventually they prescribed in "what conditions and within what limits" allegorical figures and real props could be used together to restage violent moments in the recent history of the Revolution.

This prescription tells the story that is otherwise well hidden in Neoclassical discussions of why allegory should be excluded from the epic and all similarly historical genres. Invoking the first and most-quoted advocate of this principle, the Abbé Dubos, Quatremère de Quincy objected to using allegorical figures to represent the history of the Revolution, and Jacques-Louis David deplored the use of "odious allegories" in the public funeral/revolutionary festival staged to honor Jacques Simonneau, the mayor of Étampes who was lynched by rioting peasants.[35] Yet festival organizers like Quincy and David could hardly represent the Revolution without allegory. More than the living tableau of the English Williams speaking for and as Liberty, monumental allegorical statues and spectacles provided the ideal, larger-than-life images the Revolution needed.

At times those allegorical images reflect Neoclassical values, much as David, throughout his writings, used emblematic moments like the oath of the Horatii or even (when it became necessary to invent emblems for the Revolution) the death of Marat to convey a view of history that is essentially static and memorial. Some images, like those that appear on the playing cards St. Simon devised for a new political culture, veer away from Neoclassical assumptions about history as well as allegory. In a 1789 engraving titled "L'Hydre Aristocratique," the eponymous Aristocracy is a colossal figure described as "mâle et female" (so much for the momentary exhilaration of a female Liberté) who is losing its heads, blow by blow (fig. 7). Unlike the classical historical moment David preferred to depict or create (*The Death of Marat*), the moment of this engraving is the present, the action ongoing. Beside the ramparts of a Bastille that is still standing, Frenchmen repel the Aristocracy. This is no task for a single Hercules; moreover, since many heads, some with ecclesiastical hats, remain, the French have more collective labors to

Figure 7 "L'Hydre Aristocratique." 1789. Color etching.

perform. A prostrate human figure in the foreground who wears robes that display the royal fleur-de-lis still has his head. This 1789 engraving is a prospective warrant of choices that may lie just ahead, as indeed they did. Unlike Michelet's vision of history as a unified narrative in which the future and the past and the Revolution itself articulate a coherent, progressive evolution,[36] here an allegorical image specifies early stages in a radical series of changes that promises to be violent and to require many French hands (and heads).

In the opening stanzas of *France: An Ode*, first published in 1798 with the title *The Recantation: An Ode*, Coleridge casts revolutionary France in the image of colossal allegorical figure:

> When France in wrath her giant-limbs upreared,
>   And with that oath, which smote air, earth, and sea,
>   Stamped her strong foot and said she would be free,
> Bear witness for me, how I hoped and feared!   (*Coleridge* 245)

Elsewhere he views allegory with more fear than hope. The young poet who imagined France in much the same way revolutionary festivals imagined her, Liberty, and other allegorical virtues was even then more likely to plot allegorical characters and narratives along Neoclassical lines. It is little wonder that Addison's "Vision of Mirzah" looks like a template for Coleridge's "Allegoric Vision," composed in 1795 and subsequently revised with different audiences in mind. When it was used as the preface to Coleridge's first theological lecture, its satiric target was the Church of England. In 1811 it was published in *Courier*; by then its target was the Church of Rome. In the version he adapted for its 1817 publication with *A Lay Sermon*, it takes aim at the "falsehood of extremes."[37] Although the allegorical referent shifts from one version to the next, all these versions would have satisfied the sternest Neoclassical critic. Firmly reined in by the speaker of the "Vision" and easily matched to well-identified (albeit shifting) targets, Coleridge's allegory never strays into the hazard zone where allegorical ideas meet colossal forms that move, but move "not like living men." Precisely because she does move and act, the figure of revolutionary France in his 1798 ode suggests a measure of what Coleridge learned to fear about an allegorical figure so engaged in bodily and narrative movement and fury that she might do some real damage. For this figure, like the Revolution it represents, is caught in the folds of allegory's ancient and modern alliance with *phantasia* and its English cognates, among them "fancy" (the chief antagonist) and those dream-like shapes or images produced by fancy when thinly disguised as "phantasms." Coleridge's writing is studded with recognitions of this alliance, although he is mostly vigilant about giving it prejudicial treatment. In "The Eolian Harp" the speaker half-chides his "many idle flitting phantasies." Heavily ventriloquized by the speaker, his imagined female interlocutor more harshly indicts them as "shapings of the ungenerate mind," a formulation that retains the ancient and Miltonic identification of such shapes with *phantasia* (*Coleridge* 101–2). When the speaker of *Dejection: An Ode* declares that he has lost his "shaping spirit of Imagination," Coleridge reinstates *phantasia* in a covert operation with a built-in sting (*Coleridge* 366). The Mariner of *The Rime of the Ancient Mariner* invokes the etymological affiliation of "shape" with *phantasia* and Milton's allegorical "shapes" of Sin and Death: "a certain shape, I wist. / A speck, a mist, a Shape, I wist"; "full many Shapes, that shadows were" (*Coleridge* 192, 205). In the *Biographia Literaria* Coleridge mocks the reading habits of those who visit the circulating libraries by comparing the scene to "the moving phantasms of one man's delirium" (*BL* 1:48n.). And in notes for lectures he delivered in 1818 and 1819, he insists that the pleasure he finds in Spenser's vivid, dream-like images, the poetic equivalent of rhetorical *phantasia*, has nothing to do with the allegory.[38]

This last assertion is unpersuasive but not unimportant, for it implicitly acknowledges, among other effects, that together allegory and *phantasia* make it possible to figure people as things. This figurative move might easily be diverted to justify using people as things – a possibility writ grotesquely large in the phantasmagorias, automatons, and freak shows of early nineteenth-century London.[39] To put this anxiety in more explicitly philosophical terms: allegory is an intransigeant reminder of the unremitting problem of universals and their material or figural substantiation. Coleridge tries to resolve this problem by claiming that the imagination and the symbol together supervise the transcendent passage between universals and particulars, whereas fancy works entirely within the realm of material and human particulars (*BL* 1:82–83). The flaw hidden in this assertion is exposed in the *Logic* when he considers how theorizing and abstraction become so passionate in early revolutionary France that they produce "glowing figures of fancy" (*Logic* 242–43).[40] A similarly unwanted conjunction persists in the midst of Coleridge's

most prodigious efforts to separate "idea" from the material and
sensorial fetters of its Aristotelian identification with *phantasia* (*Logic*
236–38; "SM" 30–31).

For reasons that are peculiarly his own but which Romantic and
post-Romantic culture absorbed, Coleridge's uneven declarations
about symbol and allegory (stronger in some texts than others and
stronger in 1816–18 than before or after) silently recognize that the
problem with allegory is not that it is stiff or fixed, but that it is
involved in the philosophical difficulties I have outlined.[41] Because
allegory transforms persons into personifications and abstractions,
Coleridge wants to bar it from the workings of the transcendent
imagination. By the same logic, the symbol is the positive sign of
much that he requires. These assumptions constitute Coleridge's
"gordian knot" – a tightly implicated nest of problems that cannot
be fully unravelled without disturbing his idealist and Kantian
reply to empiricist and Humean principles of knowledge and
personhood.

Yet his anti-allegorical stance is disturbed by what Jerome Christensen calls "the symbol's errant allegory" – Coleridge's penchant
for revising texts and ideas over time, undoing some arguments on
the way to others. It is also disturbed by the argumentative path of
the *Biographia Literaria*, which assumes that the task of telling one's life
history requires a recognition of its temporalities. This recognition,
evidently akin to de Man's understanding of poetic temporality, is
also at work in revisions of the *Rime*, which collectively dramatize the
unlikelihood of a coherent symbolic universe.[42] The central text in
de Man's analysis of this errant allegory is Coleridge's "Statesman's
Manual" defense of the "translucence" of the symbol ("SM," *Lay
Sermons* 30). If the symbol allows us to see through its visible and
cultural shape to apprehend its meaning, this hermeneutic activity,
de Man observes, looks very much like that of allegory as a figure
that always refers beyond itself. On these grounds, he charges
Coleridge with "ontological bad faith."[43]

In the broader set of discriminations between Romanticism and
modernity inaugurated by this critique, de Man takes skeptical aim
at the project Coleridge defends with every philosophical argument
and seeming digression: his belief that persons can write and live
authentic and coherent histories. From this vantage point, poet and
critic are uncannily well-matched antagonists. For de Man as for
Benjamin, allegory is the necessary angel of ruin, historical fragmen-

tation, and commodifying energies that turn persons into abstractions and things. On similar grounds but for contrary reasons, allegory is the demon figure Coleridge hopes to cast aside lest it undermine the coherence of persons and of the Scriptures as true revelations and histories.

Writing against early nineteenth-century assaults on claims for the historical reality of Scripture, Coleridge requires the simultaneity of the symbol to argue that biblical texts are historical narratives which convey the continuous truth of revelation. By the same logic, allegory, or "allegorism" as he and Blake also call it, undermines the truth of Scripture by making it merely the vehicle, not the substance of revealed truth and genuine history. For all these reasons, the distinction between symbol and allegory matters more to Coleridge than it does to his German contemporaries, who eventually adopt either term to describe qualities formerly assigned to the other.[44]

I rehearse these familiar objections because they indicate the broader set of philosophical difficulties that accrue to allegory as a figure that deals in abstractions and generalities. This alliance is evidently not news, for Coleridge or for us, but it offers an unexpected point of entry into those philosophical convictions he defends against modes of thought whose unacknowledged metafigure is allegory. The deep logic of Coleridge's resistance to allegory begins with his beleaguered definition of *idea*. Much of what he asserts about this term can be found scattered or collected in the "Statesman's Manual," his early lectures on literature, and *Biographia Literaria*. The somewhat later *Logic*, a redaction of Kant's *Critique of Pure Reason*, gives Coleridge ample opportunity to explain how his Kantian, idealist, and Platonic understanding of *idea* challenges early modern versions of Aristotle's definition of *idea* as notions derived from sense impressions. As marketed by empiricist or, as Coleridge calls them, "experimental" philosophers, the term *idea* is lodged in the experience of the material and phenomenal world, not the transcendent reality that is for Coleridge the only possible ground for thought. In the *Logic* he insists to the contrary that the *idea* is "anterior to all image" and for this reason has nothing in common with abstraction or generality, which extract principles from images and things (63). In the form given this argument in the *Biographia Literaria*, he explicitly opposes this claim to Aristotle's *On the Soul* consideration of ideas that might follow from the perception of visual images or shapes. Coleridge's more immediate target is the empiricist and skeptical use of Aristotle's *On the Soul* to argue that sense impressions lead, albeit in complex ways, to ideas in the mind (*BL* 1:98).

Located on the opposite side of images and things from ideas in this scheme, abstractions look very much like the paintings of Milton's Death that Coleridge judges inadequate in his 1811 lecture:

sundry painters ... had made pictures of the meeting between Satan & Death at Hell Gate and how was the latter represented? By the most defined thing that could be conceived in nature – A Skeleton, perhaps the dryest image that could be discovered which reduced the mind to a mere state of inactivity & passivity & compared with which a Square or a triangle was a luxuriant fancy. (*Lectures 1808–19* 1:311–12)

Painted in oils (or on velvet), Death is a stand-in for the "hollowness" of allegorical abstractions ("SM" 28). Benjamin West's popular *Death on a Pale Horse* goes down for the count here. As Coleridge insists in the "Statesman's Manual," abstractions excavate elements from particular shapes and forms – hollowing them out to produce thoughts and concepts and, later, a second order of abstraction that yields generalities about classes and species that are once removed from particular images and things and twice removed from Coleridgean ideas. The irony that impels this brief opposition between a passive image and the "luxuriant fancy" of a geometrical figure allows fancy, albeit briefly, to deal in figures that prompt mental activity, a concession he later disallows in the *Biographia Literaria*.

What goes unsaid in this account is at least as intriguing. Coleridge neglects to mention not just that Milton's Death is allegorical, but that this figure is a brilliant poetic instance of a hollowed-out abstraction, that "other shape, / If shape it might be called that shape had none / Distinguishable in member, joint, or limb" (*PL* 2.666–67, p. 49). Read against the chorus of Neoclassical complaints about Milton's use of allegory, this omission looks like a dodge with an end clearly in view. To have called Sin and Death allegorical figures would have disrupted his praise for Milton's poetic conception.

When Coleridge returns to public discourse on this topic in his 1818 lecture on the allegorical tradition, he more consistently isolates what he admires in allegorical narratives from the contaminating effect of allegory:

if the allegoric personage be strongly individualized so as to interest us, we cease to think of it as allegory – and if it does not interest us, it had better be away. – The dullest and most defective parts of Spenser are those in which we are compelled to think of his agents as allegories – and how far the Sin and Death of Milton are exceptions to this censure, is a delicate problem which I shall attempt to solve in another lecture. (*Lectures 1808–19* II:102–3)

If Coleridge did attempt to solve this "delicate problem" in his next lecture on Milton, no record of what he said remains.[45] It is more likely that these and similar observations – with some praise for Bunyan because his allegorical characters seem like "real persons" – constitute what Coleridge had to say about allegory. His closing rant begins with Tasso's explanation of the allegorical meaning of *Gerusalemme liberata* and ends with the merest glimpse of a further declaration about Spenser's *Faerie Queene*. Luckily for us, Coleridge argues, what Tasso says about his allegorical characters quickly slips out of mind, "having the very opposite quality that Snakes have – they come out of their Holes into open view at the sound of sweet music, while the allegoric meaning slinks off at the very first notes – and lurks in murkiest oblivion – and utter invisibility – /and in the Faery" (*Lectures 1808–19* II:103). True to its genre, this critique of allegory turns into an allegorical vignette in which the Snake of allegorical meaning, like the evil spirit it is, slinks off because it cannot stand sweet, poetic music. Instead, it is consigned to invisibility and oblivion, along with Milton's Death and *The Faerie Queene*.[46]

Coleridge's much reworked definition of allegory conveys its limitations by debasing *imagination* to mean little more than the act of recognizing visual images. The definition is resolutely conventional, even to the extent of making the imagination a pseudo-Neoclassical analogue for the eye:

we define allegoric composition as the employment of one set of <agents and> images . . . so as to convey, while we disguise, either moral qualities or conceptions of the mind that are not in themselves objects of the Senses, or other <images,> agents, actions, fortunes and circumstances, so that the difference is every where presented to the eye or imagination while the Likeness is suggested to the mind. (*Lectures 1808–19* II:99).

When he prepared the *Biographia Literaria* and the "Statesman's Manual" for publication in 1816–17, Coleridge was no longer willing to allow imagination this much proximity to images, particularly allegorical ones. Early in the *Biographia Literaria*, he tries to make this argument stick by splitting the imagination from its etymological shadow *phantasia*.[47] He asserts that while it is not "easy to conceive a more apposite translation of the Greek *Phantasia*, than the Latin

Imaginatio," the history of their usage offers a special instance of the process by which the "instinct of growth, a certain collective, unconscious good sense work[s] progressively to desynonymize those words originally of the same meaning" (*BL* 1:82) – that is, words which have the same etymology.

Desynonymization is an artifact of eighteenth- and nineteenth-century language theory, which claimed that, as language develops, it moves from concrete to abstract meanings.[48] Wary of abstraction though he is, Coleridge here finds it useful for presenting a shift from *phantasia*'s highly material and "experimental" view of images as what the eye gains from "sense impressions," to the synthetic, "esemplastic power" of the imagination. Although he had developed this principle years earlier, its function in the *Biographia Literaria* is more specific than general: to rid the imagination of its unsavory double so completely that it will disappear even as the "original likeness" of a word's ancient pronunciation will finally be "worn away" after centuries of phonetic variations (*BL* 1:83n.). This argument draws heavily on recent German philosophical attention to these terms, particularly that of Jean-Paul Richter, who suggests that imagination ("Einbildungskraft") is inferior to fancy ("Phantasie"), which "makes all parts whole," "totalizes everything, even the endless universe" ("totalisiert alles, auch das unendliche All").[49] Coleridge will in the end reassign fancy's synthesizing power to imagination.

In the next chapter of the *Biographia Literaria*, he returns to *phantasia* by a circuitous route. This return is also half buried in a long note which reviews the problematic definition of *idea* in early modern philosophy, beginning with Hobbes's mechanistic equation of sense impressions with ideas (*BL* 1:96). Against Hobbes and his empiricist descendants, Coleridge defends the Platonic conception of the Greek term *idea* as roughly equivalent to the noun "Ideal." To illustrate this use of the term, he quotes a passage from Jeremy Taylor's *Sermons*:

St. Lewis the King sent Ivo Bishop of Chartres on an embassy, and he told, that he met a grave and stately matron on the way with a censor of fire in one hand, and a vessel of water in the other; and observing her to have a melancholy, religious, and phantastic deportment and look, he asked her what those symbols meant, and what she meant to do with her fire and water; she answered, my purpose is with the fire to burn paradise, and with my water to quench the flames of hell, that men may serve God purely for the love of God. But we rarely meet with such spirits which love virtue so metaphysically as *to abstract her from all sensible compositions, and love the purity of the idea.* (*BL* 1:97–98n.)

Modern editors note that Coleridge probably wrote the final sentence, which does not appear in Taylor's text. As a gloss on the anecdote, this emphatic declaration minimizes the curious blend of the sensible and the abstract that makes the woman's deportment "phantastical" in the sense of being outlandish and highly visible. Were this consanguinity of terms not expressly foreclosed by Coleridge's parallel desynonymization of symbol and allegory, we might say that the woman's appearance and speech recognize no difference between the allegorical idea and the world of things – that she witnesses an allegorical truth by symbolic means.[50]

The rest of Coleridge's long note adduces two intervening historical examples of how modern philosophers have used the term *idea*. The first is from Locke's *Essay*, which equates it with *phantasm*, among other terms; the second is from Hume's *Treatise*, where ideas are presented as equivalent to the mind's "faint images of its most violent and forceful impressions" (*BL* 1:98n.). Coleridge categorically insists that these alignments between idea and phantasm or image mistake the universal, Platonic *idea* he wishes to defend. Yet in the next paragraph of the main text, he lets *phantasia* return, this time with a distinctly philosophical cachet. Now he explains that for the Spanish philosopher Juan Luis Vives, a disciple of Erasmus, "Phantasia … express[es] the mental power of comprehension, or the *active* function of the mind; and imaginatio the receptivity (*vis receptiva*) of impressions, or … the *passive* perception" (*BL* 1:99).

These several returns of *phantasia* in the *Biographia Literaria* look like a consciously willed return of the repressed. For what returns in Taylor's anecdote about the "phantastic deportment" of a woman in the grip of profound religious faith is an allegorical vision of the world and its things. By way of this narrative, Coleridge offers a distinction between imagination and *phantasia* that contradicts his own in the preceding chapter, where it is presented as an example of the salutary consequences of desynonymization. Finally, the long-deferred chapter on the imagination corrects this half-correction by making *phantasia* unequivocally a lesser and distinct operation of the mind.

To do this, he begins with a passage from *Paradise Lost* where fancy is subordinated to a higher power of mind that Milton identifies as a reason "more spirituous and pure" than earthly, material things. Not incidentally, this reason looks very much like Kantian pure reason, a temporary place-holder in Coleridge's philosophical approach to the transcendent, esemplastic imagination. A second epigraph, taken from Leibniz, and presented in translation, excepts "the purely mathematical and what is subject to fancy [*phantasiae*]" from the category of material things whose existence cannot be understood unless we appeal to a higher, Platonic "formal principle" (*BL* 1:295). The special status Leibniz gives to fancy implies that it, like pure mathematics, is always already apart from the material world such that it has some unspecified relation to the higher principle that is another temporary place-holder in Coleridge's narrative for the imagination.

The value Leibniz assigns to fancy/*phantasia* disappears in the account of imagination and fancy Coleridge offers abruptly and without commentary as the conclusion of his chapter. Even here, however, at the culmination of the long, highly interested disquisition on the history of philosophy that has occupied thirteen chapters, *phantasia* and allegorical figures remain oddly necessary figures of the revolution in philosophy Coleridge hopes to effect. At the point in the chapter where asterisks mark a sudden halt in the argument thus far, he claims to have stopped writing after receiving a letter of advice from a solicitous friend and fellow reader of the work this far. The "friend" is, as Coleridge's earlier journal of the same title makes clear, Coleridge himself. Reading the author's history of philosophy and consequent definition of the imagination thus far is, the letter-writing "friend" reports, like finding oneself

alone, in one of our largest Gothic cathedrals in a gusty moonlight night of autumn. "Now in glimmer, and now in gloom"; often in palpable darkness not without a chilly sensation of terror; then suddenly emerging into broad yet visionary lights with coloured shadows, of fantastic shapes yet all decked with holy insignia and mystic symbols; and ever and anon coming out full upon pictures and stone-work images of great men, with whose names I was familiar, but which looked upon me with countenances and an expression, the most dissimilar to all I had been in the habit of connecting with those names. Those whom I had been taught to venerate as almost super-human in magnitude of intellect, I found perched in little fret-work niches, as grotesque dwarfs; while the grotesques, in my hitherto belief, stood guarding the high altar with all the characters of Apotheosis. In short, what I had supposed substances were thinned away into shadows, while every where shadows were deepend into substances:

> If substances may be call'd what shadow seem'd,
> For each seem'd either! (MILTON. (*BL* 1:301)

In Coleridge's friendly letter of advice to himself, "fantastic shapes" make a stunning case for the imaginative displacement of static images (and reputations) by a new order. Under its dispensation, a gothic phantasmagoria makes the great grotesquely small and the grotesquely small great. This reshuffling is obviously staged to place Coleridge's reputation above that of the many philosophers whose arguments the *Biographia Literaria* canvasses. Moreover, like London phantasmagorias and like those magic-lantern shows that also depended on the illusion of great size or sudden shifts in apparent size, Coleridge's gothic horror picture show tries, *avant la lettre* and with this letter, to persuade readers of the truth of an argument concerning the imagination that they will never see, an argument for which the concluding paragraphs on imagination and fancy are an emblematic, rebus-like text designed to be understood only by those prepared to grasp its meaning. The Miltonic tag the "friend" uses to close this section of the letter tacitly compares the movement of its "fantastic shapes" to the appearance of Sin and Death, whose theological lack of substance is paradoxically the only substance they have. The fact that Milton's Death is an allegorical shape who swells monstrously *as he speaks* conveys the hidden logic of Coleridge's citation.

Coleridge himself tacitly refuses this logic, first in 1811, when he uses the same passage to discuss the sublimity of Milton's figure of Death, and again in the *Biographia Literaria*. For though his description of "fantastic shapes" that grow great or shrink evidently recalls Burke's defense of sublime obscurity ("A clear idea is ... a little idea"),[51] Coleridge refuses once more to identify shapes and figures that evoke the Miltonic sublime with allegorical ideas. By 1816, this silent antagonism erupts in his notes for public lectures, the "States-man's Manual," and above all the *Biographia Literaria*, where allegory becomes the shadow figure in opposition to the imagination.

Yet in the *Biographia* and by way of Milton, Coleridge lets allegorical abstraction back in by another door to get the authoritative weight of these figures behind him as "characters of Apotheosis" capable of elevating his reputation just when it might otherwise be compromised by a long disquisition on the imagination. In all the registers conveyed by its Romantic attachment to metaphor and personification as "allegory in epitome," allegory is the implied and real agent for figures that swell in shape, assume greater powers, and seem to come alive. For although Coleridge does not describe these images moving, it is easy to imagine them doing so as they change places such that location and increasing size are the index of their value.

In the concluding paragraphs of this chapter, Coleridge moves decisively to limit fancy to "fixities and definites" supplied by "the law of association," whose lifeless rigidity he had dispatched in earlier chapters and works. These limitations – which exceed the terms of the chapter 4 desynonymization of *phantasia*/fancy from imagination – look as though they are designed to countermand the ferment of "fantastic shapes" and Miltonic allusion in the "friend's" letter. To do this, Coleridge must also reframe his earlier claim that fancy's images endure in the mind (*Lectures 1808–19* 1:81). Now he suggests merely that such images are quasi-mechanically stored in the memory (*BL* 1:305).

By positioning fancy, and allegory as its unacknowledged familiar, on the side of fixed, lifeless images, Coleridge isolates abstractions from individuals. In doing so, he keeps personhood and human feeling safe from the spectacle of a culture in which persons might easily become things, objects put on view off, as well as on, the stage. In the earlier lecture on Spenser, he makes this preference clear by insisting that Spenser's characters cease to be allegorical when they become individuals, with recognizably human feelings and dispositions. Thus, whereas Una is statue-like, hence unparticularized (and conveniently immobilized), Grief is allegorically at fault because he both grieves and pinches others' hearts with grief. At once "agent and patient," Spenser's Grief defies the separation between allegorical abstraction and pathos that Coleridge, like Neoclassical writers, seeks to preserve. Coming from Coleridge, whose definition of the imagination insists on its substantiation in the world, this old chestnut looks like special pleading. It is also contradicted by his earlier praise for Shakespeare's invention of female characters who embody "that mixture of the real & the ideal which belongs to woman." Of such a woman, Coleridge says, a man "could say 'Let that woman be my supporter in life; let her be the aid of pursuit and the reward of my success'" (*Lectures 1808–19* 1:298). The weight of marital alienation, desire, and self-pity that colors this remark conveys the pathos that Coleridge elsewhere holds back from allegory. Folded into allegorical persons and narratives, pathos marks a fleeting convergence between ideas and the world of real persons and actions.

I conclude this chapter with Wordsworth's *Prelude*, book 7, description of "allegoric shapes" because it looks like a visual riddle whose solution demands re-thinking the difference between "men and moving things" (*Prelude* 7.158, p. 234). Like much of the book from which it is taken, these lines are studded with what Cynthia Chase has aptly named "rhetorical devices requiring the complicity of the reader."[52] Chief among them is the ekphrastic invitation to interpret the look of the words on the page as well as their meaning. In their verbal as well as visual registers, these lines let the distinction between animate human figures and inanimate ones cave in under closer scrutiny.

Wordsworth's "endless stream of men and moving things" is a case in point. Either they are pushed, or move of their own will, or – to split this difference – they are so cleverly mechanized that they seem to move on their own, like the ingenious automatons that were exhibited in London and on the Continent, beginning in the 1740s.[53] I think Wordsworth's text splits the difference. Like the puppeteer–narrator in Kleist's "On the Marionette Theater," who is surprisingly ambiguous about who or what controls the puppets' actions, Wordsworth is careful not to tip his hand. Like those who flocked to see automatons engaged in activities so various that they almost seemed real (or super-real: one violinist figure was said to play faster than a human musician could), readers are free to imagine that such figures take on a life of their own.

Lined up on the page, "the comers and goers face to face – / Face after face – the string of dazzling wares, / Shop after shop" that Wordsworth's speaker sees in this "endless stream" look like interchangeable particulars. As points along this continuum, they are substitutable one for the next. Insofar as they say which tradesmen occupy the shops, the indexical task performed by the "symbols" and "blazon'd names" on the shop signs overhead is mimetic. As popular adaptations of the emblematic blazon, however, they are also allegorical. As this textual field of construed resemblances mutes the differences between faces, shops, and signs, the pun embedded in the term and phrase "*fronts* of houses" (my emphasis) looks necessary, not digressive. That is to say, the lexical fact that *front* means face or forehead as well as the side of a building that faces the street marks, on the level of figure, a local resemblance between the human and the inanimate that is endemic to Romantic figuration. The "huge" letters

inscribed over those "fronts" and "stationed . . . like guardian saints"
make this point explicit. Construed by this chain of resemblances,
allegorical signs are not necessarily distinct from mimetic ones.

As Wordsworth's speaker turns from "here" to "there," he reels in
another unexpected resemblance, this time between "allegoric
shapes" and "physiognomies of real men" – that is, statues or busts
that represent famous Englishmen. Using a taxonomy of facial traits,
especially "fronts" (foreheads), physiognomy asserts that those traits
accurately predict the specific temperament and intelligence of those
who exhibit such traits. By this logic, "physiognomies of real men"
are, like "allegoric shapes," public as well as visual embodiments of
an abstract idea, principle or system.[54] The heightened lexicality of
these lines thereby specifies both their abstract function and the fact
that they are the "guardian" of particular houses and occupants.
This is a rhetorical sleight-of-hand, but it is one that must occur if
figures and abstractions are to have some binding and public relation
to life and history.

In most of book 7, the term "shapes" designates spectral figures, or
ones that invite the speaker's interior vision. Scattered among more
sharply delineated types – the Italian, the Jew, the Turk, each with
his characteristic wares – are "less distinguishable shapes" that
incontestably echo Milton's description of Sin and Death in *Paradise
Lost*.[55] Like their Miltonic forebears, these "shapes" are insubstantial. Although the blind beggar is read as an "emblem, or apt type"
of all we can know, that lesson is offered as an private insight, not a
public emblematic text presented for others to read: "on the shape of
this unmoving Man, / His fixed face, and sightless eyes, I look'd / As
if admonished from another world" (*Prelude* 7:621–23, p. 208). When
the speaker refers to "things which I had shaped / And not yet
shaped, had seen, and scarcely seen" (7: 514–15, p. 206), these
"things" straddle the line between what is real and what is imagined,
as Wordsworth's figures often do. Still other London "shapes" are so
mysterious to the speaker that he compares them to "a second-sight
procession, such as glides / Over still mountains, or appears in
dreams" (7:601–3, p. 208).

Even these spectral or interiorized shapes are figural witnesses for
Wordsworth's fascination with London spectacles, many of which
featured ghosts and other spectral emanations. The showman Paul
de Philipstal's highly successful *Phantasmagoria*, a magic lantern show
he staged in London in 1801 or 1802, introduced dead heroes of the

French Revolution with clouds of smoke (presumably sulphuric) billowing around them. In describing the scene, Sir David Brewster could not resisting quoting Milton's famous description of Hell as "darkness visible."[56] In Wordsworth's poem, Jack the Giant Killer is an unabashed, low-tech advertisement of the fact that such spectacles are illusions. Wearing a dark cloak with the word "invisible" written "in flames" across its back, Jack makes a public spectacle of his "invisibility." In return, the public makes this fiction work by not contesting it, or perhaps by not snitching to the giant.

As I read Wordsworth's figural logic in book 7 of *The Prelude*, London spectacles interest him because they work, as do the figures of this book, at the extremities of representation. Much of what the speaker encounters is exaggerated, false, freakishly large or small, monstrous or deformed: gigantic letters over doors, giants and dwarfs, a disembodied "face" in the crowd, puppets and automatons, wax-works, conjurors, deformed human beings and animals (sometimes portrayed by the same human actor from one year to the next), a "parliament of monsters" (human and animal) at Bartholomew Fair. All these figures are unreal or super-real, patent exaggerations of and departures from a realist norm, that belong to a world of phantasms and to rhetoric. As de Man puts it, "something monstrous lurks in the most innocent of catachresis. When one speaks of the legs of a table or the face of the mountain, catachresis is already turning into prosopopoeia, and one begins to perceive a world of potential ghosts and monsters."[57] For the speaker of *The Prelude*, this world is an "unmanageable sight," one that can no longer be controlled as his earlier comparison of theatrical "Spectacles" to a miniature model had imagined such sights might be. Exaggerated figures like catachresis, prosopopoeia, and synecdoche are what allegory requires to make its border raids on what is real, or what mimesis represents as real, even as allegory figures itself as something "other" to reality. Thus if the spectacles and sights catalogued in book 7 are not necessarily allegorical (some are, some are not), they put figures to use which in turn make it possible for allegory to contort the aims and means of mimetic representation. This contortion is inherently monstrous, unnatural, and most of all anti-organic because it emphasizes parts, including body parts, over organic wholes. The palpable difference between the figural disposition of allegory and the Romantic aesthetic of beauty and the organic symbol is brilliantly conveyed by Shelley's Frankenstein as he surveys in horror what he has made: "His limbs were in proportion, and I had selected his features as beautiful. Beautiful! – Great God! His yellow skin scarcely covered the work of muscles and arteries beneath; his hair was of a lustrous black, and flowing; his teeth of a pearly whiteness; but these luxuriances only formed a more horrid contrast with his watery eyes" (*Frankenstein* 52). In the botched Petrarchan imagery of this description, synecdoche goes wildly awry. Instead of being indexical signs for a larger whole, these are dismembered body parts badly put together and made animate. Shelley's story of mangled creation dramatizes one view of what Romantic allegory does as it animates figures with the same disregard for the distinction between animate and inanimate forms that Frankenstein shows when he ransacks cemeteries for bodies.

Like the superscripts and emblematic shop signs of Wordsworth's London, allegory is a bold "front" for what other, less declared Romantic figures do to and with particulars. As such, it is the necessary surplus or excess of figure writ large. Without this surplus, language and meaning are confined to the same dull round of a radically programmatic model of language, crafted and mapped to exclude the play of meaning across and by way of figures. Within allegory, abstractions and particulars are each surplus to the other. In formal aesthetic terms, this allegory is neither the perfect and disinterested form of the beautiful imagined by Burke and Kant, nor is it merely sublime in the sense that it assents to a rational, intellectual separation from lived, historical life. Because its alterity is instead made for and in a time and place, allegory plays an ambivalent but integral role in Romantic culture. Marked by history, yet persistently exceeding the measure of fixed abstractions and images, it moves on to be remade, recast, or (since this too is always possible) cast in stone.[58] Wordsworth's most rivetting performance of this third possibility occurs in his *Convention of Cintra* pamphlet. There he defensively represents Napoleon by invoking a string of abstractions that ends with the image of a Colossus that will eventually shatter "upon a shock which need not be violent" (*WProse* II:334).

For all these reasons, allegory participates in the crisis of representation scholars have identified with the Romantic era and, before then, the long trajectory of modernity that begins in the seventeenth century. In its political form, this crisis deals with questions about which individuals or categories will be represented by a society or body politic. If traditional answers such as those Burke derives from custom and habit will finally not suffice, imagining other ways to construe the parts and wholes of political systems may require substituting new figures for old. As a figure that inherently defies or exceeds mimetic representation – insofar as it has to do with the world as we know it and see it – Romantic allegory suggests how to reimagine the task of representation as having to do with both particulars and abstraction. This task requires strange figures indeed. At a cultural moment when the task of reimagining parts and wholes seems, as it still seems to many, unclear and unfinished, synecdochic comparisons with allegorical ends in view are disorienting or enabling or both. Precisely for this reason, they are appropriate signs of how Romantic culture approaches the work of representation.

To the world of Spenser's faery romance, as mediated by eighteenth-century neo-Spenserian poets, Romantic allegory offers the flesh and blood that Hunt's formula for reading Spenser wishes to exclude. To the decorum of Neoclassical allegory, it replies with phantasmagoric and monstrous figures. Working against or with the emergent demand for realism, it co-opts realistic details to deform or transform them, in spite of themselves, into something "other" such that the role of abstraction in all acts of representation cannot be put aside. To the emptying of human traits and motion from later eighteenth-century poetic personification, it replies with figures animated as well as prompted by passion such that they cannot be excluded from the scene of Romantic figuration. To the presumption that allegorical meaning is elsewhere, visionary, or hidden, Romantic allegory offers in opposition its hunger for spectacular images and figures. This oppositionality is creative and double-jointed: it ratifies the prominence of visual images in allegory since the Renaissance, but uses those images to reorient (and disorient) that tradition. Allegory's shapes are no longer Platonic but provisional and temporizing. Even as Proteus adopts then sheds successive shapes to evade those who would capture him and force him to reveal the future, so does Romantic allegory evade the fixed, ahistorical, and determinate meaning toward which allegory always tends (remember Malbecco) and toward which it was impelled by the Neoclassical insistence on simple allegorical ideas and images.

Romantic allegory is a two-handed engine. It can inaugurate new directions by challenging the law of figure as shaped by custom – the figure Milton skewers in *Areopagitica*. At any moment in its history and identity, however, allegory can also rigidify, and may do so violently, into a bloodless, pedigreed abstraction dismissive of particulars and change. As the unequivocal agent of a specific ideology or cultural norm, this version of allegory exposes the backside of Burke's custom and tradition or Bourdieu's "habitus."[59] In this incarnation, allegory makes symbolic violence possible, even likely. It thereby performs with its gloves off the violence some critics have identified with the Romantic symbol. Allegorical violence covertly or publicly compels assent, much as the vises and chains of Diderot's dream are the machinery used to coerce unquestioning belief in the reality of illusionist spectacle.

CHAPTER 6

Romantic ambivalences II

An allegorical being, however much it may be given a human shape, does not attain the concrete individuality of a Greek god or of a saint or of some other actual person ... It is therefore rightly said of allegory that it is frosty and cold.

Hegel, *Aesthetics* 1:399

What, have you let the false enchanter scape?
O ye mistook, ye should have snatcht his wand
And bound him fast; without his rod revers't,
And backward mutters of dissevering power,
We cannot free the Lady that sits here
In stony fetters fixt, and motionless.

Milton, *Comus* 814—18, *PR* 259—60

When Hegel writes explicitly about allegory, he dismisses it as he does here for its coldness and abstraction. This hardly constitutes ambivalence. Yet in the folds of his analysis of the symbolic form of art lurks a version of allegory that goes by the name of "imagination" or, more precisely, *Phantasie*, the term he uses to refer to the production of images, as distinct from *Einbildungskraft*, the concept of image making.[1] Much as Coleridge finds it difficult to extricate symbol and allegory from the figure of *phantasia*, so does Hegel find it difficult to extricate the symbolic form of art from *Phantasie*. This term disturbs Hegel's analysis of the relation between abstract idea and sensuous form or shape – the philosophical problem to which his philosophy always returns. Because of *Phantasie*, at key moments the symbolic form of art looks more like allegory than symbol, and more like trouble.

This philosophical wrangle with allegory and *Phantasie* dramatizes an attraction to the ideal that is differently but as pervasively marked in Shelley and Keats. Whereas Hegel plots a solution to the dual problem of abstraction and sensuous shape by way of Romantic

subjectivity – the Hegelian synthesis ever at work – Shelley and
Keats are more interested in the conflict between idea or spirit on
the one hand, and sensuous shape on the other. The poetic figures of
this conflict are by turns grotesque, monstrous, and rigidly abstract,
and almost always identified, either distantly or at close range, with
eroticism and female figures. The "backward mutters of dissevering
power" that Milton's narrator says will be necessary to free the Lady
from Comus's enchantment conveys the poetic logic at work in these
allegorical figures, which extend in one direction toward stony
abstraction and, in the other, toward particular beings and cultural
moments. Stretched taut in this poetic device, some female figures
break under pressure and thereby convey the absolute limit of the
Romantic experiment with allegorical figures.

In part this poetic experiment echoes the emblematic, and often
misogynist, tradition in which, for example, Flattery is a woman
whose honeyed speech deceives and cuckolds men or a condescending hypocrite with a rosary in one hand and in the other meager
alms for the poor.[2] The brief moment during the French revolutionary period when Liberty was a woman should not obscure the
ideological use, then as well as before and after, of female allegorical
figures to "consolidate the power of the state." By making women
into allegorical spectacles, this tradition excludes them from action
and history.[3] Neither Keats nor Shelley frees allegorical female
figures that are, like Milton's Lady, "in stony fetters fixt." Nonetheless, the poetic means they deploy to bind them specify the
strength and limitations of such figures and the narrative desire they
command. Hegel is so eager to exclude such figures that he names
them everything but allegory and banishes them to art of the Indian
subcontinent.

Hegel's view of allegory under the aegis of *Phantasie* in his *Aesthetics*
draws on a more schematic distinction between sign and symbol in
his *Encyclopedia of the Philosophical Sciences*, first published in 1827.
There he argues that, whereas the sign is arbitrarily related to what
it signifies, the meaning of the symbol "more or less corresponds,
essentially and conceptually, to the content it expresses as a
symbol."[4] In the later, more elaborate argument of the *Aesthetics*,
where the symbolic form of art often looks more like allegory than
symbol, the vehicle for this unlooked-for and problematic resemblance is imagination or, more precisely, *Phantasie*.

In the *Aesthetics* Hegel tries to put this problem aside by aligning sensuous shape and imperfection with allegory, and thus against the world of becoming as the true realm of the symbolic and the spirit. Yet because the Hegelian symbolic is embedded in a series of unstable relations between abstraction, spirit, and form or material shape, it dramatically revisits the abiding concern of his *Science of Logic* – how to ground the abstract idea in a particular form. In that work he argues that only subjective philosophical reflection can effect this critical relation (*Logic* 44). In the *Aesthetics*, however, two versions of allegory stand in the way of this achievement. The first of these he calls allegory. The second, which he calls *Phantasie*, governs the conflicted middle space between abstraction and sensuousness. Hegel assigns both to cultural forms whose allegorical strangeness and estrangement inevitably afflict Western eyes (*Aesthetics* 1:519–32).

Hegel at first characterizes *Phantasie* as an activity of the imagination, but then cautions: "fine art cannot range in wild unfettered fancy" ["in wilder Fessellosigkeit der Phantasie"] (*Aesthetics* 1:5, 18). Although he asserts that one of the aims of art is to "let *fancy* [*Phantasie*] loose in the idle plays of *imagination* [*Einbildungskraft*] and plunge it into the seductive magic of sensuously bewitching *visions* [literally "intuitions," *Anschauungen*]" (*Aesthetics* 1:46), *Phantasie* is a persistent liability in the examples of symbolic art Hegel lingers over. For if the symbolic releases objective nature from a "jungle of finitude and the monstrosity of chance" (*Aesthetics* 1:84), it does so at some cost. Its name is the "fantastic" (*phantasievoll*), a cognate of *fantasy* that implies exaggeration, disguise, and a surface that is wildly separate from an inner spirituality. Hegel claims, for example, that "an unknown block of stone may symbolize the Divine, but it does not represent it ... when shaping begins, the shapes produced are symbols, perhaps, but in themselves are fantastic and monstrous" (1:76n.).

In the global vision of art and culture to which the *Aesthetics* subscribes, *Phantasie* is an oriental despot whose proliferation of sensuous shapes to represent divinities works against the emergence of the spiritual in art. Hegel insists that to understand the form of the romantic as the repository of inner spirit, we must preserve that form from the predations of the sensuous, whose liabilities he assigns to foreign cultures, past and present, that exemplify the earliest, least evolved, moments in his history of art. Under the sign of the symbolic, he orientalizes allegory so that it can, in hidden as well as exposed ways, perform the alienation his preference for the symbol requires.

Hegel's defensive maneuvers on behalf of the symbol, whose highest expression he identifies with the romantic form of art, confront two risks to the ascendancy of spirit. The first is abstraction, whose rigidity would rob the symbolic of phenomenal shape. The second is sensuous shape itself, which can lure consciousness away from spirit. This, he argues, is what happens in the early stages of the symbolic form of art, which he identifies with the multiple divinities and shapes of Indian art. In the *Aesthetics* the tripartite division of art into three stages or epochs – the classical, the symbolic, and the romantic – articulates a sliding scale of differences and traits that Hegel reiterates in his *Philosophy of History*.[5] Whereas classical art displays a perfect, beautiful but fleeting match between spirit or ideality and external form, and the self-consciousness of romantic art imbues form with the subjectivity and spirit that for Hegel constitute fine art, the symbolic form of art unevenly defines the terrain between the classic and the romantic. In its most evolved stages, symbolic art like that of the Egyptians registers the immanent, if as yet unrevealed, authority of spirit over sensuous shape. In its least evolved forms, which he identifies with Indian art, the symbolic collapses into seductive, multiple forms that draw the eye and mind away from spirit and divinity. Thus the romantic form of art is achieved when human self-consciousness learns or draws out the spirit that the sensuous shape can only approximate (*Aesthetics* 1:76–89).[6]

Hegel thereby rejects Kant's argument in the second and third *Critiques* that aesthetic and purely rational judgments operate *a priori*, outside the realm of things. Against this theory of art and reason, which Hegel identifies with spectral, shadowy abstractions (*Logic* 47), he urges the interplay between spirit and shape that reaches its highest moment in romantic subjectivity. What I find striking about this schematic is the safe distance it interposes between abstraction and sensuous shape, two equally if differently hazardous extremes. Tilted toward abstraction, art is emptied, hollowed out, and thus unaffecting. Tilted toward sensuous shape, art fills mind and eye with seducing images and thereby leaves no mental space for spirit without which, Hegel insists, there can be no fine art (*Aesthetics* 1:39).

Hegel finds both extremes in the symbolism of Indian art which is, he asserts, replete with signs of a striving toward an ideal that Christ will later embody by joining His perfect divinity with a particular, human, and temporal shape. Against the unity of this figure, Hegel arrays the plural, monstrous shapes of Indian art whose shortcomings, he asserts, are typical of the early stages of the symbolic form of art: abstraction, multiple or changing shapes, fantasy and the fantastic, contingency or its opposite, fixation or fixed emblematic images.

Challenging Western theologians who claimed that the Indian god Trimurti was a version of the Christian Trinity, Hegel declares:

Starting from Brahma and Trimurti Indian imagination [*Phantasie*] proceeds still further fantastically [*phantastisch fort*] to an infinite number of most multitudinously shaped gods ... they put the greatest hindrances in the way of a clear understanding because of the indeterminacy and confusing restlessness of imagination [*Phantasie*] which in its inventions deals with nothing in accordance with its proper nature and overturns each and every thing ... The fancy [*Phantasie*] of this people in its images and shapes is inexhaustible). (*Aesthetics* 1:343–44)

Hegel's diagnosis of what is wrong with this moment in the symbolic form of art is unequivocal: in such art "what is inward, and comprehended as meaning ... merely comes and goes, now sinking here and there directly into externality, now withdrawing therefrom in the solitude of abstraction" (1:349–50). So understood, *Phantasie* is a lord of misrule whose lawless ferment engages and disengages at will with spirit or shape such that neither benefits from the other. These shifts in shape and idea are, moreover, sudden and seemingly contingent – any will do and none for very long. At one end is the erotic lure of sensuous shapes like those of Indian deities in various forms and erotic entanglements; at the other is the "solitude of abstraction." All around is a restless anarchy of meaning and form.

What Hegel fears in myths of the Indian Trimurti and thus in the symbolic form of art is what early moderns and moderns have feared about allegory: a swift, unchartable movement between form and idea; abstraction, coupled with an unnerving attachment to pictorial and sensuous shape; the erotic implications of its semiotic proliferation; and an air of manic contingency (if not this form, then some other), offset only (and with dubious rewards) by the fixed, self-evidently allegorical figures for which Hegel reserves the term *allegory*. In its "unconscious" form, the restless ferment of the Hegelian symbolic perpetually insists that the human and animal forms it takes on are spurious, made up. The effect of such alteration is to foreground the erotic invitation of the "sensuous shape" and its distance from the spirit toward which that shape is ostensibly, if imperfectly, striving.

Hegel's prudish description of the procreative couplings and transformations of Indian deities registers his philosophical and theological aversion to the semiotic instabilities let loose by the spectacle of divine erotic play. Because his theology and aesthetics depend on the uniqueness of Christ, he could not but take issue with what he later calls the "plastic polytheism" of other, ostensibly less advanced, cultures. At the same time, his response to Indian art conveys a plangent desire to lodge the symbolic not in "sensuous shape," much though art requires it, but in the romantic or subjective apprehension of how forms convey an idea whose "abstraction" gives way before the subject's recognition that the idea is, as in the body of Christ, incarnate in the form.

Despite his programmatic wariness of *Phantasie* for its involvement with the erotic dance of sensuous shapes and images, Hegel is willing to turn this restless ferment to advantage, arguing that the fantastical is valuable because its very unrest can lead the observer or artist to recognize that external forms are not adequate to represent an as yet unarticulated inner spirit (*Aesthetics* 1:333–34). He rehabilitates *Phantasie* under the sign of the symbolic by praising Egyptian art as a form of unconscious symbolism in which inner spirit rules over external form and neither is sacrificed to abstraction. In monuments to the dead, the Egyptians create forms "fantastically" (*um phantasievoll*) (1:352) whose very hieroglyphic mysteriousness insures our notice of the sacred spirit hidden within. By this negative path, says Hegel, we recognize that the human forms depicted on Egyptian funerary monuments are – like the divine figures of Isis and Osiris – "no mere personification" (1:359).

As were other Romantic writers and travellers, Hegel was fascinated by the Egyptian colossi of Memnon at Thebes, one of which was said to "speak" at sunrise, when the massive stones which comprised its upper body began to expand in the "heat of the day."[7] Thus by speaking or seeming to speak, the colossus of Memnon prefigures a crucial moment in the early stages of the romantic form of art when inner spirit as sound or "voice" and material agency converge (*Aesthetics* 1:359). Unlike Egyptian art, which preserves inner spirit by hiding it in riddles or speaking statues, allegory (in Hegel's restrictive usage) exposes what ought to remain mysterious (unless brought into shape by a romantic form of art). Allegory seeks rather "complete clarity" such that "the external thing of which the allegory avails itself must be as transparent as possible." The first goal of such activity is to personify abstract situations or qualities without however managing to "attain the concrete individuality of a Greek god or of a saint or of some other actual person." This symbolic activity is "bleak," its personifications "empty," and its specific externality "only a sign" or merely "attributes" (1:399–400).

These claims evidently reiterate Neoclassical discussions of emblem and allegory. The problem with this view of allegory – or, by another turn of argument, its advantage – is its indenture to the visual surfaces of image and text. For by quarantining the meaning of allegory in this way Hegel cancels out the play of meaning between those surfaces and hidden or unarticulated referents. This definition in turn authorizes a strategic blindness to the formal instabilities Spenser inaugurates in *The Faerie Queene* with the story of Britomart. Given Hegel's resistance on this point, his eventual return to ekphrasis in the *Aesthetics* is surprising, especially so because he presents it as the mode whose witty interchange between form or its description and meaning preserves the cooperation so critical to, and yet so unstable in, the philosophical unity in the romantic form of art. The route of this return is instructive about how pathos guards against the abstraction Hegel identifies most of all with allegory. Here the suffering or pathos of Christ performs a key service because in suffering He makes himself available to contingency, to the fatal accidents of human mortality. With this fortunate fall into mortality, Hegel argues, Christ redeems the radical contingency of pagan polytheism and harnesses that redemption to historical, temporal reality (these Pharisees, this Roman governor, this Judas).

The romantic artist who imitates Christ's example performs a similar task by making "contingent reality in its boundless modification of shapes and relationships" the subject-matter of art (*Aesthetics* 1:595). Thus both Christ and the artist bind sensuous shape to abstraction, defying the history of their fissures which is, in one sense, the story of Hegel's *Aesthetics*. Shape is in fact less apparently sensuous now than it is full of human feeling, of pathos in the older, more general sense of the term derived from classical rhetoric. The difference between Christ's suffering and that chosen by the early martyrs shows how Christ's human/divine pathos checks the abstraction Hegel identifies with the barbaric and fanatic disposition of the early martyrs. Their spirit, he explains, turned "with its concentrated force of piety against everything that, as the finite, stands contrasted with this inherently simple infinity of religious feeling: against all specific human feeling, against the many-sided moral inclinations, relations, circumstances, and duties of the heart" (1:546). Hegel calls this state of mind "fanaticism of sanctity," "horrible selfishness" and "barbaric religiosity of heart" worse than even the penitence of Indian self-torture. The key failing of Christian martyrdom lies in its tilt toward "the abstraction of its purely intellectual satisfaction," which "can trample violently under foot every other kind of enjoyment" (1:547–48). Whether Hegel intended it or not, this personification summarizes the most disturbing aspect of modern allegory, whose figures often look as though they might take action in the service of ideologues, be they friend or foe of the English Stuart monarchy or French Jacobins.

For Hegel, the romantic form of art "falls to pieces" either "into the imitation of external objectivity in all its contingent shapes" (thereby giving up its spiritual inwardness) or "into the liberation of subjectivity, in accordance with its inner contingency, in humour" (1:608). The second of these alternatives is in effect another fortunate fall back into the play of meaning and form Hegel finds in its "first and simplest shape," the Greek epigram, whose text is not merely "an inscription or epigraph" but a "felicitous witticism, an ingenious reflection, and an intelligent movement of imagination which vivify and expand the smallest detail through the way that poetry treats it." As "poems to or about something" (1:609), ekphrastic poems wittily negotiate the distance between form and meaning, hooking one to the other such that the eventual dissolution of the romantic form of art is kept at bay.

In these final paragraphs on the romantic form of art, Hegel uses *Phantasia* and its cognates exclusively to designate the work of imagining. This choice has much to do with the value of its etymology for characterizing the representational work of ekphrasis as the description of art objects or objects in general. As a term which means in Greek "image" or the power of creating images, *Phantasia* is precisely what ekphrasis must do. It is also, he notes elsewhere in the *Aesthetics*, a free-wheeling play of mind. Against the grain of this polemic, Derrida unites these features when he calls Hegel's theory of imagination "a phantasiology or a fantastics," a science whose logic of images is fantastic, hence dream-like and exaggerated.[8] This advantage in the end draws Hegel back to other kinds of oriental art, despite the "restless ferment" they share with Indian art. To illustrate the "imaginative" (i.e. fantastic or *phantasie-voll*) wit of the Greek epigram, he turns to Persian and Arabic art, praising "the eastern splendour of their images, the free bliss of their imagination [*in der freien Seligkeit der Phantasie*] which deals with its objects entirely contemplatively" (*Aesthetics* 1:610). This rehabilitation of *Phantasie* under the aegis of romantic contemplation registers the complicated appeal of allegory in Hegel's *Aesthetics*, where it exists in part as an unacknowledged sponsor of the restless, unfettered ferment of sensuous shapes and images to which Hegel warily but frequently returns.

As the English Romantic poet whose reputation among early twentieth-century critics was that of a visionary poet with a "weak grasp of the actual," Percy Shelley's use of allegory is hardly surprising. Political poems like *The Mask of Anarchy* deploy rigidly defined allegorical figures reminiscent of eighteenth-century allegory. In *Prometheus Unbound* and *The Triumph of Life*, allegorical figures are more subtle and more subject to instabilities that demand readerly intervention, whether performed by readers themselves or by characters within these works that investigate the meaning of events and characters. By turns an exhortation against the tyranny of the patriarchal state and a difficult exploration of the limits of representation, *The Cenci* sketches a view of allegory whose remainders only half-resemble the "excess of flesh and blood" Hunt finds in Spenser. In this and other poems, Shelley's excesses move in the direction Hegel identifies with allegory and *Phantasie* – toward abstractions that may quite deliberately wash out nuances of flesh and passion, leaving behind allegorical figures that make or impel figured narrative. As Hegel does not, Shelley scrutinizes the idealizing, abstracting powers of allegory, in full view of its "sensuous shapes."

Two female figures, Medusa and Intellectual Beauty, dramatize the extremes of Shelleyan allegory. In his 1816 "Hymn," Intellectual Beauty is the transient, evanescent idea whose "hues" consecrate "human thought or form," even as its light, with its strong kinship to mist and music, gives value to "life's unquiet dream." This demi-presence is well suited to the array of changing shapes that people the idealist vision of poems like *Prometheus Unbound* or "To a Skylark." It is equally suited to Shelley's repeated use of oxymoron or doubled negation[9] to explain or represent the "other speech" of allegory, the fact that what it is must necessarily lie beyond the frame of words and images. De Man's notice of the temporality of such figures aptly registers their productive as well as oblique relation to historical events and narration in Shelley's poetry. For if, as many have suggested, the unspecified referent for poems like *Prometheus Unbound* or even *The Cenci* is recent English and French history, allegorical figures handily negotiate the figured distance between their fictional status and what we call history. Even for poems like *The Mask of Anarchy* or *Ode to Liberty*, whose allusions to recent English history are hardly oblique, such figures give a wider heft and application.

Of all the English Romantics, Shelley is the only one who openly insists that allegory can be an imaginative and moral agent precisely because it is, as William Ulmer puts it, a figure of "the difference latent in metaphor."[10] Yet Shelley is also wary of allegory's tendency to self-petrify – what Fletcher calls its demonic agency.[11] Whereas Intellectual Beauty is "awful," hence sublime in the aesthetic vocabulary of the early nineteenth century, the loveliness of the Medusa is mixed with "terror" to specify her danger to the bodily and mental safety of those who look at her.[12] Her gaze suggests the work of a highly schematic, "astonied" allegory that threatens to turn readers to stone. In poems written during and after 1819, the year in which Shelley wrote the Medusa poem, he warily records this impulse in allegorical figures. In *Prometheus Unbound*, the torturer turns out to be a Blakean reification of Prometheus himself, a psychic embodiment of rage whose name is Jupiter. In *The Triumph of Life*, it is the "Shape all light," who does to Rousseau's brain what the stone head of Medusa does to the gazer.

Although "shape" is not the only term Shelley uses to identify allegorical figures ("form" and "shadow" are nearly as frequent), its frequency, together with manuscript evidence that he drew sketches as he composed poems, suggests, as Nancy Goslee wryly notes, that this poet's "deep truths" are not wholly "imageless."[13] This material evidence also puts the idealist reading of Shelleyan allegory into doubt. Tracking this term in the early poems suggests why. In *The Daemon of the World*, published in 1816 with *Alastor*, the Daemon's "shape," which rides in a chariot drawn by "four shapeless shadows," soon meets the "shape so wild, so bright, so beautiful" of the sleeping mortal Ianthe (59, 63, 71, *PW* 417). Journeying with the Daemon in a dream of futurity, the spirit of Ianthe sees first "shadows, and skeletons, and fiendly shapes" that "blast [ ] the hopes of men" (257, 261, *PW* 419–20), then a king with a threefold crown (the newly restored Bourbon king or George III) surrounded by the "motley shapes" of bowing sycophants (272–75).

In the second part of the poem, unpublished in Shelley's lifetime, "shape" also refers to the visible representation of abstract ideas. When the Daemon returns the spirit of Ianthe to the present, he assures her that "ruins" of faith and slavery will not "leave a wreck behind." Instead, "their elements, wide scattered o'er the globe, / To happier shapes are moulded" as the "universal mind" attunes itself "to individual sense / Of outward shows, whose unexperienced shape / New modes of passion to its frame may lend" (222–24, 248–50, *PW* 423). The double-jointed syntax of these lines, like other instances of Shelley's "reflexive imagery,"[14] implicate external shapes and interior passions, as though one might assist in the experience of the other: either the "unexperienced shape" lends its own "frame" "new modes of passion," or those "new modes" lend an "unexperienced shape" to the frame of those "outward shows." This syntax registers a singular Romantic understanding of how the passions might refigure abstractions.

"The Tower of Famine," published in 1820, bitterly commemorates Ugolino's starvation of prisoners as an emblem for a loss of political liberty which all of Pisa now suffers. Comparing the tower to a "spectre of a shapeless terror" that will gradually absorb "ladies fair ... till they to marble grew" (16–22, *SWorks* iv:62), Shelley makes Famine yet another Romantic offspring of Milton's figure of Death, a "grisly terror" whose "shape" is no shape at all: "If shape it might be call'd that shape had none" (*PL* 2.667, p. 49). In Shelley's poem the power such figures have to absorb the life around them registers an abiding Romantic anxiety. As it is in his poem on the head of the Medusa, the figure of that anxiety is marble statuary.

In *Laon and Cythna*, the unexpurgated version of the poem Shelley withdrew, amended, then republished as *The Revolt of Islam*, "shapes" may be foul or fair, many or one, female or male, old or infant, real or fancied, ethereal, mighty, like statues, of stone, of light, winged, or footed. Many are allegorical figures and some represent abstract ideas. Her sanity restored during a long captivity, Cythna describes her mind as a treasure-house of wisdom about necessity, love, life, the grave, justice, truth, and time. The signs she draws on the sand of her cave-prison to convey the woven texture of these ideas are "Clear, elemental shapes, whose smallest change / A subtler language within language wrought" (*SWorks* 1:105). By substituting "shapes" for "signs" in an early draft, Shelley insists on the visible materiality of those signs. For Earl Wasserman, this language within language is poetry; for Cythna, it is allegory, whose shapes craft that "subtler language."[15]

The central emblem of *Laon and Cythna*, the snake and eagle wreathed (and writhing) in fight, echoes Coleridge and Milton on "shape." A special instance of de Man's more universal claim that allegory is re-reading, Shelley's presentation of this figure follows a crucial Romantic itinerary. Watching the horizon, the narrator sees a shadow against the white moon, that becomes larger as it approaches:

> A speck, a cloud, a shape, approaching grew,
> Like a great ship in the sun's sinking sphere
> Beheld afar at sea, and swift it came anear –
>
> (*SWorks* 1:258)

At close range, this figure resolves into the compound image of the snake and eagle. With a slight adjustment, the first of these lines quotes Coleridge's *Rime*, where the speck or shape turns out to be the nightmare ship carrying Death and Death-in-Life, who play a game of chess to decide who gets the Mariner. The Miltonic echo in the last two lines is more lightly indicated. In *Paradise Lost* Milton's narrator compares Satan's approach to the gate of Hell, where he will meet his incestuous and allegorical relations, Sin and Death, to the distant sight of a fleet on the horizon, "As when far off at Sea a Fleet descri'd / Hangs in the Clouds" (*PL* 2.636–37, p. 48). Whereas this figure, which Wordsworth quotes and discusses in the 1815 edition of his *Poems* (*WProse* III:31), conveys the enormity of Milton's Satan (as big as a fleet seen far off, hence monstrous up close), Shelley's telescopic revision balloons a "speck" into the "monstrous sight" of "An Eagle and a Serpent wreathed in fight" (*SWorks* 1:259).

This reconfiguration shows how extreme contrasts or adjustments in scale mark the presence of an allegorical, rather than realist, narrative. Like those figures on the wall of Diderot's dream cave whose projected size far exceeds their real size, Shelley's poetic alternative to the MGM lion holds sway over the narrator and the meaning of the poem. Thus when the narrator is horrified by the sight of a serpent curled up at Cythna's breast, she sets him right by explaining that this serpent is to be understood emblematically as the figure whose eternal resistance to the eagle will eventually foster the revolt against absolute rule – both in the harem where she is held captive and in the European nation state.

In the political poems of 1819 and 1820, where allegorical figures might be expected to serve a coded, but hardly veiled, political agenda, some of those figures muster figural power in unexpected ways. The most remarkable instances occur in *The Mask of Anarchy*, which Shelley wrote rapidly during September 1819, after learning about the August massacre of civilians who had gathered in St. Peter's Field near Manchester to hear speeches in favor of Parliamentary reform, only to be fired upon by drunken militia and cavalrymen who had misunderstood their orders.[16] The poem begins with a parade of allegorical villains whose names and features make them particular as well as abstract. Walking in the "visions of Poesy," the speaker first meets "Murder" who pointedly has "a mask like Castlereagh." The seven "bloodhounds" that follow him at the ready to consume any human hearts thrown their way may represent the seven-nation agreement with Britain to postpone abolishing the slave trade or the pro-war "bloodhounds" of Pitt's administration. Such particulars, implied or explicit, have always been the stuff of political allegory. What makes Shelley's figures unusual is his insistence that Murder is a man who, like his bloodhounds, is fat with gore; that Fraud is Lord Eldon, whose tears turn to millstones; that Hypocrisy is Sidmouth, who rides by on a crocodile and an allegory. In an era when allegory was so often charged with abstraction, this particularity humanizes abstraction with something like figural vengeance.

The rest of the poem, which even Leigh Hunt dared not publish until 1832, puts aside similarly actionable particulars. Instead, "Anarchy" is a figure whose absolute power is supported by various agents of government oppression. Deliberately modelled on Benjamin West's famous painting of Death on a pale horse, Anarchy wears the crown of absolute monarchy and boasts of having been educated for 10 million pounds, at the expense of the nation. After more than a decade of political caricature in which the Prince Regent, later crowned George IV, was represented as a fat, self-indulgent royal nuisance and expense to the nation, no reader among Shelley's contemporaries could have missed the implied referent. Once the "Shape" arrives, looking like the Lady of *The Sensitive Plant* and a Venus/Morning star, Hope walks and Anarchy lies dead. The Shape's rhetorical questions about the nature of Freedom direct the poem toward a surprising conclusion. After attacking "paper coin," the Shape forecasts the arrival of Justice, Wisdom, Peace, Love, Science, Poetry, Thought, Spirit, Patience, and Gentleness, then urges nonviolence and trust that the laws of the land will be fair "arbiters of the dispute." It is hard for readers to know whose political argument this allegory serves. For although this is Shelley's vision for the future, it was intended for the English people at large, who would surely have been ill-advised to stand still with an eye on futurity while the militia took aim.[17]

In "England in 1819" Shelley levels a punning, ironic attack on England's "Golden and sanguine laws."[18] The etiology of the oddly placed call for nonviolence and civil obedience in *The Mask of Anarchy* becomes clearer in the *Ode to Liberty* of the next year, which chronicles the history of the world, beginning with the reign of chaos when Liberty was not. After identifying the moment of Liberty's birth with ancient Greece, the speaker compares her nurture of infant Rome to that a "Maenad" nurse-mother gives to her wolf-cub. This disquieting analogy forecasts Liberty's dubious nurture of the Roman republic's deeds of "terrible uprightness." In an important analysis of how Shelley's drafts of the rest of this stanza and accompanying sketches gradually make the figure of Liberty less particular and more abstract, Nancy Goslee notes that as Liberty assumes the "palpable, more physically present" image of a nursing mother, she also becomes dangerously ambiguous. Shelley then backs off, trading in this particularity for a synecdochic representation of Liberty's "robe of vestal whiteness"[19] that exchanges the nursing mother for a vestal virgin who wisely quits Rome.

After a thousand-year absence, Liberty reemerges in medieval Italy, only to succumb a few centuries later to Napoleon I, "Anarch of thine own bewildered powers." This is the unspecified risk of the Shape's invocations to Freedom in *The Mask of Anarchy*, that Liberty bewildered can become anarchy. Like that of the older, more conservative Wordsworth, Shelley's backward glance at post-revolutionary France acknowledges this difficult truth and its unwelcome consequence – that the birth of English liberty might crumble into anarchy.

In poems whose allegorical figures serve explicitly political ends, Shelley particularizes the allegory with words whose materiality echoes that of the sketches he drew in manuscript notebooks, but only when it is politically wise to do so. When it is not, he may leave its "Shape" unspecified, or he may specify it by parts for absent or soon-to-be-absent wholes, like Liberty's "robe of vestal whiteness."[20] As a transcendent idea or abstraction indicated at best by words or images, allegory is inherently synecdochic. Whereas Neoclassical critics make this a reason to distrust allegory, Shelley suggests that allegory manifests the degree of separation between figures in general and the world of things. By such means, allegory both allows and disallows realism's hold on particulars, whether these are attached to or separate from wholes.

As Shelley acknowledges in his "Preface," *Prometheus Unbound* is inhabited by "poetical abstractions" (*SPP* 134) that witness an intra-psychic, then world-wide, renewal of love and political liberty after Prometheus's long and, in Shelley's version of the myth, self-imposed incarceration and torture.[21] In a deft rehearsal of critical objections to the poem, Rajan notes that many of its explicitly allegorical figures seem hollowed out. They talk, some may even walk, but few convey interior or psychological realism. Turning de Man's argu-ments concerning the rhetoricity of such figures back to Hegel, Rajan compares the poem's allegorical figures to mere signs, hollow abstractions like those that Hegel finds wanting in his *Aesthetics*.[22]

I argue here that the materialist edge of Shelley's idealism evades the neat polarity Hegel asserts. Even in *Prometheus Unbound* the term "shape" remains stunningly available to abstraction on the one side and material particularity on the other. As it does elsewhere in Shelley's writing, "shape" may refer to visible forms, including sketches he drew beside early drafts of the poem and even in the fair-copy transcription he sent to his publishers.[23] In the climate of this poem, the same term may be used to designate "unimaginable shapes" as well as figured abstractions. From our sublunary perspec-tive as readers of this poem, this second usage is oxymoronic; for Shelley it is an index of how allegorical ideas and material forms share the same poetic space.

As *Prometheus Unbound* begins, rigidly objectified, abstract figures inhabit this space. By making Jupiter the projection of Prometheus's own hatred,[24] Shelley dramatizes the self-involved polarities of an allegory whose fixed figures and conflicts can go nowhere. The ensuing allegory of intrapsychic and cosmic rebirth kneads in particulars that check the potential tyranny of abstractions. As I read the figural conflict of the poem, it is between allegory and allegory, not between a state of being "congealed in allegory" and a subsequent release into the more malleable, hence vital, powers of metaphor.[25] Against this description of allegory, I array the assembled allegorical "shapes" of Shelley's argument.

Embodying *phantasia*'s most disagreeable cognates,[26] the Phantasm of Jupiter is left, as it were, holding the negative allegorical weight of Prometheus's curse, a vituperation wrought up to such a pitch that it finally becomes what it sees – the figure of absolute tyranny in the "Shape" of Jupiter (1.226, *SPP* 142). After this figure drops out of the poem, Prometheus and the narrator encounter first no shapes, then terrible "shapeless" sights, "execrable," "foul," and "barbaric shapes," and the "thick shapes of human death." The Second Fury explains why "shape" is necessary: "the shade which is our form invests us round, / Else are we shapeless as our Mother Night" (1.471–72, *SPP* 150). In the fair copy transcript of the poem, Shelley crossed out "shape" and substituted "form" to avoid an evident redundancy (*PU* 185). This slight change marks how thoroughly this word invades his allegorical practice. Demogorgon is "shapeless," but also a sublime "awful shape."

Once the curse is retracted, the "Shape" of Love, other "air-born shapes," and Prometheus arrive on the scene.[27] As the Fourth Spirit rhapsodizes in act 1, poets take the "shapes that haunt thought's wildernesses" and transform them into "forms more real than living man" (1.742, 748–49, *SPP* 157). In a similar vein Panthea later declares that the future will be "Peopled with unimaginable shapes" (4.244, *SPP* 201). Once Jupiter falls back into Demogorgon's realm of shapelessness, the poem lists highly particular emblematic signs of the power and tyranny that disappear, among them "anchors," "beaks of ships," gorgon-headed targes" (archers' shields or bucklers), "scythed chariots" used in battle, "the emblazonry of trophies." Collectively named "sepulchured emblems" and "prodigious shapes," all of them depart, leaving behind (for good or ill) "Man," whom the narrator recognizes for what he is, a "many-sided mirror / Which could distort to many a shape of error / This true fair world of things" (4.289–300, 382—84, *SPP* 202—4). Score one for Shelleyan idealism. Thus if human language, along with human action, remains responsible for all "thoughts and forms, which else senseless and shapeless were" (4.417, *SPP* 205), Shelley's act 4 use of particular things to specify generalities and near-abstractions insists that all are tangible and distinct, whether foul or fair.

It is, admittedly, difficult to keep the edge of materiality in this idealist drama in sight. We tend to overlook, for example, the brief exchange between Ione and Panthea as they watch the "train of dark forms and Shadows" that passes by "confusedly" at the beginning of act 4 (8–10, *SPP* 194). Ione inquires about the identity of their "dark forms" and Panthea answers that they are the "Hours." Then each nymph asks a question that conveys the material, visible standard against which even these dark shadows are to be measured. "What charioteers are these?" asks Ione; "Where are their chariots?" asks Panthea. The verisimilar expectation is unequivocal: when they see charioteers, they expect to see chariots.[28]

Like sketches in other Shelley manuscripts, those in the early and fair copy drafts of *Prometheus Unbound* show the poet at work and at play with key motifs – sailboats, caves, details of landscape.[29] Even as he transcribed the poem for publication, he continued to sketch and may have left a few pages blank for more sketches. Since these are not preserved in the first edition of the poem, their presence in the fair copy seems at once gratuitous yet necessary, as though Shelley believed them part of his poetic labor. The most finished sketch appears on a pastedown at the end of the third notebook and includes an island cliff with a cave open to the sea, and at least one sailboat nearby.[30] Although this scene has no exact counterpart in the text, it resembles the cave retreat Prometheus describes for Asia (3.1.10–45, *SPP* 184–85). To inaugurate the sequence of events that will end in this future retreat, the Spirit of the Hour must first blow into the "curved shell which Proteus old / Made Asia's nuptial boon" and which completes the emblematic seascape for which Shelley's notebook sketch is a material witness (3.3.24, 41–44, 65–67, *SPP* 185–86).

In the fair copy transcript this emblematic impulse checks the poem's idealism. Although most of the blank pages in these notebooks include line notations to reserve space for lines of text not yet supplied, on two occasions Shelley may have left space for a sketch – whether on paper or in the mind of the reader. The first of these follows the Fury's exclamation in act 1, "Behold, an emblem," which introduces a brief account of what happens to humankind when Jupiter's authority is challenged (*SPP* 154). In the fair copy, the remaining three-quarters of the page on which these lines appear is blank except for a cluster of leaves and a pen clearing. On the next page the Fury describes what Prometheus sees: "Blood thou canst see

& fire; & canst hear groans / Worse things unheard unseen remain behind" (*PU* 218–19). In the published text Shelley interposes a new speech in which Prometheus describes the scene of the Crucifixion but does not name Christ, whose name has "become a curse."

Prometheus describes a scene whose iconography is so well known that it can be imagined without naming names. As a verbal sketch, his speech carries the force of the visual or imagined emblem that might otherwise have "occupied" the same space in the notebook. The historical itinerary this speech travels does in words what emblems do: carry the reader/viewer back on a figural and mental path through the tradition indicated by its image and text. Where the fair copy transcript leaves a blank for a sketch that would probably have depicted what the Fury later says Prometheus can see, the published version supplies a verbal emblem instead. With this intervention, the poem reduces the role of the visual image as a guide to transcendent ideas.

A different hermeneutic negotiation takes place in the fair copy transcript of Jupiter's speech at the beginning of act 3. In mid-speech, he is interrupted by the stage direction "the Car of the Hour arrives. Demogorgon descends and moves towards the Throne of Jupiter." The next page in the notebook is blank. On the top of the following page, Jupiter continues, "Awful Shape, what are thou? Speak!" (*PU* 385–89; *SPP* 181). Because Demogorgon is also "shapeless" and the presiding spirit over a Platonic black hole for all potential shapes, the intervening blank page and Jupiter's horrified exclamation make odd sense out of the way Shelley attaches a species of materiality to allegorical figures. In the Platonic register which Demogorgon occupies, he can have no visual shape. Yet because he is vast and sublimely awful, he invisibly takes up the material space indicated by Jupiter's exclamation and Shelley's blank page.

The Triumph of Life dramatizes the potential undertow of allegorical abstraction. "Shape" specifies Life itself (the blind driver of the chariot that tramples its human captives), the winged team that pulls the chariot, "Nature's Proteus shape," and the female "Shape all light" (*SPP* 457–58, 462, 465). As de Man and others have noted, these figures do not bode well for Rousseau, the speaker who identifies them. Once he drinks what the female "Shape all light" offers, his brain becomes "as sand," a trackless waste. As this female shape fades, a new, harsher vision presents itself to the hapless

Rousseau's unsteady consciousness (352—405, *SPP* 465–66). So ends the unfinished poem that is Shelley's "death masque."[31]

Against the deconstructive punt of de Man's reading, Schulze argues that the "Shape all light," whose "evanescence" is the guarantor of the "pure potentiality" that human thought requires, disperses the inflexible allegory vested in the figure of Life, who tyrannizes history and human beings.[32] In lines she drafted for "Fields of Fancy," Mary Shelley suggests instead that this shape is a disturbing figure of mutability: "all minds, as mirrors, receive [nature's] forms – yet in each mirror the shapes apparently reflected vary & are perpetually changing."[33] In *The Triumph of Life*, the kinship is emphatic. Obvious though it is, the fact that both Life and this female are called "shapes" is not adventitious. In lines he cancelled in manuscript, Shelley had also used this term for Rousseau, Caesar, Catherine the Great, and the "many" or "lowly" "shapes" chained to Napoleon as he fell (*TL* 175, 179, 191, 223, 235, 261). In the last version we have, the same triple rhyme, "form"/"storm"/"deform," characterizes both Life and the female "Shape" (*TL* 71) and both mean trouble for human beings and historical memory (*SPP* 457, 466).[34] As I read Shelley's unfinished argument in this poem, it pits the allegorical fixation of these "shapes" against history and human particularity. Whereas Neoclassical writers worried about the volatile historical record kept alive by allegorical figures during and after the English civil war, Shelley worries here about the specter of an allegory so powerful that it erases history.

The Cenci belongs among those family romances of incest and murder that Hunt and Paulson have read as displaced fictions of the French Revolution.[35] Shelley's Pope specifies the alliance between patriarchy and monarchy that supports this reading:

> Parricide grows so rife
> That soon, for some just cause no doubt, the young
> Will strangle us all, dozing in our chairs.
> Authority, and power, and hoary hair
> Are grown crimes capital.　　　(*Cenci* 5.4.20–24, *SPP* 297)

The calculated irony of this speech, which immediately precedes his condemnation of Beatrice, shows who is in charge of this allegory. Parricide may be rife, but the rule of the father will prevail.

Behind this political allegory is another whose focus is Beatrice, Shelley's front woman for crimes committed in the name of allego-

rical abstraction – by poets as well as women. Whereas the manuscript record for *Epipsychidion* shows how Shelley transformed Teresa
Viviani into Emily to create a poem about a Dantesque pursuit of a
feminine ideal,[36] *The Cenci* makes Beatrice look like a scapegoat for
the way such figures can drain language of particularity. Feminist
critics who defend Beatrice's murder of her father sometimes put the
blame on patriarchal and papal authority or on the repression this
authority entails. Because she cannot name her father's crime,
unspeakable in itself and unspeakable to the community where his
rule is law, she murders him. Others put the blame on Shelley for
giving Beatrice over to the wolves, yet arguing in the preface that she
should have "convert[ed] the injurer from his dark passions by peace
and love" (*SPP* 240).[37] Yet as villains go, Cenci is surely among the
most uneducable; by his own admission he is wholly involved in
"sensual luxury" and "revenge" (1.1.77–81, *SPP* 245). For some
readers, Shelley's imperviousness in the preface to this moral and
political dead-end looks like political weakmindedness.[38] From all
these angles, Shelley's advice looks at once idiotic and sadistic.

What interests me about this interpretive knot is the way the
highly marked pathos of Shelley's preface puts this underlying (or
exposed, depending on who reads the play) sadism in relief. Asserting
there that the story of Beatrice is true and that he tells it in the "real
language of men" instead of the language of a single class, he
thereby draws on the rhetorical weight of Wordsworthian verisimilitude and human feeling. In the same passage he implicitly echoes the
older poet's strictures against personification. Shelley asserts that to
avoid creating characters that are merely "cold impersonations of
my own mind" (*SPP* 240), he chose a real person whose portrait
moved him thus:

In the whole mien there is a simplicity and dignity which united with her
exquisite loveliness and deep sorrow are inexpressibly pathetic. Beatrice
Cenci appears to have been one of those rare persons in whom energy and
gentleness dwell together without destroying one another: her nature was
simple and profound. The crimes and miseries in which she was an actor
and a sufferer are as the mask and the mantle in which circumstances
clothed her for her impersonation on the scene of the world. (*SPP* 242)

This deft mix of pathos with theatricality makes Beatrice the
inadvertent bearer of a false show, a brief stage impersonation "on
the scene of the world." Like Dante's sympathy for Paolo and
Francesca, Shelley's thoroughly staged and self-reflexive sympathy

for his heroine repeats her tragic flaw and fall – those figural "impersonations" that allow her to abstract pathos and human particularity from the name of her father. The Aristotelian moment of pity and fear prompted by the spectacle of her and Shelley's "abstract[ing] imagination" might be one in which readers recognize themselves in the mirror: by such means might anyone take refuge from self-knowledge.

Like Milton's Satan, according to the contemporaneous "Preface" to *Prometheus Unbound*, Beatrice is adept at "casuistry" (*SPP* 133, 240). She lies so well that she persuades her father's assassins that they, not she, are guilty of the murder she hired them to do. To others she explains that because Cenci was no father to her, she is guiltless of parricide and thus the very figure of Innocence. As I read Shelley's point regarding Beatrice, she is the play's tragic protagonist not because, or not simply because, she resorts to violence, but because she codes it in ways that disguise it and then cut off pathos, leaving only figures from which all feeling has been abstracted.[39]

At the beginning of act 3, after Cenci has raped or tried to rape Beatrice (he says early in the play that he is less capable of "sensual luxury" than he once was, *SPP* 245), her initial response is full of disordered images of blood and pollution. By making the off-stage incest the silent, absent occasion for the play's on-stage action, and emphasizing the word "parricide" in several speeches, Shelley specifies which crime the ethos of the play's time and place prefers not to broadcast. When Beatrice can speak, she says, "Like Parricide ... / Misery has killed its father; yet its father / Never like mine ... O, God! What thing am I?" (3.1.37–39, *SPP* 262). This syntactic disorder prefigures other, deeper ruptures that begin when Beatrice proclaims (with provocation) that her father is "a spirit of hell" whom they must harry "out of a human form" (4.2.7–8, *SPP* 278). To do this, she will take shelter in abstractions. In sharp contrast, the hired assassins who also hate Cenci make pathos the reason they hesitate to kill him:

> We dare not kill an old and sleeping man;
> His thin grey hair, his stern and reverent brow,
> His veined hands crossed on his heaving breast,
> And the calm innocent sleep in which he lay,
> Quelled me.   (4.2.9–13, *SPP* 280)

Talking like Lady Macbeth, Beatrice scorns and threatens them until they agree to do the deed. When one of them is captured, she denies

having ever seen him and so loudly proclaims her innocence and her
father's depravity that even the captured assassin reneges on his
testimony. Beatrice's proclaimed innocence is by now a magisterial
allegorical abstraction: "Our innocence is an armed heel / To
trample accusation" (4.2.160–61, *SPP* 285). After a brilliant speech in
which she reminds one of the luckless assassins and her audience of
her father's ways and calls for justice, she asks: "Am I, or am I not /
A parricide?" The assassin completes this line and her line of
argument by replying "Thou art not!" (4.2.156–57, *SPP* 292). Her
fear that her father will wind his arms around her in her coffin
(5.4.57–69, *SPP* 298) registers the material, unabstracted body she
otherwise erases from the stage of her rhetoric after his off-stage
attack. To keep this horror at bay, she must not ask: "am I the
murderer of my father?"

Beatrice exposes the fault line in Shelley's poetics where allegorical
abstractions and pathos part company. In a note to her edition of
Prometheus Unbound in which she explains Percy's attraction to
Aeschylus, Mary Shelley remarks: "The father of Greek tragedy does
not possess the pathos of Sophocles, nor the variety and tenderness of
Euripides; the interest on which he founds his dramas is often
elevated above human vicissitudes into the mighty passions and
throes of gods and demigods – such fascinated the abstract imagination of Shelley" (*SWorks* 11:268). In *The Cenci*, Beatrice is a remarkable
figure for what happens when human vicissitude collides with the
language of abstraction. Jewett suggests that this intersection may be
the epistemological and political arena of Shelley's skepticism – a
virtual laboratory of figures and actions where the poet investigates
the possibility of agency within language as well as within action.[40]
Beatrice's rhetoric – by turns masterful and accusatory or terrified
and disoriented – is a rivetting illustration of the fundamentally
contestatory nature of representation, personal and political. For all
her ekphrastic particularity in Guido's painting and in the story
people were still talking about when the Shelleys moved to Italy,
Beatrice operates in an arena where abstract allegorical ideas have
human names and exercise absolute power over her body and
identity. As she responds in kind (a point readers on all sides note),
we see how questions about figure, agency, individuals, and politics
are enmeshed and, what is more, written on bodies and in speech.

Keats's evidently "made-up" poetic figures dramatize allegory's
strange, yet productive, shape in Romantic culture. Whereas his

early critics claimed such figures were evidence of his "Cockney" style, more recent critics have observed that this objection is neither disinterested nor wholly belletristic, since "Cockney" means not simply lower-class and therefore too uneducated to learn what one needed to know to write poetry – beginning with the classics – but also politically radical and, what is more, "feminine." This last salvo charges that Keats is not only self-indulgent and weak, but untutored in the masculine virtues of English poetry.[41]

By insisting on the poetic and careerist advantages of Keats's excessive figures, Ricks and Levinson have turned this critical reception on its head. Levinson notes that Keats engages in a "life of allegory" precisely because he uses poetic figures that are strategically alien, even perverse. As the New Critics and other post-structuralist readers do not, she argues that Keats becomes a poet within and against, as well as above, the fray of Romantic politics and jealousies.[42] Yet she also reads Keats half-dismissively, with a sharp eye for the verbal surfaces of his poetic figures, but comparatively little interest in how those figures work within and against a complicated allegiance to emblem and ekphrasis. I contend that this allegiance is crucial to Keats's understanding of what it means to have a "life of allegory." As he presents it, that life is stubbornly poised on the verge between material, mimetic figures and those whose artifice insists on their unreality. In his poems those figures may be female, grotesque, monstrous, or all three.

When they didn't put the blame on Leigh Hunt, Keats's early critics blamed Spenser for the stylistic and figural excesses of *Endymion*.[43] These "faults" cast a long shadow over Keats's career-long exploration of the gains and losses of enchantment and romance, most notably in poems like "The Eve of St. Agnes," "Isabella," or "La Belle Dame sans Merci," where the poetic argument turns away from romance.[44] What finally attracts Keats to Spenser is not didacticism[45] but allegorical figures whose narrative paths show how abstraction and fixity hover over human particularity, and narrative signs of how particularity destabilizes abstractions.

This recognition, not a naive, overly sensuous pictorialism, directs Keats's investigation of Spenserian language and the mechanism of poetic figures in general – how they work, how they are true or not, how they lack or take on life. His youthful enthusiasm for Spenser's phrase "sea-shouldering whale" is a valuable indication of these concerns.[46] As Spenser's figure gives the sea a flicker of whale-like animation, it straddles the divide between pictorialism and its figural other – the emblematic assumption that "images" like this one exceed mimetic requirements in order to become figures. Throughout his career Keats reenacts the hermeneutic relation between pictorial vignette and figurality in Spenser by imagining narrative and history as so insistently attached to material details that they refuse, as the *Hyperion* poems finally do, the progressive or spiralling models of history and art that Winckelmann suggests and Hegel later theorizes. Keats's poetic resistance to what Hayden White has aptly named the "metahistory" of the nineteenth century is harnessed by a complex ekphrastic desire to represent the pressing, material reality of works of art and of life, and a pungent recognition that idealized abstractions offer safe haven.

Because they work within this force field, Romantic figures that are immobilized and thus "abstracted" from reality thereby poach on the domain of real things and human pathos. By such means, Keats evaluates the cost and benefit of calcifying poetic figures, from the Grecian urn to the stony figure of Saturn in either of the *Hyperion* poems. *Not* to preserve some hybrid category in which art looks like life or vice versa would acquiesce to the Neoclassical charge that allegories which contain some element of the human are grotesque, yet without this grotesqueness what is left is cold form, be it pastoral or frozen epic action. In either case, the possibility of narrative is lost or forgone, as it always is when lyric pictorialism is unchallenged. Within lyric as well as narrative frames, Keats measures degrees of allegorical fixity and abstraction in poetic figures, with a sharp eye and ear for their profit and loss.

Keats's return to the problem of pure allegory and pure history is to imagine both as adjacent and mutually invasive poetic spaces that exceed the material confines of lyric and the image. For if it is true that these two are theoretically separate, this separation cannot and perhaps should not be sustained in the world, the only arena where human poets and readers can entertain allegorical ideas. Pure allegorical abstractions such as Spenser's Florimel simply do not do well *in* history: until Britomart's character becomes intertwined with her history and destiny, she is pure allegory and nearly pure menace.

In several letters Keats suggests how materiality, pathos, abstraction, and misogyny negotiate the representational space available to allegory in his poetics. Writing to his publishers John Taylor and James Hessey in May 1817 as he drafted *Endymion*, he thanks them for loaning him twenty pounds or, as he puts it, for "your liberality in the Shape of manufactu[r]ed rag value £20" (*LJK* 1:145–46). This mix of abstraction and materialism forecasts the shape of the "nice little Alegorical poem" he goes on to imagine. To conquer the "Minor Heads of that spr[i]ng-headed Hydra the Dun," he will not need a sword since he has a pen, and he will not be misled, like the Red-crosse knight, by the false enchanter Archimago. Other details in this slight allegory map the narrative and monetary demands of the Romantic marketplace, among them "the Bank Note of Faith and Cash of Salvation," a "Castle of Carelessness," and (thanks to Taylor and Hessey) a "Draw Bridge of Credit."

This Bunyanesque mini-narrative of the perils of credit has, as Keats says of Wordsworth's poetry, a palpable design on its readers. For although Keats is just fooling around, as he often does in letters, his playfulness has a commercial end in view. By way of thanks, he makes a witty, literary return whose value as manufactured rag might be construed either as a fair return on twenty pounds or the first installment on a credit plan. As the last installment, *Endymion* might be read as a lesson from the nineteenth century about the risks of futures trading. The debt to Spenser Keats acknowledges in this allegorical game of thanks goes beyond pictorial effects and an archaic style, the hallmarks of the Spenserian revival. For the game assumes what neo-Spenserian poets of preceding generations mostly forgot – that allegory is a narrative enterprise whose invented figures carry the game forward because they are fictive agents for higher truths, in this instance, future poetic achievement (the young Keats is unquestionably brash).

Echoing Spenser's definition in a gossipy 1819 letter to his brother and sister-in-law, Keats asserts, "A Man's life of any worth is a continual allegory." His examples are evenly split between real and literary figures: "Lord Byron cuts a figure – but he is not figurative – Shakespeare led a life of Allegory; his works are comments on it" (*LJK* 11:67). Here "getting a life" means creating figures with narrative lives of their own, figures whose particularity is legitimately understood to be "lifelike." Put this way, Keats's "life of allegory" brushes aside the eighteenth century's interminable wrangling about allegory's inherent opposition to real life and human character. This point is even more striking when we read Keats's phrase back through what precedes it, a detailed account of the "circumstances" of Benjamin Bailey's stumbling efforts to find a wife. As Keats tells it, this story of amorous misadventure is alive with human particulars and foibles. During a period when Benjamin seemed to be devoted to Mrs. Reynolds and her daughters, he courted Marian Reynolds. Later he courted a Miss Martin. After his ordination and after he had moved to Carlisle to take up a curacy there, Benjamin finally succeeded in getting a wife (thereby getting a life) in the person of a Miss Gleig, to whom he showed his "correspondence with Marian." Keats acidly comments, "his so quickly taking to miss Gleig can have no excuse – except that of a Ploughman who wants a wife."

The "life of allegory" at work in this story is a crudely sexual plot, one in which a woman becomes a wife in the same way a piece of property, once acquired, becomes land to till. Keats is nearly as sharp about the conduct of the Reynolds women, despite (or because of) his closeness to the daughters and the mother:

All this I am not supposed by the Reynoldses to have any hint of – It will be a good Lesson to the Mother and Daughters – nothing would serve but Bailey – If you mentioned the word Tea pot – some one of them came out with an a propos about Bailey – noble fellow – fine fellow! was always in their mouths – this may teach them that the man who rediculed romance is the most romantic of Men – that he who abuses women and slights them – loves them the most – that he who talks of roasting a Man alive would not do it when it came to the push – and above all that they are very shallow people who take every thing literal A Man's life of any worth is a continual allegory – and very few eyes can see the Mystery of his life – a life like the scriptures, figurative – which such people can no more make out than they can the hebrew Bible. (*LJK* 11:67)

Because the Reynolds women read Bailey's attentions literally, they miss the underlying allegory – that he wanted a wife, any wife. Critics have quite accurately observed that Keats's antagonism toward the Reynolds women belongs to a fairly consistent pattern. Either Keats charges real women, including Fanny Brawne, with assorted faults or he invents female figures whom he subjects to poetic or fictive torture, binding them Andromeda-like within the constraints of the sonnet, giving them brothers who kill their sister's lover (Isabella), blaming them for the seduction and death of knights, kings, warriors (*la belle dame*), or putting them through transformations that look more like torture than delight (Lamia).[47]

This misogynist record, which I may have slightly exaggerated, participates in the rhetorical tradition, prominent in medieval and Renaissance culture, which imagines rhetorical excess as the province of women's speech and female figures. Personifying metaphor as a modest, deferential figure "who ought to have an apologetic air, ... as if it had come with permission, not forced its way in" (*De Oratore* 41.165), Cicero uses the imperative mode to indicate that the rhetorical modesty of figures is required, not natural. In the Renaissance, an explicitly gendered version of the classical imperative that metaphors should be submissive, even apologetic, commands that metaphor redirect literal meaning toward figurative ends in a manner that is "*shamefest,* and as it were *maydenly,* that it may seeme rather to be led by the hand to another signification, then to be driven by force."[48]

Parker notes that similar prescriptions in Renaissance texts require a female "other" – the monstrous and female excess of catachresis, of metaphors gone wild, artificed, and made-up like a woman.[49] No wonder Locke rails about "the perfect cheat" of a female Eloquence (*Essay* 3.10.34). No wonder the "effeminate" Cockney Keats resists and mines the resources of females whom he figures. And no wonder Lanham's modern discussion of catachresis uses examples that are prejudicial to women. To illustrate the first of two definitions, "words wrenched from common usage," he quotes Hamlet: "I will speak daggers to her." The figure of "a weeping woman's eyes become Niagara Falls" illustrates the second definition, "an extravagant, unexpected, farfetched metaphor."[50] Both suggest the peculiar energy available to figures of women in Keats's poetics. Like the woman whose eyes become Niagara Falls, the pathos of those figures makes them necessary but also alien, evidently rhetorical, and in some sense monstrous, as is the woman who weeps so copiously that someone (probably male) may drown or at the very least be captured by a rhetorical figure (that "perfect cheat") he had hoped to resist. Like Hamlet, Keats may intend some form of poetic violence for such figures.

Keats's struggle with and against women, in life and in art – at times self-defensively misogynist, at others erotic – foregrounds the extent to which rhetoric under the sign of the female prompts or displays the pathos Longinus argues is essential to the production of figures. Like Wordsworth's conflicted defense of strong figures in the "Preface" to *Lyrical Ballads,* Keats's return to pathos legitimates strong, even exaggerated, figures. The misogynist edge that marks this return is inextricable from the rhetorical work that such figures make possible. One consequence of this mix of resistance, half-

indicated violence, and erotic feeling is Keats's invention of female
rhetorical figures that dramatize the risks of turning real things into
figures. Keats typically imagines these figures as abstractions – the
best of which is Beauty (the worst are also beauties) – that are
susceptible to poetic (or not so poetic) violence.

Consider, for example, "la belle dame sans merci." In the poem
that is named for her, two male narrators and a chorus of knights,
kings, and warriors make the figure of the "belle dame" what it is – a
fetishistic sign of *eros*, alienation, and death – in short, an abstraction.[51] Yet the knight's story of his enthrallment is also marked in
every version of the poem by the speaker's pathos for the lady's
predicament. This pathos exerts some influence on readers too, who
have suggested that the poem allegorizes either the Romantic poet's
erotic entanglement with imagination, Keats's own entanglement
with Fanny Brawne, or both. This intersection of abstraction and
pathos works within as well as against the poem's seductively
misogynist narrative of an errant knight and a faery woman who
makes *eros* exactly like death.

In several letters in which Keats recognizes the value of abstractions to a mind "beset by images" of his dying brother Tom or
various women, pathos is clearly marked or implied. Writing to
Charles Dilke in September 1818, Keats explains that, because
poetry distracts him from thinking about Tom, "I am obliged to
write, and plunge into abstract images to ease myself of his countenance his voice and feebleness" (*LJK* 1:369). Thinking about fame in
the same letter, he admits that he lacks the "self possession and
magnanimity enough to manage the thing othe[r]wise." The unspecified antecedent is Tom's illness – the countenance, voice, and
feebleness that Keats transforms into abstractions in "Ode to a
Nightingale," composed late in the following spring, some months
after Tom's death in December 1818. In a world dominated by "the
uneasiness, the fever, and the fret," "Youth grows pale, and spectre-
thin, and dies," and thinking means being "full of sorrow / And
leaden-eye despairs" (*Keats* 370). The plural "despairs," which one of
Keats's early reviewers criticized, registers the tilt toward abstraction.
For if a singular "despair" might have suggested a state of mind,
"despairs" is an abstract company that crowds out the single human
death to which these personifications in part refer.

Writing to John Reynolds a day later, Keats makes abstraction
into a refuge from his desire for a woman whose "voice and shape"

haunt him so that he plunges again into the "feverous relief of Poetry," which now seems less a "crime" than it had the day before. Nearly vanquished by that voice and shape, which may belong to the "Charmian" Jane Cox or to Fanny Brawne, whom Keats had just met, Keats reports that "Poetry has conquered" and that he has "relapsed into those abstractions which are my only life" (*LJK* 1:370). In another letter he characterizes himself as a man who "loves beauty in the abstract" (*LJK* 1:373); in a fourth he invokes "the mighty abstract Idea I have of Beauty" as an amulet to ward off the seductive entanglements of marriage, wife, and children. Writing to Fanny Brawne in July of 1819, Keats insists "I am not a thing to be admired. You are, I love you; all I can bring you is a swooning admiration of your Beauty" (*LJK* 11:133). Keats's oddly material abstraction of Fanny (a "thing of beauty") is half-implicit in the exchange of him for her. It is also an abstraction that helps him keep from being absorbed by Fanny Brawne, a loss of identity he once told her he feared as much as death.[52]

The "mighty abstract Idea … of Beauty" Keats offers to Georgiana and George Keats as his reason not to marry stabilizes erotic possibilities conveyed earlier in this letter when he describes accompanying Mrs. Isabella Jones home to her lodgings. He finds there a "tasty sort of place with Books," but asserts he has "no libidinous thought about" the lady. For her part, Mrs. Jones offers to send some game home to Tom Keats, but refuses brother John's offer of a kiss. Despite Keats's effort to manage this story and Mrs. Jones, as he imagines himself of service to her "in matters of knowledge and taste," the story suggests that it is Mrs. Jones who controls the erotic potential of the moment (*LJK* 1:402–3). In this narrative context, Keats's succeeding paean to the "abstract Idea I have of Beauty" transforms female beauty into an abstraction less disturbing than the woman herself, or women themselves.

My last example returns to the Reynolds sisters. Writing to Bailey from Scotland, Keats explains that he had not visited them before leaving London because with "books to read" and "subjects to think upon," there was only time to visit Charles Brown at Wentworth Place. Having declared his intellectual and fraternal priorities, Keats admits that he is ill-tempered and suspicious when he is with the Reynolds women. He generalizes this state of mind and temper to include all women: "I am certain I have not a right feeling towards Women." Several explanations for this "obstinate

Prejudice" ensue: real women "fall beneath" his boyish conviction that a "fair Woman" must be "a pure Goddess"; real women are sensitive to insult, as is Keats himself, yet he finds himself thinking insults about women in their company; in sharp contrast, the company of men produces "no evil thoughts, no malice, no spleen" and none of the "Suspicions" that crowd his mind in the company of women.

Keats tries to mitigate this line of rhetorical march against women by asserting that he rejoiced in his brother George's marriage and "shall do so" when any of his friends marry. Yet after Bailey and two other friends married in 1818 and 1819, Keats did not rejoice. He was instead caustic about the institution and its victims (*LJK* 11:66, 240). In his letter of 1818, Keats remarks: "I must absolutely get over this – but how? The only way is to find the root of evil, and so cure it 'with backward mutters of dissevering Power' That is a difficult thing; for an obstinate Prejudice can seldom be produced but from a gordian complication of feelings, which must take time to unravell[ed] and care to keep unravelled" (*LJK* 1:342).

Keats closes the subject with a patch of self-defensive rancor: "after all I do think better of Womankind than to suppose they care whether Mister John Keats five feet hight likes them or not." By echoing "Z," the correspondent to *Blackwood's* who had used the phrase "Mister John Keats" derisively to attack the poet's effeminate style,[53] Keats magnifies rather than dismisses the question of the poet's effeminacy. The term "gordian," which here refers to the knotted complexity of his prejudice against "Womankind," turns up again a year later in his description of Lamia as the female serpent whose "gordian shape of dazzling hue" undergoes a painful transformation into a "woman's form" and "shape" (*Keats* 453–55). As Wolfson puts it, quoting Derrida, by crossing the "line of demarcation" between female figures and male poets, Keats thereby "risk[s] impurity, anomaly or monstrosity."[54] Yet this rhetorical impulse also releases figures, much as the character in Milton's *Comus* warns that the Lady cannot be released until someone grabs Comus's wand and breaks his spell over her.

This Miltonic possibility is already at work in *Endymion*, the poem early critics excoriated for its Spenserianism and poetic excess. In the Glaucus episode of the poem, Keats introduces transformations that go beyond those which Ovid's and Homer's versions make available. As theirs does not, his Glaucus becomes young again and is reunited

with a frolicking, amorous Scylla. If this outcome reminds us just
how often *Endymion* indulges the wishes of its eponymous hero, the
poem's emblematic figures provide an allegorical survey of the risk
and possible fraud that attend those willing to be enchanted by
figures, by women, or both.

Endymion is repeatedly exposed to this risk. Early in the poem he
swoons when he remembers his immortal lover. After others try to
revive him without success, he goes into a "fixed trance" so deep that
he looks "as dead-still as a marble man, / Frozen in that old tale
Arabian" (*Keats* 114). That old tale in *The Arabian Nights*, in which a
young man is a man to his waist but black marble below, is less
extreme than Keats's compressed redaction, which deadens and
freezes the entire body. In book 2, the eponymous hero nearly
follows an emblematic butterfly ("upon whose wings / There must
be surely character'd strange things") over a cliff (*Keats* 143). Had he
continued, Endymion would have been "froze to senseless stone"
(*Keats* 138).

The emblematic scenery on Glaucus's blue cloak offers more
evidence of the risks of figural and actual enchantment. "Overwrought with symbols by the deepest groans of / Ambitious magic,"
the cloak graphically displays evidence of Circe's magic (3.198–99,
Keats 169). The passive syntax of this description ("*by* ... groans *of* ...
magic") obliquely indicates too that abstraction works like death to
deny human agency. As other symbols on the cloak make clear, this
process is not bound by fixed figures or values:

> The gulphing whale was like a dot in the spell,
> Yet look upon it, and 'twould size and swell
> To its huge self; and the minutest fish
> Would pass the very hardest gazer's wish,
> And shew his little eye's anatomy.   (3.205–9, *Keats* 169)

The size of the cloak itself, "ample as the largest winding-sheet"
(3.196, *Keats* 168), more baldly recognizes that this rough magic may
be lethal. Even before Glaucus tells his story of Circe's lethal
enchantment of besotted men, the speaker exercises a version of the
enchanter's magic by offering a portrait of her victim. The old man's
features are "lifeless," he seems "not to see," and even after he
wakes as though from a trance, his brows

> Went arching up, and like two magic ploughs
> Furrow'd deep wrinkles in his forehead large,

> Which kept as fixedly as rocky marge,
> Till round his wither'd lips had gone a smile.
>
> (3:222–25, *Keats* 169)

Like the sculptured forms of the fallen Titans in the *Hyperion* poems, Glaucus is a figure of human pathos who weeps when he sees that Endymion may refuse to stop or help. Recognizing this, Endymion (all high indifference till now) regrets he may have "brought /Rheum to kind eyes, a sting to humane [human] thought" (3:285–86, *Keats* 171). Although "human" is an 1818 variant that disappears in revision, it registers the pull of feeling that makes Glaucus's last, Keatsian, transformation possible.

At the other end of the figural argument of the episode is Circe, the terrible but perfect (because female) Keatsian figure for the tyranny of figures that change people into grotesque monsters and cold abstractions. Like the *belle dame* and Lamia, Circe is the abjected sign of what the poet's figures do: they excite pathos and desire. They also hazard or perform transformations not unlike those that Circe visits on one of her victims. As Homer tells this story, Circe turns men into pigs. As Ovid tells it, she turns them into dogs and lions as well. As Keats tells it, Circe turns them into "shapes, wizard and brute" whose "deformities" not even Charon could dream of. Among them is an elephant so tormented by his heavy, monstrous bulk that he pleads "in human accent" to be released from "this heavy prison," to "die, / Or be deliver'd from this cumbrous flesh, / From this gross, detestable, filthy flesh" (3:541–52, *Keats* 178). This creature is apparently Keats's innovation, since there is no elephant among Circe's captives in Homer or Ovid, nor is there one in Peacock's *Rhododaphne*, though Keats's figure may recall Napoleon's installation of a three-story plaster cast of an allegorical elephant of the Revolution on the site of the Bastille.[55]

Keats's elephant is a trenchant emblem of the movement of personified figures away from human identity and toward the fixed, trapped abstractions at one extreme of allegory. For Circe's terrible enchantment guarantees this victim a paradoxical and burdensome materiality – a heavy, weighted set of values that freezes figures and sets them apart. In "La Belle Dame sans Merci" and *Lamia*, Keats figures this extreme in erotic terms, but with an unsteady edge of sympathy for these enchantresses. In *Lamia*, where this sympathy is most complex, it echoes Glaucus's joy at being able to shed his "serpent-skin of woe" to assume his earlier, youthful shape. For though Lamia also sheds her serpent skin, other woe lies ahead and another, final transformation and disappearance. With these turns of figure, Keats makes the figure of women abused and in pain an occasion for exploring pathos and abstraction.

The *Ode on a Grecian Urn* makes this borderland the site of its reply to the lingering Romantic debate about the sister arts and ek-phrasis.[56] In the ode, an unexpected alliance between historical consciousness and Romantic allegory veers away from the pure, ahistorical abstraction which the urn's beauty and its truth convey. The ode begins with terms of address whose mix of endearment and hostility readers have always found arresting. Calling it a "sylvan historian," the speaker says the urn can "express / A flowery tale more sweetly than our rhyme." As a "still unravish'd bride," the urn is threatened with ravishment at some future moment. Seen against the larger record of antiquity and ruin that was available to Keats as he looked at urns and fragments of the Parthenon frieze in the British Museum, the alienation and potential violence embedded in these figures[57] may specify what the speaker's idolatry of the urn as a superior "historian" has suppressed. If he does not want to break this idol, he may well want to break its hold on him, its potential silencing of his "rhyme" as less sweet, less pure than those "ditties of no tone" he identifies with the pipes depicted on the urn. As the "foster-child of silence and slow time," the urn may also be at risk once it enters the space and time of ekphrastic speech, even as being quietness's bride may mean being ravished in time and by time.

By restricting ekphrastic description to a series of questions in the next stanzas, Keats's speaker gradually shifts attention from the self-contained beauty of the urn's form toward the history it does not represent. By most critical reckonings, the urn depicts three scenes: a collective "pursuit" of "maidens loth" in the first stanza; a "Bold lover" who never quite kisses the "she" of the second stanza; and in the fourth a sacrificial procession that includes a lowing "heifer." The intervening third stanza proclaims the happiness of the lovers in the preceding one. Although the "mad pursuit" and "maidens loth" could be an earlier moment in a narrative that proceeds toward the "Bold lover" and "she" in the second stanza, the shift from singular to plural encourages readers to imagine these two scenes as isolated vignettes from different stories. The scenes depicted by the urn resemble the episodic, fragmentary vignettes whose discrete frames

eighteenth-century scholars eventually identified with Etruscan
urns.[58] With this slight rehearsal of a century-long debate on the
relative merits of Etruscan and Greek urns, Keats gives his
"Grecian" urn a narrative handicap that later stanzas amplify.

The third stanza makes this point more directly by transforming
G. E. Lessing's "most pregnant moment" (*Laocoön* 19–20) – the
moment in a story that the judicious painter represents because it
indicates what happens before and after – into a liability. For with
each manic repetition of "happy" ("happy, happy boughs,' etc.),
readers are more likely to conclude that being forever young, not
kissing or unkissed, may be far too much of a good thing. Similarly,
the repetition of Keats's already double-edged "still" in this stanza
argues against believing in the urn's "still moment" of happiness.
Then the inverted syntax of the line "All breathing human passion
far above" catches readers by surprise with a home truth: the
depicted lovers do not exemplify this passion because they are "far
above" it.[59] Although this irony echoes Hazlitt's 1816 declaration
that the beauty of Greek statues raises them "above the frailties of
pain or passion" ("On Gusto," *Works* IV:79), Keats now reformulates
that praise as something less. Whereas Hazlitt, Haydon, and others
insisted that the Elgin Marbles looked alive, Keats says that the
arrested lovers depicted on the urn "are above" living passion.

The liability of this exalted status is more openly declared in the
fourth stanza, which describes a procession of people and a heifer
toward a sacrificial altar and a "little town" that is not depicted on
the urn. The speaker's uncertainty about which "town" and "green
altar" emphasizes what the urn and pure allegorical abstraction
cannot – that the story to which this procession belongs starts and
ends off the urn. For if it is true that this speaker can at best only
imagine or speculate about the provenance of the people in that
procession, this "fantasy" is much more than the work of a belated
speaker who does what he can with what the urn and antiquity have
left for him to do.[60] It is nothing less than the work of history in the
sense of the term suggested by *historia*: "a method of learning by
inquiry"[61] – precisely what the speaker does by addressing the urn,
whose very nature resists such inquiry: it is what it is and has no time
for inquiry.

For the doomed heifer of this stanza that "low[s] at the skies ...
her silken flanks with garlands drest," the procession is an apt, ironic
example of the moment Lessing had argued the artist must depict.

We may not know precisely how the heifer got there, but we do know what will soon happen to her. This heifer is close kin to one Keats described in a verse letter in which he insists that a heifer being led to sacrifice is "touch'd into real life" by the "Titian colours" of the poet's reverie (*LJK* 1:260). Jack's suggestion that the visual source for this earlier figure is not an urn but a cow depicted on one of the Elgin Marbles brings this genealogy home (so to speak) to the pieces of Parthenon sculpture that had prompted Keats's interest in the pathos of antiquity.[62]

The heifer of Keats's ode embodies traits Hazlitt assigns to the "ideal." Arguing against Joshua Reynolds's widely influential argument in the *Discourses* that what is particular cannot be ideal and vice versa, Hazlitt contends that what is truly ideal will also be historical. For this to happen, face and figure must be particularized – this beard, this expression, this shape of muscle and bone. Both the argument and the example inevitably recall Reynolds's career as a portrait painter. What makes such a face historical for Hazlitt is "passion" or pathos – the expressive energy that unifies face or figure into a particular and recognizable identity ("On the Ideal," *Works* xviii:83). Keats's lowing heifer and the speaker who mourns the town forever emptied of its inhabitants are figures of passion – pathos in its most inclusive rhetorical sense – whose expressive gaze focuses our attention on the history which the urn cannot tell, or the history it chooses not to tell to preserve the ekphrastic fiction of its perfect form. Like other bound female figures of Keats's poetics, this heifer creates an occasion for recognizing via pathos (and bondage) what the authority and shadow cast by the urn would screen out. Much as, Hollander argues, the figure of the bound Andromeda, in the sonnet "If by dull rhymes," releases a deft poetic argument about poetic freedom and constraint,[63] so does this heifer's plaintive voice introduce this stanza's argument about another scene of pathos that the urn creates but does not represent.

The poetic fiction that the speaker knows or imagines what the urn cannot dramatizes a restless historical consciousness that is critical of the urn's willingness to suspend time in order to make pictures. For in this stanza an imaginative turn away from the urn's representations contends that its images are isolated, forever sealed off from worldly existence, temporality, and above all history. As the marker of the recognition of a truth the urn does or would conceal, pathos insists on the particular and the historical, over against the universalizing, eternal aesthetic impulse for which the urn so brilliantly "speaks."[64]

Yet for all its resistance to ekphrasis as a device that seals itself off from historical and cultural embeddedness, even as the objects so represented are sealed off, Keats's ode is enmeshed in ekphrastic desire. Were it not, it could not have served formalist analysis as well as it has done and will continue to do.[65] As technical terms that refer to classical shape and line, the speaker's last figures of address ("O Attic shape! Fair attitude!") explicitly recognize the urn's classical form. Although succeeding lines betray an edge of irritation with the power of the urn's "overwrought" and "silent form" to "tease us out of thought," the ode concludes by delivering the urn's message. Or almost: I read the last line and a half of the poem as the speaker's reply to the urn. For the narrative and historical consciousness of the preceding stanza suggests that the aphorism "Beauty is truth, truth beauty" is the urn's truth, not the speaker's.[66] The fact that the ode, as lyric and as ekphrasis, conveys this point obliquely tells us something about the shape of history in Romantic allegory. Working against the seductions of the urn's aesthetic form, the historical consciousness of the ode defends a version of idealism that is historical, particular, and animated by passion: "what men or gods are these? what maidens loth?" the speaker asks.

By placing the urn's story of beauty and truth within the humanizing lens of pathos, Keats rejects the pure allegory of fixed, emblematic objects in favor of a less pure, contingent allegorical vision in which a Benjaminian sense of ruin and impending death demand all three features of Hazlitt's "ideal" – history, particularity, and human pathos. The sense of history I have in mind is not a fixed schematic but a bending, often wounding, passage of time whose momentary truths and particularities fleetingly glimpse their own "life of allegory." Moreover it is by way of particulars – this heifer, this little town, this speaker – that such a life takes shape. Making pathos the vehicle for this recognition suggests that even the abstract weight of this allegory has to be felt in order to matter.

By way of ekphrasis, Keats propels allegory into the space of thought and history. Because time's ravages to the present are always going on, history can be indicated, but not encased, by poems and works of art. Both work instead like indexical signs that point (obscurely or explicitly) to events, other material objects, beliefs, feelings, and suppositions about how all these do or do not impinge on each other – the whole array of phenomena that constitute what we know or call history. Shaped by Benjamin's theory of history, this observation returns modern historical consciousness to its Romantic antecedents ("Theses," *Illuminations* 257). Within the mixed space of history and particularity, Romantic allegory becomes more recognizably a sublunary enterprise, the work of human beings who seek out an alien "other speech" to convey the mixed freight of human life.

Whereas G. E. Lessing insists that the grief and pain expressed by the figure of Laocoön and his sons struggling in the coils of a giant serpent argue against the pictorial wholeness that is for Winckelmann the essence of classical beauty, Keats uses the heifer and emptied town to record the historical weight of impending pain and emptiness. In both cases, what is ruptured is the closure of an ideally beautiful form. Goethe's reply to the Laocoön debate specifies the Romantic consequences of Keats's poetic argument. In his 1798 remarks on the statuary, Goethe argues that its ideal representation depends on what comes before and after, not on the moment selected for pictorial representation. In other words, this moment of bodies in pain is shocking, but it is also "passing," "fugitive," or "transitory."[67] So characterized, this moment points elsewhere and away from itself. This revision of Lessing and Winckelmann on the sufficiency of Greek sculptural representation might also radically transform how we read the Laocoön statuary, one Greek urn, and one ode. No longer a self-contained, translucent symbol in the Coleridgean sense, these material shapes exemplify the disposition of allegorical signs to gesture beyond the limits of material signifiers, to make riddles that readers and viewers are invited to unravel by moving forward and backward in time.[68] At the same time and in ways Keats's ode emphasizes, pathos humanizes allegorical representation by folding abstraction back into the world of suffering and mortality. Along this narrative and interpretive path, material signs must be sustained not because they make a case for self-absorbing forms but because they prompt and recognize pathos.

In Keats's *Hyperion* poems questions about the fixity or mobility of its divine, quasi-allegorical figures take particular note of their material shape or form. In *Hyperion* Keats uses the term "shape" to describe Mnemosyne, and Saturn calls his fellow Titans "the first-born of all shap'd and palpable Gods" (3:61, 2:154, *Keats* 354, 345). In both poems this term specifies a broader argument about massively sculptured personifications. In *Hyperion* the Titans are frequently compared, individually and as a group, to statuary: Thea and Saturn look like "natural sculpture in cathedral cavern"; Thea like the Memphian Sphinx, and "the bulk / Of Memnon's image at the set of sun"; the rest of the fallen Titans, who have "limbs / Lock'd up like veins of metal, crampt and screw'd," look like "a dismal cirque / Of Druid stones, upon a forlorn moor" (*Hyperion*, 1:40, 86, 2:373, 2:24–25 and 34–35, *Keats* 341–42). *The Fall of Hyperion* uses a more abbreviated version of this vocabulary to describe the fallen Titans (*Fall* 225, 299–300, 383–84, *Keats* 483–87). In this "very abstract poem," as Keats describes it for Fanny Brawne with a whiff of condescension (*LJK* 11:132), the poet–speaker is similarly at risk. First he sinks down in a "cloudy swoon ... Like a Silenus on an antique vase" (55–56, *Keats* 479). Writing to George and Georgiana Keats in early 1819, Keats explains that "heavy and spirituous" wines "transform a Man to a Silenus" (*LJK* 11:64). Keats's poetic figure goes one step further by making the god a fixed element in the relief design on a vase. When the poet of *The Fall of Hyperion* tries to climb the marble steps of Saturn's altar, the goddess Moneta threatens him with, as Homans puts it, "death by freezing."[69] Here and elsewhere in his poetry, misogynist portraits like this one advance intriguing inquiries about what figures can do.

Whether frozen, marble, or like the "natural sculpture" of a limestone cavern, the Titans in both epics and the poet of *The Fall of Hyperion* mark the reification and abstraction that relegate the Titans, like the Egyptians, to their historical position as superannuated gods in what Keats elsewhere calls the "grand march of intellect."[70] In this epic design, these gods will be put aside by Apollo, the Olympian god of reason and poetry whom Keats's early poems celebrate. The pathos that divides Saturn "the frozen God," from his divinity puts this design in jeopardy. He complains to Thea: "tell me if this feeble shape / Is Saturn's" (1:98–99, *Keats* 332). The "mortal oil" or "disanointing poison" which Fate has poured on Saturn's head also makes the speaker suffer the "frailty" of strong human passions (2:96–98, *Keats* 343). By such turns, Keats examines the oscillations between abstraction and pathos as necessary if unequally apportioned terms – too much pathos makes abstraction impossible; too little makes figures inconsequential. Captured though they are in sculptured forms, like Keats's marble man, the Titans are vulnerable, darkened mirror images of Hazlitt's comparison of the Elgin Marbles to "living men turned to stone." As the Titans mourn their new, unwanted resemblance to mortals who suffer and die (*Hyperion*, 1:332–35, 2:97–100, *Keats* 339, 343), they dramatize a wrenching renegotiation of the putative figural distance between abstract personification and human suffering.

This renegotiation, not the seductive power of the lyric or ekphrasis, is what prompts Keats to linger with the Titans. When he gets to the moment in *Hyperion* just before Apollo's ascendancy, the story he tells is still about suffering. For if knowledge enormous makes a god of Apollo, getting that knowledge means having to suffer. When he transfers this exchange and requirement from the newly divine Apollo of *Hyperion* to the human poet–speaker of *The Fall of Hyperion*, Keats entangles his poetic identity in the same gordian knot that traps his female figures, including the Cockney Keats.

In *Lamia* Keats returns to these and related problems of figure. Like Circe and *la belle dame*, Lamia is both a magical enchantress and a victim who has to undergo a grotesque transformation. Lamia's fairy charm probably recalls Jane Cox, whose beauty and self-possession put him "more at ease," Keats wrote to his brother and sister-in-law – so much at ease in fact that "I forget myself entirely because I live in her" (*LJK* 1:395). The same could be said of Lycius. Shedding her "gordian shape" for a "woman's shape," Lamia submits to a near-death experience that echoes what Apollo, and then the poet–speaker, undergo in the *Hyperion* poems:

> She writh'd about, convuls'd with scarlet pain:
> A deep volcanian yellow took the place
> Of all her milder-mooned body's grace;
> And, as the lava ravishes the mead,
> Spoilt all her silver mail, and golden brede.
>
> (154–58, *Keats* 456)

This fantastic use of geological figures to present elemental change as volcanic eruption makes Lamia painfully real and yet full of artifice. Her pain authorizes the grotesque and oddly material energy of figures that pull toward and away from recognizably human forms. Nor is it an accident that her transformation looks like a demonic, or sadistic, view of taking off make-up. Like seventeenth-century paintings in which female make-up is a figure for overdecorated and deceptive rhetoric,[71] Keats's narrator offers a figure of a serpent-woman who is "nothing but pain and ugliness" underneath, a bad rerun of Spenser's false Duessa. In the highly colored rhetorical surface of Keats's poem, cast in the decorous format of Drydenesque couplets instead of the looser, couplet rhymes that had so exercised critics of *Endymion*, Lamia is a new, or newly exposed version of Rhetoric. And so is Keats.

Lamia, whose transformation revises Lemprière's description of African "lamiae," ought to be Keats's figure of the phallic woman.[72] Evidently well-schooled in "woman's love" (325, *Keats* 461), she seduces, then dominates, the youth from Corinth. The narrator is quick to note her duplicity. Lately transformed from snake to woman (or back to woman if we believe Lamia's version of her history), she becomes, quite impossibly, "a virgin purest lipp'd, yet in the lore / Of love deep learned to the red heart's core" (188–90, *Keats* 457). Deploying the resources of "Cupid's college," she beguiles Lycius: "so delicious were the words she sung, / It seem'd he had lov'd them a whole summer long" (249–50, *Keats* 459).

Despite ample evidence throughout the poem that this narrator subscribes to the misogynist analogy between deceptive female talk and overdecorated rhetoric, made-up just like a woman, he is at times unmistakably sympathetic. Thus although her claim to be a woman unhappily transformed into a snake seems ontologically unlikely, if naming can here be understood as a generic label for what she is, the narrator half-grants the premise (or fiction) when he imagines what the woman Lamia must have dreamt of in her "serpent prison-house" (203, *Keats* 457). He also turns finally on Apollonius, the philosopher who unravels the "knotty problem" of Lamia's identity, and whose accusation that she is a snake finally makes her vanish. The "gordian complication of feelings" which Keats had earlier used as a figure for his prejudice against women now includes Apollonius, who himself becomes a lamia according to the horrified Lycius: "Mark how, possess'd, his lashless eyelids stretch / Around his demon eyes!" (288–89, *Keats* 474).

Among the sources Keats used to write the poem, Philostratus's *Life of Apollonius* describes him as a Pythagorean and a sophist – i.e. a rhetor – whom rulers and priests consult for his knowledge, wisdom, and prophecy. By virtue of his goodness, Apollonius can perform miracles, including slipping out of his chains while imprisoned by the Roman emperor Domitian. Just before his birth, Apollonius's mother was visited by Proteus, whose identity as a shape-changer and prophet Philostratus interprets as a sign that the child would be wise and favored by the gods. Recognizing the possibility that

Apollonius might also change shape to escape confinement, Domitian chains the philosopher, much as Menelaus confined Proteus until the god had run through his repertory of elemental shapes. Domitian, who knows his Ovid and his Homer, tells Apollonius that he will be chained "until you become either water, or a wild beast, or a tree."[73]

In Keats's poetics the transformation that matters is that into figure, the "abstract idea" or "image" his letters describe. For although his Lamia belongs to the species William Godwin had earlier defined as "demons, who assumed the forms of beautiful women, and whose favourite occupation was supposed to be first to entice young children ... and [then] devour them" (*Pantheon* 102–3), Keats displaces the vampirism common to Godwin's definition and Philostratus's *Life of Apollonius* onto Apollonius or, more precisely, onto his rhetorical question to Lycius: "And shall I see thee made a serpent's prey?" Immediately, we are told, "Lamia breath'd death breath" (298–99, *Keats* 474). As woman and as rhetorical figure, Lamia makes it possible for Keats to initiate those "backward mutters of dissevering Power" he said would be necessary to undo his prejudice against women. Even so, this figure and process do not, as they do in Milton's *Comus*, free the lady, the philosopher, or the poet from fixations and abstractions which each harbors.

Keats's poetic interest in sensuous shapes, especially female ones, continues a long tradition in which allegorical figures are often female and as often chastized. The pathos he feels for poets and male protagonists similarly seized up makes a productive settlement with the way grotesque transformations and artificed figures mark the intersection between sensuous reality and abstraction in allegorical figures. As these concerns unravel and ravel in his poems, they create distinctly un-Hegelian alignments between sensuous, particular shapes and abstract ideas. As they are not for Hegel, such alignments are temporary and temporizing, caught up like Shelley's Beatrice in a culture and time whose pressures cannot be evaded or foreclosed.

CHAPTER 7

J. M. W. Turner's "Allegoric shapes"

> Thus incorporeal spirits to smallest forms
> Reduced their shapes immense, and were at large.
> Milton, PL 1.789–90, p. 29

> wading through the rubbish, that deformed our walls or ceilings,
> in the shape of allegorical absurdities, we shall clear all away for
> the purpose of giving West the honour of laying the foundation
> stone of the Historical school of painting in England.
> Anon., "Historical Painting in England" 65

Unlike many of his contemporaries, including this anonymous critic
for the *Art Union*, J. M. W. Turner was not at all queasy about
allegory. He often painted mythological and classical subjects traditionally identified with allegory; he also appended poetic tags to
landscape paintings to evoke the visual/verbal structure of the
Renaissance emblem.[1] My argument concerns a feature of Turner's
allegorical practice that is untraditional: his use of extremes of scale
to push away from realist norms and interpretation. Whether
excessively large or small, his choice of subject and medium frequently conveys an allegorical disposition that coexists with realist
surroundings and historical anecdote.[2] This practice occurs even in
late works that have been identified as evidence of his "impressio-
nist" style.

First exhibited in 1840, at the beginning of Turner's last decade,
The Slave Ship, or *Slavers throwing overboard the Dead and Dying – Typhoon
coming on*, shows how realistic details and a well-documented practice
among nineteenth-century slave traders support an allegorical
reading. To lighten the load or to capture insurance money that
would not be available in port for slaves who were ill or diseased,
captains of ships carrying slaves to ports in the New World would
throw weakened slaves overboard to drown. Turner appended these

verses from his manuscript poem "The Fallacies of Hope" to the exhibited painting:

> 'Aloft all hands, strike the top-masts and belay;
> Yon angry setting sun and fierce-edged clouds
> Declare the Typhoon's coming.
> Before it sweeps your decks, throw overboard
> The dead and dying – ne'er heed their chains
> Hope, Hope, fallacious Hope!
> Where is thy market now?'[3]

Although the first exhibition of *The Slave Ship* coincided with royal proclamations against slavery and increased abolitionist activity between 1839 and 1840, the figurative energies of Turner's verse and image push the scene away from the documentary toward the emblematic. Beginning with "hands," a common nautical synecdoche for sailors at work, the verse presses toward figured abstractions, among them the "angry" sun and "fierce-edged" cloud; the apostrophized "Hope"; and nominalized, hence generic, phrases – "the dead and dying" instead of "dead and dying people." In this crowd, "Typhoon" looks like an angry god of wind and sea.

The painting amplifies this allegorical reading (fig. 8). In the foreground iron chains float above the water as, in some cases, the only sign of drowned slaves thrown overboard. In realistic terms this detail makes no sense, for iron chains would sink faster and lower than the arms or legs to which they were attached. This visual detail instead advertises the series of synecdochic figures that collectively sponsor an allegorical argument. By holding these human body parts aloft in a grotesque display, these chains reduce the dying slaves to their working appendages. Allied figurative dismemberments govern other visual details. The unseen slavers of Turner's title are known only by their actions: violently displaced images figure what they do to others and what the painter does to them. This metafigural logic suggests too that the murderous turbulence of the water as the typhoon moves is itself a figure for the human rapaciousness left on board ship. With emphatically painted mouths that are larger than they would be in nature, the fish are similarly hyperbolic figures.

With these metonymic refigurings of a real event, Turner reinvents the abstracting, fragmented energy of the Renaissance emblem. Here numerous iconographic details invite viewers to read them

Figure 8 J. M. W. Turner. *The Slave Ship.*

allegorically. The cue for such readings is a distortion or exaggeration akin to that of chains that bob above the water, holding up
hands and feet just where we would not expect to see them. These
exaggerations are not accidental but patently theatrical. No one
knew better than Turner how to draw to scale: he began his career as
a topographical painter and in 1807 was appointed the professor of
perspective at the Royal Academy.[4] As a painter whose early friends
and acquaintances included artists who created spectacles or painted
the panoramic views that spectacles soon made popular,[5] he could
not have failed to notice that theatrical spectacles after 1780 relied on
elaborate machinery and stage illusion to make small scenes look
enormous. Like Diderot's imaginary technicians, the organizers of
revolutionary festivals, and London theater managers from whose
productions he borrowed, Turner knew how to create a spectacle by
manipulating realist expectations.

In the 1780s Philippe de Loutherbourg, whose topographical art
Turner imitated at the beginning of his career, invented the *eidofu-
sikon*, a relatively small, recessed box which he used to project scenes

so that they would seem immense to spectators sitting in a London drawing room. To indicate objects close or far in the limited space of this box, Loutherbourg probably used different-sized pieces that had been miniatures in the Drury Lane theater sets he designed when he was first employed there in the early 1770s. Illusionist spectacles soon became more grandiose. In 1794 Robert Barker completed an enormous building on the edge of Regent's Park to house his Panorama of London, a massive circular fresco to be viewed from an interior dome-like platform modelled on the dome of St. Paul's. Altick explains that the building did away with "the limiting frame and standard of size and distance external to the picture itself" – features that reveal the role of illusion in representational art.[6]

Whereas nineteenth-century entrepreneurs tried to insure the illusion of reality with spectacular effects that emphasized exaggerated scale and perspective, Turner uses these effects to turn the logic of spectacle inside out. Instead of presenting imitations of the world that encourage spectators to believe what they see, he invites a different order of reading and seeing by presenting images that are complexly allusive. The history such images represent is almost always stratified, mixing ancient and recent pasts, contemporary scientific or popular topics, and biographical details relevant to Turner's view of himself as "a painter of historical landscape etc."[7] Thus in an early canvas titled *Army of the Medes, destroyed in a Desart by a Whirlwind – foretold by Jeremiah chap xv vers 32, and 33* (exh. 1801) – which one nineteeenth-century critic lumped among Turner's "ragged attempts at history" – Napoleon's recent, unsuccessful Egyptian campaign may be the unspecified, intermediate event that links a biblical defeat and prophecy with the historical present. The stratified historical perspective created by seeing the biblical story of the army of the Medes through the lens of Napoleon's Egyptian campaign makes an oddly skewed return to the pattern of figure and archetype in biblical exegesis. Now the Old Testament stands in for a "modern" event whose chief actor is not Christ but Napoleon Buonaparte. By such means, the representation of history moves close to the generic, even universalist, perspective of allegory, biblical and modern.

In later works where contemporary historical events are the acknowledged subjects, Turner's characteristic indirection supervises multiple and often ironic relations between the depicted event and a surrounding text and narrative. Unlike Manet, whose art conveys a "sense of complete and synoptic presentness" even in paintings whose subjects look cut off,[8] Turner creates images that unravel outward in several directions, toward biographical statements, toward historical events past and present, toward allegorical meaning, engaging technical concerns and marketplace economics as well as compelling pictorial representation. What he thereby accomplishes is not the displacement of history, but the invention of pictorial fictions that obliquely register the materiality of history and provide their own readings of that history. So reimagined, displacement is the mediation that facts, persons, and events require to become the narratives we call history.[9]

My reading of how these competing interests support allegory under unfriendly fire begins with Turner's 1820 *Rome, from the Vatican*, a canvas whose topographical subject looks away from the artistic turmoil within the picture space. The middle section of this chapter deals with Turner's career-long interest in the St. Gothard Pass in Switzerland, which he represented in different media beginning in 1802, when he sketched several views in notebooks, and continuing into the 1820s and '30s, when he used the same visual motifs in the much-reduced size required for his vignette engravings for Samuel Rogers's *Italy*. In the chronological middle of this experimentation with the miniature vignette, Turner painted the large oil sketch and finished canvas *Ulysses deriding Polyphemus* (1828–29). Both versions use spectacular effects to represent landscape as an allegorical emblem and history. Among his late works, *War: Exile and the Rock Limpet* (1842) summarizes the allegorical impulse that accrues to similar deformations of realistic scale throughout Turner's career.

Rome, from the Vatican, exhibited in 1820 and subtitled *Raffaelle, accompanied by La Fornarina, preparing his Pictures for the Decoration of the Loggie*, commemorates the 300th anniversary of Raphael's death. In the painting Turner celebrates the occasion by offering a visual pastiche of works by Raphael and others (fig. 9). The inclusion of a seventeenth-century colonnade by Bernini suggests that to see Raphael's art in Rome we must now see it through intermediate layers of history suggested by this colonnade, among other details, much as Turner saw it on his first visit to Rome in 1819.[10] The painting also commemorates Raphael's relation to his mistress La Fornarina, who plays with jewels on the parapet as he looks at the loggia.

Figure 9 J. M. W. Turner. *Rome, from the Vatican.*

By clustering art-works around these two figures, *Rome, from the Vatican* invites an allegorical reading. The canvas in the foreground bears the inscription "Casa di Raffaello," to identify the Claudean scene with a small garden house between the Villas Medici and Borghese in which Raphael painted frescos and placed portraits of La Fornarina for his own, rather than his patrons', pleasure. The inverted history of art proclaimed by using a Claudean vocabulary to represent Raphael's private domain of art and love elaborates a tension in Turner's painting between public, commissioned works of art and private pleasures.[11]

This tension centers on Raphael's relation to his mistress as he stands in the papal loggia. The erotic and divisive energies associated with La Fornarina are specified by her placement in the picture space. Turned away from Raphael and his art to examine jewels spread out on the balcony, she also has her back to the portrait of the Madonna della Sedia, a female inspiration of quite a different kind. Both figures extend the thematic range suggested by Raphael's *Expulsion from Paradise* – represented in Turner's painting by an easel painting in which the figure of Eve is suggestively hidden by the left half of the painting of the Casa di Raffaello – and the *Creation of Eve* panel in the second bay of the right perspective. "Implausibly bright," McVaugh notes, this bay acts as a point of contact for the implied narrative of Raphael's glance, which "traverses the *Creation of Eve* on its way to *The Building of the Ark* beyond the upper right corner."[12]

The painting's argument about art, love, and the Fall suggests a more elusive but parallel one about art. Of all the canvases propped up on the balcony, only the *Madonna della Sedia* corresponds to an actual Raphael canvas; the rest translate his frescoes onto canvas. By twisting the facts in this way, Turner implies that, like him, Raphael was primarily a painter and not also a sculptor.[13] The painting's arrangement of Raphael's "canvases" and the loggia bays suggests a more explicitly visual distortion. An early reviewer of "this strange wonderful picture" objected to its "crossing and re-crossing of reflected lights about the gallery" and "the perspective of the foreground."[14] As great frescoes become smaller canvases, so does the monumental sculpture of a reclining male figure seem life-size (or canvas-size) because of the truncated recession Turner uses to define its relation to the canvases between it and the foreground. There the Vatican is reduced to the size of the bound architectural plans inscribed "Pianta del Vaticano" and heaped in the center.[15]

The miniature winged figure perched on the knee of the reclining sculpture both does and does not correct these distortions. Despite the apparent contrast between its size and that of the larger sculpture, the winged figure is a miniature. As such, it will necessarily make any other object look large beside it. The problem is not that there are no scalar values in the painting – the contrast between the miniature and the immense space of St. Peter's Square makes quite the opposite point – but that competing scalar values are at work. The diminished scale of Raphael's frescoes and sculpture puts them on a level (literally that of the balcony where they are placed) with an all-too-human Raphael, half turned from but half involved with La Fornarina, whose primary interest here is at best aesthetic, at worst mercantile, as she examines the jewels spread out on the parapet.

The interpretive logic of the twisted architecture and compressed space in which these elements are placed is more difficult to work through. The loggia arcade is "twisted boldly so that its third arch enframes the central city scape," while an exaggerated recession compresses the other two bays at the right. With this "wrenching" of building and perspective, McVaugh explains, viewers are drawn into the picture space even as the compressed scale and disorder of the foreground push them back.[16] This visual double bind calls attention to the kind of viewing going on inside it. The reclining sculpture gazing over the parapet, identified variously as a river god, the Tiber, Raphael's sculpture of Jonah, or Michelangelo's *Day* (at least in the configuration of its crossed legs),[17] may recall the House of Commons debate about the Elgin Marbles, in which experts frequently mentioned two sculpted figures, the River God and the Theseus. Payne Knight preferred the River God, which he dated "from the time of Hadrian," to indicate he thought it was Roman of the first century AD. One fellow of the Royal Academy, Richard Westmacott, preferred the back of the Theseus. A third witness whose testimony might have interested Turner was Benjamin West, then President of the Royal Academy, who compared these and other figures to works by "Raffaelle in the Vatican." The abstract of the subcommittee report that appeared in the *Annals of the Fine Arts* summarized West's position: "the great improvement of our British artists, may be expected from this acquisition, as *it is in these marbles which is seen the source from which they grew* ... and as RAFFAELLE was benefitted by them, so may our British artists."[18]

Turner could not have ignored this acrimonious debate, which concerned whether English imperialism had fostered this cultural acquisition at the expense of a besieged Greece under Turkish rule, and the appropriate role of institutions of patronage, royal or otherwise, in the future of British art and culture.[19] Eames, the editor of the *Annals of the Fine Arts*, and its contributors, notably Haydon, tried to make the Marbles a pawn in the institutional rivalry between the British Institution, supported by the *Annals*, and the Royal Academy. Turner's first contact with the origins of this controversy occurred in 1799, when he chose not to join Elgin's expedition as its artist because the salary was too low.[20]

The bickering fueled by the public inquiry concerning the Elgin Marbles is not clearly or necessarily at issue in Turner's *Rome*, but the river god of the painting, if that is what he is, may be a blurred image (either Greek or Roman or both at once) of the classical history to which Raphael and Turner are both heirs in West's vision of Greece and the Marbles. Whatever his identity, the reclining sculpture and the winged miniature perched on his knee are the only figures inside the picture frame who look at the scene described by the main title of the painting, *Rome, from the Vatican*. La Fornarina looks down at her jewels, Raphael looks at his loggia – albeit diffusely, as if several pictures there occupy his mind and eye. Only the painter and the viewers outside the picture frame gaze in the direction indicated by the reclining statue's turned head and the title. This shared gaze suggests a common view and perspective, and thus a momentary relief from the cluttered foreground and distracted gaze of Raphael, his mistress, and the portrait of the Madonna, who looks directly out at the painter and the viewer. Absent from this painting is the self-theatricalized absorption Fried finds in the figures of eighteenth-century French art, whose gaze inward solicits our gaze from without.[21] In brief, too many gazes in *Rome, from the Vatican* convey a stratified history that points in several directions: personal, public, Renaissance, classical, or early Roman.

Turner calls attention to this aspect of the painting by presenting the whole composition as a crowded stage. The balcony on which works of art, the artist, and La Fornarina are crowded is a displaced image of a theater balcony, pushed forward, as it were, to stage a view of another stage, the Rome of the title. And because the twisted third arch of the loggia is cut off by the top of the painting and as a result also cut off from the vertical mass of the same building and (presumably) the same arch in the left foreground, thus "enframed" the composition seems more like a stage set than an architectural reality. By these means, obvious artifice foregrounds a view of the history of art whose allegorical theme is artistic greatness made small or large. By altering the scale of great works, by making them seem just or only life-size, Turner puts monumental works of art back into the life and histories they both invent and record. Or, to argue this point in more careerist terms, he restages Raphael's art to fit the historical perspective and ambition of a nineteenth-century painter who is Raphael's admirer and successor. For in this view of Rome and Raphael, Turner creates a fractured frame and framed works of art (even when the actual works are frescoes) that make it impossible to ignore pictorial illusion.

Rome, from the Vatican demonstrates how the allegorical representation of history is for Turner caught up in questions about theater and spectacle, at least by 1820 and probably long before. Before, during, and after the Revolution, Burke's great "tragic-comic scene" that soon afterward found its way onto the English stage, London entrepreneurs produced spectacles that extended the illusionist machinery of the early magic lantern shows. In post-revolutionary France, the scenes represented by such means often included violent revolutionary events. In London theaters and other viewing halls, spectacles depicted natural cataclysms, literary episodes such as Milton's Pandemonium in Hell, and events in history or recent news that were violent or cataclysmic.[22] Implicit in these spectacles was a peculiarly lurid interpretation of Lessing's "most pregnant moment" of dramatic and pictorial representation. Made powerless by spectacle, viewers could be and were caught up in the sweep of images or the sweep of history such images were supposed to represent.

The power of spectacle and its political agenda during the revolutionary and Napoleonic periods suggest how the representation of history becomes enmeshed in Romantic allegory. Whether the spectacle at issue is a "phantom train of images" – Terry Castle's evocative description of the phantasmagoria[23] – or a single image, it often assumes a central figure or figures who magisterially control the "progress" of events and the captive viewer – at once the ambition and the terror of French revolutionary history. Fascinated by theatrical spectacles, Turner is skeptical of the "truth" they seem to offer, precisely because he too knew how to paint spectacles that would capture spectators. The lure of spectacle is evident in many of his works, including several canvases that depict the burning of the Houses of Parliament in 1834; the 1840 *The Slave Ship*; and the 1810 oil *Fall of an Avalanche in the Grisons*, praised by Ruskin as the first visual representation of "a stone in flight."[24] In *Rome, from the Vatican*, Turner invites viewers to resist a similar lure by making the illusionism of his representation of Rome a key to its argument.

Beginning in 1802, when he visited Switzerland during the Peace of Amiens, Turner sketched the St. Gothard Pass from at least two directions and several different positions (some of them imagined) along the narrow track through the pass. As he later repeated these early sketches in watercolor, oil, and different engraved formats, they seem to comprise glimpses in a visual narrative – not single moments that imply what comes before and after, but "cuts" in a longer narrative about passage through time whose visual vocabulary depends on sharply incommensurable scalar values and some quite impossible points of view, at least within the realm of human dexterity. As these distortions exaggerate the geological antiquity of the site and the arduousness of human passage through it, they assume an oddly emblematic status. Indeed, their articulation of what Ruskin calls "that marvellous road" through the Alps[25] becomes so generic that Turner eventually extracts some details to convey in miniature the larger, emblematic narrative to which they belong.

Throughout the nineteenth century, the St. Gothard pass was a narrow track through the Schollinen gorge, punctured at one end by a long tunnel built in 1707 to accommodate pack mules and their drivers, which could only be reached by walking over a treacherous rock causeway. Along it, Dorothy Wordsworth reported in 1820, were crosses to mark where travellers had perished.[26] In 1802 Turner sketched several views in the pass itself. Following the course of the Reuss, he depicted scenes in the gorge and at either end of the route, from near Altdorf to the north to the Pass of Faido in Italy, in addition to the two views he repeated most often: the Devil's Bridge in the St. Gothard Pass and the view from the bridge. A third view from somewhere suspended in the gorge shows the tunnel blasted into the rock wall in one direction; a fourth looks down on the bridge from above a waterfall that cascades down into the ravine toward the bridge. In an 1848 watercolor, titled *Descent of the St. Gothard* and sometimes identified as his last work, Turner depicts a point farther south, probably near Airolo or Bellinzona.[27]

In the two 1802 sketches of the pass whose views he repeats more often than any other – the bridge itself and the view from it – Turner emphasizes the verticality of the ravine and the cliffs. The view from the bridge, which is the more insistently vertical, emphasizes the difficulty of this Alpine passage, whereas that of the bridge calls attention to the achievement of its passage over the ravine.[28] In both views an arch or arch-like opening – indicated by the bridge in one view and by the walls of the ravine in the other – structures the representation and draws the viewer toward the ravine, as if through an opening, yet insists on the mystery of what lies beyond the opening.[29] The Devil's Bridge in Turner's sketch thus revises the compositional and thematic functions of the "bridge in the middle distance," the most common Claudean "furnishing" in English land-scape painting of the late eighteenth century. Because of its place-ment, the Claudean bridge unified compositions by drawing the eye toward the middle and background values of the picture space.[30]

In Turner's St. Gothard redactions of this pictorial motif, unity is less at issue than tenacity. Lower in the picture space than its Claudean antecedents, the Devil's Bridge is a slender link between the massive walls of the gorge, dividing them from each other and dividing the lower and upper parts of the ravine (fig. 10). The image warrants the description John Murray would later give for the bridge Turner would have seen in 1802. Writing after a second bridge was constructed higher up in the same place, Murray remarks:

The old bridge, a thin segment of a circle, spanning a terrific abyss, had originally an air at once of boldness and fragility ... The single arch of slight masonry, suspended in the air at a height of 70 ft. above the Reuss, with scarce a parapet at the side, and with barely breadth to allow two persons to pass, almost seemed to tremble with the rush of the torrent under the feet of the traveller. Modern improvements have deprived the bridge and its vicinity of much of its terror and sublimity.[31]

Later oils, watercolors, mezzotints and steel engravings elaborate these two views. In a large 1803–4 oil titled *The Pass at St. Gothard*, the view from the bridge includes a human figure kneeling, perhaps praying, before a cross (fig. 11).[32] Turner's visual figure for the fragility of these monuments, which Dorothy Wordsworth character-ized as "so slightly put together that a child might break them to

Figure 10 J. M. W. Turner. *Devil's Bridge.* Watercolor.

pieces ... yet they lie from year to year as safe as in a sanctuary,"[33] is
to place the cross at the extreme edge. Behind it is a cloud which,
like the patches of white in the sketch of the bridge, makes the ravine
the focus of the image.

The theme of the St. Gothard watercolors and oils of 1804 is the
hazard and difficulty of this route for those who travel it. A second,
more or less contemporary, version of the view from the bridge, the
large finished watercolor titled *The Passage of the Mount St. Gothard* (fig.
12),[34] shows two pack animals travelling away from the bridge
toward another cross and figure. Bands of deepening blue intensify
the recession of the ravine away from the bridge and travellers. After
1802, Turner also altered the rock buttress so that it would overhang
the stone causeway, thereby calling even more attention to the way
the track is hewn, just barely, out of the rock of the mountain for
which the pass is named.

Figure 11 J. M. W. Turner. *The Pass at St. Gothard.* Oil.

By 1802, the St. Gothard was famous as the scene of battle in 1799 between the French, who controlled the Swiss Alps, and Austrian and Russian forces who temporarily routed the French in a series of extraordinary encounters. This event and the pass itself were spectacular in ways fortuitously adapted to Turner's sense of spectacle: a

Figure 12 J. M. W. Turner. *Passage of the Mount St. Gothard.* Watercolor.

deep, Romantic chasm, "sublime" by anyone's definition except Kant's, where men and horses and munitions tumbled down or struggled across the Devil's Bridge, which was partly dismantled by the French as they retreated. Resourceful Russian troops threw planks across to continue their pursuit. By one count, 900 men died in a single skirmish. The Russian general Alexander Suvaroff's account of this struggle was soon translated into English. For a new edition of his popular *Travels in Switzerland* published in 1801, William Coxe added extracts from Suvaroff's account to help bring the original 1784 edition up to date by detailing this and other evidence of French tyranny over the Swiss since the French Revolution.[35] According to Coxe, the Devil's Bridge is one of those "sublime scenes of horror, of which those who have not been spectators, can form no perfect idea; they defy the representations of painting or poetry." Of this as the scene of the 1799 skirmish, Suvaroff is supposed to have said, "it is beyond the powers of language to paint this awful spectacle of nature in all its horrors."[36] Turner's representations heighten this sense of sublime spectacle, yet with hardly any notice of the military history identified with the pass after 1799.

In only one view of the St. Gothard pass and route does Turner give a hint of this military history. In an oil exhibited in 1804, two soldiers who may be French walk along the causeway toward the Devil's Bridge. One is armed and looks down into the ravine, either to indicate where many had been lost during battles in the pass or to exclaim about the depth of the chasm, a point always noted in the early guidebooks (fig. 13).[37] Even in this oil, the history that matters is geological, not human. In this view and the one taken from the Devil's Bridge, the smallness of the human figures is made more emphatic by their proximity to the massive verticality of the rock walls of the gorge. The recession Turner achieves through the narrow opening of the pass in either direction presents depth of field as a spatial figure for the geological history of the gorge.

Turner never was, as Gage has put it, "very ambitious in his choice of topographical subjects."[38] In part this lack of ambition in a remarkably ambitious painter can be explained by marketplace economics. He characteristically sketched subjects that could later be worked up in oil or other media on commission. To sketch a scene of no interest to his contemporaries would therefore not have been

Figure 13 J. M. W. Turner. *Devil's Bridge*. Oil.

profitable and Turner both needed and wanted to make a living of his art. Moreover, he had other reasons for sketching famous scenes. Trained in the topographical tradition, he returned to scenes made famous by earlier topographical artists to indicate his indebtedness to this tradition and to challenge it. The first English painter to represent views in the St. Gothard Pass had been William Pars, whose watercolor *The Devil's Bridge in the Canton of Uri* was exhibited at the Royal Academy in 1771, then engraved and published in 1773 and 1783.[39] The differences between Turner and Pars argue two attitudes toward Alpine sublimity, an established aesthetic by the late eighteenth century.

In Pars's flattened, broad-angle view of the bridge, it is an easy, nearly pastoral Alpine crossing for shepherds and animals. In Turner's view, the bridge looks, to use phrases repeated in the nineteenth-century guidebooks, "thrown across" or "cast" over the ravine.[40] Whereas Pars domesticates the St. Gothard and especially his view of the Devil's Bridge, Turner heightens the uncanny, treacherous character other travellers assign to this Alpine passage. The most telling difference between the two artists is their choice of point of view. In Pars's 1771 watercolor, the point of view is anchored on one side of the ravine to suggest where the artist might have stood and where viewers could imagine themselves standing as they look at the scene. Although contemporary accounts of the gorge indicate several possible points of view Turner might have used, the perspective recorded in the 1802 sketches and later oils and watercolors suspends painter and viewer over the ravine to create a sense of vertigo that does not exist in Pars's watercolor. Much later, in an 1832 watercolor of Loch Coriskin designed for Scott's *Lord of the Isles*, Turner chose a high point of view to exaggerate the verticality and height of the mountains flanking the lake. Gage suggests that Turner did so to play out the scalar implications in a description of the same scene by an eminent Scottish geologist John Maccullough in a work published as a series of letters to Scott, a friend since the 1790s. Noting that the "hugest masses of rock" around the lake had looked like "pebbles" from a distance, Maccullough says of the scene at close range: "I felt like an insect amidst the gigantic scenery, and the whole magnitude of the place became at once sensible."[41] As it is in the much earlier St. Gothard images, the exaggerated verticality of Turner's Loch Coriskin is a visual figure for the long geological history of scenes in which geologists and travellers (though perhaps not painters) are tiny and inconsequential.[42]

Turner's *Liber Studiorum*, a series of mezzotint engravings issued between 1808 and 1819 that classifies landscapes by type, includes three scenes along the St. Gothard route. The first, titled *Mont St. Gothard*, depicts the tunnel and pack mules moving toward it along

Figure 14 J. M. W. Turner. *Mont St. Gothard* from *Liber Studiorum*. Mezzotint.

the causeway (fig. 14). The second, published a year later and titled *Little Devil's Bridge*, records a less precipitous section and bridge farther to the north near Altdorf. The third mezzotint, never published and mistakenly titled *Via Mala* for some time, presents the Devil's Bridge itself. Its correct title is *Swiss Bridge, Mount St. Gothard* (fig. 15).[43] Although the titles of plates in the *Liber Studiorum* include local place names, generic designations such as *Bridge and Cows*, and occasional literary or mythological subjects, this is the only title to mix a place name with a generic one. Collected in a book of landscape types, the view of the St. Gothard bridge and pass merits double notice as a particular landscape and as a type.

As a type, the St. Gothard images helped Turner shape other roads through the Alps as well as extensions of the route through the pass, among them a late watercolor which shows the new bridge above the old one (fig. 16). Ruskin suggests that the rock buttress and arch, which appear in the 1802 sketch of the bridge, in the oil of the same view, and in the unpublished *Liber Studiorum* plate, also reappear in the 1843 watercolor *The Pass of Faido*. In this image, says Ruskin, the right bank of the Ticino is transformed into a rock buttress and

Figure 15 *Swiss Bridge, Mount St. Gothard.* Also called *Via Mala.* Etched by Frank Short, after J. M. W. Turner.

arch to signify its resistance to the stream. This and other differences between the actual topography of the Pass of Faido and its "Turnerian" topography are the figurative consequence of its proximity to the St. Gothard Pass, since travellers who follow the Reuss through that pass may then proceed down to the Italian Pass of Faido. For Ruskin at least, it is all one road to someone familiar with Turner's St. Gothard images. Thus the ravine in the background of *The Pass of Faido,* though "not in itself narrow or terrible, is regarded nevertheless with awe, because it is imagined to resemble the gorge that has been traversed above; and, although no very elevated mountains overhang it, the scene is felt to belong to, and to arise in its essential character out of, the strength of those mightier mountains in the unseen north."[44]

Turner himself identifies the Reuss with a scene farther to the southwest in verses from his manuscript poem "Fallacies of Hope," which he included in the catalogue entry for a watercolor titled *The Battle of Fort Rock, Val d'Aouste, 1796,* probably painted between 1805 and 1810 but not exhibited until 1815.[45] The "battle" in question is a

Figure 16 J. M. W. Turner. *Devil's Bridge.* 1841–43 watercolor.

skirmish in another Alpine pass between French troops under General Napoleon Buonaparte and Austrians. Turner's verse compares the conquering French army that "forc'd its way" into Italy to "the wild Reuss" as it tumbles down "the pass," and then concludes: "thus rapine stalked / Triumphant; and plundering hordes, exulting, strew'd / Fair Italy, thy plains with woe."[46] Made a rhetorical and visual figure for a plundering, destructive *force* (north of England dialect for "waterfall" or "cataract"), the Reuss is figuratively displaced from the St. Gothard to the region near Fort Rock. In the actual topography of the Alps, the Reuss flows north into Lake Lucerne. The river that flows south from the St. Gothard is the Ticino, whose headwaters arise only two miles from those of the Reuss, as Coxe's popular guidebook explains.[47] In the verse extract for Turner's 1815 watercolor of a 1796 battle in the Val d'Aousta, the "Reuss" flows south, like the Ticino and like the conquering French army. A parallel figurative logic governs Turner's transposition of the rock buttress and arch on the causeway to the Devil's Bridge to the banks of the Ticino in the 1843 *The Pass of Faido*. Both topographical "mistakes" witness Turner's gradual transformation of the St. Gothard from a single Swiss pass into an allegorical emblem in which recent and ancient stories of Alpine passage and conquest vie for notice.

In *Snowstorm: Hannibal Crossing the Alps*, exhibited in 1812, Turner reinterprets Hannibal's passage over the Alps as something less than heroic spectacle to present an allegorical revision of David's (and Napoleon's) view of history. Making ironic use of Lessing's advice that a painting should depict the moment in an action which implies what comes before and after, Turner abandons the moment chosen by earlier painters (and by Turner himself in a 1798 sketch) – Hannibal's triumphant arrival at the summit of a snowbound Alpine pass.[48] Instead he presents a mêlée of figures in the foreground and a barely discernible Hannibal, well below the summit and about to be engulfed by the approaching storm. The appended verses explain first that the painting depicts Hannibal's hapless rearguard, set upon by local mountain-dwellers, and, second, that this scene is a harbinger of worse to come once Hannibal reaches Capua and, soon after, as he finds himself embroiled in the beginning of the second Punic War. Turner's visual narrative of Hannibal's history as a confusing swirl of storm and action gains its specific rhetorical weight from the appended verses. Read together, verse and image inhabit an unstoppable hermeneutic circle in which "an apparent victory can appear from another point of view to be a defeat," and defeat may yield "a positive end result from the larger perspective of history."[49]

Snowstorm: Hannibal undermines both the "great man" theory of history and the Neoclassical theory of history painting which the story of a triumphant Hannibal would have confirmed. Turner's insistence that the painting had to be hung low during its first exhibition despite its size extends this argument to the viewer. Discovering that the Hanging Committee placed the painting "above the line," over a doorway in the Great Room, he demanded that the painting be hung much lower, persisting for days until the Committee agreed to do so.[50] To understand Hannibal and the history Turner gives him, viewers must recognize that Hannibal's position is roughly their own, not that of an elevated hero whose spectacular struggle awes mere human spectators. Placed squarely in front of the canvas, spectators become participants.

Less directly but in ways that are characteristic of Turner's layering of contemporary and ancient history and mythology, *Snow-storm: Hannibal* also rewrites the heroic scale of Jacques-Louis David's *Napoleon at the St. Bernard Pass*, which Turner had seen in Paris in 1802.[51] In David's painting a triumphant Napoleon rears up on horseback at the barren summit, dominant against a stony Alpine background that looks like the backdrop of a stage set. To establish the military and imperial ancestry he wanted, Napoleon had David inscribe three names in the rock: "Hannibal," "Charlemagne," and "Bonaparte." The theatricality of the painting is unabashedly nineteenth-century: its central figure strikes a pose whose iconography is unmistakable at first glance. David and Napoleon well understood the value of a working relationship between ideology and theater. As a Jacobin revolutionary, David had been responsible for staging revolutionary festivals and other political spectacles. Napoleon took acting (and posing) lessons from the popular actor Talma.[52] In *Snowstorm: Hannibal* Turner replies to David's *Napoleon* with a different, if equally theatrical, counterargument about how to read spectacular figures, great and small.[53]

This counterargument draws on a well-established satiric tradition in which exaggerated size troubles the usual or comfortable definitions of heroic scale. As Swift's Gulliver remarks in the land of the Brobdingnags, "nothing is great or little otherwise than by comparison."[54] In English political prints of the first decade of the nineteenth century, Swiftian parallels specify the English reception of Napoleon, who is caricatured as a Lilliputian, a Brobdingnagian, or even an imperial Gulliver who eyes the throne of the English Brobdingnag. By 1801, satirical prints also echo or invert the mythography of size that imagined Napoleon a colossus, a new Alexander or Hannibal. Rarely content to represent Napoleon in a recognizably human scale, the satirists make him either a colossus or giant, or a monkey, a Corsican fly, a toad, a shuttlecock, or a tiny fairy (fig. 17).[55] In these caricatures gigantism signifies Napoleon's ambition and power; his miniaturization, an oversized ego and (the English hoped) eventual defeat.

Particularly in the 1830s and '40s, Turner's visual rhetoric of distorted scale and perspective assists a densely figured understanding of history and allegory. In the 1829 canvas *Ulysses deriding Polyphemus – Homer's Odyssey*, Turner makes the Homeric legend carry another, more allegorical narrative about the power of artist and image. The implications of earlier experiments with scale emerge

Figure 17 George Cruikshank. "The Corsican Shuttlecock." April 10, 1814.

definitively in this painting, which Ruskin called "the *central picture* in Turner's career."[56] Echoing the scalar extremes of *Snowstorm: Hannibal*, a miniature Ulysses taunts a gigantic Polyphemus who gestures, blind and impotent with rage, from the top of the Cyclops's volcanic island (fig. 18). The scene follows its indicated literary source, the end of book 9 of *The Odyssey*, when Odysseus has for the moment evaded destruction by blinding Polyphemus. As readers of the poem are of course well aware and as the maritime emphasis of Turner's painting may also imply, Poseidon will continue to harry Odysseus as he sails for Ithaca.

The figurative visual logic of *Ulysses* aligns Polyphemus with a group of personifications that includes the horses of the Morning as they lead Apollo's chariot in the lower right and the Nereids or nymphs with stars on their foreheads who swim around Ulysses's ship. Apollo's horses are the most traditional figures in this group, yet even they specify a more contemporary pictorial source – early nineteenth-century drawings of the east pediment of the Parthenon. The nymphs are not in Pope's translation of Homer, to which

Turner's image is faithful in other ways, although they may recall
Hesiod's claim that the Nereids personify "the different qualities and
various effects of water" – always a consideration in Turner's
representations of the sea. A more immediate occasion for Turner's
nymphs is suggested by late eighteenth- and early nineteenth-century
discussions of the effects of phosphorescence on water, which
Erasmus Darwin had compared to "little stars" that look "like bodies
electrified in the dark."[57]

The giant Polyphemus offers an even richer configuration of
classical and scientific sources. Part rock and part "volcanic
vapor,"[58] Polyphemus objectifies Turner's fascination with volcanic
activity, a favorite subject in nineteenth-century theatrical spectacles.
At least two classical arguments direct this representation: the
identification of the other Cyclops with thunder and lightning,
phenomena related since the eighteenth century to volcanic activity;[59] and Odysseus's reiterated complaint that the Cyclops are
primitive, unaware even of basic rules of hospitality to strangers
(especially those who make visits on the sly). In one modern translation Odysseus calls Polyphemus "a monstrous man" and "a monstrous wonder" who has "a lawless mind." In Pope's translation the
parallels to Turner's painting are sharper still. Polyphemus is "a
form enormous ... As some lone mountain's monstrous growth he
stood."[60] Turner half-literalizes Pope's simile by making Polyphemus
look like part of a mountain. The figure of a volcanic or demi-
volcanic Polyphemus may also rework contemporary associations
between volcanic eruption and political turmoil, specifically revolution, and an earlier identification of volcanic activity on the island of
St. Helena with an exiled, but still potentially disruptive, Napoleon.[61]

With a playful sense of the available permutations, Turner
elaborates Polyphemus's identification with natural monstrosity.
Two arched rocks occupy the middle distance to the left of the sun's
(or Apollo's) rays. The one nearer the foreground and fully visible is
gigantic in contrast to the ship sailing close by. A similar pair of
arches appears in a contemporary Turner oil titled generically *Italian
Bay*, where they look like no more, if no less, than a geological
formation often found along rocky coastlines. In Turner's *Ulysses*, the
same formation is made to look like the back view of a giant lower
torso.[62] Bent so that it seems to stagger toward the Cyclops's island,
it looks bizarrely displaced from the shoulders and head of Poly-

Figure 18 J. M. W. Turner. *Ulysses deriding polyphemus — Homer's Odyssey*. 1829.

phemus, which it tries to rejoin even as Ulysses prepares to rejoin his fleet. As lurid as this reading is, it fits the theatrical character of the painting, influenced, Turner insisted, not just by Homer but also by a popular song from a London melodrama.[63] Turner's first biographer Walter Thornbury explained that the arched rock accurately depicts the geology of the island identified with Homer's story of the Cyclops. Thornbury also complained: "Not that I am fond of the arched rock; we have had too much of it in theatrical scenery, and I always associate it with sham smugglers, cocked eyebrows and enormous horse-pistols."[64]

As an exaggerated figure of a giant, a rock, or both, Polyphemus suggests the role of personification in allegorical narratives, where ideas walk like human forms that are larger than life. Spacks cites two telling eighteenth-century examples: Conscience ("Why thus thy swelling for rear to gigantic size?") and Jealousy, who becomes "in size more huge."[65] Made grotesquely large or small, personifications call attention to their figurative enterprise. In *Ulysses*, visual relations between the figure of Polyphemus and images of fire and light suggest that Homer's story of Odysseus and the giant specify the allegorical power of visual figures in Turner's art. Beginning with Apollo's horses as they bring up the sun, and including the starry foreheads of Turner's nymphs, the glow of Polyphemus's cave, and finally the smoky vapor surrounding Polyphemus himself, these figures replace the bloody episode at the center of Homer's narrative: Odysseus's blinding of the Cyclops with a wooden pole heated in the giant's own fire. In *Ulysses* the narrative center is evidently Odysseus making his escape from Polyphemus. The allegorical argument constructed in and through the pictorial elements that comprise this narrative concerns Turner's parallel management of light, fire, and gigantic forms. Together these elements radically assimilate traditional personification to nineteenth-century accounts of colossal forms in nature.

In *Snowstorm: Hannibal*, the early St. Gothard images, and works (early and late) in which natural spectacles such as avalanches or waterfalls dominate the composition, they also dominate tiny human figures. In *Ulysses*, the opposition between gigantic and miniature figures, derived from Polyphemus's angry taunt in Pope's translation, favors Ulysses and the painter who has made Polyphemus the lump of nature he is. After Ulysses shouts his real name to the Cyclops from the ship, the anguished giant remembers the ancient prophecy that has now come to pass: he has been blinded and disfigured by Ulysses. Polyphemus says he did not recognize Ulysses when he arrived because he had been expecting

> some godlike Giant to behold,
> Or lofty Hero, haughty, brave, and bold;
> Not this weak pigmy-wretch, of mean design,
> Who not by strength subdu'd me, but by wine.[66]

Polyphemus is either too dumb or too defensive to notice that he has been subdued by strategem not size, since Ulysses gives his name as "no man" until he is safely away from the Cyclops's island. Still, the giant's taunt about the pigmy size of his adversary is a crucial element in the argument of Turner's full title, *Ulysses deriding Polyphemus – Homer's Odyssey*. In Homer's text the derision is mutual, not one-sided, as the two combatants gesture and shout across the distance between the island summit and the ship below. In Pope's translation the giant keeps yelling "imprecations" long after Ulysses's last, scornful curse. As Pope explains in his note, Ulysses, whose "manly stature" the Phaeacians "wonder'd at," looks dwarflike to Polyphemus because he is a giant. Turner's pictorial management of the moment in the story indicated by his title is subtly weighted toward the "pigmy-wretch." Although Turner includes the giant's upraised arm, he omits the boulder he hurls, which grazes the hero's ship, and his unspecified "imprecations," which are heard by Neptune, Polyphemus's father, who acts immediately, stirring the waves angrily to imperil the Greeks' escape. In Turner's painting the miniature hero has the last or the only words to specify his mastery of a gigantic figure, much as Turner's representation of Polyphemus exerts its own mastery over the conventional terms of personified figures and visual allegory.

One motive for (or evidence of) this disposition to assign more value to small or miniature figures is probably technical. By 1827, Turner had begun to create watercolor designs that would be reproduced as steel-engraved vignette illustrations for Rogers's *Italy*, first published with these engravings in 1830. During the 1830s, Turner created other designs for steel engravings for editions of Walter Scott's prose and poetry, other poems by Rogers, Thomas Campbell, and Thomas Moore's *The Epicurean*.[67] The technology of steel engraving, new at the time, required that preliminary designs be more or less the size of the engraved vignettes, which were usually no more than $3\frac{1}{2}$ inches square and not always perfectly square. As he had for earlier engraving projects, Turner paid close attention to the technical processes this new method of engraving demanded, for at least two reasons. Steel engraving was highly successful for commercial reproduction; moreover, he was always interested in how the resources of one medium might be adapted to another. Beginning around 1800, he had experimented with adapting water-color techniques to the requirements of oil and mezzotint.[68] In the 1830s, the technical requirements of steel engraving prompted him to investigate the resources of a small-scale composition destined to be an end- or tail-piece on a page of printed text. This new pictorial context required scaled-down images; this format in turn fostered an unusual emblematic relation betweenTurner's image and the printed page.

Turner's extensive work in this new format during the 1830s may also challenge one side in the earlier English debate about the value of miniature painting, a debate that began in 1805 with Martin Shee's verse attack on bad painters of miniatures.[69] Shee soon found himself in the middle of a minor pamphlet war when the miniaturist W. H. Watts responded with a rehearsal of the late misfortunes of miniature painters at the Royal Academy. Whatever Turner's view of this complaint about the Academy (at the time he was probably not sympathetic to the miniaturist case), by the early 1830s he had modified his earlier tendency to ally great size with a parallel great-ness in subject by presenting the figure of Ulysses as victorious and small. In the 1812 *Snowstorm: Hannibal,* the equally small figure of Hannibal had been by contrast heading for disaster and was not clearly victorious even in the Alps. By the late 1820s, Turner was committed to producing small designs for images and subjects he had earlier handled on much larger canvases.

The consequences of these adaptations for the representation of history are suggested by the first set of vignettes for which he prepared watercolor designs, the vignettes for Rogers's *Italy.* Two vignettes for Rogers's poem extend the historicized image of Alpine passage in Turner's *Snowstorm: Hannibal.* The first represents Napo-leon at the foot of the Alps during the battle of Marengo and the second, Hannibal in the Alps. In both Turner is attentive to the thematic implications of representing great figures and scenes in little. The result is not Virgilian pastoral but an intriguing counter-point between the vignette, the surrounding white space, and

Rogers's text. Although the basic compositional format of Turner's vignettes is rectilinear and emphasizes horizontals and verticals, its box-like structure is challenged by diagonal contrasts. The "almost geometric logic" supplied by this opposition between rectilinear and diagonal forces is in part what makes Turner's vignettes for Rogers's poem so compelling as miniature compositions. Presented in this way, they invoke the nineteenth-century cult of the miniature. They also recall what Holcomb calls "a correspondence between macrocosm and a microcosmic compass containing the relationships of [that] larger structure" – the cosmological relation on which traditional allegory had depended. De Luca's notice of the power of Blake's "radically condensed vignettes," or Coleridge's admiration for the "allegorical miniatures" that stud Milton's prose might be extended to Turner's vignettes, in large measure because they invite comparison with the figurative and visual "shorthand" that traditional emblems use to convey much in little.[70]

In Rogers's *Italy*, Turner's vignettes extend the layering of history and texts that goes back to *Liber Studiorum* and earlier images. His visual shorthand in these vignettes recalls Byron's vision of history in *Childe Harold's Pilgrimage*, whose narrator is frequently absorbed by parallels between the recent and the classical past. In canto 3 of *Childe Harold*, he compares the carnage at Waterloo with that at Cannae, the Apulian scene of Hannibal's victory over the Romans in 216 BC.[71] Although Rogers layers history in similar ways, he does not reproduce the irony of this typically Byronic example, which dryly and bitterly notes that Napoleon's defeat involves as much carnage as did Hannibal's victory over the Romans (a victory that did not however lead to the capture of Rome). Rogers prefers to leave the unsettling afflatus of such comparisons unspecified.

Turner's vignettes on the Alpine passages of Napoleon and Hannibal offer a Byronic (or Turneresque) commentary that implies what Rogers does not say. The Napoleon vignette appears at the end of a chapter titled "The Descent," which narrates Napoleon's descent of the Great St. Bernard Pass on his way to Marengo. As other scholars have noted, Turner's vignette is busy with visual echoes of David's *Napoleon at the St. Bernard Pass*. The most obvious of them is Napoleon's pose, which is identical. Turner's inscriptions "Marengo" (on a fallen stone marker in the foreground) and "Lodi" (beside the marker) substitute early victories (and probably imply by contrast Waterloo as the scene of Napoleon's final defeat) for the

Figure 19 J. M. W. Turner. *Marengo*. Vignette. Samuel Rogers, *Italy, a Poem*.
London, 1838.

military and imperial associations indicated by David's inscriptions
(fig. 19). The heroic iconography of David's painting is further
undermined by the scale of the vignette. Turner's earlier painting of
this image, *Snowstorm: Hannibal*, is a large canvas, approximately 5 ft
by $7\frac{1}{2}$ ft, as is David's, which measures about 6 by 7 ft. The Hannibal
and Napoleon vignettes for Rogers's *Italy* each measure $3\frac{1}{2}$ by $2\frac{3}{4}$
inches. My point is not simply that the figure of Napoleon has shrunk
in the vignette, which is certainly the case, but that this figure is small
even within the usual scale of a miniature composition. The vignette
quite literally puts Napoleon in perspective by situating him in a
recessional plane that includes the stonemarker in front of him, the
scene of battle behind him, and behind these the Alps, which further
define the depth of field. Sheila Smith has suggested that in this
context Napoleon's theatrical pose takes on a different value. Here
David's figure of a triumphant Napoleon looks like someone "indifferent to the sufferings" of the troops fighting behind him,
sufferings emphasized by Rogers's text.[72]

The Hannibal vignette, which appears at the beginning of a later
chapter titled "The Alps," is intricately if surreptitiously related to
the image of Napoleon at Marengo. The narrative project of
Rogers's poem – to describe a tour of Italy via Switzerland – seems

thrown off track by this chapter, which has Rogers crossing the Alps again, having already done so via the St. Bernard Pass. Holcomb has suggested that in this later chapter Rogers describes the Simplon Pass, which he crossed during the 1820–21 tour on which the poem is based.[73] Yet he mentions just two passes by name in the chapter, the Simplon and the Splügen, then settles on a third. Rogers's model for such inclusiveness may be, once again, canto 3 of *Childe Harold*.

In a passage written in 1816, when Byron was, thanks to the Shelleys, heavily dosed with Wordsworthian and French Alpine sublimity, the narrator proclaims: "High mountains are a feeling."[74] As Rogers does in the beginning of his chapter on "The Alps," Byron's narrator records a pleasure in the Alps as an aggregate, not as individual scenes or passes. A similarly generic pattern is at work in Rogers's text until he echoes the epithet Byron also uses for Hannibal – "the Carthaginian on his march to Rome" via the Alps.[75] At this point Rogers's generic image of Alpine passage gives way to a multiple image of famous Alpine travellers over the St. Bernard Pass, indirectly named when Rogers says that three well-known travellers crossed the Alps "over the Drance," a river whose headwaters are located near the Great St. Bernard Pass. The travellers are Hannibal, Charlemagne, and one hapless "Abbé de St. Maurice," who fell into the Drance "with carriage, horse, cook and driver."[76] Although at least one late eighteenth-century writer argued that Hannibal had crossed the Alps over the St. Bernard Pass, other passes were more usual candidates, among them the Val d'Aousta (the choice indicated by verses appended to Turner's *Snowstorm: Hannibal*) and Mt. Cenis. Charlemagne had in fact crossed the Alps over Mt. Cenis, not the St. Bernard Pass, on his way to conquer the Lombards in 773.[77] The famous traveller excluded from Rogers's list is of course Napoleon.

Turner replies to this obvious suppression (Rogers is not likely to have been unaware of where the Drance flows or where Napoleon had crossed the Alps in 1800) by inserting his own iconography of Alpine passage. The watercolor design and the vignette both feature the St. Gothard bridge and pass view of the unpublished *Liber Studiorum* plate (fig. 20). By 1830, Turner had travelled through all the Alpine passes Rogers mentions at least once and so would have recognized that travelling "over the Drance" meant crossing the Alps at the Great St. Bernard Pass. Nor would Turner have missed Rogers's omission of Napoleon from his list of travellers in this pass.

Figure 20 J. M. W. Turner. *Hannibal.* Vignette. Samuel Rogers, *Italy, a Poem.*
London, 1838.

Turner's parallel omission and substitution tell their own story. To
illustrate the chapter on the St. Bernard Pass, he chose not the scene
of Napoleon's descent but the battlefield at Marengo, with ironic
adjustments. To illustrate the chapter on "The Alps," Turner again
chose not to use the topography of the St. Bernard. He had even
stronger visual reasons for not choosing the Simplon. Between 1801
and 1806 Napoleon had transformed the Simplon from a narrow
mountain track like the St. Gothard into the first carriage road over
the Alps. To do this, his corps of engineers built 611 bridges, one of
which Turner sketches in a late watercolor of the Simplon route.[78]

As the St. Bernard and the Simplon passes could not, the St.
Gothard could represent the hazards of Alpine passage as Hannibal
might have experienced them, before Napoleon and other travellers
had complicated the figure of Hannibal with other layers of history
and a triple-exposed image of imperial ambition on the march
through the Alps. Turner would have been directed toward the St.

Gothard imagery by Rogers's text, which mentions the Devil's Bridge in a note for the preceding chapter, and by accounts of the pass Hannibal had used. In the chapter titled "Marguerite de Tours," Rogers describes a place "where the rock / Is riven asunder, and the Evil One / Has bridged the gulf, a wondrous monument / Built in one night." In the note to these lines, he adds: "Almost every mountain of any rank or condition has such a bridge. The most celebrated in this country is on the Swiss side of St. Gothard."[79]

At least one eighteenth-century account (as well as Livy and Polybius, whose narratives Turner knew well) characterize Hannibal's Alpine passage in these terms:

After they had for some days marched through narrow, steep, and slippery ways, they came at last to a place which neither elephants, horses, nor men, could pass. The way which lay between two precipices was exceeding narrow; and the declivity, which was very steep, had become more dangerous by the falling away of the earth. Here the guides stopped; and the whole army being terrified, Hannibal proposed at first to march round about, and attempt some other way: but all places round him being covered with snow, he found himself reduced to the necessity of cutting a way into the rock itself.[80]

The topographical similarities between Hannibal's passage and the St. Gothard Pass are made emphatic by the suggestion that modern travellers, like Hannibal, depended on a way cut through rock to get across. In the final design for the Hannibal vignette, Turner makes the image as confused in its own way as Hannibal's Alpine passage in *Snowstorm: Hannibal*. In the center foreground of the vignette for Rogers's *Italy*, a black African archer seems to signal a someone (probably Hannibal) who is seated on an elephant. A battle scene occupies the left foreground and a ribbon of figures on both sides (harder to spot in the engraved vignette) proceeds toward (or from) the bridge and pass. Like the 1812 oil, this vignette presents a scene whose narrative sequence is hard to specify. Are the figures in the lower left dead opponents to Hannibal's army (some are clearly dead or dying) or are they a rear or advance guard for Hannibal? In which direction are the processions of figures in the pass travelling? These questions indicate the uncertainties that mark Turner's representation of the less qualified view of Hannibal in Rogers's poem.

Turner's use of the St. Gothard as a type of Alpine passage suggests how a particular landscape and history might come to supervise an allegorical idea. By extending the range of Hannibal's struggle in the Alps to imply that all who use a passage like this one confront similar difficulties, Turner indicates a larger narrative vision of Alpine passage whose allegorical impulse gestures away from the heroic scale and perspective of traditional history painting. For, to read these vignettes, we must read them with (and sometimes against) the text they illustrate and the generic and historical energies they invoke.

In other vignettes of the 1830s designed for Scott's *Life of Napoleon*, Turner's presentation of Napoleon as a miniature figure explores a middle ground between satire and a version of the Tory Scott's sympathy for the exiled emperor. In part, this miniaturization probably echoes the same motif in the earlier political prints. It may also challenge B. R. Haydon's portraits of a colossal Napoleon in exile on St. Helena. Over a few years, beginning in the late 1820s, Haydon painted between twenty-five and forty versions of this subject.[81] In Turner's vignette of Napoleon at Fontainebleau in 1814, as he directs envoys to convey his abdication to Paris, the scale of the image makes it impossible to identify Napoleon, as Finley notes, by "physiognomy" or "dress." The theatrical positioning of an isolated figure at the head of the steps, however, virtually assures that he is Napoleon.[82] In the vignette of Napoleon on the British ship *Bellerophon*, after his surrender in July 1815 to its captain, he is similarly isolated on the deck of the ship, in sharp contrast to the tourist-like bustle of boats whose occupants row out to make a spectacle out of him. The miniaturization of the political prints during the years of Napoleon's rise and fall is repeated without a satiric edge in these vignettes. But in the 1842 *War. The Exile and the Rock Limpet*, gigantism and miniaturization return in a Napoleonic figure that reexamines the implications of scale and perspective in earlier political prints, *Ulysses*, and the vignettes of the 1830s.

War was first exhibited at the Royal Academy beside *Peace – Burial at Sea*, which commemorates Turner's friend and rival painter, Sir David Wilkie, who died in 1841 during a return voyage from the Middle East. Wilkie was buried at sea off the Gibraltar coast. The subject of *War* is Napoleon, whose ashes were brought back from St. Helena in 1840 for state burial in Les Invalides. Like *Peace* and a number of major oils Turner painted during this decade, *War* is a smaller canvas ($31\frac{1}{4}$ inches square) (fig. 21). Like its pendant, *War* was first exhibited in an octagonal frame.[83] As a pair, *War* and *Peace* contrast the lonely burial of Wilkie with that of Napoleon, the man

Figure 21 J. M. W. Turner. *War. The Exile and the Rock Limpet.* 1842.

of war whose posthumous reputation eventually made a public state burial politically expedient. Since the mid nineteenth century, Turner's *Peace* has fared better than his *War* (so little does art imitate life). Whereas earlier critics suggested that the ship in *Peace* "resemble[d] a burnt and blackened fish kettle" and insisted that both paintings would look "as well upside down," modern critics single *Peace* out for special praise and *War* for still more blame. Martin Butlin and John Rothenstein remark: "unfortunately he chose to pair this masterpiece [*Peace*] with *War: The Exile and the Rock Limpet* in which the mastery of his handling of the setting is nullified by the grotesque superimposed figure of Napoleon."[84]

In more extended fashion, the early reviewers of Turner's *War* urge much the same point. The critic for the *Literary Gazette* argued that "the continuous reflection" of Napoleon's black boots "in the water give[s] him the appearance of being erected upon two long back stilts, and the whole thing is . . . truly ridiculous." The critic for *The Times* called the picture "an elongated Napoleon . . . running to see in a redhot atmosphere of brimstone and brickdust'; and the critic for the *Athenaeum* charged that Turner's *War* is

> yet odder than his *Peace*. In the midst of a canvas with every shade of rose colour, crimson, vermillion, and orange, is set up a *thing* – man it assuredly is not – . . . an effigy of Napoleon rolled out to colossal height . . . Below the feet of the modern Prometheus lies something about the size of his cocked-hat, called in the Catalogue "a rock limpet."[85]

At the end of *Modern Painters* and despite his repeated defense of Turner's *War* in earlier volumes, Ruskin admits in a note that he had been unable to guess what the painting meant and gave up after Turner spent fifteen minutes "giving me hint after hint in a rough way."[86]

Like other late paintings that one exasperated nineteenth-century reviewer dismissed as "painted riddles," Turner's *War* is puzzling because its title invites a mimetic reading which the absurdities of scale within the painting frustrate. One critic has suggested that the key to the meaning of *War* might be Turner's antagonistic relations with the most vocal of his contemporary reviewers.[87] Although this is certainly possible, his attention to scale in *War* reiterates earlier arguments about heroism and scale, most notably in *Snowstorm: Hannibal crossing the Alps* and *Ulysses deriding Polyphemus*. *War* also echoes the iconography of the earlier political satires. Thus the reflection of Napoleon's boots in the water, which one reviewer complained made him look as though he were standing on stilts, recalls an 1814 satiric print in which a still gigantic Napoleon teeters on breaking stilts (fig. 22).

Precisely because this stilt-like reflection connects Napoleon to the rock limpet in the unrealist register of the painting, it suggests that both figures constitute Napoleon's double image, colossal before his final exile and microscopic since. The verse appended to the painting in the catalogue speaks to the same point with an intriguing mixture of obviousness and indirection. Extracted from the manuscript poem "Fallacies of Hope," the lines imagine Napoleon's address to the rock limpet:

Figure 22 Anon. "Du Haut en Bas ou les Causes et les Effets." April 1814.

Ah! thy tent-formed shell is like
A soldier's nightly bivouac, alone
Amidst a sea of blood –
– But you can join your comrades.[88]

The apparent relation urged by Turner's simile (that of a limpet's shell to a soldier's tent) points to the unspoken, visual analogy between the two figures: the rock limpet is to Napoleon what his present existence is to his past military and imperial self. If *War* is a speaking picture, as this relation between its visual and verbal parts implies, it defies what Fineman calls the "specular mimetics" of the sister arts.[89] For if we try to read the painting as a mirror or reflection of the reality it names, its grotesque deformations of realistic scale make us think, as its early reviewers mostly believed, that Turner's *War* presents a funhouse of distorted representations of Napoleon, the rock limpet, and perhaps a viewing public whose credulity must be stretched to accommodate what it sees.

In part these distortions echo those used to depict Napoleon in earlier political prints, especially after his final exile, when he is frequently represented as simultaneously gigantic and miniature. In George Cruikshank's *Boney's Meditations, or the Devil addressing the Sun*, Napoleon is colossal and Satanic (fig. 23). In another Cruikshank

Figure 23 George Cruikshank. *Boney's Meditations on the Island of St. Helena or The Devil Addressing the Sun.*

caricature published in December, 1815, and titled *State of Politicks at the close of the year 1815*, the Allies, including a plump Prince Regent, support the Bourbon French king in the foreground, while a small figure of Napoleon appears in the background, where he is literally and figuratively less important than the figure in the foreground. The satiric point of this print is less Napoleon's frustrated ambition than the motley crew of two-faced French courtiers, Allies, and Catholic supporters of an obese Louis XVIII. Even this notice of Napoleon's relative unimportance at the end of 1815 insists that he is larger than life, dwarfing St. Helena in a distant, miniaturized version of his former stature as the Colossus of Europe. Cruikshank gives the same point another, more dismissive twist in *Royal Christmas Boxes and New Year's Gifts*, published two weeks later. Here Napoleon is presented as a colossus who stands on St. Helena, but the entire image is a miniature designed to fit on top of, or in, royal gift boxes. Like other contemporary caricatures that represent Napoleon as a caged animal, this print recalls Gulliver's captivity among the Brobding-nags, and Napoleon's among nearby sentries on St. Helena. Kept as a kind of British toy or pet, Napoleon is, like Gulliver, a spectacle for royal delectation.[90]

These caricatures of the exiled Napoleon, which intensify the theme of exaggerated scale found in earlier prints, can of course be read two ways. In part exaggeration works against Napoleon. Colossal though he was once, he is now little more than a toy for the triumphant Allies. A parallel exaggeration in caricatures of his English adversaries, including a gargantuan John Bull and Prince Regent, suggests a more sympathetic view in Turner's vignettes for Scott's *Life of Napoleon* and the verses appended to the 1842 *War*.[91]

In a larger sense implied by the history of Napoleonic caricature, *War* specifies the figurative value of its flagrantly unreal distortions of normal size and perspective. Such exaggerations turn visual and verbal discourse away from the emergent norms of nineteenth-century realism to insist on an allegorical reading of Napoleon's foreshortened place in history. In Turner's art more generally, allegory supervises a complex rhetorical and visual enterprise that is often inseparable from the representation of history as landscape. Because they specify a hermeneutic logic at odds with realist or naturalist style, gigantism, miniaturization, and related deformations of realist perspective supply the key terms in Turner's allegorical practice. This is the figural lesson of Alice's experiences with the mushroom in Lewis Carroll's tale. Whether too great or too small, neither her body nor her realist logic fit Wonderland. Here and in Turner's art, the figural argument of both extremes is that neither is "better" in the sense of being true to realist scale. As Turner experiments with different formats and smaller compositions during the 1830s and 1840s, a similar logic emerges from his use of smaller or near-miniature formats for subjects earlier represented in large, "heroic" six-foot canvases. These new formats and shapes (circle, octagon, and square) recall and adapt the spatial geography of traditional emblems and impresas. In the telling reflex of this visual allusion, the older Turner offers new allegoric shapes that work against the emerging norms of realist art.

CHAPTER 8

Allegory and Victorian realism

The form of wood, for instance, is altered if a table is made out of it. Nevertheless the table continues to be wood, an ordinary, sensuous thing. But as soon as it makes its entrance as a commodity, it changes into a thing which transcends sensuousness. It not only stands with its feet on the ground, but, in relation to all commodities, it stands on its head, and evolves out of its wooden head grotesque ideas, far stranger than if it were to begin dancing of its own free will.

Marx, *Capital* 1:163–64[1]

Even the most valiant attempt at lively figuration, one that might dazzle the rhetorically untutored, can thus be expected to reveal the deathly cogs of a tropological automaton.

Gary Stonum, "Surviving Figures" 207

Marx's figure of a table that stands simultaneously on its feet and on a "wooden head" dramatizes the strangeness of allegory's interventions in Victorian literary culture. The table-become-commodity reproduces what commodification does to things: it turns them over and upside down, thereby standing value on its head by substituting a "fantastic form" ("*phantasmagorische Form*") (*Capital* 1:165) for real wood and real labor. It also turns them into grotesquely unreal things, like Marx's figure.[2] To represent the hidden, mystified relation between the commodity form and falsifying abstractions like "Profit," Marx invents allegorical persons and body parts that walk, talk, or come up with ideas that are crazily bereft of good sense.

Stonum's remark about lively figures that conceal their rhetorical mechanism provides another point of entry into Marx's figure and Victorian allegory. In a culture that was fascinated with automatons and especially with mechanized puppet shows that were amazingly lifelike, the image of a wooden table that metamorphoses into, at the very least, a puppet's wooden head reproduces the voyeuristic world of the Victorian grotesque, where exaggerations and odd body parts are the "norm," and where human spectators admire the motorized puppets that are their bizarre competitors – a flautist who plays better than a human musician or a violinist whose technical speed surpasses its human counterpart. As Marx makes clear, such figures are highly self-conscious, staged impersonations: the table steps forth or presents itself ("*auftritt*") as though making a dramatic entrance ("*Der Auftritt*"). Like a stage puppet, its "wooden head" reenacts the absurd "metaphysical subtleties and theological niceties" that transform a table made of wood into an artificial, commodified entity with a value to match (*Capital* 1:163). Such figures bend toward allegory because they are seemingly animated representations of abstract ideas.

As Victorian writers became more skeptical of the positivist faith that fueled liberal humanist hopes for the things of this world, realism's presentation of particulars and individuals began to look less convinced about its representational status.[3] Enter allegory, either as a demonic engine that exaggerates the picture of realism run aground in its own life-like machinery, or as an ideal principle that exceeds the realist charter. My argument in this chapter thus concerns what might be called the peripheral vision of Victorian realist culture – that edge where realist values become blurred and allegory's raids on the verisimilar occur.

Because allegory is strongly identified with visual images in early modern and modern culture, it can mimic or colonize realist details. In Dickens's fiction, mantra-like repetitions of realist details nudge a Tom All-Alone or the legal world of Chancery toward abstracted, generalized figures. At the limit of Victorian realism and a rationalist faith in human and social progress are monsters like "Chancery," grotesque forms whose abstractive powers exceed or control real particulars. Indeed, Levine's account of Thackeray's fictional realism suggests that its task is in part to keep the grotesque and violent exaggeration of allegory at bay: "the seductive world of things (which the Thackerayan narrator cozily indulges) disguises a latent hostility to human ideals; the digressive plots deflate all energies directed toward the extreme, the violent, or the ideal yet imply the impossibility of narrative control."[4]

To illustrate what goes on at peripheries where Victorian realism gives way, I focus on two writers whose quite different realist commitments are laced with an attraction to figured abstractions that is at least as strong as Marx's antipathy toward anything that smacks of metaphysics or theology. The first is Robert Browning, whose grotesque figures persistently mark the difficulty of getting from particulars to ideas. Ruskin intuitively recognizes this problem when he compares getting around one of Browning's poems to leaping across crevasses.[5] The second is George Eliot, whose commitment to realism and liberal humanist faith in historical progress gradually becomes more conditional and more given over to the effort to embody and personify abstractions. Eliot's recognition of this difficulty is more sustained than Browning's and more deeply philosophical. On both counts, her last novel *Daniel Deronda* puts into play very different and explicitly competitive allegorical figures as it moves between two plots, one that is or seems resolutely attentive to a darkly realist English comedy of manners and a second that is Jewish, idealist, and above all subversive of the historical relation between cause and effect that is one linchpin of realism.

Browning's contemporary reviewers quickly identified those features of his poetic style that have alienated readers ever since – difficult or murky syntax, obscurity, and the grotesque. Late in his career, long after he claimed to have given up writing poems like the notoriously obscure *Sordello*, which Jane Carlyle says she read without being able to make out whether Sordello was "a man, a city, or a book," difficulty remained the hallmark of that style. To catalogue Browning's poetic faults, his contemporaries reinvent the old rhetorical link between allegory and *difficultas*, the figure that authorizes the use of a difficult medium or style to convey complex truths. Tennyson privately complained, "I verily believe his school of poetry to be the most grotesque conceivable. With the exception of the *Blot on the Scutcheon*, through which you may possibly grope your way without the aid of an Ariadne, the rest appear to me to be Chinese puzzles, trackless labyrinths, unapproachable nebulosities." One reviewer asked rhetorically, "Who will not grieve over energy wasted and power misspent, – over fancies chaste and noble, so overhung by the 'seven veils' of obscurity?" In 1856, still relatively early in Browning's long career, another reviewer offered this damning list of poetic faults: "a *penchant* for elliptical diction, interjectional dark sayings, *multum in parvo* (and, sometimes, seemingly *minimum in multo*), 'deliverances,' flighty fancies, unkempt similitudes, quaintest conceits, slipshod familiarities, and grotesque exaggerations" – all "unhealthily on the increase."[6]

Though his contemporaries hardly praised him for it, they recognized that Browning's figures and syntax are intriguingly (or idiotically) adhesive to the visual or material vehicle for a given allegorical tenor – a practice that runs sharply against the grain of Coleridge's insistence that Milton's Sin and Death are sublime because so *in*distinct. If this assertion does an end run around eighteenth-century objections that Milton's figures are insubstantial *and* material allegorical agents, Browning's poetic experiments in grotesquerie force allegory to a material limit. Although Browning later attributed the difficulty of *Sordello* to youthful ineptitude, the internal or figural complexities of *The Ring and the Book* and other poems he published after his marriage, particularly after Elizabeth Barrett's death and suggest that he was to the end unrepentant.

At its rhetorical best, Browning's difficulty posits truth as something longed-for, half-postulated, but perennially not found in the "shows o' the world."[7] Using multiple sources, informants and narrators, he reasserts the ancient rhetorical link between allegory and irony as figures whose meaning is extended as it is played through different narrative registers. His poetic lingering over visual details, especially grotesque ones, grants them emblematic status in ways that make nineteenth-century realism turn round and return as a figure whose implied ground is elsewhere – abstract and general more than concrete and individual. Browning's early engagement with Shelley – as much for the idealist, allegorical impulse of his poetics as for his subjective or quintessentially Romantic point of view – never really dissipates, despite the disillusion that followed the publication of his 1852 *Essay on Shelley*.[8] By insisting that the status of allegory and transmission has to do with materiality and psychological realism as well as realistic detail, Browning makes the transgressive relation between allegory, figure, and reality tell and retell the role of abstraction and materiality in his poetics.

Browning's poems of the 1860s and '70s emphasize realistic details so grimy, so scandalous, and so grotesque that they leave little room for allegorical idealism. At the expense of a hard-won popularity, the older Browning presses material vehicles so close to their figural tenors that they risk being absorbed or debased by the material grotesque. Three poems in the 1864 volume *Dramatis Personae* – *A Death in the Desert, Caliban upon Setebos,* and *Mr. Sludge, the "Medium"* – variously depict the work performed by monstrosity, transmission, self-deception, rhetoric, and the idea of history in the poems of this decade and the next. *A Death in the Desert* recapitulates the skepticism of the German "higher critics" of the Bible who doubted the divinity of Christ and John's gospel.[9] Like Coleridge, some higher critics attempt to save biblical revelation from the ravages of their own realist and historical expectations by appealing to another order of truth. To explain how ancient texts and later exegetes convey the "other speech" of Christian revelation, they imagined revelation as a cumulative and versional text whose end is Revelations. *A Death in the Desert* dramatizes the theological instability that marks this meta-allegorical hermeneutics. *The Ring and the Book* and poems published after 1864 extend this argument to a more secular hermeneutics of realism and historiography.

A Death in the Desert dramatizes the alienation and loss that the higher critics often experienced when they recognized the intractable distance between themselves and the life of Christ, a gap in time and culture imperfectly managed by the gospels themselves as composite records with complex histories of transmission. As he lies dying, John tries to answer those who challenge the truth of his gospel. First he says he was an eye witness to the events his gospel narrates, the touchstone of reliability according to the higher critics and Coleridge. But as his own words bear witness and as others tell him, his transmission may be faulty, incomplete, misremembered – lies in deed if not intention.

The poem begins and ends with a sharply textual sense of how much John's last words are the mediated outcome of numerous interlocutors and written transmissions. The "outside" narrator identifies the manuscript text of the story as belonging to Pamphylax of Antioch, whose description of the parchment immediately follows:

> a parchment, of my rolls the fifth,
> hath three skins, glued together, is all Greek
> And goeth from *Epsilon* down to *Mu*:
> Lies second in the surnamed Chosen Chest,
> Stained and conserved with juice of terebinth,
> Covered with cloth of hair, and lettered *Xi*,
> From Xanthus, my wife's uncle, now at peace:
> *Mu* and *Epsilon* stand for my own name. (2–9, *Browning* 1:787)

This modulation from editorial and archeological evidence to self-inscription forecasts the poem's emphasis on the humanity – flawed yet persistent, with personal interests served by the telling – of those disciples whose witness to Christ's life and death are recorded in the gospels and challenged by the higher critics. Pamphylax is in fact unclear about the source of his written record. Having said that Xanthus gave him the manuscript, he later explains that the Xanthus who attends to the dying John is "the Xanthus that escaped to Rome. / Was burned, and could not write the chronicle" (56–57, *Browning* 1:789). We are left to sort out who wrote it, and whether there were two men named Xanthus.[10]

At the end of the poem, an unidentified "one" meets Cerinthus's silence about the parchment manuscript he has read with a counter-affirmation of Christ's humanity and divinity. Without this affirmation, the "one" asserts, humankind is "lost." The outside narrator laconically adds, "But 'twas Cerinthus that is lost." The revelatory bias of Browning's conclusion places the argument of the poem in a middle space between higher critical invectives against the person and authority of John and the divinity of Christ, and a naive faith in the authority of biblical texts and their transmission. In the poem that space is defined by John, who describes warrants available for the truth of the gospels at various stages in their transmission.

Although he offers himself as the eyewitness whose reliability his disciples count on, John is very old and admits his confusion of past and present:

> So is myself withdrawn into my depths,
> The soul retreated from the perished brain
> Whence it was wont to feel and use the world
> Through these dull members, done with long ago.
> Yet I myself remain; I feel myself:
> And there is nothing lost.   (76–81, *Browning* 1:789)

Despite this last assertion, we may well suspect that John's testimony is enfeebled by its distance from the events he recalls. Moreover, his admission (not indicated in his gospel) that he fled Christ at the time of his arrest in Gethsemane (310, *Browning* 1:795) contradicts his claim to have witnessed all the events he thereafter describes for those who had not known Christ:

> I went, for many years, about the world,
> Saying, "It was so; so I heard and saw,"
> Speaking as the case asked: and men believed.
>   (136–38, *Browning* 1:791)

A critical voice in the poem objects that others cannot be expected to believe if John has the facts wrong (513–30, *Browning* 1:800). Readers of John's gospel and the Book of Revelation never get what this interlocutor seeks: plain facts and a text free of figure, of parable, of allegorical presence. What they get instead is a flawed eyewitness whose own actions do not measure up to the spiritual truths he offers.

Although *A Death in the Desert* exposes the flaws that human speech always harbors, the poem does not fully register the pessimism and betrayal that marks Renan's *Life of Jesus* and similar doubts about Christ's existence and divinity.[11] Browning's sublunary argument suggests instead a view of spirit, revelation, and human knowing that repeatedly invokes the instabilities of flesh as an intermittent guide to the spiritual meaning that allegorical figures convey.

Like the Quarles's emblem on which it is based,[12] the "optic glass" vision John claims to have is tilted toward the clarity of figural distance, which permits the telescoping of events into identifiable patterns, a process of abstraction whose outcome is easier to manage than the confused mass of evidence seen in close-up:

> Look through his tube, at distance now [objects] lay,
> Become succinct, distinct, so small, so clear!
> Just thus, ye needs must apprehend what truth
> I see, reduced to plain historic fact,
> Diminished into clearness, proved a point
> And far away: ye would withdraw your sense
> From out eternity, strain it upon time,
> Then stand before that fact, that Life and Death,
> Stay there at gaze, till it dispart, dispread,
> As though a star should open out, all sides,
> Grow the world on you, as it is my world.
>
> (233–43, *Browning* 1:793)

The Blakean expansion and contraction of this image argues that being able to identify a larger, abstract pattern prompted by the fact of Christ's life and death is itself assurance, the guide to belief in the love that remains for John the truth of that life as both abstraction and lived particular.

In later poems Browning conveys a more skeptical understanding of how abstraction and particulars meet in poetic figures. This allegorical disposition is harder won and more permeable to facts than John's, along lines suggested by the Romantic reinvention of traditional figures, but more resolutely interested in the textual friction between literal vehicles and figural meaning. Consider

Caliban, whose rhetoric and theology remain as earth-bound as the dying John's are not. As the self-styled "rank tongue" that "blossom[s] into speech" (23, *Browning* 1:805), Caliban talks with a mind and eye for detail and sense largely absent from John's narrative. Deliberately monstrous and grotesque in speech and action, Caliban displays the poetic energy Browning gains in this and later poems from the uneven, alienating style and rhythm Elizabeth Barrett had once argued he ought to avoid because it put readers off.

As a comic reinvention of the newly minted deism of the Bridgewater tracts,[13] Caliban's deism summarizes what remains of theology without revelation and thus without apparent inclination toward allegorical speech. Thus his speech typically works figures from a material base to construct his natural theology. Even so, Caliban produces a rhetoric capable of intriguing figural resonances. To account for the logic of divine creation (and the inherent bad temper and spite of his God), Caliban compares God ill at ease with his place "i' the cold o' the moon" to an icy fish's longing for some other element (31–43, *Browning* 1:805–6). The epistemological tact of the speech mirrors the limits it records: Caliban says "the other kind of water" instead of "air" to maintain the argument that air is alien, unknown to the fish. Alliteration and contraction here create an aural texture that imitates the material basis of the figure. Like the icy fish, what is alien or "other speech" to Caliban has no proper name. The Quiet mentioned as a dimly perceived alternative to Prospero remains outside the aural and material specificities of Caliban's internal dialogue.

Mr. Sludge, "the Medium" dramatizes the potential fraudulence of allegorical speech, the proximity of fiction to lying, and, to put it neutrally, problems inherent in the transmission of spiritual truths into speech as well as print. Although he is a spiritual charlatan modelled on those whom Browning learned to despise over a long, unwilling acquaintance with mediums and mesmerism,[14] Sludge's self-comparisons with "your literary man" – writers of novels and poems – and his claim to provide supernatural accounts on a par with the Bible and history expose the unbound and fraying edge between fact and fraud in the secular as well as religious culture of the later nineteenth century. As Armstrong and David Goslee have argued, this unsavory speaker rehearses key issues in Browning's poetry: the nature of truth, personal revelation, and art.[15] Put baldly, Sludge is a deliberately grotesque medium, one who inevitably contaminates his Browningesque message about spiritual truth and its opposites.

If the poem begins with open season on its protagonist, the duplicity and crassness of his rich American accuser and auditor complicate the satirical target, as does Sludge's account of how the gullibility of an idle leisure class prompted him to imagine himself a medium who takes the main chance in the midst of the "raree-show" and "market-mob" he gulls (910, *Browning* 1:844). These echoes of Wordsworth's satirical description of London's Bartholomew Fair (*Prelude* 7.174, p. 237) have several targets: the Romantic imagination, the higher criticism, historiography and hermeneutics, and art as a godlike exercise of mind and spirit. Much as the garrulous sea-captain narrator of Wordsworth's "The Thorn" parodies the poet's fascination with odd characters and quasi-haunted places, Sludge caricatures what Browning the poet most values. The mesmerist's view of the "palace of art" radically undermines the value Browning had assigned to Abt Vogler's "palace of music." Sludge confides that it is "all half real, / And you, to suit it, less than real beside, / In a dream, lethargic kind of death in life" (1415–17, *Browning* 1:857).[16]

The grotesque exaggerations of characters like Caliban, Sludge, and more unsavory figures like Guido Franceschini of *The Ring and the Book* insist on the potential decay of figures, those rhetorical guides to speech that extend its range beyond the quotidian, the here and now. They interrupt and query allegory's claim to be "other speech." Their grotesque speech displays, as Armstrong puts it, "the centri-fugal movement of Browning's poems; they throw words outwards, leaving a litter of linguistic wreckage for the reader to reconstruct, a wreckage which has a curious way of demanding more attention than it seems to deserve."[17] At times, Browning's excessive demand on the reader's attention marks the residue of a coherent allegorical plot gone awry in the material and figural stresses of the rhetorical grotesque, which acts as a reality check on human efforts to create or approximate the "other speech" of allegory.

The Ring and the Book offers the most sustained exposition of Browning's allegorical temper, from its narration of fairly sordid legal and popular accounts of familial treachery and murder to its idealist portrayal of Pompilia, the innocent victim. Briefly put, as commentators – themselves actors who have their own interests to protect – tell this story, their conflicting narratives become the only available medium for getting at the truth of these events and their meaning. Linguistic confusion and betrayal are endemic to this process. De Man's understanding of allegory as the figure of deferred and constantly disfiguring meaning registers a version of Browning's exuberant and skeptical demonstration of figural decay, as does Benjamin's claim that allegorical meaning is the outcome, almost the phosphorescence, of fragmentation and disintegration.[18]

Purchased in Florence a year before Elizabeth Barrett died, the "Old Yellow Book" in which Browning found the story of Pompilia seems later to have prompted a longing, yet also conflicted, mental exchange between Browning and his dead wife. The exchange thus imagined concerns transmission – how to transmit meaning across barriers as impermeable as that between death and life, how to sustain or undermine the original meaning of translated works or documents, how to make figural language very nearly concrete – "real" in the nineteenth-century sense of the term, by insisting on its material resources, whether erotic, violent, or grotesque (often all three). As the metafigure that theorizes difficulties in transmission, allegory dramatizes the logic of Browning's poetic difficulty.

In a more specifically textual sense, the grotesque figures in *The Ring and the Book* mine the literal to invent the figural. In this and other late poems, allegorical speech uses the same figural path. Browning's use of the grotesque deliberately exaggerates the impact of material, literal referents on poetic figures. The story of necks, especially Guido's, tells the tale. Guido begins his final monologue shorn of title, shortly to lose his head at the neck, and verbally obsessed with necks, beginning with his "soft neck and throat" (*RB* 11.128, p. 540). He refers to "the way a head is set on neck," to "those lithe live necks of ours" (*RB* 11.284, 290, p. 544). He bitterly recalls Pompilia as the child "whose neck writhes, cords itself against your kiss" and finally asserts his right to "wring her neck" (*RB* 11.1019, p. 564 and 11.1359, p. 573). When he insists that the mob, rather than the Pope and clergy, should judge him, he offers the neck as the virtual seat of the soul:

> Born-baptized-and-bred Christian-atheists, each
> With just as much right to judge as you, –
> As many senses in his soul, or nerves
> I' the neck of him as I, – whom, soul and sense,
> Neck and nerve, you abolish presently.
>
> (*RB* 11.709–13, pp. 555–56)

Guido's compulsive return to his neck creates a figural net that binds his terror of death to its origin, his assumption that he could wring Pompilia's neck as though she were a captive bird (who nonetheless lives long enough to sing).

Browning refused to modify or reduce the grotesque imagery of *The Ring and the Book* despite a long exchange of letters on the topic with Julia Wedgwood, who repeatedly questioned his preoccupation with characters like Guido, unidentified Roman voices from the crowd, the self-serving lawyers on both sides of the case, and other occasions for vulgarity.[19] The figural pyrotechnics of the poem, which burn innocent as well as guilty parties, forecast his deployment of similar figures in later poems and, more indirectly, the poetic logic of his interest in rough, literal translation in the 1870s. In each instance, grotesque, often violent, figures like those Guido musters to talk about Pompilia's neck and his own make apparent the way that material, literal facts will, under the pressure of feeling, become figures. In this regard, Browning's grotesque style insists on a potentially damaging contact between the resources of human rhetoric and its gesture toward the "other speech" of allegorical narrative and meaning.

The figuration of *The Ring and the Book* punts toward contradiction and dissonance by implying unwelcome affinities between Pompilia and Caponsacchi – the characters whose testimony the Pope and Browning's narrator trust the most – and the sordid speakers and characters who dominate the physical space of the poem, including Guido, Violante, Pietro, the Abate, and the two lawyers. All these characters are at different moments in the poem compared unflatter-ingly to snakes and dogs. This oddly random approach, which Walker aptly names a "shotgun blast of imagery," demands that readers evaluate the applicability of such figures by examining the speakers and arguments served in each instance. The "strong imagistic undertow" of such figures is suggested by the succession of bird figures the Abate uses to depict Guido's capture of a wife.[20] The narrator is The Other Half-Rome, but the sentiments are ascribed to the Abate and, behind that figure of marital bliss and authority, Guido:

> Since if his simple kinsman so were bent,
> Began his rounds in Rome to catch a wife,
> Full soon would such unworldliness surprise
> The rare bird, sprinkle salt on phoenix' tail,

> And so secure the nest a sparrow-hawk.
> No lack of mothers here in Rome, – no dread
> Of daughters lured as larks by looking-glass!
> The first name-pecking credit-scratching fowl
> Would drop her unfledged cuckoo in our nest.
>
> (*RB* 3.332–40, p. 120)

The slippage from phoenix to cuckoo is a cumulative bad omen, forecasting Pompilia's capture by Guido, who elsewhere imagines her as his hawk to wound or imprison as he chooses. To be sure, as she dies, Pompilia rises phoenix-like from the disasters of her birth and marriage to God ("And I rise"). Yet the preponderance of bird images used for her throughout the poem works against this figure of resurrection.[21]

Browning's personifications also work the figural terrain between human and animal, animate and inanimate: Pompilia compares her marital predicament to that of a goat standing on a pile of sticks as its master removes them one by one, calling that goat and thus herself "A shuddering white woman of a beast" (*RB* 7.609–10, p. 341); Guido's household becomes, in the mill of Tertium Quid's narrative, "the two, three creeping house-dog-servant-things" (*RB* 4.1077, p. 188); Browning's narrator calls the lawyer Bottinius "the scrannel pipe that screams in heights of head" (*RB* 1.1201, p. 55); as Caponsacchi listens to the "stone lungs" of the cathedral with its "scrannel voice" of dead passion, he sits "stone-still" until dawn (*RB* 6.1000 and 1023, pp. 292–93); and The Other Half-Rome uses synecdoche to personify the primitive violence temporarily hidden in Guido's observation of his wife's exchanges with Caponsacchi, presented namelessly as "tooth and claw of something in the dark" (*RB* 3.786, p. 132). Guido's description of his guillotine offers a still more chilling exchange of human and inanimate or animal figures: "there the man-mutilating engine stood / At ease, both gay and grim, like a Swiss guard / Off-duty" (*RB* 11.207–9, p. 542).

Like "snow" – verbal chatter or white noise – repeated syntactical patterns erode the integrity and specificity of speech in the poem. The most obvious is the use of prepositional contractions by the most cynical speakers of the poem and even Browning's narrator, who introduces this pattern: "arm o' the feeler," "mouth o' the street," "curd o' the cream," "flower o' the wheat," "sense o' the city." This pattern is often applied to Pompilia: Tertium Quid sardonically notes the "sudden existence, dewy dear, / O' the rose above the dungheap, the pure child / As good as new created" (*RB* 4.246–48, p. 165); Guido derisively names her "dirt / O' the kennel," "dust o' the street" and "denizen o' the dung." This pattern becomes a verbal tic in the poem, used by all speakers but particularly those who are the most cynical and most aware of the possibilities for rhetorical sleights of speech.[22]

These and my earlier examples of dissonant aural and figural density complicate the poem's central ring figure. For some, this density supports an organic plenitude that does not contaminate or undermine the moral claims of the Pope and the narrator about the truth of the story.[23] For others, it demonstrates the post-structuralist, deconstructive impulse at work in Browning's longest poem, corrosive to the claims regarding truth offered by the Pope and the narrator.[24] The first view grants moral authority to these speakers, whose convictions reflect the progressive, secular as well as spiritual, revelation Browning uses in *A Death in the Desert* to defend John's weaknesses against the deepest anti-theological skepticisms of some of the higher critics. When the Pope declares,

> Truth, nowhere, lies yet everywhere in these –
> Not absolutely in a portion, yet
> Evolvable from the whole: evolved at last
> Painfully, held tenaciously by me   (*RB* 10.228–31, p. 482),

he indicates the role of progressive revelation in secular as well as spiritual life. Throughout the poem, Browning's narrator indicates ample grounds for assenting to the Pope's judgment of Guido, thereby discounting the excuses and justifications offered by other speakers. Implicitly, then, the poem seems to grant the spiritual and moral legitimacy of moral choice founded on progressive (speech) acts of revelation. When the narrator specifies the human obstacles to knowing truth in the last book ("our human speech is naught, / Our human testimony false, our fame / And human estimation words and wind," *RB* 12.834–36, p. 627), he acknowledges the difficulty of revelation without denying it as a principle of knowing.

This is not to say that the poem displays the organic wholeness readers have wished on it. The deconstructive insight that figural language decays is apt for this prolix poem, which gives ample evidence of such decay.[25] The interpretive problem is not so much figuring out what happened – all versions agree on the essential details of the plot even when they disagree about motive and actual speech – but figuring out figures, getting a grip on the rhetoric of the poem. This, I think, is an important dimension of the poem's argument, one that demonstrates the verbal, rhetorical "way o' the world," the miasma of speech, chatter, deception, and self-presentation that infects and animates the only language humans have with which to articulate their sense of human and divine revelation. The path of figure in *The Ring and the Book* is for Browning the one which human thought must travel, with more obstacles than clear guides.

Browning remained adamant on this point in the early 1870s, risking recent good favor in the reviews by writing poems whose characters and situations were at least as sordid as some in *The Ring and the Book*. Two of these poems, *Fifine at the Fair* (1872) and *Red Cotton Night-Cap Country* (1873), exploit grotesque figures to make spiritual arguments. The strategy produces especially lurid results in *Red Cotton Night-Cap Country*, a poem based on a contemporary event which Browning pursued through legal documents, much as he had done in writing *The Ring and the Book*. The story concerns a middle-class French jeweler named Mellerio who falls in love with a woman who fakes her parentage, but later admits lower-class origins. In a fit of madness (or inspiration, suggests Browning), Mellerio (renamed Miranda in the poem) burns his hands off in a fire and retreats with his lover (variously named Clara or Mille-fleurs) to the country. There he later leaps off a church parapet to his death.

Doing more violence to the facts than he had in writing *The Ring and the Book*,[26] Browning reimagines the jeweler's character as that of someone who finally leaps to his death out of faith in the Virgin, whom he expects to save him (she does not). Browning's poetic assessment of this final act emphasizes its spiritual conviction, however superstitious and flawed, as superior to, and more consistent than, any other action in Miranda's life. As the poem begins, a Browningesque narrator brings a friend to the place where Miranda jumped and died, points to the ground and hints about the circumstances of the jeweler's death, without saying more. This ghoulish toying with the audience introduces the organizing figure of the poem: the turf below signifies the secular, fleshly existence that preoccupied Miranda for so long; the tower, the spiritual values to which he finally assents. A more marked spirit of grotesquerie and absurdity governs the graphic description of Miranda's earlier self-mutilation, Clara's character, and Miranda's "Cousinry." In a temporary fit of spiritual disgust for his life with Clara, Miranda burns his hands off:

> and there again smiled he,
> The miserable hands re-bathed in fire –
> Constant to that ejaculation "Burn,
> Burn, purify!" And when, combining force,
> They fairly dragged the victim out of reach
> Of further harm, he had no hands to hurt –
> Two horrible remains of right and left,
> "Whereof the bones, phalanges formerly,
> Carbonized, were still crackling with the flame,"
> Said Beaumont.   (2594–603, *Browning* 11:142)

The narrator's use of this moment is unsettling. He follows it with an account of Miranda's beatified convalescence over the next three months, quoting him extensively as he waxes rhapsodic about spiritual gain and claims to feel no pain. Then, without warning, the narrator laconically reports Miranda's sudden return to Clara's arms as soon as he is strong enough to get into a carriage (2717–25, *Browning* 11:145–46). Similar failures in what might be called rhetorical tact occur throughout the poem as Browning puts those burned stumps to extensive figural use. Asserting that there was no "recrudescence" in Miranda's character when he retreated to the country with Clara, the narrator compares this (non-recurring) "rescrudescence" to a "wound, half-healed before, / Set freshly running – sin, repressed as such, / New loosed as necessity of life" (2815–17, *Browning* 11:148). Equally grotesque diction marks the narrator's account of how the clergy treats Miranda:

> There was no washing hands of him (alack,
> You take me? – in the figurative sense!),
> But, somehow, gloves were drawn o'er dirt and all.
>   (3106–8, *Browning* 11:155)

On other occasions Browning uses grotesque figures that are rhetorically apt, such as his account of Clara's transformation from parasitic grub to butterfly (*Browning* 11:172, 11:180–83). In the conclusion, the character who has listened silently to this tale thus far remarks (two years after Miranda's death and burial) that it might be best to "draw your very thickest, thread and thrum, / O'er such a decomposing face of things, / Once so alive, it seemed immortal too!" The next line insures that readers won't miss the ghoulish pun:

"This happened two years since" (4145–47, *Browning* 11:181). *Red Cotton Night-Cap Country* works hard to yoke its bodily grotesque to the story of Miranda's soul. In the end, the spiritual and potentially allegorical frame indicated by its turf-and-towers imagery seems at least half cancelled out by its deliberate exploitation of Miranda's self-mutilation. As such, the poem is a limiting instance of the relation Browning seeks between a compelling spiritual referent and figures whose strangely material basis can be used to evoke some sense of allegorical possibility in human speech.

In *Fifine at the Fair* the monologist is Don Juan, who tries to convince his wife Done Elvire that his pursuit of women like Fifine, a girl they have seen at a fair, is in fact a fleshly yet allegorical pursuit of the true amid the false or human representations of love and beauty. The scorn which he imagines his wife would heap on his "make-believe" or "false shows of things" dramatizes the exasperated skepticism with which the poem corrects its protagonist's self-serving argument.[27] Yet Browning also frames that argument such that he gives it some credence. The "Prologue," subtitled "Amphibian," is narrated by a swimmer who wishes he could survive in air as well as water. Like the butterfly flying above him, which would die if its wing touched the water, however, Don Juan cannot survive in air. This analogy is animated by Browning's longing for Elizabeth Barrett, figured here as a woman who has slipped from an earthly chrysalis and taken to the air. The poetic vehicle for the speaker's flight, were it possible, would be "passion and thought," which together "substitute" poetry for heaven (*Browning* 11:5–7). The true amphibian would be someone who could sport between the flesh (the sea) and the spirit (the air). In rhetorical terms, the pathos of Browning's longing for his dead wife animates the figures of the "Prologue" and the poem that follows. This use of pathos indicates the figural logic of Browning's allegorical temper: to find figures of passion that convey human speech across the distances and barriers described here and in the "Epilogue," where a cranky "householder" greets his dead wife's unexpected return with complaints about the domestic tedium he has endured since her death.

In every physical sense of the term, Don Juan is also amphibian. He enjoys the "play o' the body" in the sea, an apt figure for the kind of fleshly existence he prizes: constant sexual desire and conquest. Anticipating his wife's charge that he is incapable of fidelity, he claims to be driven by a metaphysical need to find or approach the ideal feminine being through just this "play o' the body." He invokes Eidothee, the daughter of Proteus, to argue that to find the feminine "one," he must have "the many." As the Greek root of her name implies, Eidothee fixes the multiform reality of desire, telling Menelaus how to capture her father before he changes his elemental form to elude capture. Don Juan assures his wife that she will never meet this rival except "i' the soul's domain, why, there / She ravishingly moves to meet you" (789–90, *Browning* II:30).

Even so, this urbane rhetoric cannot entirely dispel Don Juan's erotic grotesquerie, whose figural counterparts are the fakes and deformities of the fair itself, including the beast exhibited one year as a "six-legged sheep" that had been the "Twin-headed Babe, and Human Nondescript" the previous year (123–25, *Browning* II:11). Like these, Fifine and her compatriots strip off layers of seductive female costume to "bounce forward, squalid girls transformed to gamesome boys" (26, *Browning* II:8). Ryals argues that this exposure, like Don Juan's tricky rhetorical self-defense, shows how *Fifine at the Fair* "systematizes what is sensuous and relativistic" and "utterly excludes what is transcendental or metaphysical."[28]

Yet the freaks and wayward girls of Browning's fair, like the London fair in book 7 of *The Prelude*, tell a story that is oddly pitched toward a Wordsworthian recognition of "allegoric shapes" amid a "parliament of monsters."[29] All are shape-changers in a fleshly or moral medium; they adopt or shed false disguises to assume others that are also false. The same charge is justly made about poetic figures and particularly allegory, as an exaggerated, at times grotesque, metafigure for the power of figures. Changeability is the law of figure, even as it is the self-serving "law" of Don Juan's sexual and aesthetic appetite as he loses interest in a Raphael when he decides to acquire a Doré engraving (*Browning* II:22–28). Describing a "prodigious fair" of human beings in Venice, Don Juan claims,

> A love, a hate, a hope, a fear, each soul a-strain
> Some one way through the flesh - the face, an evidence
> O' the soul at work inside; and, all the more intense,
> So much the more grotesque.   (1718–21, *Browning* II:55)

Approaching this spectacle as "a groundling like the rest" (1738, compare Wordsworth's narrator in *The Prelude*, who stands on a platform far above Bartholomew Fair), he conveys both its abstract and its particular human features:

> – whereas so much more monstrosities deflect
> From nature and the type, as you the more approach
> Their precinct, – here, I found brutality encroach
> Less on the human, lie the lightlier as I looked
> The nearlier on these faces that seemed but now so crooked
> And clawed away from God's prime purpose. They diverged
> A little from the type, but somehow rather urged
> To pity than disgust.   (1740–47, *Browning* 11:55–56)

As Don Juan elaborates this view of human limitation and striving, he argues that human, bodily particulars cannot be separated from souls: "one must abate / One's scorn of the soul's casing, distinct from the soul's self" (1789–90, *Browning* 2:57). *Fifine at the Fair* makes the hardest possible case for understanding how a story might be inextricable from allegorical meaning. This union, made adhesive rather than naturally so, is neither expected nor easy to grant when the literal narrative is the deft rhetoric of a Don Juan who parades his traditional biases and failings.

The epigraph that begins the poem, a selection from Molière's *Don Juan* which Browning loosely translates, suggests that this problem is analogous to that of translation. When Molière's Done Elvire asks sardonically, "*Vous plaît-il, don Juan, nous éclaircir ces beaux mystères?*", Browning translates: "Don Juan, might you please to help one give a guess, / Hold up a candle, clear this fine mysteriousness?" A few lines later, Done Elvire mockingly remarks, "*J'ai pitié de vous voir la confusion que vous avez.*" Browning translates, "You move compassion, that's the word – / Dumb-foundered and chap-fallen." She finally asks, "*Que ne me jurez-vous que vous êtes toujours dans les mêmes sentiments pour moi, que vous m'aimez toujours avec une ardeur sans égale?*" In Browning's translation, this statement becomes,

> Why don't you swear and vow
> No sort of change is come to any sentiment
> You ever had for me? Affection holds the bent,
> You love me now as erst, with passion that makes pale
> All ardour else.   (8–12, *Browning* 11:4)

With each translation, Browning adds a figure that does not occur in Molière's text: "hold up a candle," "dumb-foundered and chap-fallen," and "passion that makes pale." These slight figural interventions are instructive about the role Browning assigns to figures used in translation. The ancient rhetorical affiliation between *translatio*, metaphor, and allegory defines translation as a technical figure for the way that speech other than our own is inherently different and thus alien, as Benjamin's essay on translation emphasizes.[30] In translating Molière Browning could have minimized this feature by excluding figures of his own devising. He instead chose to include such figures, much as he permits Don Juan's half-ironic citations of Aeschylus in different narrative contexts.[31]

At the end of the manuscript of *Fifine*, Browning appended two Greek passages which link the difficulty of the poem to Greek drama. The first, taken from Aeschylus's *Libation-Bearers*, implies the stylistic affinity between Browning and Aeschylus. Dated several months after the publication of *Fifine* in June 1872, it reads (in translation): "speaking an inscrutable word at night he brings darkness over the eyes, and by day he is no clearer" (*Browning* 11:975). This difficulty is allegorical. Browning later added a second inscription from Aristophanes which might refer to his reader or to Browning himself as the "savage" householder of the "Epilogue":

> What avails me? Shall I make a speech?
> His savage nature could not take it in.
> True wit and wisdom were but labour lost
> On such a rude barbarian.   (*Browning* 11:975)

An uncannily similar critique reverberates in contemporary reviews of Browning's own translation of the *Agamemnon* (1877). Readers complained, with some reason, that his rough, highly literal translation is at best a grotesque, perversely distorted caricature of spoken and written English. For example, he translates a Greek synecdoche used to characterize Clytemnestra, γυναικός ἀνδρόβουλον ἐλπίζον κέαρ (a woman's man-willed hopeful heart), as "The man's-way-planning hoping heart of woman." In the scene that presents Agamemnon's sacrifice of his daughter Iphigeneia, Browning makes the roughness of Aeschylus's syntax a material figure for the violence of the father's command:

> Kid-like, above the altar, swathed in pall,
> Take her – lift high, and have no fear at all,
> Head-downward, and the fair mouth's guard
> And frontage hold, – press hard
> From utterance a curse against the House
> By dint of bit – violence bridling speech. (250–53, *Plays* 409)

A similarly rough handling of English syntax and vocabulary throughout Browning's translation of *Agamemnon* displays the figural violence for which this scene is a material witness. By insisting on the alien, unstable relation between his translation and its source, Browning suggests the difficulty inherent in the semiotic traverse between signs and meaning. As it has been at different moments in its rhetorical career, allegory is the metafigure of that difficulty. Here and in other late poems, Browning suggests that material violence of allegorical figures is the apparent sign for an implicit affinity between abstraction and figural violence. Abstractions can take possession because they mimic reality, borrowing its life much as nineteenth-century realists hoped to do, but with quite different ends in view.

From its first serial publication, Eliot's *Daniel Deronda* has vexed readers, not because its figures are difficult to the degree that Browning's figures often are, but because the novel gradually dissipates the realist, or seemingly realist, commitment of its opening chapters.[32] Other readers make the idealism of the Jewish plot bear the brunt of their critique. As if to defend Eliot's novel against the incursion of a narrative that disrupts its realist fiction and rational historiography, they argue that Deronda's narrative, erotic, and religious entanglements with Mordecai and other Jewish characters vitiate the stronger, more emphatically realist role he could have had in the English plot. Those who dislike Daniel Deronda from the opening scene (and many do) contend that as his desire for a higher, moral life settles on a future in the "East" for Jewish zionism and culture, this bloodless, patronizing hero becomes still less personable and more vague. A similar antagonism dominates criticism of the novel's other, "refined," Jewish characters: Mirah is adamantly pious and deferring as Gwendolen is not; Mordecai's impassioned zionist rhetoric and Cabbalist claims about twinned souls are tedious, long-winded or vague.

Although neither the novel nor its characters are flawless, these complaints look excessive. At times they defend Gwendolen against Deronda or, more precisely, against the tragic scheme Eliot uses to bring this beauty down. To counteract this novelist's treatment of her heroine, readers tend to exaggerate Mirah's liabilities. For although she refuses theatrical display and visual power as Gwendolen does not, the Jewish singer is not all submissiveness and crossed hands, as one early critic insists.[33] More to the point, how she feels and acts receives the same realist scrutiny given the main characters in the English plot. If Daniel is at times aloof and always wary of becoming enmeshed by Gwendolen's needs, the narrative provides ample psychological warrant for this behavior. Mordecai is less tedious and long-winded that his English counterparts in *Middlemarch*, the novel Eliot's readers tend to prefer. In that work at least as much, and perhaps more, narrative space is taken up with Brooke's ambling, garbled syntax and Casaubon's tedious, self-focused pedantry.

The snappishness that often erupts when readers of *Daniel Deronda* criticize its characters or the way Eliot deals with its English heroine may finally have less to do with characterization than it does with the novel's unsteady realism, which is awkwardly poised between two incommensurable plots. Although Eliot had at least once before taken up the cause of disinherited races, this novel is her first (and last) in which a member of one such race moves to the narrative center, with devastating consequences for the plot of this highly plotted work.[34] Critics of the Jewish plot and Mordecai in particular have pointed out with some justice that the novel gets caught in the undertow of a creeping idealism that finally takes over. Eliot's long-standing realist and historiographic commitments, together with G. H. Lewes's polemical insistence that whatever is not realism is "falsism,"[35] offer some grounds for this complaint.

After nearly two volumes in which the narrative looks firmly entrenched in its satiric and realist comedy of manners, the Jewish plot inaugurates a swerve away from the demands of realism toward something else, call it idealism, religious fanaticism, or allegory. The last and most deadly blow to the novel's realism is administered by Mordecai when his earlier, seemingly wishful "prediction" that Deronda was born a Jew turns out to be right. By such "backward mutters of dissevering power," the dying Jew rewrites Deronda's known history as a well-educated Englishman of means as well as mysterious birth. Chase has argued that because Mordecai's wish-come-true is narratologically the belated cause for which Deronda's Jewish origin is the desired but earlier effect, the Jewish plot also unravels the relation between prior causes and subsequent effects that makes rational historiography and Eliot's realism possible.[36]

Even readers who admire the philosophical idealism vested in Mordecai make a similar point about the novel's faltering commitment to the vision of social and moral improvement that Eliot aligns with realism and historiography until relatively late in her career. As the focus of this novel's realist energies, genteel English society could hardly be more sharply indicted for its unexamined sense of cultural and social privilege and near-manic elevation of pleasures that depend on inherited wealth. The misanthropy of this portrait is unmistakable and damning: given this society, the narrative swerve toward Mordecai and Jewish zionism implies, the only option left is to leave England, as Deronda does, and try to reclaim an ancient nation-state that is separate and Jewish.[37]

The extremism of the novel's swerve away from the realist narrative of its first third is arresting and instructive. For if Eliot's earlier novels exhibit some partiality toward ideal types and more reluctance to find them earthly mates (readers will think of Dorothea Brooke–Casaubon–Ladislaw), most advance a realist, progressive vision of historical change and most imagine individual characters as the particulars that collectively illustrate this vision, which Eliot denies only in her last novel and only within the terms dictated by its Jewish plot. Thus the figure of Gwendolen as presented early in the novel prompts this characteristic passage from a particular being to a social type:

> Could there be a slenderer, more insignificant thread in human history than this consciousness of a girl, busy with her small inferences ... ? in a time, too, when ideas were with fresh vigor making armies of themselves, and the universal kinship was declaring itself fiercely: when women on the other side of the world would not mourn for the husbands and sons who died bravely in a common cause ... What in the midst of that mighty drama are girls and their blind visions? They are the Yea or Nay of that good for which men are enduring and fighting. (109)

As this rhetoric moves from Gwendolen to "the Yea or Nay" of good for which men elsewhere fight, looping in a few allegorical possibilities along the way ("when ideas were with fresh vigor making armies of themselves"), it conveys Eliot's certainty that even a self-absorbed character like Gwendolen Harleth can be lined up with a larger principle. At its grandest, this disposition assumes a universal history of human development. As Eliot puts it in a late essay on *Antigone*, "the struggle between Antigone and Creon represents that struggle between elemental tendencies and established laws by which the outer life of man is gradually and painfully being brought into harmony with his inward needs."[38]

As *Daniel Deronda* vests its sense of history in the Jewish plot, this epistemological vision unravels. Readers have tracked Eliot's late pessimism and anti-realism to Schopenhauer, to the skeptical branch of the higher criticism that Browning paraphrases in *A Death in the Desert*, or more generally to liberal disappointment in the likelihood of progress after the failed economic and political revolutions of 1848.[39] I am interested in the representational impasse all these impose on Eliot's realist vision. As it shuttles in ungainly fashion between the realist and idealist plots, *Daniel Deronda* pushes the allegorical dimensions of its English as well as Jewish characters into the foreground. Eliot's tendency to present the individual "as an allegorical subject"[40] wreaks a peculiar havoc in this novel, where explicit differences appear to segregate the two plots, even as the novel's narrator and various characters assume or imply a similar racial separation between English and Jew. In fact, the allegorical punt of the idealist Jewish plot works hard to neutralize the harsher allegorical possibilities of the English plot.

These possibilities are anything but hidden. Consider this motto, which introduces all four volumes:

> Let thy chief terror be of thine own soul:
> There, 'mid the throng of hurrying desires
> That trample o'er the dead to seize their spoil,
> Lurks vengeance, footless irresistible
> As exhalations laden with slow death,
> And o'er the fairest troop of captured joys
> Breathes pallid pestilence.   (xxxviii)[41]

Precisely because this advice so obviously applies to Gwendolen, whose decision to marry Grandcourt is made with the knowledge that his illegitimate children and their mother have a prior claim on his wealth, it argues for an intermingling of allegorical and realist narratives. For Gwendolen, the outcome is, at least in her eyes and Grandcourt's, a commodification so complete that she is as much his bought and sold mistress as his earlier mistress has been. By such swerves do living women become allegorical trash.

The opening chapter suggests just how this transformation might happen. The people who surround the gaming tables exhibit "a certain uniform negativeness of expression which had the effect of a mask – as if they had all eaten of some root that for the time compelled the brain of each to the same narrow monotony of action" (5). Eliot gives these characters their reward in kind by describing them as types, among them a "respectable London tradesman, blond and soft-handed, his sleek hair scrupulously parted

behind and before, conscious of circulars addressed to nobility and
gentry, whose distinguished patronage enabled him to take his
holidays fashionably" (4). Like adjacent descriptions of other gambling patrons, this one puts realistic detail in the service of a satiric
type. The scene looks so much like one of those nineteenth-century
inventions in which several robot figures play cards or make music
together that the narrator compares the monotone of the croupier's
occasional remarks to the sound that "might be expected to issue
from an ingenious constructed automaton" (3–4).

Although Gwendolen is in Deronda's view different, she too is
initially presented as a type and only incidentally named. In swift
succession she is described as a "problematic sylph" (5), a "Nereid"
(7); Gwendolen Harleth (7); a serpent-like beauty in the way she turns
her neck and, making the Keatsian image explicit, a "Lamia beauty"
(8–9), a demon. The irony of this presentation soon becomes evident:
Gwendolen prizes surfaces and reads faces like houses as mappable
and easily managed physiognomies (18). Benjamin's ironic understanding of *schein* as appearance or false show aptly records the
empty commodification of people that quickly catches Gwendolen in
its undertow. Her confidence that she can control as well as read
appearances is disturbed early in the novel by the image of a dead
face behind a trick panel at Offendene. When she first sees it,
Gwendolen angrily shuts the panel (22). Later she is terrified out of
her carefully arranged pose in a dramatic tableau when her little
sister opens the panel again (54). Like Mordecai's backward prediction of Deronda's Jewish origin, this dead face is a gothic preview of
the "white dead face" (627) of the drowned Grandcourt that haunts
Gwendolen's emergent moral conscience in the last part of the novel.

Even while he is alive, Grandcourt presents a congealed, demonic
character that comes close to allegorical abstraction. Introduced to
readers as a "prefigured stranger," the real Grandcourt hardly seems
alive. The narrator dryly remarks that "it was perhaps not possible
for a breathing man wide awake to look less animated" (97). The
obviousness of his allegorical name helps to complete this unsavory
first impression. Like many an allegorical emblem, Grandcourt's
cold, languid, passionless appearance masks a will-to-power that seeks
out victims and soon finds one in Gwendolen Harleth. Pallid and half-
bald, he comes as close to an allegorical figure of Death as one could
find in realist fiction or genteel English society. In his company or
under his influence, other allegorical possibilities tend to gather.

Meeting his discarded mistress Mrs. Glasher, Gwendolen thinks that "it was as if some ghastly vision had come to her in a dream and said 'I am a woman's life'" (137). After marrying him, she receives Glasher's "poisoned" letter with the family diamonds, then collapses Crëusa-like as she sees "reflections" of her image in the diamonds that look "like so many women petrified white." The narrator puts the truth of Grandcourt's marital disaster in allegorical terms, "in some form or another the Furies had crossed his threshold" (331). Gwendolen's flippant and inaccurate comparison of the heiress Mary Arrowpoint to "the figure of Wealth in an Allegory" (93) shows just how narrow and demeaning allegorical representation can be.

The allegorical language of the novel which thus begins in the English plot continues throughout. After Grandcourt's death by drowning, Gwendolen imagines "Temptation and Dread" moving through her mind (628); "familar Sorrow" comes to sit beside Mirah again when she imagines that Deronda loves Gwendolen (681); and Hans Meyrick half-admiringly writes to Deronda that Mordecai is "a sort of philosophical–allegorical–mystical believer" (598). Deronda's view of Mirah as she asserts her cultural and religious identity to the Meyricks (who welcome her but silently hope that she will convert from Judaism to a more acceptable, less intense religious affiliation) suggests the figurative power she commands, little clasped hands notwithstanding: "she seemed to Deronda a personification of that spirit which impelled men after a long inheritance of professed Catholicism to leave wealth and high place, and risk their lives in flight, that they might join their own people and say, 'I am a Jew'" (347). In the aggregate, these examples constitute more than simply figural decoration; they are necessary rhetorical vehicles for the strong passions and ideas that impel both plots.

The darkened pessimism that readers of the novel have identified with Schopenhauer's gothic imagery of the world and human will in irreversible decay[42] provides, in other words, a receptive medium for allegorical figures and human agents who stand ready to drag culture down into an unthinking automatism that is at the mercy of impersonal chance and a few demons. Against these forces the novel arrays the Jewish plot, whose main characters live by passionately held ideals. Animated in this way, Mirah and Mordecai often remind the narrator of allegorical figures. The auditory sign of the link between passion and ideas in the novel is voice or music, and singer–artists who convey thought by such means are mostly Jewish – Herr

Klesmer, Mirah, and Deronda. For them, as it will be for Gwendolen, suffering teaches the voice and the spirit how to feel but also how to live by ideas. When Deronda first sees Mirah, he is singing the gondolier's song from *Otello* ("No greater sorrow than the misery of remembering a happy time now past"); she is "a figure which might have been an impersonation of the misery he was unconsciously giving voice to" (171). Of this meeting, the narrator says, "the moment of finding a fellow-creature is often as full of mingled doubt and exultation as the moment of finding an idea" (178). Later in the novel, when Gwendolen's marriage has made her desperate for Deronda's help, he thinks to himself that she has "a dreary lack of the ideas that might help her" (385). To urge her thoughts in that direction, he says to her, "in all deep affections the objects are a mixture – half persons and half ideas" (388).

Readers who do not like Deronda because of speeches like this one argue he gets his comeuppance when he finally meets his dying mother, who sharply tells him (perhaps as much for Gwendolen as for herself) that he cannot imagine (though he says he can) "what it is to have a man's force of genius in you, and yet to suffer the slavery of being a girl" (588). Gwendolen unconsciously echoes Deronda's mother and, behind her, Mary Wollstonecraft, when she describes herself on the last sail with Grandcourt as his "galley slave."[43] Though readers have not and will not soon forgive him or Eliot for saying so, Deronda is right when he says Gwendolen needs ideas, a larger purpose, if she is to escape the virtual mental prison of her existence, however plush its realist accoutrements.

This is perhaps the deepest held conviction of Eliot's last novel. It is applied most prominently to Mordecai, who represents the "passionate current of an ideal life striving to embody itself, made intense by resistance to imminent dissolution" (442). The same conviction shapes Eliot's invention of Herr Klesmer, the composer–musician whose slightly ridiculous, bohemian appearance amuses the correct English (92). Klesmer has what most of the English characters lack: a highly wrought and passionate devotion to ideas and a sense of purpose informed by "creative work and theoretic belief" (622). The narrative placement of this analysis, between a description of Lady Arrowpoint's mental inventory of all the reasons why Klesmer and her daughter would not think or dare to fall in love (they already have) and one of Mr. Bult, an "expectant peer" who obtusely glories in the profits to be garnered from slave colonies, puts Klesmer in an especially favorable light. Because Derrida is someone who struggles to realize for himself work and a future with a sense of ideal purpose that will be comparable to what Klesmer has already achieved, he is both a Klesmer in the making and Mordecai's long-desired successor.

Thinking about Deronda as a neophyte helps to explain the novel's reiterated notice of his emotional sensitivity and sympathy for others, especially women. With some reason and with Gwendolen in mind, some readers will not forgive Eliot for letting Deronda feel like a woman but act like a man, a special favor she never extended to women.[44] I grant this point, which the Princess Halm-Eberstein manages to smuggle into the novel. This objection, however, may misconstrue the point of Deronda's "feminine" susceptibility to emotion, and to women. In part, this trait is a mostly hidden mark of his slight foreignness – the sort of excess one of the other English characters in this novel might expect of someone who is not entirely English, as indeed Deronda is not. It is also, like Mordecai's "enthusiasm," the affective ground that, according to Eliot individuals must acquire before they can take up ideals and put them to work. For Klesmer, Mary Arrowpoint, and Mirah, music and voice carry this passion. Deronda carries it in his being.

The figure of Mordecai as the prophet who predicts the origin he requires to make Deronda his twin-soul extends further Eliot's commitment to ideal, allegorical representation by reimagining the kind of history the novel might sponsor. Chase's observation that Mordecai's eschatological sense of history disturbs the role assigned to history and causality in nineteenth-century realism is both accurate and revelatory. For this disturbance rebounds at least twice between the two extremes of Eliot's fictional achievement: the visionary ideal commitments of, for example, the end of *The Mill in the Floss, Romola*, and the figure of Dorothea Brooke in *Middlemarch*; and the acid realism with which she effectively damns the microcosm of English gentility in *Daniel Deronda* by aligning most of its representatives with some species of limited understanding. Even the benevolent Whig Sir Hugo Mallinger who brought Deronda up, as the boy once requested, as an "Englishman," has only this advice for him when he decides to widen his experience beyond that of Eton and Cambridge: "for God's sake, keep an English cut, and don't become indifferent to bad tobacco! And – my dear boy – it is good to be unselfish and generous; but don't carry that too far. It will not do to give yourself to be melted down for the benefit of the tallow-trade; you must know where to find yourself" (168).

Knowing where one is placed and the relative economic safety of having inherited wealth and land in industrial England after the French Revolution is what Deronda eventually abandons in a series of movements that lead to his eventual decision to live separately in the Jewish community, but with the wider knowledge gained from his assimilated history. The sense of history is thus made available to the novel and dramatically enacted by Mordecai, that "sort of philosophical – allegorical – mystical believer" who passionately imagines the kind of change that is beyond the ken of Sir Hugo or the initial reaction of Lord and Lady Arrowpoint to their daughter's announcement that she will marry Klesmer. Even though the zionist project for the return of the Jewish diaspora to Israel is vaguely presented in the novel, as critics have charged, the novelistic point at issue concerns how, as passionate ideas move and animate human beings, those beings grow larger, as do their histories and their understanding of historical change.

Early in the novel Eliot's narrator remarks concerning Gwendolen Harleth: "Sir Joshua [Reynolds] would have been glad to take her portrait; and he would have had an easier task than the historian at least in this, that he would not have had to represent the truth of change – only to give stability to one beautiful moment" (102). This light rehearsal of the Winckelmann-Lessing debate about still moments and the larger histories from which those moments are extracted evidently aligns this novelist and story with history-writing or with, as Kate Meyrick says of a novel she and her sisters read, "a bit of history brought near us with a strong telescope" (180). When another sister Mab replies, "call it a chapter in Revelations," she inadvertently reminds readers that in this novel history is revelation and, as such, relies on prophecy to go forward. This history cannot be known by reading surfaces, as the story of Gwendolen's marriage painfully discloses. Only by preserving some recognition of a separate, ideal commitment, as the mystery of Deronda's origin paradoxically teaches him to do while he is still a little boy, can one's history proceed beyond the narrow track of a tradition or set of fixed expectations like those that fence Gwendolen around in the name of marriage and wifely decorum.

There is one unyielding problem with this critical defense. Throughout the novel Eliot quite deliberately shuttles between the

kind of redemption idealism might make possible, either for entire
people like the Jews or for individuals like Gwendolen, and redeeming pawn. Nor is the narration the least bit shy about invoking
the anti-semitic stereotypes it thereby makes available.[45] After losing
at the roulette table, Gwendolen pawns a necklace. The narrator
wryly comments, "Gwendolen's dominant regret was that after all
she had only nine louis to add to the four in her purse: these Jew
pawnbrokers were so unscrupulous in taking advantage of Christians
unfortunate at play" (15). Unasked and unintroduced, Deronda takes
the liberty of redeeming Gwendolen's pawned necklace and returning it to her anonymously. Gallagher assesses the unwelcome
consequences: instead of a clear economic exchange between Gwendolen and the pawnbroker in which she gets money and he gets the
necklace, she finds herself suddenly and without her permission in
another kind of debt to Deronda. This is, moreover, a debt she
cannot repay because she is now impoverished and because the
pawnbroker has sold Deronda the necklace for more than she got for
it.[46] Thanks to Deronda's first of several acts of "redemption,"
Gwendolen's debt must assume a compounded "interest." She
cannot pawn the necklace for cash again because it has even more
symbolic than economic value or, more precisely, because its value
has been fetishized within the circuit of private exchange that
Deronda has initiated.

Later in the novel Eliot extends the figurative implications of
redeeming pawn by having Deronda leave a ring at a Jewish pawn
shop so that he will have an excuse to come back and find out
whether the Jewish pawnbroker is Mirah's long-lost brother. From
this second pawnshop visit unrolls the novel's Jewish plot. The anti-
semitic bite of Gallagher's remark that Deronda eventually chooses
to become a future leader of "a nation of usurers" exposes the
troubling intersection in this novel between the language of profit,
pawn, and commodified human beings who are mostly women, and
the idealist language used to describe the redemption of women,
Jews, and two women who are Jews.[47] In the latter category are
Mirah, the young Jewess who tries to drown herself in despair but is
rescued by Deronda, and Deronda's long-lost mother, who even as
she is dying does not wish to be rescued for motherhood and the
faith of her fathers.

As the site where the two plots are created and where they
diverge, the London pawnshop of Ezra Cohen is a prominent

narrative reminder of the mercantile stereotype that is, whether we or Deronda like it or not, the quite down-to-earth figure in which the novel's idealist currency must trade. Whereas the late Browning might invest this point of intersection with something like excessive relish for its grotesque possibilities, Eliot aligns the abstracting, demonic energies of commodification with allegorical possibilities in the English plot; then imagines Mordecai, Mirah, and Deronda as human characters in whom pathos and abstract ideas might live. In both directions *Daniel Deronda* urges a hermeneutic swerve away from the forms of mercantilism and commodification that bind the two plots – the genteel English mercantilism of inherited wealth and cultural power and the more open, though financially far less significant, mercantilism of the Cohen family.

Compared to the ease with which the English characters condemn Jewish pawnbrokers for openly performing the financial transactions a moneyed class needs to support its pleasures, Deronda's class-conscious embarassment about the Cohens, whose minute regard for profit and loss the young son Jacob has already perfected, looks like small potatoes. A brief exchange between Grandcourt and Deronda about Shakespeare's Caliban makes the point concisely. Grandcourt is, predictably, on the side of colonial exploitation and absolute power; Deronda lightly declares his sympathy for Caliban (303–4). The polite anti-semitism of Eliot's novel looks like still smaller potatoes beside Marx's 1844 essay "On the Jewish Question," which thoroughly demonizes the Jew as the universal figure of "Capital" whose religious faith is, as all religious faith will be classed in *Capital*, a vehicle for mystifying, phantasmagoric ideas that obscure the real relations between people and what they make. Here is Marx on the "*everyday Jew*": "let us not seek the secret of the Jew in his religion, but let us seek the secret of the religion in the real Jew. What is the profane basis of Judaism? *Practical* need, *self-interest*. What is the worldly cult of the Jew? *Huckstering*. What is his worldly god? *Money*."[48] Beside Marx's vitriolic against the race of his forefathers, Eliot's condescending yet sympathetic family portrait of the Cohens looks mild.

The ungainliness with which *Daniel Deronda* and its hero tack between the English and Jewish plots, and between idealist and materialist views of what it means to deposit or redeem pawn, is an allegorical mark of the figural argument that is enmeshed in its materialist vehicle. This contamination or seepage, essential to the business of allegory in modernity, seems to be part of the herme-neutic invitation the novel extends to its English readers. By catching them, including Deronda, in the narrowly materialist plot of their anti-semitism, Eliot may hope to draw them toward the idealist vision she admired in late nineteenth-century zionism. Such an invitation is deeply allegorical in a modern key. Look hard at these literal and materialist surfaces, it urges, until you recognize the allegorical argument they animate.

By plotting the novel against the grain of realism and a historical vision anchored by visible causes and effects, Eliot opens contin-gency, even gaming, to this allegorical invitation. In *Middlemarch*, the gaming table or den is a sulphuric, hellish place. In *Daniel Deronda* gaming and economic failure articulate the reckless underside of genteel English culture. Predictably, Grandcourt is said to have been a gambler.[49] Yet irrational chance and coincidence are also crucial to the redemptive plot of this novel. Of all the ways Deronda might have chosen to look for Mirah's long-lost mother and brother, whose family name was Cohen, he chooses the least rational: he simply wanders in the Jewish quarter of London until he sees a pawnshop with the name Cohen.[50] What could be more ludicrous or more adventitious than the ensuing discoveries? A common Jewish name produces the brother after all, though he is unrelated except by race and religion to these Cohens. Other coincidences produce Deronda when Mirah attempts suicide and when Gwendolen most needs to see him. Deronda's role as the man of feeling who also redeems women in distress by the odd Humean coincidence makes chance, not a rational sequence of events in which causes precipitate effects, the guardian of redemptive possibilities in the novel.

Together with the allegorical tendencies of the novel's Jewish plot, its Lucretian swerve away from historiographic realism toward the aleatory extends human possibilities beyond the limits of realism and the fizzled idealism at the end of *Middlemarch*. It is also a rivetting sign of Eliot's modernist vision, which puts this story of individuals in the path of contingency.[51] I would put the relation between chance and allegory in *Daniel Deronda* still more emphatically. Because allegorical figures and ideas reach beyond the verisimilar, they act as agents for possibilities that exceed the reality at hand. The highly detailed, materialist surface given to the novel's realist vision of English gentility and Jewish poverty calls attention to its own hard limits and thus to the need to move in other ways. Not to do so is to risk absolute enslavement to a demonic, if comfortably well-off, Grand-court and the settled vision of culture and hierarchy for which this character is his own bad allegory.

On the other side, the novel's idealist, prophetic gesture toward the future also tends to rid itself of material, realist details, thereby letting slip the opportunity to "embody," as the narrator says of Mordecai's desire and character, the "passionate current of an ideal life."[52] There is finally no way to resolve this contradiction, more marked in *Daniel Deronda* but evident throughout Eliot's long career as an essayist, translator, and finally novelist. As if in a quarrel with itself, this last novel spurns a realist achievement in the early volumes as finely particular and material as any comparable scene in *Middlemarch*, unwilling perhaps to give realism a crack at embodying an ideal life.

The paths allegory takes through Victorian literary culture could hardly be more different in Browning and Eliot. Indeed, the extremity of that difference suggests just how difficult the Victorian accommodation between these two modes became. At times Browning's poetic style leans so hard on material vehicles and syntax that its allegorical point caves in. Eliot leans away from the terms of her own conflicted realism, as though she has finally had enough of an era crowded with its things and occasionally too well-upholstered by its positivist vision of what things can do for people. Marx's mid-century call for a society in which the "allegoric," "moral," and "political" side of man would be one with the "real," "sensuous," "authentic man"[53] seems from the double perspective offered by Eliot and Browning a difficult goal or, more precisely, a goal made difficult by the doubt that lingers within the scheme of representation itself, which relies on individuals, specifics, and things to convey ideas.

CHAPTER 9

Conclusion

The dangers of fraudulence, and of trust, are essential to the experience of art.

Melville, "Reemergence of Allegory" 87

As the metafigure of irony and fantastic invention, allegory hovers playfully and seriously over late modernity's turn from realism toward something else whose hybrid nature is one sign of its resilience – call it Latin American magical realism, philosophical or science fiction, postmodern or postcolonialist political fable, or critical theory.[1] In all these modes, allegory authorizes "meta-commentary" and improvisation; it may also harden into automaton figures with a strong hermeneutic grip on the means and ends of their production. Allegory's survival in recent theory and fiction dramatizes this truth, even as it signals the necessity and advantage of trusting its metafictional fraud.

My point of entry into this argument is Angela Carter's novel *Nights at the Circus*. In the opening scene the heroine Fevvers, a famous aerialist, is being interviewed by a skeptical American reporter. She tells him she was not born by "*normal channels*" (her emphasis) but hatched, "just like Helen of Troy." Eyeing the reporter as if daring him to "Believe it or not," she rips off one false eyelash and flounces around her dressing room while the reporter Jack Walser eyes her bulging shoulder blades, which house the great wings that are another sign of her unusual (perhaps divine?) parentage. Wondering, like everybody else, "how does she do that," Walser is vigilant for every hint that Fevvers is a sham – from the peroxide blond hair and two layers of false eyelashes, to dyed wing tips (*Nights* 7–8). Coarse, funny, and the consummate mistress of her own self-promotion, Fevvers flaunts her outrageous difference and offers a life story to match.

Left a foundling on the steps of a late nineteenth-century whore-house in Whitechapel, she is tenderly brought up and kept from the rigors of the house for years by posing first as a Cupid with budding wings and later, when those wings miraculously unfurl, as a winged Victory who graces the drawing room. Evidently this is no ordinary angel of the house. The metaphysical madam of the establishment, makes neo-Platonic statements about time, calling it the "dead centre" of day or night and "the hour of vision and revelation" (*Nights* 29), and has nurtured a similarly philosophical strain in Fevvers, who compares her disastrous maiden flight to the fall of another angel at the beginning of another history:

Like Lucifer, I fell. Down, down, down I tumbled, bang with a bump on the Persian carpet below me, flat on my face amongst those blooms and beasts that never graced no natural forest, those creatures of dream and abstraction not unlike myself, Mr Walser. And then I knew I was not yet ready to bear on my back the great burden of my unnaturalness. (*Nights* 30)

Pausing for dramatic effect, she lets Walser take all this in, or be taken in. In the end, he does both by falling in love with her. In the course of adventures as fantastic as any in or out of the allegorical tradition, he gets "hatched out of the shell of unknowing" (*Nights* 294) – so much for the fact-finding *wunderkind* of American journalism on the cusp of the new century. Finally married to Fevvers, he ends up by his own report "smothered in feathers and pleasure." Those wings are dyed, but they're real.

Whatever else Fevvers is, she is a perfect ringer for modern allegory on the cusp of its fashionable liaison with postmodernity. She looks (and is) made up, but she achieves even this effect by using real props and real wings. She finally manages to sweep away even Walser's documentary *pudeur*. Looking very theatrical and a little shabby against the backdrop of fact and documentary realism, Fevvers thrives anyway. Hovering and swooping over the heads of a slightly endangered modern audience (Fevvers is a big girl), she shows how modern allegory is held aloft by magic, fraud, trust, and real wings. If Carter's earlier work at times generates rigid allegorical schemas, the rather different allegorical impulse of *Nights at the Circus* challenges those who would list a "love of allegory" among this novelist's weaknesses.[2] Or, to put this point less contentiously, this late novel shows that allegory is also one of Angela Carter's strengths.

In the person of Fevvers, modern allegory looks like a buoyant version of Benjamin's tragic vision of allegory as ruin, hence recognizable only in the phosphorescent decay of its material signs. This odd intersection between Benjamin's tragic understanding of allegory and the grandly comic Fevvers indicates in brief how modern allegory survives somewhere between philosophy and literature. On this border, as on others, allegory dramatizes more than one way to understand Calvino's distinction between "the phantom lightness of ideas and the heavy weight of the world" (*Uses of Literature* 49). Benjamin's allegory is heavy, weighted down with history and impending ruin, as are some recent works of metafiction. Fevvers is no lightweight herself, and life in the circus turns out to include the heavy weight of the world, and a good deal of philosophical rumination about the promise or burden of the twentieth century. Fevvers's gamesmanship, no less than that of the novelist herself, registers the penchant for combinatorial, fictive play that characterizes modern allegorical fiction, whether comic or tragic, heavy or light.

As the modern writer whose tragic understanding of allegory initiates the modern reinvention of allegory – a reinvention whose historical trajectory begins in the seventeenth century – Benjamin works out three related claims about allegory that have strongly influenced postmodern critical theory: it is the shared domain of fragment and ruin; it is caught up in time such that its meaning and signs are always marked by time passing; and it is either a hidden, redemptive agent in the onslaught of material and figural decay that is modern culture or the desiccated sign of this decay. He introduces most of these to characterize German Baroque tragedy in his 1928 *The Origin of German Tragic Drama*. He later extends them to Baudelaire and, in the unfinished *Passagen-Werk*, to the commodified world of the nineteenth-century Arcades project for central Paris. In "Theses on the Philosophy of History," the 1940 essay that was published with this title after his death, Benjamin includes two patently allegorical figures – a wizened, hidden dwarf who controls the material expression of historical culture and Klee's "Angelus Novus," an ironically redemptive angel of modernity who looks back on the cumulative wreck of history as it flies (or flees) backward toward eternity. Both figures convey his understanding of the allegory and history under the darkened sign of the twentieth century.

As Benjamin moves among these topics and epochs in his earlier writing, he favors allegorical motifs that belong as much to his own era as to the Baroque: ruin, melancholy, montage; the strolling eye's view of culture represented by Baudelaire's *flâneur*; the dialectical image; an ironic or shock view of history that repels Hegel's teleological view of history; and a question to which he returns by different paths and emphases – how can modernity's materialist, commodified culture be harnessed to a redemptive allegorical vision?[3] Looking backward through his later work on Baudelaire and nineteenth-century Paris, we can see how his early study of seventeenth-century allegory helped Benjamin recognize the time-ridden and rapidly decaying pace of early modern and modern culture.

By placing the history of modernity under the sign of allegory as fragment and ruin, Benjamin challenges the neo-Hegelian historicist model of history as *telos*, as unified set and theory. For Benjamin, the isotopic decay of allegorical ideas into figures and images is the true nature of history. To study allegory is thus to amass a cultural record that extends from the seventeenth to the twentieth centuries, but to do so in ways that declare no unified project, no *telos*. In part, this conviction must also chasten the backward glance I use to chronicle Benjamin's long and diffuse engagement with allegory. With Benjamin at my back, or perhaps before me looking back at the catastrophe of history and criticism as he speeds backwards, like Klee's "Angelus Novus," toward eternity, I want nonetheless to locate the argument of his early study of German Baroque drama in the context (but hardly a unified set) he gradually amassed for its argument, those theoretical statements about allegory, Baroque and modern, that crop up in various forms in later essays, many of them related to or part of the unfinished Arcades project. I proceed in this way, risking the lure of teleology and historicism, to suggest that Benjamin's refracted, diffused retelling of allegory under the intermediate sign of Baudelaire and the commodity shows how different cultural and historical moments provide material for allegory's reinvention in modernity.

In the 1938 essay "Central Park," Benjamin looks back over more than a decade of writing and research to reflect on the differences between Baroque and modern allegory. The focus of this essay is Baudelaire, the nineteenth-century poet whose tragic sense of the modern recalls for Benjamin the pathos of Baroque tragedy, with some key differences for the kind of allegory each epoch sponsors.

Common to both is the persistent, indicative function of some version of the emblem as a signifying image that conveys abstractions by way of personification and stereotype. Whereas German Baroque tragedy looks back to antiquity via the emblem and thus allegory, argues Benjamin, Baudelaire looks back on modern life via the commodity. For Benjamin, emblem and commodity are, along with personification and stereotype, dialectical images whose abstractions or abstracting energies are lodged in material and visual forms that gesture beyond themselves, frequently into the past. Whether allegory or commodity, the double signpost or dialectical image of this backward glance is ruin.

In the same essay Benjamin argues that conceptual and material violence might explode a false, because teleologically generated, view of history. Understanding history as ruin, as punctured by small fissures, he allies history to allegory. As commodities of nineteenth-century industrial culture, material objects that resist incorporation into a seamless historical narrative shock us with the fragmentary reality of modern life. Acknowledging itself as a fictive compositor of ruins and fragments, allegory prohibits myths of continuity by showing us history as montage, the modern counterpart to the roughly joined parts of a Renaissance woodcut emblem, where the material roughness of the form of the art foregrounded its made-up, as opposed to organic and continuous, nature (Benjamin, "Central Park" 41–43).

According to Benjamin, Baudelaire can look back on the modern as though it were the past because the commodified world of late nineteenth-century Paris insures the rapid decay of material things. Their usefulness slips away soon after they are produced, much as the theological and political anchors for traditional allegory rapidly decayed in German Baroque drama. But whereas decay was then a melancholy, plodding affair, in modern culture it is very nearly instantaneous and, as such, a shocking sign that decay and ruin, not continuity, make history. Thus whereas Baroque allegory offers exterior signs of its isotopic decay, most notably the corpse, modern allegory is interior; its alienated sign is the souvenir, which represents the past as a "dead possession." Having vacated the exterior world, allegory has hidden inside, as recollection or *Erlebnis* (Benjamin, "Central Park" 49).

Here, as elsewhere when Benjamin writes about dialectical images, the referential status of these images is difficult to fix. Like traditional emblems and the modern commodity, the dialectical image is – and on this point he becomes ever more insistent – material and visual. Yet it is also indexical in that it points to a referent that is elsewhere. So, the modern souvenir is at once material and suggestive of a recollection that is hidden and perhaps alienated from it, whereas Baroque allegory offers emblematic images that are, as it were, skeletal reminders of a structure of meaning that is decaying even as it is being re-presented.

Whereas the decomposition within the German *trauerspiel* occurred gradually, with a sorrowful but stately grandeur, "Baudelaire's allegory bears … traces of a wrath which was at such a pitch as to break into this world and to leave its harmonious structures in ruins" (Benjamin, "Central Park" 42). That wrath is "spleen," the personified agent whose ironic, destructive energies constitute the ambience of *Les Fleurs du Mal* and Benjamin's modern and postmodern placement in a world where spleen hovers and erupts to challenge assumptions about continuity and survival. In some measure, the comparison between the immobilized, masque-like emblematic tableaux of seventeenth-century German *trauerspiel* and the careening, eruptive spleen of Baudelaire's Paris offers a distinction without a difference. For behind the static, emblematic dramaturgy of these plays is the history of, and potential for, violence.

The German *trauerspiel* designates a body of German plays written during the Thirty Years' War. Literally a "play of sorrow," the *trauerspiel* usually features an aristocratic male protagonist and tyrant whose difficulties prompt him to ask questions about the nature of kingly sovereignty and historical sequence posited on the rights of kingship. At a critical moment when he is expected to act as though he believes in the divine right of kings, he becomes indecisive. Such a protagonist dramatizes the version of traditional allegory whose rigid, theocratic control over narrative adamantly resists change. Invoking the Renaissance doctrine of humours, Benjamin argues that such a character is typically melancholy and saturnine. The characterological dead-end thus indicated for the *trauerspiel* is made explicit by its dramaturgic preference for pageant-like allegorical representations of death, cruelty, and violence (Benjamin, *German Tragic Drama* 69–72, 187–89).

As seventeenth-century writers and artists adapted Renaissance emblems, and as editors of emblem books and books on iconography deployed new typographic methods to complicate the simpler images in Renaissance emblem books, the Baroque emblem became more clearly marked as an elaborate visual and verbal fiction. Its components demanded a reader attentive to a montage-like relation among parts, or a reader ready to supply the interpretive links to make those parts (text, inscription, motto, or even the iconographic visual "bits" that increasingly cluttered the visual image) cohere. For this reason, the Baroque emblem and the emblematic and allegorical set pieces of the *trauerspiel* offer ample evidence of how images might also be ruins, montage-like assemblages of material from the past. Benjamin's reiterated figure for such images is death or ruin or, more precisely, the *facies hippocratia* (*German Tragic Drama* 342–43) or death's head whose *rigor mortis* makes clear how an unnatural, inorganic visage displaces its organic past. So mortified, the past has no organic, natural connective to the present; it is always "other" and thus under the sign of allegory. This Baroque reading of the emblem, as much as the subject matter of German Baroque *trauerspiel*, is the immediate occasion for the pervasive, tragic melancholy of Benjamin's allegory.

Under the sign of Saturn, the world of German *trauerspiel* is bound to and by its potential for violent disruptions of the state. Indeed, in English Jacobean tragedy of the same period, violence – conceptual, linguistic, and actual – is the dramatic order of business, at a time when Puritan iconoclasm authorizes violence against material images, including allegorical ones. Looking back to this epoch and culture, Benjamin is the first modern allegorist to reject openly the "stable, hierarchized" world and vision that once sustained allegory's will-to-power as an engine or mechanism that grinds up narrative and character on its way to preordained abstractions.[4] What he sees in the Baroque is evidence of the cultural and historical moment when allegorical will begins to take new forms.

This recognition, which Benjamin repeats a decade later in "Central Park," supervises what he calls the dialectical image, an allegorical vehicle that is distinctly modern but also Spenserian. On one side, the inevitable decay of such images shows that meaning lies elsewhere in the juggernaut of time's swift, mortal passage. On the other side, such images register the violence that suddenly breaks up or breaks in upon a world where appearances are thought to be transparent to and coherent with meaning – that is to say, appearance under the auspices of the Romantic symbol. Given this formulation, Benjamin's surprising claim that allegory's dialectical image is or might be redemptive seems counterintuitive. It also asks a good deal of readers of traditional allegory who emphasize its firm utilizations of stable, referential truths. In exchange for abandoning this stability of reference, he offers the prospect of allegorical redemption *via* ruin and decay. This itinerary would probably only be attractive in an era as ironic as our own. Yet precisely because the alliance between irony and allegory is also part of its ancient as well as modern history, Benjamin's irony warrants attention.

One target of this irony is the German Romantic defense of symbol against allegory, a defense that Coleridge quickly adapted to his own philosophical project. Insofar as the symbol is isolated, complete, and momentary, its alienated other is allegory, which emphasizes instead its incompleteness, its factitious and provisional reference to some other world and meaning whose complete totality must be inferred and taken on faith. In the *trauerspiel* and thereafter, Benjamin challenges the "naturalism" of the symbol and thus organicism by emphasizing how organic life is made what it is by the fact of its mortal being – on the decline even as it lives its existence. By contrast, the logic of allegory requires, in Benjamin's words, "the contemplative calm with which it immerses itself into the depths which separate visual being from meaning" (Benjamin, *German Tragic Drama* 165). Thus whereas the symbol is putatively transparent to its meaning, allegorical images posit something like an impervious material cover whose gesture toward some "other" cannot be read as the spiritual thing itself.

To break the hold of organic figures and the ideology of the symbol sustained by such figures, Benjamin insists that the spectacle of decaying organic figures is a double signpost of the passing, time-drenched status of allegorical meaning and figure. Under the sign of allegory, we can no longer take refuge in the optimism of Romantic organicism. Exposed for what it is, the organic body becomes the decaying corpse, filled with and defined by time passing. To identify allegory as Schelling does with the "fleeting experience of the infinite" is from Benjamin's perspective merely to foreground the momentary, historically located mode of interpretation that belongs to the allegorical.[5] The visible agent of redemptive possibility in so negative a path to allegorical meaning is still ruin – the ruin of medieval and Renaissance political culture, the Baroque, and the cumulative, accelerating ruin of modern culture that Benjamin chronicles in his later writing.

In the closing argument of *German Tragic Drama*, Benjamin imagines the redemptive potential of Baroque allegory as a figural "springing back" or "jump around" that reverses the material free fall of emblems in decay. In Bahti's firmly deconstructive reading of this passage, this free fall of emblems and ultimate reversal looks like a turnstile with all exits closed, such that the material decay of emblems exposes a distance between allegorical signs and what they represent that is so vast and so absolute that it makes allegory "the denial of the sign."[6] I read the movement at the bottom of this free fall differently. Benjamin says,

Ultimately in the death-signs of the baroque the direction of allegorical reflection is reversed [Bahti translates "jumps round"]; on the second part of its wide arc it returns, to redeem. ... In God's world the allegorist awakens ...[thus] these allegories fill out and deny the void in which they are presented, just as, ultimately, the intention does not faithfully rest in the contemplation of bones, but faithlessly leaps forward [*uberspringt*; Bahti translates "springs over"] to the idea of resurrection. (Benjamin, *German Tragic Drama* 232–33).[7]

Being "faithless" to the emblem or allegorical image allows us to "spring over," to imagine resurrection as the reverse or hidden sign of the emblematic coin. The mental springing over or turn about at the bottom of the material decay or fall of emblems is, I suggest, something like what Virgil has Dante experience at the bottom of Hell. As the two climb down to the bottom, they must traverse Satan's gigantic body to get out of Hell. Suddenly Virgil makes a peculiar backwards leap that somehow reverses his direction. Dante is (along with his readers) initially confused: if Virgil has changed his direction, they ought to be climbing once again back up Satan's body and thus back up through the circles of Hell. Instead they are now seated on the rim of the bottom of Hell, looking down at Satan's flailing legs. Now Satan is upside down and they are, thanks to Virgil's reverse leap, sitting upright, with Hell below and behind them.

This reversal, which puts readers and travellers on the path toward resurrection, is what Benjamin claims as the redemptive opportunity offered by allegorical images and emblems. For when readers recognize that decaying emblems are just decaying signs, they recognize the world of eternity and resurrection to which allegorical signs point. What Bahti calls the "improper" nature of figures – the fact that they are not proper names but signs that refer elsewhere and mean nothing in and of themselves – in fact witnesses their fundamental allegorical decorum. To understand how this peculiar semiotic dead-end (in the sense that signs cannot successfully deposit their meaning in material forms that do not decay) is redemptive, readers must see how, as Benjamin put it, a death's head can become an angel's face.

In the "Theses on the Philosophy of History" the angel is Klee's "Angelus Novus," who flies backward toward eternity, looking back on history as a series of catastrophes unfolding before its angelic eyes (Benjamin, "Theses," in *Illuminations* 257–58). To think of history in this way is to "spring over" or turn around a vision of history as *telos* and so, in Benjamin's eyes, redeem the material and allegorical truth of history. This view of allegory and history does away with the whole array of attributes traditionally assigned to allegory, among them its secret arbitrary rule over what Benjamin calls a "realm of dead objects." In their place is an allegory more cognizant of its necessary, transient factitiousness and for this reason as free as it ever can be from fixed, inflexible codes and receptive to the productive, material decay of its modern figures.

The text of this argument has, however, ironies enough for poststructuralist readers. From the angel's perspective, what we see as *telos*, "a chain of events," is just "one single catastrophe which keeps piling wreckage upon wreckage" ("Theses," *Illuminations* 257). This angel would like to stay to perform the work of apocalypse: "awaken the dead, and make whole what has been smashed." It cannot because it is propelled backward by a wind from paradise that holds its wings open, dragging it back with a heavenly (or demonic) jet propulsion. If this allegory about history is also an allegory about allegory, as I think it is, the angel's inability to make history whole or continuous, except in the ironic sense that it is a "single catastrophe," marks the limits modernism places on allegorical agency, which operates as best it can, with its shrunken theology hidden, because the world it faces (or flees) is centrifugal, flying off cataclysmically from itself and as such alienated – such is the special, mortal intensity of modern allegorical alienation – from the theological framework of the medieval and Renaissance allegorical traditions.

Benjamin's theory of allegory is at once skeptical and hopeful about the distance between allegorical images and what they represent. Even with the transcendent referent of allegorical speech forever in recession (or making its escape backward into eternity), forever hidden or buried, or otherwise out of reach (*always* the allegorical norm), the traditional relation between the allegorical image, allegorist, and "other speech" is still at work in this modernist understanding of what allegory is. Despite the fact that it is difficult or impossible to fix the precise relation among these terms, this effort is the focus of the allegorist's inquiry and longing.

These special circumstances, so marked in Benjamin's writing and so often invoked in recent critical theory, may help to explain the baffling status of his unfinished *Passagen-Werk*. The nature of this project is most evident in the "Konvoluts" Benjamin developed to describe it – topical categories and schemas that encompass an extraordinary array of cultural material.[8] This evidence typically invites two contradictory assessments. One asserts that only someone like Benjamin (that is, no one else) would have been able to finish such a project. The second contends that the project was by definition inexhaustible, and that Benjamin would never have completed it had he lived, or had the Nazis not made it imperative that he try to get out of France into Switzerland in May 1940.

The evidence that remains – voluminous notes together with published and unpublished essays written between 1928 and 1940 – shows him hard at work imagining and re-imagining schemata that would contain the cultural phenomena he collectively named the Arcades project. In the end, the Arcades project is the unfinished work of an allegorist for whom material artifacts are a necessary, if also stubborn and thus resistant, element of allegorical practice. In *One-Way Street*, published in 1928, well before he began the Arcades project, Benjamin projected his interest in categorizing phenomena onto children at a construction site. Arguing that children are drawn to the "detritus" or "waste products" of building or housework or gardening, he observes that they do not use these products as adults do. Instead, children "bring together, in the artifact produced in play, materials of widely differing kinds in a new, intuitive relationship" (*One-Way Street* 69).

Two impulses in Benjamin's adult intellectual life are contained in this observation of children at work and play: collection and innovative schemes, the "Konvoluts" of the *Passagen-Werk*. As children collect the waste products of their culture and reorder them in unexpected ways, so does Benjamin. Both create a new artifact out of left-over, discarded material artifacts. By calling the product of this kind of assemblage an "artifact," Benjamin conveys his desire to affix material status to the work of the allegorist. Hence the special position that images (*bilder*) and material objects occupy in this theory of allegory. As sensuous images and things decay, the effect is akin to phosphorescence – a sensuous because light-full (or light-emptying) process whereby things become allegorical signs.

Material artifacts and objects are not, as earlier and some modern discussions of allegory argue, a veil which the world casts over the transcendent world of allegorical truths. On the contrary, Benjamin insists, you cannot do allegory without signifying objects. This reply to nineteenth-century realism asserts then that what is real is necessary to allegory, not antithetical to it. If the two terms are antagonistic, and to some extent they are, this is so because they are stuck together as they patrol a shared boundary. They may not want to share it, yet each needs the other to say what it is – allegory's need is especially subversive because it requires objects to craft its "other" speech.

Like his reading of Klee's "Angelus Novus" in "Theses," Benjamin's story of a chess-playing automaton illustrates the peculiar working relationship he imagines for materiality (or historical materialism), allegory, and history. Bahti quite accurately notes that both figures and accompanying narrative vignettes illustrate "the allegorical structure of the emblem," which is to say that each offers an image or *bild* that is literally and allegorically placed with a story or *inscriptio* and its commentary or *subscriptio*.[9] In the first of these texts or theses, Benjamin tells (or retells) a story about an automaton "constructed in such a way that it could play a winning game of chess."

This story is encrusted, like a traditional emblem, with signifying pictorial details: the automaton is "a puppet in Turkish attire ... with a hookah in its mouth"; a system of mirrors fools observers into thinking that all sides of the table are transparent, i.e. unoccupied except for the puppet; however a dwarf (who is also a good chess player) is hidden inside the table (Benjamin's French version of the essay makes this placement clear) and directs all the puppet's moves. To this image and story, Benjamin adds a brief and quite stunning commentary which specifies the allegorical function of the story. The puppet is "historical materialism"; it will win "all the time" because it has enlisted theology in its service (as the German text puts it). Thus the story is that, although theology is now shriveled and must keep out of sight, historical materialism gives up its own sense of agency to become the puppet/automaton that theology, from its hiding place under the table and behind mirrors, directs to make the winning moves.

This rather bitter anti-theological tale has mirrors of its own. Briefer than the text it explicates (relatively unusual in the annals of long-winded allegorical commentaries), Benjamin's commentary looks like an inscription. Its form is lapidary, epigrammatic – just the sort of text a Renaissance emblematist might choose to place with an engraved or woodcut image. Bahti finds other mirror images at work in the relation between this commentary (cunningly made to look like an inscription) and the story itself. Whereas many readers have tried to argue that it is the hidden dwarf who controls the puppet, Bahti notes that the text, or at least the German text, says otherwise: "*sie* [the puppet] *die Theologie in ihren Dienst nimmit*" (it takes Theology into its service).

The wording of Benjamin's French text ("*elle s'assure les services de la théologie*")[10] sanctions Harry Zohn's looser, more equivocal English translation, where the whole sentence reads: "It [the puppet] can easily be a match for anyone if it enlists the services of theology, which today, as we know, is wizened, ugly [*hasslich*] and has to keep out of sight" ("Theses," in *Illuminations* 253). Bahti argues instead that the German text exposes an endless figural shuttle between the signifying image or figure (the puppet) and the real agent (the dwarf), and between historical materialism and theology. Thus if one is merely a mirror of the other, there can be no material or theological ground in Benjamin's allegory. Instead, "the rhetorical 'apparatus' – the puppet, historical materialism – is in control of, or masters, the philosophic topic."[11]

In the French version, which Benjamin also wrote in 1940, theology retains some agency ("*Elle* [the puppet] *n'aura aucun adversaire à craindre si elle s'assure les services de la théologie*"; the puppet will have nothing to fear if it assures itself of theology's services (*GS* v:3:1260, my translation). Here it looks as though the dwarf Theology is an allegorical knight-in-arms who puts himself in the service of his puppet, even as the Red-crosse knight devotes himself to the service of Spenser's Faery Queen. If who takes whom into whose service is not at issue, how we are to understand the agency available to each figure is. If the puppet is the sire, and the dwarf his knight-at-arms, as the French text's chivalric diction would have it, the puppet is still just that, a mechanical figure manipulated by an unseen agent. To establish who is the agent would thus require pulling puppet from puppeteer, or allegorical vehicle from its controlling, winning theological tenor.

Benjamin's highly crafted counterpoint of text, image, and commentary marks this necessity. The dwarf cannot act in the open, but the puppet cannot win by himself. Like it or not, Benjamin seems to say to those among his contemporaries who debated the relative dominance of Jewish theology or Marxist dialectics in his thought, you will have to work together. This odd partnership in an equally odd, if resonantly allegorical, world recalls the complex understanding of authority and priority in Roman and medieval theories of translation and allegory. Benjamin's two versions supersede each other under the guise of mutual translation, much as Copeland has argued Roman writers produced translations of Greek texts that claimed in some measure to supersede their source or original. One far-reaching consequence of these Roman and medieval rivalries with source materials is the creation of hermeneutics as a mode of criticism confident of its own inventional practices.[12]

As the chief metafictional representative of these practices, allegory is also implicated in Benjamin's satiric view of dialectical materialism. For to claim that it is an automaton, even one capable of taking others into its service, is to insist that rigidity and artifice are its preeminent features. Often accused of being mechanical and thus anti-human, allegory here relies on two deformed, transformed versions of the human body. The dwarf Theology is such because this identity is the one assigned him by modern culture and perhaps dialectical materialism, which declares theology ugly or wizened to mirror its shrunken, hidden role in modern culture.

On the other side of the bifold between human agency and such figures is the chess-playing automaton. Beaune's interpretive survey of the classical age of automata from the sixteenth to the nineteenth century reminds us that the special fascination of automata is in part derived from the fact that they are "monstrous doubles" of the human body. The automaton of Benjamin's essay invokes what Beaune calls "1950s fantasies" of machines that would fulfill the cultural desire for absolutes, for computational perfection so complete that it could be lodged in a machine.[13] The longer trajectory of cultural interest in automata specifies what is implied by the hope for an unbeatable robot chess-player. Whether the automaton mimics the mechanical operations of a human arm, a human musician playing an instrument or – to condense the role of play and illusion even further – a group of human beings playing cards, it projects a close, if illusionary, resemblance to human beings and activities.

The long debate extending from Descartes to Diderot regarding sentience in animals turns on exactly this point – whether the machine-like properties of animal and human physiology make us more or less like machines or animals or both.[14] Even ideas could, if arranged cunningly enough, become cultural automata, like the "total and systematic machine, characterized by an optimism as yet untainted by Borgesian anxieties" of Diderot's *Encyclopédie*. The illustration Beaune places just below this statement offers an emblematic visual commentary in the shape of an early eighteenth-century engraving of "a peculiar and practical desk for scholars." That desk is a wheel whose spokes are book shelves full of books. The seated scholar looks as though he will consult the books in the order of their shelving – it would be hard, with such an arrangement, to do otherwise, to browse at one's leisure from shelf to shelf and back again. The wheel looks too heavy and cumbersome an apparatus to permit Borgesian movements.

I call attention to these moments and images in the history of automata to suggest the special baggage that the automaton chess player brings to the opening paragraph of Benjamin's "Theses." The machine-like regularity that has consistently fascinated the inventors and observers of automata is in this case valuable emblematic property: with the dwarf in its service, the automaton will always win. This is a special version of what early modern writers often identified as the liability of allegory: a machine-like, rigid imposition of meaning not susceptible to human control, but in fact eager to exercise its powers by inventing rhetorical shapes for allegorical ideas that look and move like human beings but are not. If this view of allegory depends in some measure on its critical double – the eighteenth-century effort to redefine allegory narrowly and rigidly – it quite accurately records the willfulness that drives allegory toward abstraction, even as it goes by way of complex, humanized figures. This concern directs de Man's epistemological and rhetorical attention to Kleist's Romantic story of puppets whose automated movements surpass the grace of human dancers. The seductive pull of abstractions on figures – human and rhetorical – is for de Man crucial evidence of the dangers of an aesthetic ideology so complete that it seduces us into believing that automatons are superior to dancers.[15]

As evidently, this allegorical tableau of theology and Marxism engaged in illusionist trickery (for very high stakes) reminds us that allegory, like automata, presents theatrical doubles of human shapes who may speak for and of a world of fantasy and luxury, whether in the material form of expensive toys with moving parts or in the form of highly elaborated, highly crafted, emblematic figures. By way of such emblems, allegory is productively laminated to a culture and reality where theology had best, for various reasons, stay out of sight.

Elements of this tragic vision are at work in recent allegorical fiction whenever pathos, loss, and alienated speech are at issue, and they often are. At the same time and often in the same work, a comic, half-bogus buoyancy like that of Angela Carter's Fevvers speaks for a different, but no less allegorical, preoccupation with combinatorial play, improvisation, and the manufacture of unexpectedly ideal types who are essential to the narrative. As it has throughout this study, my argument deals with works that take on Western modernity from within by making an issue of the unsettled ground that realist detail and allegorical argument now share. I take this ground to be what is peculiarly modern about allegory in the present time and, as such, also peculiarly indicative of the troubled logic of postmodernism.

The novels I have chosen to illustrate these claims, Carter's *Nights at the Circus*, Iris Murdoch's *The Sea, the Sea*, Calvino's *Cosmicomics*, and Hoban's *Riddley Walker*, register versions of an allegorical impulse that has flourished in much recent fiction, particularly from Latin America and Europe. As the narrators and characters of these novels try to sort out the meaning of the narratives they inhabit, they replay the most prominent features of allegory after the Renaissance: its referent to an "other" or "truth" that is under construction; its odd but productive relation to realism and history; its interest in art objects as special versions of the spectacular, fixed aspect of allegory; and verbal permutations of figure and plot that assist volatile allegorical arguments.

I begin with a recent work of cultural anthropology which dramatizes the way contemporary allegorical fiction shuttles between local details – the stuff of realism – and a self-consciously allegorical narration. This interpretive move asserts a larger point about the productive interchangeability of allegory and *allegoresis* in modern allegory. At times, *allegoresis* does the work of allegory so deftly that it produces an allegorical narrative. For ancients and moderns, this transformation is not a problem but a symptom of allegory's critical and productive relation to hermeneutics.

Writing about her field-work in the late 1970s among the Mzeina, a Bedouin subgroup who live in the Israeli-occupied Sinai desert, Smadar Lavie describes a frightening episode late in her stay with the Mzeina, who taught her to how to move safely among the men and women of this subgroup, and put their cultural authority behind her. As Lavie makes clear, one crucial allegorical feature of this story is her mixed heritage. Born of an Arab mother from Yemen and a Lithuanian father, she is an oddly displaced Israeli because she is both "other" to the Mzeina, whose cultural values the Israeli occupation army tends to dismiss, and yet Arab kin. Because she spends nearly three years writing and retelling Mzeina culture, they come to identify her as "the one who writes us." As an Israeli, however, she is also an outsider whose identity is temporally defined by the Israeli occupation of the Sinai which had strained the limits of Mzeina hospitality, a concept that is essential to the Bedouin sense of honor and right conduct.[16]

Soon after returning from a Mzeina pilgrimage to an ancestral tomb, a pilgrimage in which, as she has been instructed, Lavie travels with the Mzeina elders, she asks the designated "Fool" of the Mzeina whether she might travel to a well near the then-proposed boundary set by the Camp David accords of that year (1978). He indicates why not, scoffs when she suggests renting a camel and insists she can go on foot. The Bedouin, he further assures her, still camp at this well twice a year, in summer as well as winter. So she goes, only to find that the well is deserted and has been since the previous winter (it is late September). After she spends a day there alone without extra food and in some terror, a Bedouin woman arrives and treats Lavie as a guest, according to the hospitality of the tribe.

In retelling this tale to the Mzeina, who are infuriated with the Fool for having deliberately misled a guest, Lavie emphasizes the Bedouin woman's hospitality, thereby telling back to them (as is customary in Mzeina story-telling) an essential cultural ideal. At the same time she is well aware that the Fool saw a chance to give at least one Israeli a fair return on the Israeli occupation of the Sinai, and he took it. This story and her narration of it are allegorical at every level (even now allegory works on levels). Telling it back to a

Western audience in written form, she constantly marks the narrative shift between talking and thinking like an anthropologist, and talking like an individual who has been dangerously tricked. By birth and profession, Lavie is "other" to the Mzeina in at least two ways. First, she is alien because she is Israeli (if complexly so) and because she is a woman who dresses like a man and spends time with both sexes while living among the Mzeina. Second, as the one who "writes" them, she impersonates or personifies a cultural ideal of hospitality which she tells back to them at a time when the Israeli occupation brings a host of Western tourists who have no clue, and could not care less, about Bedouin ways and values. This invasion puts an enormous strain on the Mzeina code of hospitality. How, the Mzeina ask themselves, is it logically possible to be hospitable to an army of occupation, or to tourists whose public undress and sexual activity at a nearby fake-Bedouin resort flout Bedouin values?

As someone who represents and narrates their cultural ideals, Lavie becomes an allegorical model because her "other speech" is critical to the world of the Mzeina. Precisely because this model is in jeopardy in the late 1970s, it is even more needed than before. What she learns from her situation about the nature of allegorical types constitutes an ethnographic scene of instruction that can help us think about how allegory works in recent allegorical fiction. Those characters or ethnographers who personify ideal, hence allegorical, types improvise on tribal or cultural forms by adjusting them "poetically," as Lavie puts it, to the "lived experience of the present." "Poetically" means here by way of figure, or by making oneself into a personification that can, because one is also alive and human, bend to accommodate new situations and thereby attach them to cultural ideals or norms. As an allegorical figure, in other words, she shows how conjecture and improvisation help to shape identity.[17] This thoroughly allegorical understanding of self and world, which we may adopt more readily in moments of personal, cultural, or political crisis, challenges the claim that identity is organic or inherent – a claim that wears its affinity to the Romantic symbol on its sleeve. By such turns of figure and thought, allegory accommodates itself to the modern and postmodern understanding of the task of selfhood and cultural identity in a world where contingencies work against a ready assimilation of an older allegorical and theological view of human existence.

Italo Calvino's *Cosmicomics*, a cluster of tales that illustrate scientific or pseudo-scientific descriptions of early events in the creation of the cosmos, wittily recasts science and fact as strange, engaging fables. Somewhere between parables and allegorical narratives, these tales record the allegorist's fascination with combinatorial play and patterns of events as puzzles about the meaning of existence and, at a more theoretical level, as parables about how narratives work. In "The Distance of the Moon," the story imagines what would happen if, as one George H. Darwin claimed, the earth and moon were so close that early beings could travel so easily between them that they would not at first recognize when the two bodies began to drift apart with a change in the moon's orbit. Full of bits of scientific or mock-scientific detail about the moon-milk that is transformed into cheese by a complex, intergalactic fermentation process, the story chronicles what happens to those left behind on the moon as its orbit changes, each amorous for something or someone that pulls away toward someone else, just as the moon pulls farther away from earth with each orbit.

In the end, Qfwfq longs for the woman who chooses to be left behind on the moon, and she becomes what makes the moon what it is and why the dogs howl when it is full. Located somewhere on the border between myth and allegorical fable (a border that often disappears in commentaries on early myths and becomes paper thin in Calvino's fiction), this tale uses a particular set of circumstances and a particular woman, Mrs. Vyd Vyd, to show how the moon became identified with amorous desire and longing. Here and throughout *Cosmicomics*, particulars act as fixatives or fermenting particulars that turn something general or even abstract into a "solid" – by way of personification.

Consider "The Aquatic Uncle," a wry tale of an unexpected courtship conducted by the fish protagonist who is an embarrassment to younger members of his extended family that have evolved into amphibian creatures. The nephew-narrator, Qfwfq again, hopes to evolve still further by mating with a fetching young land animal named Lll. Reluctantly, he takes her to meet his retrograde uncle, who so captivates her that she decides to abandon her higher evolutionary status and become a fish. Like "The Distance of the Moon," this ironic parable about those who smugly occupy the "top" of an evolutionary pyramid uses apparently realistic, scientific details to make a deftly figurative argument that lightly mocks empiricism and modern science by exposing the *naïveté* of their underlying assumptions. Calvino's parable also dramatizes the way allegorical irony unsettles and re-sorts consensus by introducing an unlooked-for erotic contingency – that the progressive Lll might find the fish uncle exotic and alluring by virtue of his very difference.

Linguistic systems and a tail-biting deconstructionist fervor receive a similarly ironic treatment in two parables about signs in space and authorial control. In "A Sign in Space," the omnipresent Qfwfq makes the first such sign, recognizing its fundamental importance as an orienting mark in the universe and his virtual signature. Once the galaxy and Qfwfq with it have whirled through space for several millennia, he forgets what the sign looks like and anxiously waits for the moment when the galactic orbit will return to the spot. When it does, he finds that the sign has been wiped out. He later discovers to his despair that someone named Kgwgk from another galaxy has erased his sign, then copied it or versions of it elsewhere in space. Now Qfwfq begins to inscribe false signs, which the envious and evidently duplicative Kgwgk also erases. As the galaxies evolve, others put up signs until "a general thickness of signs superimposed and coagulated, occupying the whole volume of space" make it impossible to find Qfwfq's first sign and equally impossible to imagine space without using signs to name points in space (*Cosmicomics* 39).

The reduplicative lexicality of gestures and signs becomes even more frustrating for Qfwfq in "The Light-Years" when he tries to figure out the author and referent for the "I SAW YOU" which he sees written in space "a hundred million light-years away" (*Cosmicomics* 127). Racking his brain and diary to figure out what he was doing that many light-years ago, he discovers it was something he wanted to hide forever, so he initially writes nothing back and hopes that the visible record of his existence will nullify the bad impression of this one action, hidden for all space and time except during the one light milli-second when somebody saw him. When the same sign starts popping up at other intervals, he puts up signs of his own: "OH REALLY? HOW NICE," "FAT LOT I CARE" and so on. After a few millennia and other exchanges about other moments in Qfwfq's existence, during which galaxies turn and species evolve, this defensive strategy becomes part of Qfwfq's make-up as a nervously successful academic scientist whose "famous prolusion at the University of Göttingen" (136) prompts the cautionary, and probably ironic, message from space, "WATCH OUT FOR DRAFTS."

Like other "comics" in this collection of tales, this parable about the factitiousness and necessity of signs provides an emblematic snapshot, a miniature cartoon whose implications can be, and soon are, writ large across narrative and across the universe. In the modern and postmodern worlds that Calvino's science-fiction myths capture in a retrospective mirror, contingency becomes the virtual occasion for narrative and at times allegory, which prospers now precisely because it is inventive, endlessly adaptive, and open to a calculus of time and change as more stable systems of representation are not, including some that were once called allegorical.[18]

As parables about those who systematically (and egotistically) try to make meaning only to find themselves frustrated by the envy of others and the sheer randomness and contingency of the universe, these tales send up academics and, more generally, the desire to control meaning absolutely for oneself. As allegorical tales about the impossibility of moral and logical absolutes, *Cosmicomics* undermines absolutes within the allegorical framework supplied by its ironic, sci-fi version of creation myths/science. Calvino's penchant for tightly figured allegorical patterns is clearer still in *The Castle of Crossed Destinies*, where travelers who find themselves mute and captive inside a castle or a tavern must tell their adventures with tarot cards. In both works Calvino challenges the drive for absolute allegorical control – a metafigure for narrative control – not to suggest that all reference or meaning must be washed out by the force of contingency and the unravelling of the tightest narrative patterns, but to emphasize the impossibility that is bitten into this deeply allegorical narrative and human desire.

In Murdoch's *The Sea, the Sea* the narrator and protagonist Charles Arrowsby is consumed for most of the novel by the allegorist's passion – for the most part explicitly erotic – for meaning and pattern, as long as they are his own. This collusion between erotic longing and allegorical pattern very nearly caricatures an impulse that is present in Murdoch's other fiction and persistent throughout the allegorical tradition. A famous London theater director, Charles, has, by his own smug admission, been widely revered and feared as a demi-god or Prospero figure, someone who stage-manages human lives as if they belonged to him. In Murdoch's fiction characters like Charles nearly always mean trouble, for others and for themselves, because their blind conviction that their fantasies are real makes them dangerous to everyone else.[19] At first, Charles's penchant for ordering the world looks simply ridiculous in its late twentieth-century hedonism. In early chapters he fussily describes the odd, putative gourmet menus he puts together in the tower retreat by the sea. There, he claims, he will rest from the theatrical career that wilted him "spiritually" (*The Sea* 4). Instead of the stage, he avers, he will have the sea: "how huge it is, how empty, this great space for which I have been longing all my life. Still no letters" (15). The trailer exposes the deceptive theatricality of his claim to have left the stage and his wide circle of friends – more precisely victims and acquaintances.

Before and after assorted uninvited or half-invited guests arrive, Charles becomes convinced that the tower and nearby sea are haunted. First he thinks he sees a sea monster, then he imagines seeing a face framed by a window that opens from one of the outer rooms of the tower onto a two-story inner room (*The Sea* 19, 69). Obviously emblematic of his unexamined and undeveloped inner life, this awkwardly situated room becomes a mnemonic space and a virtual stage set where Charles repeatedly acts out his spiritual and narratorial blindness to the reality of the human lives and desires he still tries to manage.

Early in his retirement he discovers that Hartley, his long-lost adolescent love, has retired in the same village with a dull, jealous husband. Charles is instantly convinced that she must still love him, that he never stopped loving her, so he decides that she needs and wants to be rescued. He secretively makes contact and pesters her until she arrives at his tower to ask him to leave her alone. He insists instead that she stay. She soon escapes, but only to be recaptured by stratagem. Using the adventitious arrival of Hartley's estranged son Titus as a lure, Charles gets her back for another "visit," then locks her in the tower, certain that she will soon recognize the wisdom of his actions. Mostly inchoate and deeply miserable inside the tower and Charles's dream vision of who she is and what she wants and needs, Hartley somehow manages to tell him he has dreamed her. Later his Buddhist cousin James delivers much the same message, as do others who have arrived, and as does the son Titus. Finally, they convince him to release Hartley and one of them drives her home. During this sequence of events, Charles twice dreams of Hartley's death by drowning or suicide. Instead Titus drowns while swimming in a heavy sea because he cannot climb back up the rock cliff to the tower.

Believing for a time that Titus was murdered – James calls this a "vision" – Charles eventually realizes that he is responsible for the boy's death. For *"out of vanity"* he never told him not to dive off the rocks (*The Sea* 402). That vanity imagined both that he could pretend to be the boy's athletic equal without causing harm and that Titus's youth and strength would make him invincible. The egregiousness of this self-deception is measured by two details. Early in his "autobiography" he mentions that he attaches a rope, soon frayed, to the steps leading from the sea to the tower. Thereafter he repeatedly notes that the rope needs to be longer, that climbing out of the sea and over the cliffs is difficult or near-impossible (*The Sea* 4–5, 16, 25). Shortly before Titus drowns, Charles is unable to get out of a heavy sea by using the rope and steps. Although James and Titus somehow manage to save him, he realizes then that under similar conditions even a good rope would not be enough – that even the tower steps are unusable except in a calm sea.

These details, which convey Murdoch's persistent commitment to realism, are fundamental to the novel's allegorical vision, as distinct from Charles's self-absorbed allegorical visions of life with or without him. Within this deluded narration, his Buddhist cousin James speaks persistently for the affiliation between realism and allegory in the novel. From the moment he arrives, James notices and describes things Charles never mentions and apparently never sees. Instead of seeing the coils of a sea monster in what the narrator calls an otherwise "remarkably empty sea," James sees "that bay with the spherical boulders" and "that huge rock out in the sea covered with guillemots" (*The Sea* 321). Charles prides himself on noticing small things, but he cannot see things whole or great, and he does not understand the sea any more than he can see things in it. Working hard to make Charles see what he cannot see, James persistently asks his cousin about the reality of what he imagines to be true, whether it is sea monsters, Hartley's affection, or the various imagined or real perpetrators of murder and attempted murder against which the narrator rages.

Most of these turn out to be fantasy in the negative Platonic sense of this term which Murdoch prefers – ego-involved dreams that willfully exclude the truth. The one claim Charles gets partly right – that someone pushed him into the sea when he nearly drowned – is only about half-right: Charles's assailant is not, as it turns out, Hartley's jealous husband Ben but another instance of the type with stronger cause, an old "friend" in the theater whose wife Rosina the narrator seduced years before, then dropped. The typological rigidity and repetition in this doubling in the plot points to the allegorical world Charles creates and inhabits, a world where identifiable types recur with variations so slight that they look for all the world like the embodiments of Freud's theory of obsessive, compulsive repetition and even more like Spenser's Malbecco.

As one embodiment of this type, Charles is the "monster" he imagines coiled out in the sea. Here too, Murdoch employs James's enlightened version of Tibetan Buddhism – which holds that inner fantasies of the sort Charles builds a life on are "monsters" – to monitor the limitations of allegorical types whose chief trait is their numbing, repetitive predictability. What Charles doesn't see for most of the novel but James does is the way fantasmatically real details, like the coils of an imagined sea serpent, are allegorically figured truths. Even when he recognizes "the bite of the serpent of jealousy" (*The Sea* 378) in his bitter notice of how James attracts people, especially the young Titus, Charles is blind to the material resonances of this figure and thus to the way that even allegorically figured truths carry some weight in real life. In this way allegorical figures turn materiality inside out.

The Buddhist James belongs to what Lorna Sage calls Murdoch's "outer space" – liminal characters, scenes, or events that are virtual "vanishing points" in her novels. Where they disappear would be, if Murdoch chose to put her fictional energies there, the realm to which allegorical narratives and figures point.[20] When James dies the death of an enlightened one – according to his Indian physician – Charles becomes heir to artifacts, books, and poems that hint at a pattern or design he now sees cannot be packaged or managed. Instead he waits, probably for death and the Buddhist version of Purgatory that James has described and Charles will so evidently require.

Like other characters in Murdoch's fiction who try to impose patterns on reality so that they can read them magisterially, like an allegorist or a god, Charles exposes the danger of allegory and art in general, insofar as both display a compulsive need to supply a (moral) order that would master the contingent, unmanageable nature of the world and experience. In this sense Plato's charge that art lies indicts allegory as the most artificed, most fictive of fictional modes. Even so, Murdoch specifies the value of allegorical designs on our attentions in a modern Platonic dialogue in which she imagines Socrates speaks. Trying to work out why human beings long for patterns in art, he observes, "some say that the gods are always doing geometry. Perhaps they are always composing music too" (*Acastos* 25). In the patterns it sets up and the harmonies it proposes, allegory is one form of art one imagines the gods might do. This Socrates also puts the relation between what gods do and human reality this way: "reality resists us, it is contingent, it transcends us, it surprises us, language is a *struggle*, we live on a borderline" (*Acastos* 36).

What this statement does not fully convey is the fragile but necessary alliance between realism and allegory that persists in Murdoch's fiction. Convinced that the tactile, sensory world will sooner provide "work for the spirit" than will "demons of abstraction,"[21] she imagines characters who discover (or refuse to discover) an allegorical path toward goodness that weaves through contingent reality, turning up at surprising moments with contingencies of its own. Until late in the novel, the narrator of *The Sea, the Sea* imagines in the muddy reflection of his own mind and fantasy that he sees the world as it is. James's different view of an always tentative and vulnerable relay between the real world and allegorical truth requires instead letting go – perhaps at the right time, perhaps not, and not always with the desired result.

The history of James's failures to let go or hang on at key moments can be understood as a fictional lesson about the hazards of writing allegorical fictions in the present time. Once, in a high Himalayan pass, James wrongly believed he could use the Tibetan Buddhist trick of maintaining a body temperature high enough to warm two people to keep the young Sherpa guide he loved alive through a bitterly cold night. He was mistaken. In the midst of Charles's tragi-comic scene of romance and abduction, James lets his mental grasp on Titus loosen, worn out from having used another Tibetan trick to climb down into the sea to rescue the drowning Charles. The boy wanders off and drowns instead. As Murdoch's novels often insist, human will and intentionality are simply no match for the contingency of reality. People are responsible and things happen, but not within a predetermined design.

It is just this kind of design that has such appeal for Murdoch. When she pushes it past the contingencies that hover in realist fiction, it risks becoming unspecified abstraction or, as Sage says of two minor characters in Murdoch's *Henry and Cato*, "an emblematic blur in the middle distance"[22] – a version of the seemingly macular disorder that afflicts Charles in *The Sea, the Sea* when he sees a coiled sea monster instead of a bay with spherical boulders and a rock covered with guillemots.

Set in a postnuclear landscape and time, Russell Hoban's *Riddley Walker* is an allegorical tale in which characters negotiate for space and survival in a world that is postmodern with a vengeance. The distinction between the world of postmodern literary theory and the cracked cartography of this novel's postnuclear corner of England, with Canterbury or what was once Canterbury as its decentered hub, is a measure of what seems most suspicious about postmodern theory: the unearned vacillation between euphoria and despair in its account of a world or worlds where Western nationalism and coherent belief systems need not apply.

This is an accurate description of the world Riddley Walker inherits when he comes of age on the day his father dies, but it fails to describe Riddley's view of his circumstances. On that day, Lorna, the old (i.e. middle-aged) woman whose prophetic "tells" he and others have relied on for some measure of guidance, teaches him about sex and her view of human existence. As she grows older, she tells him, she becomes ever more aware of "some kynd of thing it aint us bet yet its in us. Its looking out thru our eye hoals." "Lorn and loan and oansome" in the fractured speech of the novel, this thing is fundamentally alien or, as Lorna puts it, humans aren't "a naturel part of it" and it "dont think the way we think." For this reason, it "puts us on like we put on our cloes" (*Riddley* 6–7). The allegorical cast of this anti-organicism is indicated by its differential view of alienation. Humans are not "naturel" to this thing; they fit it badly. Whereas Romantic theorists are wary of allegory precisely because it is unnatural and inorganic, Riddley accepts this allegorical understanding of what it means to live in the world in part because he has no choice – this is how things are. His baffled sense of what this means is quite literally postmodern and allegorical: "Our woal life is an idear we dint think of nor we dont know what it is. What a way to live" (*Riddley* 7).

The patent strangeness of the language of this novel, which looks like a phonetic transcription of a dialect in which compressed, altered forms of late twentieth-century English barely survive,[23] is demotic, excessive, figural, and most of all allegorical. Using this language as best he can, Riddley acts out his name, as do many traditional allegorical characters. He tries to riddle out the mysteries and history of the nuclear blast and the present era and he keeps on walking around the ring of changes and episodes that is for better or worse energized by "Cambry," the blasted core of what is left of the seat of the English church and a nuclear reactor from the late twentieth century.

By using place names which echo John Clare's 1841 *Journey out of Essex* and his writing on natural history, Hoban punningly redistributes the Romantic value of naming places such that their emblematic function becomes more overt. Echoing Clare's remark about an inn named "The Ram," Hoban reassigns the name to an island separated from the mainland by a bay named "Ram Gut" (Ramsgate). The place-names he invents for the geography of southeast England are wildly allegorical elaborations of the coarseness of Clare's dialect speech: "Do It Over" (for Dover), "Sel Out," "Moal Arse," the island "Dunk Your Arse," and "Bernt Arse." This trio of place-names, particularly the last, echoes the local name Clare gives for a will-o-the-wisp: "Jenny Burnt Arse" (Clare, *Journey*, in *Autobiographical Writings* 153–64). "Pooties," Clare's term for snail shells, reappears in Hoban's novel as the female puppet figure "Pooty" (Judy) whose staged altercations with "Punch" get more violent and more evidently allegorical as the novel proceeds (*John Clare* 477–79; *Riddley* 205). Finally, Hoban transforms the flint heap that Clare rests on one night into multiple post-nuclear, iron-age work sites – a bitter, ironic revision of Romanticism's desire to go back to the future.

The pathos of language and narrative Hoban vests in *Riddley Walker* in part by echoing Clare recalls the highly rhetorical, highly speechified pathos of Romantic figures and, more broadly, the problem posed by the signifying practices of modernity over the long haul from the Renaissance to the present. Without pathos, representation slips into the absolute generality of abstraction or into disoriented, isolated particularity. With pathos, figures and the task of representation that figures so powerfully dramatize realize the desire to figure and refigure each extremity in order to think about where, how, and whether individual subjects figure in their worlds.

The "EUSA" story Riddley and other characters tell is the story of the thermonuclear power plant which the USA created or detonated or both near "Cambry." How to figure out what to do about the power that remains in the superstitious, burned-out, and once-again aboriginal civilization that the novel presents is the problem before all the characters. Riddley deals with it by "roadying" on, learning what he can from a strange dog and even stranger human mutant characters like his "Ardship." What Riddley Walker does as he walks is try to map a terrain, its inhabitants, and events as though all were or might be signifiers of a coherent system or world that he knows in the sense of inhabiting it, but cannot quite grasp. From the moment early in the novel when his father is crushed to death, Riddley is on his "oansome," befriended from time to time by characters that seem prophetic or admonitory but never stay long. A "connexion" man like his father, he is invited to offer his own "tells" – half-inscrutable, allegorical interpretations of events and old stories.

Goodparley, one of Riddley's patently allegorical and unreliable counterparts in the novel, suggests the difficulties that accrue to such interpretations when he tries to explain "The Legend of St. Eustace," a point by point explication of a lost fifteenth-century painting:

What this writing is its about some kynd of picter or dyergram which we dont have that picter all we have is the writing. Parbly that picter been some kynd of a seakert thing becaws this here writing (I dont mean the writing youre holding in your han I mean the writing time back way back what this is wrote the same as) its cernly seakert. Its blipful it aint jus only what it seams to be its the syn and foller of something else. A Legend thats a picter whats *depicted* which is to say pictert on a weall its done with some kynd of paint callit *fidelity*. *St* is short for sent. Meaning this bloak Eustace he dint just tern up he wer sent. (*Riddley* 124)

Clueless about the referent for this legend as the original readers of the writing Riddley holds in his hands would not be, Goodparley decodes it as yet another version of the "Eusa" story. The point of this episode is not I think to insist on Goodparley's "error" but to indicate the dark pathos of allegorical interpretation – the fact that it will and must go on construing meaning and finding patterns in a world where there are no fixed guides. If this activity is an extreme redaction of allegory and interpretation in the present time, it is also a compelling story of how and why allegory survives and of the necessity of that survival.

Riddley's adult career as a puppeteer in Goodparley's traveling minstrel show exposes the uncertainty about agency that confounds human actors or figures in allegory. As he does the Punch and Pooty show which he as a child watched Goodparley and his cohorts perform, Riddley cannot decide whether he plays Punch or Punch or someone else "plays" him. This version of questions about human agency and automatism suggested by Kleist's *puppentheater*, Benjamin's figure of a chess-playing automaton, and the enraged air conditioner in *The Brave Little Toaster* redramatizes the tug of abstraction always at work in allegory. For it is not the case, as de Man argues against Yeats, that allegory can release us from the tyranny of symbols in which the human dancer is inseparable from the idea of dance – Yeats's conclusion in "Among School Children."[24] This tyranny is also embedded in allegory or, more precisely, in the way abstraction and idea get figured in and by human figures and beliefs. Allegory, as distinct from symbol, resists this internal mechanism because its delight in recombinatory play meets contingency by remaking accidents into new patterns, "roadying on" as do Riddley Walker, Calvino's Qfwfq, Murdoch's plots, and Carter's Fevvers, whose train trip across Russia and successive accidents make space for one wild tale after the last.

As I read these novels, they exemplify a version of postmodernity in contemporary fiction that differs sharply from that offered by recent critical theory. In different essays Jameson presents very nearly contradictory assessments of the decentered, fragmented world of postmodernism. On the one hand, it is the specter of post-industrialist consumer culture, embodied in Los Angeles's Bonaventure Hotel. On the other, it is the heartening face of allegory in postcolonial literature and theory.[25] Against this optimism, I offer the aging dictator of García Márquez's *The Autumn of the Patriarch*. As he grows old and goes mad (or madder), his identity depends on and sustains an allegorical dispersal of his power into parts – an elephantine foot, a "pensive hand" – and various acts of violence he has authorized but thereafter denies or simply finds vaguely puzzling (García Márquez, *Autumn* 8, 101). Belonging to the body of postcolonial literature and theory to which Jameson's reading of allegory refers, this allegorical figure of absolute power argues against an easy equation of allegory with postmodern virtue, an equation that some postcolonialist writers justly view with suspicion.[26] Against the claim that postmodernism and allegory together constitute an anti-aesthetic whose fragmented and decentered sensibility is unavailable to history, let alone critique,[27] these novels present surmise and construal as the work at hand.

In the works I have discussed, particular allegorical practices may seek rigid, absolute control of narratives and figures. They may also feature characters and narrators who try to piece, or hold, together the meaning of their worlds, attentive to particulars as though they were emblematic details within an allegorical image or narrative frame. In an irony that is fully sanctioned by the nature of allegory, what keeps this enterprise from being symbolic is the intransigeance of the task and the materials at hand. It just isn't possible to sustain or even arrive at the sense or conviction of the whole that Coleridge assigns to the symbol. If this is allegory by default, it is so because the world is difficult to understand, conflicted and conflictual by turn, and because human observers are sublunary, eccentric, and limited. Above all, this is a world made in narrative and in history, one that revivifies the first part of Marx's description of the relation between history and human, material existence: "men have history because they must *produce* their life."[28] So charged, allegorical characters riddle on and muddle through, keeping what they can of the spirit and matter of what they learn.

So construed, modern allegory acknowledges the temporality and historicity of figures made in time and narrative and, as such, subject to the vicissitudes of their making. For Benjamin and de Man, decay and ruin are controlling figures of those vicissitudes. Yet what makes allegory's modern intersections with history and contingency so compelling has more to do with the eccentric and difficult positions allegorical figures take up as they work within and against the realist, experiential disposition of modern thought. Here allegory's modern career toward and away from automation warrants particular notice. Precisely because it acts as a foil to its other self – the cultural authority of figures that move in lockstep to fixed meanings – allegory remains a capable figure, not because it asserts that referentiality or reality are washed up, which it does not, but because its figural interventions can clear paths and help human reason make its way. As the visual and rhetorical figure of those interventions, *phantasia* or fantasy can be disordered and illusory. It can also create a figural space for improvisation. Even now working through allegorical images and figures is one way to work things out, reasoning as best we can without having a secure, prior knowledge but with an absolute conviction that "roadying on" is the task at hand.

Notes

1 INTRODUCTION

1 Dante, *Divine Comedy, Inferno*, 1; Spenser, *The Faerie Queene* 1.10–18. Blackmore was not always this antagonistic. In the 1716 essay "Epick Poetry" he grants the role of allegorical figures in epic and cites "our celebrated *Milton*" and "the famous *Spenser*" (*Essays upon Several Subjects* 42).

2 Here *realism* and *realistic* designate the philosophical and literary understanding of these terms in modernity, whereas *"realism"* designates the Platonic theory of ideal forms; Allen, *Mysteriously Meant* 279–311; Gordon, "Ripa's Fate" 55; Murrin, *Veil of Allegory* 167–98; in 1972, just before the modern critical reevaluation of allegory began to take hold, R. Fowler defined allegory as "a major symbolic mode which has fallen into some critical disrepute" (*Dictionary* 5–6).

3 Recent scholars who argue that allegory ends with the onset of modernity include: Fallon, "Milton's Sin" 350; Braider, *Refiguring the Real* 96–97; and Francus, "Monstrous Mother" 844. The most influential modern theorists are Benjamin, *German Tragic Drama*, essays collected in *One-Way Street, Illuminations* and "Central Park"; de Man, *Rhetoric of Romanticism, Allegories of Reading*, and other essays; Fletcher, *Allegory*. See too recent work by Teskey, "Allegory," "From Allegory to Dialectic", and "Irony, Allegory, and Metaphysical Decay." Allegorical fiction is doing well in most corners of the globe, particularly Latin America, Africa, the Caribbean, and Europe, though it now appears in Anglo-American literature as well. See, for example, works by García Márquez, Kundera, Tournier, and the novelists discussed in the last chapter of this book: Calvino, Hoban, Murdoch, and Carter.

4 Poe's description reflects this hostility: "the deepest allegory" gives "a very, very imperfectly satisfied sense of the writer's ingenuity in overcoming a difficulty we should have preferred his not having attempted to overcome" (quoted by Fletcher, *Allegory* 250n.). For assessments of Anglo-American resistance to theory and abstraction, see de Man, *Resistance to Theory* and Simpson, *Romanticism* 2–6.

5 See, for example, David Collins's recent poetic epitaph, "The Death of
   Allegory"; Du Plessix Gray's comments about the "lusterless predictability of ... allegorical figures" in a recent English novel (Du Plessix
   Gray, "Cult of the Cousin"); and Kisselgoff's review of a modern ballet
   on the history of the American Indian: its "plot line, like the choreo-
   graphy, is basically simple, and its stereotypes are heightened into
   allegory. ... Pride is opposed to decline; good battles evil" (Kisselgoff,
   "Harsh yet Poetic Elegy" B3).
6 Auerbach's magisterial comparison between the scene in the *Odyssey*
   when Odysseus's old nurse recognizes her former charge despite his
   disguise and biblical typological narratives (which he elsewhere calls
   figura) opposes the mimetic character of the Greek epic to the way
   figural concerns subsume the literal story in order to point elsewhere to
   a "whole" that is mysterious and "fraught with background" (*Mimesis*
   12). Whereas mimesis insists on a kinship, whether understood as "real"
   or assumed, between its figures and life, typological narratives gesture
   allegorically toward a moral or spiritual background whose mystery is
   its providential vision of history. See as well Doris Lessing, *Marriages
   between Zones Three, Four, and Five*, the second in the *Canopus* series;
   Mitchell, "Visible Language" 95.
7 As Jameson observes, such labels are at once indispensable and yet not
   wholly satisfactory (*Political Unconscious* 19). Reiss conveys their usefulness in his account of the role of early analytic philosophy in shaping
   the dominant features of modernity (*Discourse of Modernism* 31–54).
8 See, for example, Krieger, "Symbolic Alternative to Allegory" 18–22.
9 Quilligan, *Milton's Spenser* 95.
10 Quintilian, *Institutio* 8.6.44, 54–57; 9.1.5–7; de Man, "Rhetoric of
   Temporality," in *Blindness and Insight* 226; Kellner, "Inflatable Trope"
   14–18; Bloomfield, "Allegory as Interpretation" 306; Gellrich, "Deconstructing Allegory" 201–2; Levin, "Allegorical Language" 25; and
   Fletcher, *Allegory* 5; Freccero, *Dante* 103–9.
11 Teskey, "Allegory," Hamilton 21.
12 The phrase is Wordsworth's, who uses it in *The Prelude* to register a
   version of the Romantic distrust of the power of images (6.179–80,
   p. 194).
13 Kelley, "Visual Suppressions" 37–51.
14 Freud, "Creative Writers and Day-Dreaming" ["Der Dichter und Das
   Phantasieren"], ix:9:141–54, and *Interpretation of Dreams* 366; Lacan
   discusses the role of wit, rhetorical figures, and what he calls "ideo-
   graphic writing" in the dreamwork (*Ecrits* 1:146, 470, 511). Ricoeur uses
   these passages to describe the dreamwork's rhetoric of visibility
   ("Image" 315, 307, 318–19).
15 Teskey, "Allegory," Hamilton 20, 17.
16 Murrin, *Veil of Allegory* 167–98; Quilligan, *Language of Allegory* 18–22, 29–
   32.

17 Whereas Gellrich argues that medieval theorists were strategically blind to the difficulties entailed by trying to keep allegory and *allegoresis* separate ("Deconstructing Allegory" 202–3), Copeland and Melville explain that medieval commentators (and modern translators) use *integumentum* to convey its slippery relation to both ("Allegory and Allegoresis" 170–71). See too Copeland, *Rhetoric* 35–36.

18 Fletcher, *Allegory* 49; Mitchell, "In the Wilderness" 11; Hollander, "Gazer's Spirit" 159. Robert Bridges more equivocally calls allegory "a cloudland inviting fancy / to lend significance to chancey shapes" (*Testament of Beauty*, quoted by Hollander, "Gazer's Spirit" 153).

19 Hagstrum, *Eros and Vision* 75, citing Panofsky, "Blind Cupid" 101.

20 The structure of the Renaissance emblem typically included a text or motto, an image, and a commentary (Daly, *Emblem* 7–8).

21 Brownlow, "Epochal Allegory" 294.

22 De Man, "Reading and History," in *Resistance to Theory* 66; Hertz, "Lurid Figures"; Teskey, "Irony, Allegory, and Metaphysical Decay" 406–7, and "Mutability" 115–17.

23 Girard, *Things Hidden* 105–40. Siebers discusses allegory among other "forms of violence" in *Ethics of Criticism* 7, 20.

24 Fletcher, *Allegory* 30–40.

25 The paradigmatic Romantic statement of the link between feeling and figural expression is Wordsworth's discussion of personification ("Preface" to *Lyrical Ballads*, in *WProse* 1:130).

26 Fineman, "Allegorical Desire" 49–51.

27 Nussbaum, *Fragility of Goodness* 116–17.

28 Nussbaum, *Fragility of Goodness* 133.

29 Melville, *Philosophy Beside Itself* 126–28.

30 De Man, "Rhetoric of Temporality," in *Blindness and Insight* 226, "Phenomenality and Materiality" 142–43, and "Aesthetic Formalization." in *Rhetoric of Romanticism* 263–65.

31 This is a vexed point in recent post-structuralist theory. De Man attacks the *a priori* claims of Kant's *Critique of Judgment* in a late essay in which he compares Kantian rationality to the way Kleist says puppets mimic human movement so well that they look more graceful than real human beings ("Phenomenality and Materiality" 142–43). Defending de Man and Derrida against complaints that both scorn rationality, Norris argues that they instead challenge post-Kantian avoidance of the epistemological labor Kant emphasizes in the three *Critiques* (*Postmodernism* 65–70). For a philosophical critique of relativism as the anti-rational consequence of deconstructive theory, see Putnam, *Realism and Reason* 199–200, 234–40.

32 Bourdieu, *Outline* 78; Harpham notes that allegorical interventions are or can be ethical (*Getting It Right* 58–61); Giddens calls such interventions evidence of "structuration," which he defines as the moves individuals make from within cultural systems to change them ("Structuration

Theory"). Hoerner uses principles developed by Giddens and Bourdieu
to investigate poetic agency in "Nostalgia's Freight" and "'Fire to
Use.'"

33 Sallis identifies a similar stress within mimetic representation, which
can only assert referential completeness ("Mimesis and the End of Art"
75).

34 Jameson, *Political Unconscious* 34–35.

35 Longxi, "Postmodern Allegory" 216–18.

36 Derrida, "Law of Genre" 225. Others emphasize allegory's rare
appearances in modernity: Hernadi, *Beyond Genre* 166, and Quilligan,
Allegory 158. MacQueen's monograph in the Critical Idiom series
includes no examples after the eighteenth century (*Allegory*).

37 Curran distinguishes "form operating as a structural principle" from
"genre conceived as a nexus of conventions and a frame of reference"
(Curran, *Poetic Form* 5–6).

38 Rosmarin, *Power of Genre* 18–20.

39 Colie, *Resources of Kind* 19–23. Ralph Cohen argues that genre allows for
a "receptive and productive continuity" despite historical and particular differences (Ralph Cohen, "Genre Theory" 97, and "Postmodern
Genres?" 244–45). Alastair Fowler describes allegory's generic modula-
tions in medieval and Renaissance literature (*Kinds of Literature* 192–95).

40 Jauss, *Aesthetic Reception* 93.

41 Perkins reviews these objections in *Literary History?* 1–27 and "Some
Prospects." Whereas traditional literary histories typically offer a
comprehensive image of an epochal literary history, recent literary
histories such as the *Columbia Literary History of the United States* and *A New
History of French Literature* query their own overall design or assiduously
undermine efforts to read them for such a design. Like Perkins,
Johnstone finds disadvantages both ways ("Impossible Genre" 29–36).

42 Perkins, *Literary History?* 65.

43 Stewart, *Reading Voices* 12, quoted by Brown, "Theory of Literary
History" 18.

44 Nietzsche, *Advantage and Disadvantage of History for Life* 17, 22, 20, 8–10,
28. Whereas de Man uses Nietzsche to explore the tension between
ideas of literary history and modernity and the problematic gain of a
literary history that neglects texts ("Literary History and Literary
Modernity," in *Blindness and Insight* 142–65), Perkins challenges
Nietzsche's conclusions but grants his objections to positivist and
Hegelian historiographies (*Literary History?* 175–86).

45 Barker, *Culture of Violence* 97. White suggests that Nietzsche is here
sharply if obliquely critical of Hegelian history because it imposes a
schema that cannot imagine a future except in terms of the past
(*Metahistory* 336–37). I grant this point, which might be illustrated by
Hegel's claim that what he defines as the romantic moment in the
history of art is the subjective reiteration of classical Greek art; but

Nietzsche's counter-argument that we ought instead to ruminate in the present like contented cows seems to me far worse.

46 Hobson, "History Traces" 106–7.

2 ALLEGORY, *PHANTASIA*, AND SPENSER

1 I modernize Spenser's *u* and *v* throughout.

2 [Cicero] *Rhetorica ad Herennium* 405 and *De Partitione oratoria* 4.20–21; Quintilian, *Institutio* 8.3.61 and 9.2.40; Campbell, *Philosophy of Rhetoric* II:210.

3 Freccero describes realistic depiction in the *Purgatorio* (*Dante* 202–04).

4 Whitman, *Allegory* 263–72.

5 Tuve, *Allegorical Imagery* 33–45.

6 Spenser, *Mother Hubbard* 1326; quoted by F. Hughes ("Imagination," Hamilton 392).

7 Alpers, *Faerie Queene* 200–34; Bender, *Literary Pictorialism* 35–50.

8 King, *Spenser's Poetry* 66–78; Gilman, *Iconoclasm* 61–83. Gross argues that Spenser's struggle or "allegorical agon" against his own iconoclasm endangers his argument (*Spenserian Poetics* 56–69).

9 Teskey, "Allegory," Hasmilton 19–22.

10 Norbrook uses Brecht's term to explain how Archimago's false simulacra show readers how to read with an eye for deceptive appearances (*Poetry and Politics* 111).

11 Puttenham's *Arte of English Poetrie* was published in 1589. Spenser published the first three books of his poem a year later. King notes that Puttenham's definition may owe something to the figure of "False Semblaunt" in *The Romance of the Rose* (*Spenser's Poetry* 76).

12 Pépin, *Mythe et Allégorie* 85. In early Greek, *allegory* and *symbol* share etymology. Eco discusses the notion of conjecture implied by the Greek verb *symballein* (*Limits* 9).

13 Plato, *The Republic* (2.382.e.9–10; 1:197; Cocking, *Imagination* 12–18.

14 Aristotle, *Of the Soul* 403a, 425b, 428a-b, 431a-b, 433a-b, 434a.

15 Aristotle, *Rhetoric* 1.11.6, 2.2.2, 3.1.6. Cope analyzes these passages in his edition of Aristotle's *Rhetoric* (111, 121–26) and in his *Introduction to the Rhetoric of Aristotle* (316–23).

16 Cocking's historical survey of these terms seeks retrospective confirmation of Coleridge's distinction (*Imagination*).

17 Longinus, *On the Sublime* 15.1–2. Imbert cites this passage as a retrospective warrant for wide acceptance of Stoic principles in late classical antiquity ("Stoic Logic" 182–95).

18 Imbert, "Stoic Logic" 182.

19 The Stoic Chryssipus (third century BC) is credited with having systematized Stoic logic (Kerferd, "Synkatathesis" 252–60; Imbert, "Stoic Logic" 187–201 and "Théorie" 233). Barnouw offers detailed scrutiny of *phantasia* in Plato and among the Stoics in a forthcoming essay.

20 Kerferd, "Synkatathesis" 252, 266; Imbert, "Stoic Logic" 209–12, 199.
21 Imbert, "Stoic Logic" 184.
22 Auerbach, "Figura" 11–58.
23 Quintilian, *Institutio* 8.3.87–89; 8.6.14–15, 44–59; 9.1.5–7; 9.2.41–47.
24 The confusion is noted in *Thesaurus Linguae Latinae* ("energeia," "en-argeia") and Du Cange, *Glossarium* ("enargia"); Hagstrum describes the values assigned to both terms in early commentaries on the sister arts of painting and poetry (*Sister Arts* 11–12).
25 Lausberg, *Handbuch* 1:441.
26 Eden examines the problematic distinction classical rhetoricians make between word (*scriptum*) and intention (*voluntas*) in "Rhetorical Tradition" 45–46.
27 Moran, "Seeing" 108.
28 Kellner, "Inflatable Trope" 23–26.
29 Macrobius, *Commentary* 84–91. See too the Latin text (Macrobius, *Commentarii*).
30 *Chaucer* 282. Miller discusses Chaucer's use of Macrobius in *Chaucer: Sources and Backgrounds* 44–45.
31 Niermeyer, "phantasia" and "phantastic," *Mediae Latinitatis*.
32 Copeland and Melville, "Allegory and Allegoresis" 71.
33 Quilligan, *Language of Allegory* 25–26; Teskey, "Allegory," Hamilton 16.
34 Alciati, *Emblemata* Emblem LXIX.
35 Puttenham, *Arte of English Poesie* 191.
36 Shugar discusses the Renaissance use of *phantasia* to advance a sacred, classical style (*Sacred Rhetoric* 198, 207, 219).
37 Morier, "allégorie," *Dictionnaire*.
38 Berger, *Revisionary Play* 39.
39 F. Hughes, "imagination," Hamilton 392. Puttenham uses the Greek term to anchor his discussion of fantasy or vision (*Arte of English Poesie* 18–19).
40 Guillory, *Poetic Authority* 11–16, 35–36; Gilman, *Iconoclasm* 63–71; Gross, *Spenserian Poetics* 211–34; Mitchell, *Iconology* 164–68.
41 Teskey, "Allegory," Hamilton 21.
42 Gregerson, "Protestant Erotics" 31n.; see as well Goldberg, *Endlesse Worke* 1–23.
43 Gregerson, "Protestant Erotics" 13–15.
44 Gregerson, "Protestant Erotics" 5.
45 Parker, *Romance* 99.
46 Knapp calls this the "reversibility" of personified figures (*Personification* 58–60).
47 Berger, *Revisionary Play* 166.
48 Berger, *Revisionary Play* 155.
49 Fletcher, *Allegory* 273.
50 Freccero, *Dante* 106.
51 Hagstrum, *Eros and Vision* 33–37.

52 Dante, *Divine Comedy, Purgatorio* 32.73–75; quoted by Freccero to explain the moral import of the Medusa episode (*Dante* 121).
53 *FQ* 3.12.44–45; quoted by Berger, *Revisionary Play* 90.
54 Fletcher, *Allegory* 25–69; Parker, *Romance* 99; Wofford, "Lament" 44n.
55 Wofford, "Lament" 53–57.
56 Wofford, "Gendering Allegory" 13–16.
57 Wofford notes the critique of Petrarchanism in this speech ("Lament" 31–33).
58 Lanham questions this psychological reading ("Britomart" 429–43).
59 Wofford, "Lament" 54.
60 Dees, "Ship Conceit" 218–20, cited by Wofford, 'Lament" 41n.
61 Wofford, "Lament" 53–55.
62 Freccero, "Fig and Laurel."
63 Wofford, "Gendering Allegory" 10–11; Quilligan, *Milton's Spenser* 198.
64 Berger, *Revisionary Play* 183.
65 Berger, *Revisionary Play* 187.
66 Berger, *Revisionary Play* 215–42.
67 Gross, *Spenserian Poetics* 22.
68 Neuse, "Book VI of the *Faerie Queene*" 342.
69 Puttenham, *Arte of English Poesie* 186, 191. The Duke Theseus uses the phrase "shaping fantasies" to describe what lovers and madmen see (or think they see) in *A Midsummer Night's Dream* (5.1.4–6). Montrose describes fantasy as an instrument of Elizabethan courtly language and power ("Shaping Fantasies" 61); Miller applies Puttenham's definition of allegory to Calidore ("Courtly Figure" 62–66).
70 Nohrnberg, *Analogy* 668; quoted by Miller, "Courtly Figure" 52.
71 Neuse, "Book VI" 345.
72 Plato, *The Republic* 309, quoted by Neuse, "Book VI" 345.
73 Spenser probably did not know Ripa's emblem "Self-Restraint" (*Iconologia* 126). But Ripa's iconographic source, Pierio Valeriano's *Hieroglyphica*, first published in 1556 and often reprinted, would have been available to Spenser.
74 Dees, "Ship Conceit" 220–25.

3 "MATERIAL PHANTASMS" AND "ALLEGORICAL FANCIES"

1 Fineman, "Allegorical Desire" 8.
2 Zwicker, *Lines of Authority* 9.
3 O Hehir analyzes Denham's the political allegory (*Expans'd Hieroglyphicks* 227–56); Potter (*Secret Rites* 21), Loewenstein (*Milton* 51–62), and Gilman (*Iconoclasm* 154–58) discuss the royalist pamphlet.
4 Potter, *Secret Rites* 1–25.
5 Milton added the phrase "Image-doting rabble" to the second edition (*CPW* III:601).

6   Burton, *Anatomy* ii:102; Hobbes, *Leviathan* 426; Bacon, *Novum Organum*, in *Advancement of Learning and Novum Organum* 319–20.

7   Kibbey, *Material Shapes* 2–3. The term "Allegorical Fancies" appears in Humphrey Ellis's prosecutorial account of the Franklin–Gadbury episode, which Luxon uses to specify the vexing internal contradictions in the Puritan view of allegory ("Allegory and the Puritan Self" 905–12).

8   Coppin, *Divine Teachings* 4, quoted by Nigel Smith, *Perfection Proclaimed* 322–23.

9   Peacham, *Eloquence* 186–87.

10 Kroll *Material Word* 17.

11 Kroll *Material Word* 100; see as well Kerrigan's analysis of seventeenth-century atomism ("Atoms Again" 90–91).

12 Kroll, *Material Word* 66.

13 Kroll, *Material Word* 281; Fallon compares the materialism of Hobbes and Milton (*Milton* 130–36).

14 Banks, *London* 106–07; Millar describes the ceiling and notes the striking resemblance between its allegorical themes and those of *Salmacida Spolia* (*Rubens* 18–20).

15 Nicoll describes the symbolic role of the Banqueting House (*Stuart Masques* 28–53).

16 *Book of Masques* 342n., 344; Grimal, *Dictionary* 151–152.

17 Jonson, *Masque of Queens*, 102.

18 The use of the masque as a fictive cover for real murder became a virtual commonplace in revenge tragedies, including *Hamlet*. Holinshed's *Chronicle* had suggested a historical prototype in the deposed Richard II's plan to murder Henry Bolingbroke. Spencer comments, "the masque so used implies almost unlimited opportunities of ironic reversals: a celebration turns into a bloodbath, a wedding into a funeral" (T. Spencer, *Book of Masques* 437–38).

19 The phrase is Prospero's from *The Tempest*. Nicoll uses it to mark a pertinent structural paradox: although Stuart masques required a substantial outlay of funds for elaborate scenery, costumes, and machinery, they were often staged just once (Nicoll, *Stuart Masques* 19–25 and 117).

20 Rahn discusses Roger L'Estrange's contemporary royalist account of the broadside and subsequent trial and William Cobbett's nineteenth-century *Complete Collection of State Trials* ("*Ra-Ree Show*" 80–88, 95).

21 George, who argues that College's authorship of the broadside was "accepted as common knowledge," aligns this episode with other instances of Whig agitation against the "Popish Plot" to insure James's succession (*English Political Caricature* 1:50–53).

22 Rahn quotes this statement from the record of College's trial ("*Ra-Ree Show*" 89, 94). Jennifer Carter describes the legal strictures pertaining to treasonable and related illegal acts and writing in Restoration

England ("Laws" 82). Worden characterizes the Exclusion Crisis as one of three great constitutional crises in seventeenth-century England; the other two are 1640–42 – the struggle between Parliament and Charles I that led to the outbreak of civil war, and 1688–89 – the period that includes James II's reluctant abdication and the choice of a new monarch and royal line ("Despairing Radicals" 17).

23 *CPW* III:393. Milton's text is I Kings 21:19.

24 Reedy, "Mystical Politics" 21–28.

25 Tyndale, *The Obedience of a Christian Man* folio 123 verso.

26 Korshin describes the conformist and nonconformist use of typological allegory (*Typologies* 102–28).

27 Nigel Smith quotes this rationale (*Perfection Proclaimed* 15).

28 Keeble, *Nonconformity* 254–55.

29 Niclaes, *Terra Pacis* 7, cited by Nigel Smith, *Perfection Proclaimed* 72, 83, and 149–62. For more discussion of the Ranters, female preachers, and seventeenth-century nonconformist writing, see *Pamphlet Wars: Prose in the English Revolution*, a special issue of *Prose Studies* 14 (December 1991).

30 Quoted by Keeble, *Nonconformity* 251.

31 Luxon marks these turns in Puritan allegory ("Allegory and the Puritan Self" 927–28).

32 Potter, *Secret Rites* 1–3, 10.

33 Pooley, "Anglicans" 188–97.

34 Williamson summarizes the seventeenth-century call for an English plain style (*Seventeenth-Century* 202–39).

35 Vickers, "Royal Society and English Prose" 22–24, and Pooley, "Language and Loyalty" 2–4.

36 Quoted by Pooley ("Language and Loyalty" 7–8).

37 Zwicker, *Lines of Authority* 24.

38 Kroll, *Material Word* 278.

39 Francis Christensen describes the various, and variously laundered, political pasts of Sprat, Wilkins, and other Fellows ("Wilkins and the Royal Society" 179–87), as do J. Reed ("Restoration and Repression" 408–10) and Davies ("Ark in Flames" 84).

40 Pooley summarizes the components of that style: decorum, Englishness, honesty, and simple imagery ("Language and Loyalty" 6).

41 W. B. C. Watkins, *Milton's Verse* 14. Fallon assesses Milton's monism ("Metaphysics" 69–83 and *Milton* 95–107).

42 Sirluck discusses this figural practice in his introduction to *Eikonoklastes* (*CRW* III:137–38n. See too Corns (*Development* 10). Milton's extended figure of the greedy prelate/palate appears in *Of Reformation* (*CPW* I:549).

43 Corns presents these examples (*Development* 16–18).

44 Corns, *Development* 18.

45 Milton, *Colasterion, CPW* II:737, 757, 747. Quoted by Fallon, "Metaphysics" 73.

46 Corns assesses the figural work of this phrase rather differently (*Development* 47). Echoing Sayce (*French Biblical Epic* 244), Ricks uses the term "compressed violence" to explain, the peculiar force of Miltonic figures (*Style* 32n.).

47 Corns argues that the material vehicle in this passage outweighs its tenor (*Development* 48), whereas I understand this material heaviness as part of the tenor of Milton's figure.

48 *Eikonoklastes* presents Custom at an earlier moment, when it is "begott'n and grown up either from the flattery of basest times, or the usurpation of immoderat Princes" (*CPW* III:409). See Fallon's notice of the allegory of Error and Custom as an "image of an outside without an inside" (*Milton* 93).

49 Loewenstein, "Defence" 185; Sirluck explains Milton's use of the phrase "things indifferent"("Introduction," *CPW* II:68–69).

50 See Corns, *Development* 91–92; Wilding, "Milton's *Areopagitica*" 16; and Potter, *Secret Rites* 52.

51 Potter, *Secret Rites* 10–11, 160.

52 Potter notes that Milton must verbally contend against Charles's emblematic self-representations and demeanor at the time of his execution, described by observers (including some who were not royalist) as a brilliantly pathetic and tragic performance (*Secret Rites* 165–69).

53 Loewenstein traces Milton's effort to cast Charles not as a tragic martyr but a comic figure easily vanquished by antimasque characters (*Milton* 58–62).

54 Loewenstein reports early criticisms of Milton's two *Defenses* ("Defense" 176–81).

55 Corns notes that royalists were also unwilling to allude to the body of the beheaded king, but almost certainly for different reasons (*Uncloistered* 206–7).

56 Hughes allies Milton's usage with Cicero on form/shape/*factura* (in Milton, *Paradise Regained* 489n.).

57 Steadman describes Milton's plans for such a drama in the Trinity manuscript (see appendix A, in *CPW* VIII:539–41, 554–60), cited by Fallon ("Milton's Sin" 340). In his eighteenth-century introduction to *Paradise Lost*, Hughes argues that "the gallery of abstractions" in these early plans "betrays a scenic and allegorical purpose even more abstract than that which inspired *Comus*" (xli).

58 Quilligan, *Milton's Spenser* 94; Teskey, "Dialectic," Hamilton 19.

59 Teskey, "Dialectic," Hamilton 19.

60 Philip Gallagher, "Real or Allegoric" 317.

61 Schwartz, "Shadowy Types" 123.

62 Rumrich, "Uninventing Milton" 256; Fallon, *Milton* 96–98.

63 Ferry notes the emblematic character of Sin and Death's bridge (cited by Fallon, "Milton's Sin" 122). Fallon argues (with Dr. Johnson) that

they know allegory and Milton's is no allegory. As I understand Fallon's accounts of Milton's monism in another essay and recent book, they urge a contradictory argument: in a monist universe like that of *Paradise Lost*, allegorical persons must have bodies ("Metaphysics" 347; *Milton* 79–110). Borris discusses the allegorical character of Satan's journey ("Allegory").

64 Radzinowicz notes Satan's desire for absolute monarchy over the fallen angels and humankind ("Politics of *Paradise Lost*" 204–29).

65 *PL* 10.692–94, p. 254; Quilligan, *Milton's Spenser* 126.

66 Tuve, *Allegorical Imagery* 27.

67 Ferry, *Epic Voice* 123–24.

68 Patterson, "Meer Amatorious?" 87.

69 Patterson, "Meer Amatorious?" 86.

70 Fallon reviews the Augustinian ground for Milton's allegory ("Milton's Sin" 330–31, 345–46).

71 Ricks, *Style* 49; *PL* 2.675–76, 681, 704–6, pp. 49–50.

72 Hughes discusses the pertinence of the earlier allegory (Milton, *Samson Agonistes*, *PR* 562n.).

73 Milton's implied polemic is complicated by the figure of Charles I, presented in *Eikon Basilike* as an injured Samson; in *Eikonoklastes* Milton scorns this analogy (*CPW* III:461).

74 Hughes reviews this evidence in his "Introduction" (*PR* 426–29).

75 Clifford, *Culture* 10.

76 Murrin, *Veil of Allegory* 196–98.

77 Allen quotes Phillips's remark (*Mysteriously Meant* 290).

78 Seidel, *Crusoe* 46.

4 ALLEGORICAL PERSONS

1 Addison's editor notes that no. 419 does not appear in the original draft of the essay on "Pleasures of the imagination" (*Works* III:573n,).

2 Murrin, *Veil of Allegory* 167–98, and Allen, *Mysteriously Meant* 279–311. See too Frei's discussion of hermeneutics in the eighteenth century (*Eclipse* 11–16, 29–31).

3 Pooley, "Language and Loyalty" 3. A sixteenth-century Flemish painting, Jan Prevost's *L'Allégorie Chrétienne*, brilliantly displays the inscrutable visual iconography for which later critics chastize Renaissance allegory. Now in the Louvre, this painting has challenged the interpretive skills of modern curators, who ask questions they can only partially answer about the seated figures in Prevost's allegorical tableau, the brightly painted blue cosmic globe at the center, the dismembered hands extending from another globe below, with a half-closed eyeball in its center, and the open eyeball in the globe at the top ("Une énigme iconographique: *L'Allégorie Chrétienne*").

4 Bronson, "Personification" 122.

5   Francus, "Monstrous Mother" 844. The description of women revolutionaries as Harpies in histories of the French Revolution suggests to the contrary that such figures survive well past Milton. Francus is by no means the only recent critic to argue that allegory disappears or becomes at best superfluous in modernity. See, for example, Morgan ("Rise and Fall of Abstraction" 449) and Fallon ("Milton's Sin").

6   Allen, *Mysteriously Meant* 287, 294.

7   A similar anxiety animates the long debate between Bishop Warburton and his adversaries about whether the Book of Job and other parts of the Bible are historical or allegorical narratives, and frequent harangues against Rubens for having used allegorical figures in history painting. Bohls pursues the political resonances of Reynolds's conviction that "eccentrically particularized natural objects" are deformities ("Disinterestedness and Denial" 17). Lamb reviews the allegory vs. history debate ("Job Controversy" 3–5, 14–15). Most eighteenth-century critics of Rubens echo Abbé Dubos, *Reflexions* 1:216 (Saisselin, "Du Bos to Diderot" 149).

8   More's contributions include "Parley the porter" (1796) and "Sunday Reading. The Pilgrims" (1797), both subtitled *An Allegory*; see as well works with titles like Stayley's *The Statue of truth, in the garden of allegory addressed to Lord North: containing such remarks as may not be unworthy of His Lordship's notice: useful to the managers of His Majesty's revenues, etc.* (1773). Although by no means exhaustive, an on-line search of titles published after mid-century lists these and similar titles. Omitted from such lists are numerous allegorical figures and tales which appeared in magazines during this period and throughout the Romantic era.

9   Addison, *Spectator* no. 159, II:121–26; Johnson, "Vision of Theodore" in *Works* XVI:179–212. Bond reviews the allegorical preferences of both writers (*Tatler: The Making of a Literary Journal* 152).

10 Pope, *Iliad* 4:500–7, in *Poems* VII:244–45. Pope includes Discord in his list of "Allegorical or Fictitious Persons" (*Poems* VIII:592). In Hobbes's mid seventeenth-century translation, she is "Strife" in book 4, but "Eris" in book 11, where she is sent from Heaven to call the Greeks to battle (*English Works* X:46, 119–20). In Fagles's modern translation, whose glossary omits allegorical names, she is called "Strife" (*Iliad* 160, 296).

11 Knapp, *Personification* 58–60.

12 Pope, *Iliad* 11:5–10, in *Poems* VI:35. Even if she is here a mere bystander, as Knapp suggests, her sphere of action has by now enlarged to include the entire Greek advance on Troy.

13 Kames, *Elements* III:129–30; Joshua Reynolds, *Discourses* 128. Paulson describes the Thornhill ceiling (*Emblem* 16). The allegorical ceiling in St. George's Hall, Windsor Castle, depicts the Stuart Charles II attended by representatives of Religion and Piety (Pyne, *Royal Residences* 1:176). Its motto is "*Honi soit qui mal y pense.*"

14 Hesiod, *Works* 807ff., *Theogony* 225ff. – both in *Hesiod*; Webster, "Personification" 12.

15 Knapp, *Personification* 59–60, and Fletcher, *Allegory* 25–69.

16 Aarsleff assesses the implications of Locke's position (*Locke to Saussure* 49–51, 102, 120–45).

17 Locke, *Essay*, "Epistle to the Reader" p. 10; Bk. 2, secs. 22–24, pp. 288–318.

18 Pooley notes that Locke's Whig advocacy of a plain style does not assent to the Tory model of government and society advanced by Restoration apologists ("Language and Loyalty" 12, 14).

19 Aarsleff points out that, unlike Leibniz, whose interest in the lexical concreteness of German implies some willingness to identify concreteness with some version, however corrupted, of an original, proto-hieroglyphic language, Locke repeatedly advises readers to use words whose purported basis in sense experience might offer a counterweight to vague philosophical arguments. Despite this preference for simple ideas derived from the senses, Locke's epistemology is more subtly balanced between experiential or empiricist and rationalist principles than later commentaries sometimes recognize (*Locke to Saussure* 26–31).

20 Parker tracks this motif in early modern rhetoric (*Fat Ladies* 22, 104, 154); Bennington assesses the role of Locke's figure in his theory of language ("Perfect Cheat," *Figural* and *Literal* 104–13).

21 Pocock, *Machiavellian* 435.

22 Locke, *Two Treatises* 342; Davenant, "Discourses on the Public Revenues," in *Works* 1:151; Defoe, Vol. III of *Review* no. 92, p. 365 and no. 126, pp. 502–3. Pocock discusses these examples in *Machiavellian* 435, 439, 552–55. Recent and forthcoming scholarship has begun to take the measure of this kind of allegorical figure in eighteenth-century culture. See, for example, Sherman, "Servants and Semiotics" 552–59.

23 Beginning in 1679, after nearly a century during which no new or reissued editions of Spenser appeared, a spate of new editions marked the onset of the Spenserian revival (Beers, *History* 74–80). Farmer surveys the history of Spenser illustration in "'A Moniment Forever More'" and "illustrators," Hamilton 388–92. Hughes's edition, published in *The Works* by Jacob Tonson, included both illustrations and an emblematic frontispiece. Thereafter, many artists illustrate Spenser, not necessarily for presentation between book covers. In the 1760s Henri Fuseli and Benjamin West were among the first painters to depict scenes from Spenser. After the elaborate Hughes–Tonson edition, Hughes's essay "On Allegorical Poetry" was reprinted in a 1750 Tonson edition and a 1751 edition by another publisher; it is also reprinted without attribution in Bell's elaborately illustrated 1778 edition of Spenser in the *Poets of Great Britain* set. Hughes's glossary of Spenser's difficult or arcane words is silently incorporated in a more detailed glossary for one of two London editions of 1758. In the other

edition of the *Fairie Queene* published that year – which reviews the history of editions since 1653 – the editor Church argues that modern (i.e. eighteenth-century) interest in Spenser began as "polite learning began to revive," near the end of the reign of Charles II. In 1679, the royalist propagandist Roger L'Estrange licensed a new folio edition of Spenser's works (*FQ*, ed. Church, 1758 edn. vii).

24   *FQ*, ed. Hughes, 88, Addison, *Spectator* no. 419, III:573. Addison makes this point frequently in the *Spectator*. See, for example, nos. 62, I:265; 183, II:221; 297, III:60; 309, III:119; 315, III:145–46; 357, III:337. Perhaps influenced by his friendship with Hughes, Addison gradually changed his mind about Spenser after 1694, when he declared that the poet's allegory is too long and its moral "too plain" (*Spectator* no. 183, II:221n.). In his *Dialogues on the Usefulness of Antient Medals*, he praised "natural," that is picturable, allegories (*Dialogues* 296). Ogilvie and Newbery offer a similarly mixed reading of Spenser and allegory (Ogilvie, *Poem* II:v, and Newbery, *Art of Poetry* I–13).

25   Shaftesbury, *Second Characteristicks* 380.
26   Mâle, *L'art religieux* 383–428.
27   Ripa, *Iconologia*, and Alciati, *Emblemata*. Becker discusses the 1644 edition of Ripa's text in his introduction to the modern facsimile (*Iconologia* viii–xiv). Henkel's and Schone's *Emblemata* list other editions of both works.
28   Dubos, *Réflexions* I:184, cited by Gordon, "Ripa's Fate" 63, and Mâle, *L'art religieux* 428.
29   Kelley, "Visual Suppressions" 28–60.
30   Spence, *Polymetis* 304–5.
31   John Hughes writes more tolerantly of the "liberty" available to allegory ("Allegorical Poetry" 90–91). Later in the century Newbery more vaguely praises its "boundless scope for invention" (*Art of Poetry* II:3).
32   Hagstrum, *Eros and Vision* 33.
33   Nicolson, *Microscope and Imagination* 2–5, 37–56.
34   Gulliver seems here to have forgotten his observation soon after he reaches the Brobdingnags that "Nothing is great or little, otherwise than by comparison." He seems also to have forgotten that the Lilliputians who glimpsed his exposed private parts responded with both "laughter and admiration" (*Gulliver's Travels* 78 and 125).
35   Bertelsen notes a version of the grotesque allegorical body in Christopher Smart's presentation of Pope's Dulness ("Journalism" 357).
36   Critics have long recognized this feature of later eighteenth-century poetry. See Trickett, "Augustan Pantheon" 76; Spacks, *Horror* 153–57, 175; and more recent psychoanalytic and rhetorical discussions of Collins's "Ode to Fear" by Weiskel, *Sublime* 108–19; Hartman, *Fate of Reading* 126–27; and Knapp, *Personification* 90–94.
37   William Collins, "The Passions," in *Works* 49–53.
38   Hagstrum, *Sister Arts* 276–77. Whereas Siskin argues that eighteenth-

century personifications convey a sense of a "universal human community" onto which they then graft a "select literary community" (*Historicity* 87), Brown is attentive to the shifting status of abstraction and pathos in personifications from Gray to Wordsworth (*Preromanticism* 44–63, 312–25).

39 Siskin, *Historicity* 69.

40 Paulson, *Emblem* 35–78.

41 Weinbrot assesses Lowth's impact on the emergence of a complexly nationalist idea of British culture (*Britannia's Issue* 409).

42 In the last decades of the eighteenth century and the early Romantic era, the nationalist reimagination of English culture encouraged other redeployments of allegorical figures. See, for example, characters and place-names in Maria Edgeworth's fiction, including *The Absentee, Castle Rackrent,* and the nurse in *Ennui,* as well as the more covert allegorical nationalism in some of Thomas Moore's *Irish Melodies.* I am indebted to Marilyn Butler for these examples.

43 Mitchell, *Iconology* 94–113, and Wellbery, *Lessing's Laocoön* 7.

44 Wellbery, *Lessing's Laocoön* 119–22.

45 Mitchell argues that Lessing implicitly sets the "mute, castrated, aesthetic object" against the figure of "the phallic, loquacious idol" (*Iconology* 113).

46 Nearly three times larger than the typical exhibition piece, Fragonard's painting impressed viewers with the scale and operative grandeur of its key figures (Sheriff, *Fragonard* 31 and 217n.).

47 Diderot, "Salon" of 1765, in *Salons* II:189–90 (my translation).

48 Diderot, "Salon" of 1765, in *Salons* II:195; Sheriff, *Fragonard* 55–56, and Meisel, *Realizations* 86–87.

49 Diderot's allegorical dream narrative has little in common with his "Salon" analysis of Colchin's design of a frontispiece for the *Encyclopédie,* exhibited in 1765, which Diderot interprets as a static emblematic tableau of Truth's allegorical relation to the arts and sciences (*Salons* II:230). May explains the history of Colchin's frontispiece design for the *Encyclopédie;* May also argues – against relatively late evidence of Diderot's renewed interest in allegory – that he gradually abandoned his youthful interest in this mode ("Observations" 162–63). For a discussion of Diderot's career-long ambivalence about allegory, see Fried, *Absorption* 90, 210–213n.

50 Stafford, *Body Criticism* 385–90; Fried, *Absorption* 142–43; Meisel, *Realizations* 41–42, 86–87.

51 Fried, *Absorption* 176, 95.

52 Bryson, *Word and Image* 196.

53 Diderot, *Oeuvres Complètes* 1:369. Quoted by Bryson, *Word and Image* 179.

54 Unlike the main *Encyclopédie* entry on allegory, which briefly recapitulates Neoclassical arguments, the *Supplément* includes a much longer essay in which Suzler explores the hermeneutic complexity of allego-

rical figures and reading and suggests that the categorical opposition between allegorical and historical or real persons might be too rigid ("Allégorie," *Supplément à l'Encyclopédie*). As the sole editor of the *Encyclopédie* by the time the *Supplément* was published, Diderot would have had to approve the inclusion of this material.

55   Bryson, *Word and Image* 200–3.

5 ROMANTIC AMBIVALENCES I

1   Gossman, *History and Literature* 258. De Baecque's misleading claim ("Allegorical Image" 125–27) that after 1789 French allegory depends on simplified and popular iconography (contradicted by ample evidence that revolutionary propagandists frequently used arcane allegorical images) reduces the complexity of this critical juncture in the modern history of allegory and representation.

2   White's *Metahistory* inaugurates the postmodern view of history; see too Lynn Hunt, "History as Gesture" 98–105; Anderson, "Dispensing with the Fixed Point" 277; and David Carr, "Narrative and the Real World" 124–31.

3   Byron, *Childe Harold*, 1.38–39, pp. 24–25; 2.75, p. 69; 3.18–19, p. 83; 4.104, p. 159.

4   Blessington, "Allegory," in *Sketches and Fragments* 72–79. The advantage of this kind of allegory for Lady Blessington, whose regency past might be glossed as the Perils of Pleasure, is clear. A computer-generated list of titles published between 1760 and 1810 indicates that Blessington's allegorical tale is a latecomer among works published at the end of the eighteenth or the beginning of the nineteenth century which advertise themselves as allegories.

5   Elmes, "Attributes and Allegory" *Annals* v (1820):309–26; see too the "Ghost of Barry" essays, *Annals* II (1817):127–45, 295–96, and 446–61, and one among several "Somniator" dream-visions (III (1818):229–33). In the first of his *Discourses*, Barry reiterates Neoclassical arguments about the liabilities of "continued allegory" (*Discourses*, in *Works* 1:356–57, 466–71). Curran lists other Romantic allegories (*Poetic Form* 31, 60, 93, 49–50, 166, 167).

6   Whitley, *Art in England* II:11. Fuseli reiterates Neoclassical arguments against the use of allegory in history painting ("Aphorisms," in *Life and Writings* III:126–27); the *Encyclopaedia Britannica* (1796, "metaphor") dutifully echoes received opinion; Elmes reprises Spence and Reynolds on the faults of Ripa and Rubens ("Attributes and Allegory," *Annals* v (1820):311–20).

7   Mee notes other Romantic instances of this critique (*Dangerous Enthusiasms* 71, 275).

8   Percy Shelley reads this tendency ironically in cancelled lines for *Triumph of Life* (*TL* 191) and in *Posthumous Poems* 180–81.

9 William Carlos Williams, *Paterson* 9.

10 Damon, *Blake Dictionary* 16.

11 Heppner, *Blake's Designs* 43–47, 114–15.

12 Critics who grant Neoclassical definitions of allegory tend to conclude that Blake is not an allegorist. See Hagstrum, *Poet and Painter* 109; McGann, "Blake's Prophecies," *Curran and Wittreich* 11–13. Hazard Adams uses the term *synecdoche* to describe the relation of visible part to absent whole that others identify with allegory (*Literary Symbolic* 13–18; "Synecdoche and Method" 45–47). De Luca argues (*Poetics of the Sublime* 22, 34) that Blake's view of sublime allegory is indebted to Burkean indistinction, without noting Blake's contempt for this idea ("Obscurity is Neither the Source of the Sublime nor of any Thing else," *Blake* 658). Mee mentions emblem, prophecy, and parabolism but not allegory (*Dangerous Enthusiasms* 13–27). Damrosch aligns symbol and vision against allegory, but notes that Blake's prophecies invite readers to perform exegesis (*Symbol and Truth* 91–97). On the other side of this debate are Frye, *Fearful Symmetry* 9–11, Curran and Wittreich as editors of *Sublime Allegory*, and several contributors to this volume: Rieger, "Bard's Song in *Milton*" 274; Easson, "Blake and Reader" 309; Rose, "Los, Pilgrim of Eternity" 86–93.

13 Gleckner, *Blake and Spenser* 69.

14 Gleckner, *Blake and Spenser* 100; Essick, "Altering Eye"; Spector, "*Tiriel*" 316–32.

15 De Luca, *Poetics of the Sublime 133*.

16 Essick, "Blake's Body"); Viscomi, *Blake and the Idea of the Book* 164–79. Carr asks whether each change, whether an accident of the process or an intended effect, might have mattered to Blake ("Illuminated Printing").

17 Goldsmith, *Unbuilding Jerusalem* 171.

18 Clark, "Blake, Nietzsche, and the Disclosure of Difference" 111.

19 Samuel Johnson, *Gray*, in *Lives* III:434. Blake's reading was sufficiently eccentric that he may or may not have read Johnson on Gray.

20 Tayler, *Blake's Gray* 58.

21 Gleckner, *Blake and Spenser* 17; Tayler, *Blake's Gray* 103–4.

22 Gleckner, *Blake and Spenser* 18.

23 See Blake's design for Gray's *Ode on a Distant Prospect*, plate 8. Tayler discusses Blake's use of grotesque figures (*Blake's Gray* 110–11).

24 The term *structuration* is Giddens's. Hoerner has used it productively to discuss poetic agency in Wordsworth's poems ("Nostalgia's Freight").

25 See, for example, Blair, *Rhetoric and Belles Lettres* II: 315–34. Modern critics have been increasingly attentive to the rhetorical power of Romantic figures. See, for example: Bronson, "Personification" 226–30; de Man, *Rhetoric of Romanticism*; Chase, *Decomposing Figures*; Wolfson, "Comparing Power"; Manning, *Reading Romantics*; Jacobus, *Romanticism*; Rajan, *Supplement*; Liu, *Wordsworth* and "Power of Formalism"; essays

collected in Arden Reed, *Romanticism and Language* and in Bialostosky and Needham, *Rhetorical Traditions and British Romantic Literature.*

26 *Prosopopoeia* refers to the presentation of an imaginary or absent person as if really present and speaking (or spoken to). Literally the giving of a face or voice to that which has neither, *prosopopoeia* is a disembodied, synecdochic figure for an absent speaker (Lanham, *Handlist* 83; Culler, "Apostrophe" 60–63).

27 By the 1819 edition, Campbell's phrase "prospopoeias in miniature" had disappeared. In its place, the revised text describes allegory and *prosopopoeia* as "comparisons conveyed in a particular form." Campbell's "room" may also suggest the use of fixed frames – rooms or boxed stages – to present magic lantern shows to eighteenth-century viewers. For a discussion of magic lantern shows and phantasmagorias, see Altick, *Shows* 117–19, 217–19.

28 Wimsatt, *Allegory and Mirror* 22–23.

29 Ozouf, *Festivals* 211–12; Lynn Hunt, *Politics, Culture and Class* 62–66, 89–90; Darnton and Roche, *Revolution in Print*, plate 13, no. 188; Popkin, "Pictures in a Revolution" 254–57. De Baecque argues from other evidence that the French use of allegorical images in the last years of the eighteenth century dramatizes a crisis in representation ("Allegorical Image" 134).

30 Williams, *Letters written in France in the Summer of 1790* 1.203–4, in *Letters*, vol. 1; Lynn Hunt, *Politics, Culture and Class* 64, and Favret, *Romantic Correspondence* 64–65.

31 Ozouf, *Festivals* 209–12.

32 Darnton and Roche, *Revolution in Print* 248, 286. Such evidence argues that revolutionary allegorical images were not always, as De Baecque suggests, simpler. The clear exception is the figure of Liberty, whose conventionality De Baecque documents (De Baecque, "Allegorical Image" 136).

33 Andries, "Almanacs," in Darnton and Roche 220.

34 Ozouf, *Festivals* 212.

35 Ozouf, *Festivals* 77–79; Dowd, *Pageant-Master* 68–71; Rubin, "Allegory versus Narrative" 387–90.

36 Michelet begins his history of the Revolution by presenting it as the inevitable consequence of France's luminous history (*Histoire de la Révolution* 1:v–vi).

37 *Lay Sermons* 131–37. E. H. Coleridge reviews these changes (*Coleridge* 589) as does White (*Lay Sermons* 131–32n.).

38 Coleridge, *Lectures 1808–19* II:103 and 409. See texts for these lectures which Raysor created by assembling Coleridge's notes and those compiled by members of his audience (Coleridge, *Miscellaneous Criticism* 29–33). For much of this century, critics have assented to Coleridge's influential distinction. See, for example, Barth, *Symbolic Imagination* 3–21.

39 Taylor, "Persons and Things" 163–65; Altick reviews the nineteenth-century fascination with automatons and related spectacles (*Shows* 64–72).

40 Coleridge reworks the fancy–imagination axis numerous times. See for example *Lectures 1808–19* 1:67, 81–82; *CN* II:865–66, 1034; *Table-Talk* 1:426, 439, 489–90. Simpson notes Coleridge's affiliation between fancy and dangerous French theory (*Romanticism* 82–83).

41 In his 1817 preface to "Fire, Famine, and Slaughter," Coleridge likens the density of metaphor in Milton's prose to "so many allegorical miniatures." These are presented to the "eye of the imagination," whereas the Platonist Thomas Taylor's "images of fancy" attract merely the "common & passive eye" (*Sibylline Leaves* 106).

42 Jerome Christensen, "Symbol's Errant Allegory"; Gatta, "Coleridge and Allegory"; Kearns, *Romantic Autobiography* 118–19; McGann summarizes earlier critical assessments of the *Rime*'s relation to nineteenth-century biblical hermeneutics ("Ancient Mariner" 44–47).

43 De Man, "Rhetoric," in *Blindness and Insight* 190–96, 211; Harding (*Inspired Word* 93–94) and Longxi ("Postmodern Allegory" 214) take issue with de Man. Halmi argues that by naturalizing the symbol Coleridge undermines its theological foundation ("Coleridgean Symbol" 29).

44 Schelling, *Philosophie der Kunst, Part II* 354ff.; Goethe, "Symbolik," in *Werke* XVI:855–56, and "Über Laokoon," in *Werke* VIII:161–74; Solger, *Erwin. Vier Gespräche* 218–29; Creuzer, *Symbolik und Mythologie*. For English translations, see Schelling, *Philosophy of Art* 45–50; for Creuzer, Solger, and his relevant correspondence, see Wheeler, who summarizes the German Romantic preference for symbol over allegory (*German Aesthetic and Literary Criticism* 9–17 128–35, 157–58). De Man notes Schlegel's 1823 substitution of "symbolical" for "allegorical" in *Gespräch über die Poesie*, first published in 1800. See de Man, "Rhetoric of Temporality," in *Blindness and Insight* 190–91, and Schlegel, *Gespräch*, in *Kritische Ausgabe* II:324. Other critics note when German writers question this preference: Berefelt, "Symbol and Allegory"; Hamlin, "Temporality of Selfhood" 182–86; Simon Richter, *Laocoon's Body* 173–79. Titzmann reviews this debate ("Allegorie und Symbol" 642–65). Todorov offers a briefer account in *Theories of Symbol* 198–221; Gadamer's analysis of German Romantic writing on symbol and allegory is distinctly Coleridgean (*Truth and Method* 65–73).

45 Foakes, in Coleridge, *Lectures 1808–19* II:102n.

46 Foakes notes that "Faery" is the last word on the page (*Lectures 1808–19* II:103n.). Coleridge either decided not to continue or the rest was lost.

47 Engell and Bate list eighteenth-century comments about "fancy" and note Coleridge's earlier effort to "desynonymize" fancy from adjacent terms in his *Lectures 1808–19* (*BL* 1:306n.).

48 *BL* 1:lxxxvi–lxxxvii, xcvii–civ.

49 *Vorschule der Aesthetik* 31–37. The English translation is mine. In their overview of German Romantic and earlier discussions of fancy and

imagination (*BL* 1:xcvii–civ), Engel and Bate emphasize consensus, whereas I attend to the occasional, but instructive, note of dissent.

50 Coleridge is less chary in his praise for the "allegorical miniatures" in Milton's prose, where "words that convey feelings, and words that flash images, and words of abstract notions flow together" (*Sibylline Leaves* 106).

51 Burke, *Enquiry* 61.

52 Chase, *Decomposing Figures* 48.

53 Altick, *Shows* 8n., 64.

54 Ferguson discusses other relations between persons and abstractions in Wordsworth's "We Are Seven" (*Solitude and the Sublime* 146–71).

55 See Jacobus's differently poised discussion (*Romanticism* 114).

56 Quoted by Altick, *Shows* 217.

57 De Man, "Epistemology."

58 Hodgson assesses the redundancy in Wordsworth's allegorical figures ("Poems of the Imagination" 278–80).

59 Bourdieu, *Outline* 69.

6 ROMANTIC AMBIVALENCES II

1 Knox uses "imagination" to translate *Phantasie* and *Einbildungskraft*, claiming that Hegel uses these terms synonymously, as he does pairs of terms such as *Inhalt* and *Gehalt*, or alternate names for Greek gods, and much as, Knox asserts, Coleridge does (Hegel, *Aesthetics* 1:4–5n.). In fact, Hegel maintains the distinction between *Einbildungskraft* and *Phantasie*: in the *Enzyklopädie* he identifies *Phantasie* with the activity of sign making ("*Zeichen machende Phantasie*") and "the symbolizing, allegorizing or poeticizing imagination" ("*Phantasie, symbolisierende, allegorisierende oder dichtende Einbildungskraft*," secs. 456 and 457, *Enzyklopädie*, in *Werke* x: 265–69). Derrida argues ("Pit and Pyramid" 79n.) that this distinction echoes Kant's *Critique of Pure Reason*, where *Einbildungskraft* designates the *a priori* imagination (Kant, *Pure Reason* 183). This seems unlikely given Hegel's adamant rejection of *a priori* categories.

2 Ripa, *Iconologia* 7, 232, and 308.

3 Lynn Hunt discusses the figure of Liberty in French revolutionary iconography (*Politics, Culture and Class* 93–116); Schor calls attention to the political usefulness of such female figures ("Triste Amérique"); Parker uses Laura Mulvey's influential analysis of the male cinematic gaze to talk about rhetorical figures that are gendered female (*Fat Ladies* 65).

4 *Aesthetics* 1:399; *Enzyklopädie*, in *Werke* x:270, sec. 458. The *Encyclopedia* translation is de Man's ("Sign and Symbol" 766). De Man's analysis of Hegel's aesthetics depends on the sign/symbol distinction in the *Encyclopedia*, yet in both the 1827 and 1830 editions of this work, Hegel

bypasses philosophical difficulties that surface in his longer works. Weber assesses Hegel's hostility to German Romanticism and Romantic precedents for Benjamin's theory of allegory ("Walter Benjamin's Romantic Concept" 314–18).

5 In the *Philosophy of History* (87–88) Hegel excludes "eastern Asia" from "the process of historical development." In his forthcoming *Appropriating India: Discourses and Dominance*, Balachandra Rajan discusses Hegel's "orientalism," in Edward Said's sense of the term. David Clark observes a strange mirror effect in Schelling's critique of Hegel, which compares the apparently unassuming but actually all-assuming character of Hegelian concepts and first principles to the Indian God Vishnu (Clark, 1995 correspondence). Leask surveys the English cultural climate against which Hegel's orientalism can be understood (Leask, *Romantic Writers and the East* 1–12).

6 Bahti discusses the mourning that colors Hegel's discussion of idea and shape (*Allegories of History* 95–133).

7 Tacitus, *Annals* 1:161–2. The basis for Hegel's attraction is suggested by his analysis of "abstract sound" as phonemes, building blocks of speech that are, in isolation, abstract only insofar as they represent basic speech patterns and locutions (*Logic* 802).

8 Derrida, "Pit and Pyramid" 76.

9 Herson, "Oxymoron" 379.

10 William Ulmer, *Shelleyan Eros* 85.

11 Fletcher, *Allegory* 40.

12 Jacobs, *Uncontainable Romanticism* 9–12; Hildebrand, "Shelley's Medusa Moment," Blank 150–52.

13 Goslee, "Shelley at Play" 228.

14 Keach, *Style* 79–117.

15 Wasserman uses this phrase for his landmark study of Romantic poems, *The Subtler Language*. See the early draft of this passage in *Drafts for Laon and Cythna*, in *Bodleian Shelley* XVII:81. For other instances of the role of this term in Shelley's early drafts, see *Bodleian Shelley* XIII:16 and XVII: 231.

16 Reiman and Powers give a relatively moderate account of what actually happened at St. Peter's Field (*SPP* 301n.). Calculations of the number of people present, wounded, or killed vary widely in contemporary reports.

17 The order of published political poems in Shelley's 1820 volume *Prometheus Unbound and Other Poems* may instead encourage hope for genuine reform. See Fraistat, *Poem and the Book* 141–87; Nancy Goslee, "Pursuing Revision" 180.

18 Reiman and Powers identify gold and blood as recurring figures in Shelley's poetry that represent the origins of tyranny (*SPP* 311n.).

19 Goslee, "Pursuing Revision" 172–73.

20 Goslee, "Pursuing Revision' 172–76.

21 The allegorical nature of the poem has never been in doubt. See Wasserman, *Shelley* 101–2; Keach, *Style* 101; M. H. Abrams, in *SPP* 597–98; Dawson, *Legislator* 133.

22 Rajan, *Supplement* 299–316.

23 See Fraistat's fascimile edition (*PU* 82, 424, 480) and reproductions from earlier drafts in Nancy Goslee's essay, "Shelley at Play" 210–55. Goslee extends the argument of Neville Rogers's *Shelley at Work* by examining the Bodleian materials more closely, together with notebooks in the Huntington and the Pforzheimer collections.

24 Wasserman, *Shelley* 257–58.

25 Woodman, "Metaphor and Allegory" 174–83.

26 A more ambivalent use of "phantasy" to refer to what the mind imagines not sees occurs in "Mont Blanc" (36, *SPP* 90).

27 The term "shape" is used throughout the poem but especially in acts 1, 2, and 3. For these quoted phrases as well as still others, see *SPP* 137–38, 149, 153, 164, 181, and 193.

28 Nancy Goslee, "Shelley at Play" 251.

29 Nancy Goslee, "Shelley at Play" 214.

30 Fraistat identifies three boats in his facsimile edition; only one is as fully sketched as the island cliff with cave (*PU* 481).

31 William Ulmer, *Shelleyan Eros* 158–82.

32 Schulze, "Allegory" 53, 62.

33 Timothy Clark quotes these lines from *Mathilda* and links them to Shelley's Shape (*Embodying Revolution* 242).

34 Reiman, *Shelley's Triumph* 84; William Ulmer, *Shelleyan Eros* 172; Dawson, *Legislator* 273; and Rajan, *Dark Intepreter* 68.

35 Scrivener, *Radical Shelley* 188–90; Paulson, *Revolution* 225–39; Lynn Hunt comments on the incest theme in novels of the revolutionary period (*Family Romance* 84–85).

36 Nancy Goslee, "Drafting as Plot" 111–14.

37 Behrendt, *Shelley* 154–58; McWhir, "Ab/Using Language" 148–49; Wolfson, "Shelley and Hemans" 13–15.

38 Wolfson so charges Shelley ("Shelley and Hemans" 17). At best, the charge that Beatrice should have remained passive might be read as an unsuccessful effort to pacify the reviewers, whose antagonism to the published text echoes the reason the manager of Covent Garden Theatre gave for refusing to stage the play. Reiman and Powers summarize the history of the play's reception (*SPP* 236–37). Curran notes that the 1820 reviews of the published text were very nearly unanimous in their disapproval of Shelley's sympathetic portrayal of a parricide (*Shelley's Cenci* 8–10).

39 Peterfreund says that in killing her father Beatrice becomes "a vengeful, stony patriarchist" ("Figuration and Authority" 200). McWhir argues that Beatrice uses language exactly as her father does ("Ab/Using Language" 157). These readings may move too quickly to

remake Beatrice in her father's image. Blood argues that the allegory of this play is its *allegoresis*, the divergent critical opinion about whether Beatrice is good or flawed, about how this story echoes the French Revolution ("Allegory and Representation" 363). I argue that the play's reliance on allegorical figures invites this *allegoresis*.

40 Jewett, "Strange Flesh" 321–25.
41 Wolfson, "Feminizing Keats" 320–21.
42 De Man's introduction to his edition of Keats's poetry reiterates this view of Keats. Essays in Roe, *Keats and History*, present Keats as a poet embedded in the concerns of his era.
43 Matthews 91–115.
44 Wolfson, *Presence* 290–300.
45 In his judicious study of Keats's poetic debt to Spenser, Kucich nonetheless insists that Spenserian allegory is narrowly didactic (*Spenserianism* 174, 182, 217).
46 Clarke, *Recollections* 126.
47 Kelley, "Poetics" 338–40; Homans, "Keats Reading" 356–61; Wolfson, "Feminizing Keats" 327; Swann, "Harassing the Muse" 89.
48 Fenner, *Arts of Logike and Rethorike*, quoted by Parker in an exemplary analysis of the role of female figures in the rhetorical tradition (*Fat Ladies* 108).
49 Parker, "Metaphor and Catachresis" 73.
50 Lanham, *Handlist* 21.
51 Kelley, "Poetics" 334; Swann, "Harassing the Muse" 88–90.
52 Homans, "Keats Reading" 350; Hofkosh, "Writer's Ravishment" 107.
53 Wolfson, "Feminizing Keats" 320.
54 Wolfson, "Feminizing Keats" 593.
55 Napoleon planned to install a monumental elephant statue on the site of the Bastille. Although he managed to have a plaster cast of the elephant made and placed there in 1814 (where it remained, crumbling, until 1846), he was defeated and exiled before the final bronze monument could be cast (Schama, *Citizens* 3–17).
56 Kelley, "Ekphrasis," in Roe 217–24.
57 David Watkins reads the ode's implied sexual violence as evidence of Keats's historical amnesia and silencing of women ("Historical Amnesia"). Other critics recognize that Keats often projects his fears as a poet onto female figures: Wolfson, "Feminizing Keats" 317–56; Homans, "Keats Reading"; and Manning aligns the ode's eroticism with reading ("Reading and Ravishing").
58 Brilliant, *Visual Narratives* 21–23.
59 Wolfson, *Presence* 321–23.
60 Phinney uses the term "fantasy" to devalue what the speaker imagines in the fourth stanza ("Keats in the Museum" 223); Aske rather strangely concludes that the stanza is "packed with signifiers that refuse to signify" (*Hellenism* 121); asserting that "pastness" is part of the "essence

of the aesthetic object," Trilling neglects the ode's presentation of what the urn does not represent ("Why We Read'); Eggers remarks that the urn cannot reply to the speaker's historical queries in the opening stanzas ("Memory" 994).

61 Wolfson notes the aptness of the Greek etymology (*Presence* 319).

62 Jack, *Mirror of Art* 219.

63 Hollander, *Melodious Guile* 92–93.

64 McGann argues instead for reading the ode as praise for the self-sufficient totality of aesthetic objects ("Keats and Historical Method" 44, 51–53).

65 Among those who discuss the ode as an ekphrasis are: Spitzer, "Grecian Urn"; Brooks, "Sylvan Historian" 142–52; Krieger, *Ekphrasis* 227–76; Scott, *Sculpted Word* 119–50; and Brown, "Unheard Melodies."

66 In Stillinger's edition, the last two lines are: " 'Beauty is truth, truth beauty.' – that is all / Ye know on earth, and all ye need to know" ("Keats" 373). Stillinger explains that, whereas the text of 1820 *Lamia* volume uses quotation marks to separate the urn's aphorism from the last line and a half of the poem, other transcripts by Keats's friends and the text printed earlier in the *Annals of the Fine Arts* do not use quotation marks for any part of these lines (*Keats* 654–54). In a separate essay he points out that of the four ways these lines might be distributed among speakers and audience, each has problems (Stillinger, "Who Says What" 167–73). Phinney ("Keats in the Museum" 227) suggests that the speaker addresses his last words to us as "ye." Although the archaic "ye" usually refers to a plural addressee, until the end of the nineteenth century it could also be used to speak to a singular addressee. Even this brief summary of the long-standing debate about this text suggests that deciding whether the urn's view of truth and beauty is all we need to know was not any easier for Keats than it has been for his modern readers.

67 Goethe, "Über Laokoon," *Werke* XIII:161–74. I quote from Simon Richter's translation (*Laocoon's Body* 169). A year after its first publication in 1798, an English translation, titled "Observations on the Laocoön," used the term "fugitive" (351).

68 Richter, *Laocoon's Body* 178–79.

69 Homans, "Keats Reading" 356.

70 Thomas Reed, "Gregarious Advance" 222–24; Bewell, "Classicist Aesthetics" 225.

71 Lichtenstein, "Making Up" 81.

72 Listed below Lemprière's definition of "Lamia" as the name given to female deities of Crete are "lamiae," "monsters of Africa" who were half-woman (face and breast) and half-snake (the nether part). Unlike Keats's Lamia, they could not speak, but their "hissings were pleasing and agreeable" – as Lamia's and Apollonius's are not. Lamiae could also assume the form of a beautiful woman and were purported to

entice and devour strangers or young children (Lemprière, "Lamiae," *Classical Dictionary*).

73 Philostratus, *Apollonius* 415.

7 J. M. W. TURNER'S "ALLEGORIC SHAPES"

1 Nicholson, *Turner's Classical Landscapes* 30, 46–88; Tomlinson, "Landscape into Allegory" 181–91; Graham Reynolds, *Turner* 174, 194; Kroeber, "Experience as History"; Paulson, *Literary Landscape* 64–73, 92–97. The Royal Academy premium for the best "historical picture" was awarded to Joseph Severn in 1819 for *Spenser's Cave of Despair*. Among Turner's fellow Academicians, allegory and history were not separate and unequal enterprises. Turner painted the same subject by selecting details from different cantos of *The Faerie Queene*, book 1 (Fuseli, *Life and Writings* 11:190; Chubb, "Minerva Medica" 30).

2 Rosen and Zerner consider how Bewick's miniature vignettes specify one of these extremes (*Romanticism and Realism* 3–5).

3 Butlin and Joll reprint the ms. extract from "Fallacies of Hope" and discuss the likely motivation for Turner's choice of subject (*Paintings of Turner* 1:237).

4 Finberg, *Life of Turner* 138, 369. Gage notes that while few contended that Turner lacked the expertise to give the Royal Academy lectures on perspective, they were infrequently given and often difficult to follow, though well researched and extraordinary discussions for those who could follow (*Turner : Wonderful Range* 142–45). In 1819, an anonymous review of Turner's lectures during that year began: "Mr. Turner, Professor of Perspective, delivered his usual course to students, distinguished for its usual inanity, want of connexion, bad delivery, and beautiful drawings" (*Annals* iv (1819):98).

5 Altick reviews evidence of Turner's knowledge of London spectacle (*Shows* 126, 134–36, 186–87, 413).

6 Altick, *Shows* 133.

7 This is the phrase given next to Turner's name beginning with the second "Annual Register of Artists," published in the *Annals* ii (1817):580. The evidence suggests that Turner insisted on this designation (Finley, "Turner's *Rome*" 71–72). Nicholson assesses Turner's visual invitation to readers to engage in allegorical surmise about the subject of his 1814 canvas, *Appulia in search of Appulus vide Ovid* (*Turner's Classical Landscapes* 227–34).

8 Nochlin, *Realism* 165.

9 This assessment challenges Kroeber, who has suggested that Turner painted mythological and allegorical subjects largely because he needed the money and painted on demand (*British Romantic Art* 192–93), and Heffernan, who argues that Turner displaces history by painting landscape but then acknowledges that the anti-heroic vision of *Snow-*

storm: Hannibal is historical in ways not canvassed by the Neoclassical theory and style of history painting (*Re-Creation of Landscape* 80–89, 102). McGann has argued to the contrary that poetic displacement marks a strategic suppression of history among Romantic poets, especially Wordsworth (McGann, *Romantic Ideology* 72–92).

10 Butlin and Joll, *Paintings of Turner* 1:137; Finley, "Turner's *Rome*" 62.

11 Nicholson, *Turner's Classical Landscapes* 219; McVaugh, "Turner and Rome" 393.

12 McVaugh, "Turner and Rome" 394.

13 Gage, *Colour in Turner* 93; Finley, "Turner's *Rome*" 61–62; McVaugh, "Turner and Rome" 385.

14 *Repository of Art* (1820), quoted by Butlin and Joll, *Paintings of Turner* 1:138.

15 McVaugh, "Turner and Rome" 385.

16 McVaugh, "Turner and Rome" 370.

17 Gage, *Colour in Turner* 93; Finley, "Turner's *Rome*" 63; McVaugh, "Turner and Rome" 386.

18 "Abstract of a Report from the Select Committee of the House of Commons, on the Earl of Elgin's Sculptured Marbles," *Annals* 1 (1816):229, 231, 233–34, 240–41.

19 St. Clair, *Lord Elgin* 225–60. For accusations about the initial lack of Royal Academy support for Elgin's claims, see *Annals* III (1818):67–68, 548–49. By 1809, if not before, Benjamin West, President of the Academy, praised the Marbles as the work of Phidias and urged that they be purchased. West's letters of 1809 and 1811 to Elgin are printed as appendix A in Hamilton, *Memorandum* 47–56.

20 Finberg, *Life of Turner* 58–59.

21 Fried, *Absorption* 99–101, 108.

22 Altick, *Shows* 116–33.

23 Castle, "Phantasmagoria" 43.

24 Butlin and Joll quote Ruskin's remark (*Paintings of Turner* 1:78).

25 Ruskin, *Modern Painters* v:420.

26 Dorothy Wordsworth, *Journals* II:185.

27 Wilton notes that Ruskin identified this drawing as the last one Turner did for him; an 1857 exhibition catalogue calls it Turner's "last drawing" (*Turner in Switzerland* 129).

28 Both sketches, from which Turner developed subsequent watercolors and oils, are reproduced in Hill, *Turner in the Alps* 139–40.

29 J. D. Hunt, "Wondrous Deep and Dark" 144–45.

30 Holcomb, "Middle Distance" 50–53.

31 Murray, *Handbook* 109. Dorothy Wordsworth also mentions a single arch (*Journals* II:186). Turner shows a main and a short side arch.

32 Butlin and Joll, *Paintings of Turner* 1: plate 155, catalogue no. 146.

33 Dorothy Wordsworth, *Journals* II:186.

34 Reproduced in Wilton, *Turner in Switzerland* 60–61.

35 Coxe, *Travels in Switzerland* 1:332; Murray, *Handbook* 109–10. Suvorov's Alpine campaigns soon became famous. See Anthing's 1799 *Campaigns of Count Alexander Suvorov.*

36 Coxe, *Travels in Switzerland* 1:333–34n.

37 Coxe, *Travels in Switzerland* 1:331–35; Murray, *Handbook* 108–10.

38 Gage, *Turner : Wonderful Range* 42.

39 Wilton, *William Pars* 16, 59.

40 Coxe, *Travels in Switzerland* 1:332; Murray, *Handbook* 109; Ruskin, *Modern Painters* III:294.

41 Maccullough, *Highlands and Western Islands of Scotland* (1824), quoted by Gage, *Turner:Wonderful Range* 220. Finley discusses the difference between the topography of Lake Coriskin and Turner's watercolor (*Landscapes of Memory* 135–37).

42 Finley, *Landscapes of Memory* 138.

43 Wilkinson, *Turner on Landscape* 165. The impression that Finberg reproduces was made on 1815 Whatman paper, which means that this impression would have been made in or after 1815. Turner stopped publishing the series in 1819 (*Finberg, Turner's Liber Studiorum* 313).

44 Ruskin, *Modern Painters* IV:41.

45 Wilton, *J. M. W. Turner* 103.

46 Wilton quotes Turner's verse text (*Turner in the British Museum* 47).

47 Coxe, *Travels in Switzerland* 1:338 and Murray, *Handbook* 110.

48 Nicholson, *Turner's Classical Landscapes* 100–3; Matteson, "Poetics and Politics"; Woodring, "Turner's *Hannibal*" 23–32.

49 Nicholson, *Turner's Classical Landscapes* 102.

50 Butlin and Joll review this controversy (*Paintings of Turner* 1:89–90).

51 Farington, *Diary* II:49–50, cited by Matteson, "Poetics and Politics" 395.

52 Meisel, *Realizations* 156.

53 David's *Napoleon* displays a less subtle theatricality than that Norman Bryson finds in earlier paintings, including the *Oath of the Horatii*, where a compositional uneasiness disrupts the Neoclassical certitudes other critics have identified with this painting (Bryson, *Word and Image* 204–38, and "Centre and Margins in David"). In 1815, Turner charged that "David and the French School" emphasized line at the expense of other pictorial considerations (Finberg, *Life of Turner* 230).

54 Swift, *Gulliver's Travels* 125.

55 George, *Catalogue* x: nos. 9967, 9977, 9987, 9994, 10012, 10031, 10032, 10034, 10048, 11917, 12217–18, 12245, 12254. Butlin and Joll note Napoleon's self-presentation as a new Alexander or Hannibal (*Paintings of Turner* 1:89).

56 Ruskin, *International Exhibition* (1862), quoted by Butlin and Joll, *Paintings of Turner* 1:184.

57 Gage offers both observations in his astute analysis of *Ulysses* (*Colour in Turner* 129–31).

58 Kroeber, *British Romantic Art* 196.
59 Butlin and Joll, *Paintings of Turner* 1:184.
60 Homer, *Odyssey* 118–19; in Pope's translation of *The Odyssey* 11.221–23, pp. 315–16.
61 Cruikshank, "Boney's Meditations, or the Devil addressing the Sun," in *George Cruikshank* no. 24. A later, post-Napoleonic link between political violence and volcanic activity is illustrated by the volcanic eruption near the end of the ballet *Masaniello*, the hit of the London season in 1829. As a spectacular, onstage dramatization, the eruption mirrored the revolutionary struggle in which the protagonist is killed. Along with other works in which revolution and the hope of liberation are central themes, *Masaniello* later became a source for Turner's 1846 work *Undine giving the Ring to Masaniello* (Sheila Smith, "Contemporary Politics" 44–45).
62 Butlin and Joll, *Paintings of Turner* 1:177. Turner's 1828 oil sketch for *Ulysses* lacks this visual detail and pun.
63 Gage, *Turner : Wonderful Range* 197.
64 Thornbury, *Life of Turner* 1:314.
65 Spacks, *Horror* 177, 179.
66 Pope's translation, *The Odyssey*, 11.601–4, p. 331.
67 Finley discusses Turner's illustrations for Rogers, Scott, Moore, and Campbell (*Landscapes of Memory* 27–48).
68 Gage, *Turner : Wonderful Range* 75–96.
69 Bertelsen, "Austen's Miniatures" 363–64n. Shee, whose *Elements of Art* Turner freely and often critically annotated, became President of the Royal Academy in 1830. Venning discusses Turner's annotations of Shee and Opie ("Turner's Annotated Books").
70 Holcomb, "Turner and Rogers's *Italy*" 67, 65; Gentleman summarizes Thomas Bewick's early nineteenth-century use of wood engraving for miniature vignettes (*Design in Miniature* 64–68); Coleridge, *Sibylline Leaves* 106; Hagstrum compares emblems and allegorical miniatures (*Eros and Vision* 33); Susan Stewart discusses gigantism and miniaturization in early modern and contemporary culture (*On Longing* 37–103); in an unpublished essay, Kevin Brooks notes the "shorthand" technique of Bewick's vignettes.
71 Holcomb, "Turner and Rogers's *Italy*" 78; Byron, *Childe Harold*, 3.608–10, *Byron* 64.
72 Smith, "Contemporary Politics" 42.
73 Holcomb, "Turner and Rogers's *Italy*" 85. Rogers first titled this chapter "A Retrospect" then changed his mind when the work was being prepared for publication in 1821. Hale suggests that Rogers hoped to keep his authorship a secret by obscuring the fact that this chapter is or was intended as a retrospective on his own route over the Alps in 1814 and again in 1820–21 (Hale, *The Italian Journal of Samuel Rogers* 82–83 and 108).

74 Byron, *Childe Harold* 3.680–88, *Byron* 72.
75 Byron, *Childe Harold* 3.1023, *Byron* 110.
76 Rogers, *Italy* 31.
77 "Charlemagne," *Colliers Encyclopedia*, 1947 edn.
78 Wilton reproduces the Simplon watercolor and discusses Napoleon's re-engineering of the pass (*Turner in Switzerland* 129).
79 Rogers, *Italy* 26 and 241n.
80 "Carthage," *Encyclopaedia Britannica*, 1797.
81 Gage, *Turner : Wonderful Range* 150.
82 Finley, *Landscapes of Memory* 199.
83 Wallace, "Turner's Circular, Octagonal, and Square Paintings" 112–13. A number of Turner's major works of the 1840s are smaller canvases as well as irregular shapes, including *The Sun of Venice going to Sea* (1843), *Dogana, and Madonna della Salute, Venice* (1843), *Shade and Darkness – the evening of the Deluge* (1843), and *Light and Colour (Goethe's Theory) – the Morning after the Deluge – Moses writing the Book of Genesis* (1843).
84 Butlin and Rothenstein, *Turner* 68.
85 Butlin and Joll reprint these excerpts (*Paintings of Turner* 1:249).
86 Ruskin, *Modern Painters* v:338n.
87 Stuckey, "Turner , Masaniello" 175.
88 Butlin and Joll, *Paintings of Turner* 1:249.
89 Fineman, "Shakespeare's *Will*" 57.
90 George, *Catalogue* nos. 27092 and 12700. George discusses Cruikshank's *State of Politicks* print (no. 27092 in *English Political Caricature* II:168). Paulson notes this effect (*Fictions of Satire* 167). For more analysis of Napoleonic cartoons, see my essay, "Turner , Romantic Allegory and Napoleonic Caricature" 354–73.
91 George, *Catalogue* nos. 10067, 11902, 12786, 10033; Bradley, *Napoleon in Caricature, 1795–1821* I: opposite 206 and 238; *George Cruikshank* no. 51; Rickward, *Radical Squibs* 13.

8 ALLEGORY AND VICTORIAN REALISM

1 For the German text, see Marx, *Kapital*, in *Ökonomische Schriften* 1:46. I have amended the English translation to emphasize Marx's theatrical diction.
2 Cvetkovich, *Mixed Feelings* 101–10.
3 Levine, *Realistic Imagination* 46–47, 167–70, 190–99.
4 Levine, *Realistic Imagination* 167. Stein notes the Victorian disapproval of allegory (*Victoria's Year* 225, 241, 246, 257).
5 Quoted by Tucker, *Browning's Beginnings* 11.
6 Drew quotes these and other complaints (*Browning* 70–72). The term "grotesque" has been a constant in Browning's critical reception since the 1864 publication of Bagehot's "Pure, Ornate, and Grotesque Art" (Armstrong, "Browning and the 'Grotesque'" 93–95). Among modern

critics, Dale assesses *Sordello*'s difficulty ("Stuff of Language" 361–69); Froula discusses the poem's modernist poetics ("Browning's *Sordello*" 979).

7 Browning, *A Death in the Desert*, in *Browning* 1:799.

8 Tucker reviews Browning's career-long poetic interest in Shelley ("Memorabilia").

9 Shaffer, *"Kubla Khan"* 191–224.

10 Shaffer, *"Kubla Khan"* 208–10.

11 Shaffer discusses Renan on Christ and John (*"Kubla Khan" 193–98*).

12 Hyde, "Browning's Inverted Optic Glass" 93–96.

13 Browning's editors note the popularity of these tracts in the 1830s and 1840s (*Browning* 1:1158).

14 Karlin, " 'Mesmerism,' " 65–77 and David Goslee, "Mr. Sludge."

15 Armstrong, "Browning's 'Mr. Sludge' " 212 and David Goslee, "Mr. Sludge" 40.

16 Armstrong, "Browning's 'Mr. Sludge' " 215–20.

17 Armstrong, "Browning and the 'Grotesque' " 93–94.

18 De Man, "Shelley Disfigured," in *Rhetoric of Romanticism* 93–124; Benjamin, *German Tragic Drama* 161–235.

19 Curle 135–209.

20 Walker uses these phrases to describe the effects of Browning's repetitive syntax and figures ("Dynamic Imagery" 14–20).

21 Among other examples, see The Other Half-Rome's metaphorical description of Pompilia as a small, caged bird pursued by the "tooth and claw of something in the dark, – / Giuseppe Caponsacchi" (*RB* 3.776–88, p. 132).

22 Every speaker uses this pattern; it is most frequent when the tone is skeptical or derisive. See, for example, Caponsacchi's bitter tirade about the Church's unwillingness to assist Pompilia (*RB* 311–12, 315, 316, 318); or the lawyer Bottinius's use of the pattern to tell the story of Guido's marriage to Pompilia (*RB* 443–66).

23 Walker, "Dynamic Imagery" 28–29; Woolford, *Browning the Revisionary* 176–204; Hiemstra, "Browning and History"; McGowan, *Representation and Revelation* 158–73; Feinberg, "Truth and Illusion." Critics who have questioned the figural coherence of Browning's central ring figure include A. K. Cook, *Commentary* 93, and Siegchrist, *Brutal Print* 7–10.

24 Slinn, "Language and Truth" 115–32; Shaw, "Browning's Murder Mystery." Several critics emphasize the figurality of Browning's realism: Dillon, "Browning and the Figure of Life"; Froula, "Browning's *Sordello*"; and Tucker, "Dramatic Monologue" 226–43.

25 Armstrong, "Prolixity."

26 Siegchrist, *Brutal Print* 3–8, 150.

27 When Done Elvire challenges his casuistical arguments, Don Juan charges that women lack the ability to comprehend "mental analysis" (511, *Browning* 11:22); he also argues that women "rush into," and are

absorbed by, men (1173, *Browning* 11:40). Both claims evidently serve Don Juan's purpose.

28 Ryals, *Browning's Later Poetry* 466, 468.

29 The similarity is probably not accidental. The freaks Browning names are listed in accounts of London's Bartholomew Fair of 1803, also the source for Wordsworth's account of a similar fair he visited in London. Browning's editors describe the freaks exhibited at Bartholomew Fair (*Browning* 11:977). The other likely source is Wordsworth's *Prelude* description of Bartholomew Fair, which Browning echoes in *A Death in the Desert*.

30 Benjamin, "Task of the Translator," in *Illuminations* 69–83; Steiner applies Benjamin's thesis to Browning (*After Babel* 476, 315); Prins assesses the syntactic violence of Browning's translation ("'Violence bridling speech'").

31 Prins provides literal translations of Aeschylus's Greek ("'Violence Bridling Speech'" 156–62).

32 Excerpts from the novel's early critical reception are reprinted in Carroll 382–460; Knoepflmacher critiques the novel's awkward joining of its two plots (*Religious Humanism* 126); McGowan assesses evidence of Eliot's commitment to realism and her novelistic defections from that commitment (*Representation and Revelation* 132–57).

33 *Carroll* 368.

34 Semmel discusses Eliot's treatment of problems of race and homeland for disinherited peoples in *The Spanish Gypsy* and Mordecai (*Eliot and National Inheritance* 103–29).

35 Quoted by McGowan (*Representation and Revelation* 133–37).

36 Chase, "Decomposition of the Elephants," in *Decomposing Figures* 159–63.

37 Knoepflmacher, *Religious Humanism* 116–48.

38 Eliot, *Essays* 264; Cottom, *Social Figures* 76–77, 109.

39 Knoepflmacher, *Religious Humanism* 136–48; Semmel, *Eliot and National Inheritance* 102; E. A. McCobb, "Eliot and Schopenhauer" 536–43; Houghton, *Victorian Frame* 179.

40 Cottom, *Social Figures* 79.

41 The motto disappears in the second edition, then returns a year later in the third (*Deronda* xxxiv–xxxviii).

42 McCobb, "Eliot and Schopenhauer" 546–47; Knoepflmacher, *Religious Humanism* 145–46.

43 Wollstonecraft, *Vindication* 54.

44 Cvetkovich, *Mixed Feelings* 150–54.

45 Meyer, "Proto-Zionism" 735–52.

46 Gallagher, "Eliot and *Deronda*" 49–50.

47 Gallagher, "Eliot and *Deronda*" 50.

48 Marx, "On the Jewish Question" 48.

49 McCobb reviews evidence of Eliot's distaste for gambling houses ("Eliot and Schopenhauer" 537).

50 Lerner, "Eliot's Struggle" 93.
51 Tucker, "Epiphany and Browning" 211.
52 Mintz, "Messianic Vocation" 155–56.
53 Marx, "On the Jewish Question" 46.

9 CONCLUSION

1 Among recent novelists who write allegorical fiction are: Gabriel García Márquez, Milan Kundera, Michel Tournier, Italo Calvino, Iris Murdoch, Derek Walcott, Wole Soyinka, Ben Okri, Fred Chappell, and Russell Hoban.
2 Wood, "Bewitchment" 20.
3 For differently poised accounts of this question, see Tiedemann, "Historical Materialism"; Wolin, *Benjamin* 90–131; Clej, "Benjamin's Messianic Politics" 27–29; and Walter Cohen, "Marxist Criticism" 324.
4 Lloyd Spencer, "Allegory" 62.
5 Bahti, *Allegories of History* 47.
6 Bahti, *Allegories of History* 285.
7 For the German text, see *GS* II:1.405–6. Bahti, *Allegories of History* 281–82.
8 For a partial English translation, see Benjamin, "[Theoretics of Knowledge]"; Benjamin, *Das Passagen-Werk*, in *GS* V:1–2; Buck-Morss offers an extended account of this project in *Dialectics of Seeing* 49–52.
9 Bahti, *Allegories of History* 186–87, 200; Daly also remarks that Benjamin may be the first to have recognized the emblematic character of choral maxims in Baroque tragedy (*Emblem* 7–8, 143).
10 Benjamin, "Sur le concept d'histoire," in *GS* I:3.1260–66.
11 Bahti, *Allegories of History* 200.
12 Copeland, *Rhetoric* 3–4, 151–55.
13 Beaune, "Age of Automata" 433.
14 Beaune, "Age of Automata" 437, 444–45, 462–63; the Museum of Automata in York, England, includes such a group of musicians.
15 De Man, "Aesthetic Formalization," in *Rhetoric of Romanticism* 286–90. Norris emphasizes this concern (*Postmodernism* 19–21); Caruth discusses de Man's alignment of Kleist and Kant ("Claims of Reference" 197–98).
16 Lavie, "Political Allegory" 153–55.
17 Lavie, "Political Allegory" 155–77.
18 In "Myth in the Narrative," Calvino examines the tension between a fixed combinatorial system and the desire for innovation (76–77).
19 Dipple describes Murdoch's fictional investigation of Platonic reality and literary realism (*Work for the Spirit* 9–35).
20 Sage, "Pursuit of Imperfection" 118.
21 Dipple uses these phrases, the first from Murdoch's study of Plato, *The*

Fire and the Sun, the second from her novel *The Black Prince*, to describe Murdoch's novelistic inquiry (*Work for the Spirit* 116).

22 Sage, "Pursuit of Imperfection" 119.

23 Porter describes the decaying shelf life of language and post-nuclear culture in the punning language of Hoban's novel ("Three Quarks" 450).

24 De Man, "Image and Emblem in Yeats," in *Rhetoric of Romanticism* 202–4.

25 Jameson presents the first view of postmodernism in *Postmodernism* 55–66 and the second in "Third-World."

26 Slemon assesses this double view of allegory in several recent essays ("Revisioning Allegory" 45–54, "Monuments of Empire" 7–13, and "Post-Colonial Allegory"). JanMohamed emphasizes the hegemonic, colonialist side of allegory ("Manichean Allegory" 68–69). Longxi critiques widespread use of the term in recent theory ("Postmodern Allegory" 217–18).

27 Hutcheon discusses the term "postmodernism" and its implications in *A Poetics of Postmodernism* and *Politics of Postmodernism*. For influential statements of allegory's involvement in postmodernism, see Owens, "Allegorical Impulse;" Carravetta, *Prefaces* 160–65; and essays in Foster's collection *The Anti-Aesthetic*, particularly Gregory Ulmer, "Post-Criticism" 95–99, and Owens, "Discourse of Others" 57–64.

28 Findlay quotes from Marx's marginal note in *German Ideology* to question the ahistoricality of postmodernism ("Otherwise Engaged" 388–98).

Bibliography

Aarsleff, Hans. *From Locke to Saussure*. University of Minnesota Press, 1982.

Adams, Hazard. *Philosophy of the Literary Symbolic*. Tallahassee: Florida State University Press, 1983.

"Synecdoche and Method." In *Critical Paths*. Ed. Dan Miller, Mark Bracher, and Donald Ault. Durham: Duke University Press, 1987. 41–71.

Addison, Joseph. *Dialogues on the Usefulness of Antient Medals*. In vol. III of *The Miscellaneous Works in Verse and Prose*. London: J. and R. Tonson, 1766.

The Spectator. Ed. Donald F. Bond. 5 vols. Oxford: Clarendon Press, 1965.

Alciati, Andrea. *Emblemata*. Antwerp: Plantyn, 1584.

Allen, Don C. *Mysteriously Meant*. Baltimore: Johns Hopkins University Press, 1970.

Alpers, Paul J. *The Poetry of the Faerie Queene*. Princeton University Press, 1967.

Altick, Richard D. *The Shows of London*. Cambridge, Mass.: Harvard University Press, 1978.

Anderson, Wilda C. "Dispensing with the Fixed Point: Scientific Law as Historical Event." *History and Theory* 3 (1983): 264–77.

Andries, Lise. "Almanacs: Revolutionizing a Traditional Genre." Darnton and Roche 203–22.

Anon. "Historical Painting in England." *Art Union* 2 (1840): 65–66.

Anthing, Johann Friedrich. *History of the Campaigns of Count Alexander Suvorov Rymnisksi*. 2 vols. London: J. Wright, 1799.

Aristotle. *The Art of Rhetoric*. Trans. John H. Freese. Cambridge, Mass.: Harvard University Press, 1926.

On the Soul. Ed. T. H. Page. Trans. W. S. Hett. Cambridge, Mass.: Harvard University Press, 1935.

Armstrong, Isobel. "Browning and the 'Grotesque' Style." Armstrong 93–123.

"Browning's 'Mr. Sludge, "The Medium'." In *Robert Browning*. Ed. Philip Drew. London: Methuen, 1966. 212–22.

"*The Ring and the Book*: The Uses of Prolixity." Armstrong 177–97.

Armstrong, Isobel, ed. *The Major Victorian Poets: Reconsiderations*. Lincoln: University of Nebraska Press, 1969.

Aske, Martin. *Keats and Hellenism.* Cambridge University Press, 1985.

Auerbach, Erich. "Figura." In *Scenes from the Drama of European Literature.* 1954 rpt.; University of Minnesota Press, 1984. 11–76.

Mimesis. Trans. Willard R. Trask. Princeton University Press, 1968.

Bacon, Francis. *Advancement of Learning and Novum Organum.* Ed. James E. Creighton. Rev. edn. New York: Willey, 1944.

Bagehot, Walter. "Wordsworth, Tennyson and Browning; or Pure, Ornate, and Grotesque Art in English Poetry." *National Review* 19 (1864): 27–67.

Bahti, Timothy. *Allegories of History.* Baltimore: Johns Hopkins University Press, 1992.

Baillie, Joanna. *A Series of Plays.* 2nd edn. 2 vols. London: T. Cadell and W. Davies, 1799–1802.

Banks, F. R. *The Penguin Guide to London.* 6th edn. Baltimore: Penguin, 1973.

Barker, Francis. *The Culture of Violence.* Chicago University Press, 1993.

Barry, James. *The Works of James Barry, Esquire, Historical Painter.* 2 vols. London: T. Cadell, 1809.

Barth, J. Robert, S. J. *The Symbolic Imagination.* Princeton University Press, 1977.

Beaune, Jean-Claude. "The Classical Age of Automata." In vol. 1 of *Fragments from a History of the Human Body.* Ed. Michel Feher. New York: Urzone, 1989. 430–80.

Becker, Jochen, ed. *Iconologia of Uytbeeld dinghe des Verstands.* Joest, Netherlands: Davaco, 1977.

Beers, Henry A. *A History of English Romanticism in the Eighteenth Century.* New York: Gordian Press, 1966.

Behrendt, Stephen C. *Shelley and His Audiences.* Lincoln: University of Nebraska Press, 1989.

Bender, John B. *Spenser and Literary Pictorialism.* Princeton University Press, 1972.

Bender, John, and David E. Wellbery, eds. *The Ends of Rhetoric.* Stanford University Press, 1990.

Benjamin, Andrew, Geoffrey N. Cantor, and John R. R. Christie, eds. *The Figural and the Literal.* Manchester University Press, 1987.

Benjamin, Walter. "Central Park." *New German Critique* 34 (1985): 28–58.

Gesammelte Schriften. Ed. Rolf Tiedemann and Herman Schweppenhäuser. 7 vols. Suhrkamp: Frankfurt am Main, 1972.

Illuminations. Ed. Hannah Arendt. Trans. Harry Zohn. New York: Schocken Books, 1968.

One-Way Street and Other Writings. Trans. Edmund Jephcott and Kingsley Shorter. London: NLB, 1979.

The Origin of German Tragic Drama. Trans. John Osborne. London: NLB, 1977.

"[Theoretics of Knowledge; Theory of Progress]." *The Philosophical Forum* 15 (1983–84): 1–39.

Bennington, Geoff. "The Perfect Cheat: Locke and Empiricism's Rhetoric." Benjamin, Cantor, and Christie 103–23.

Berefelt, Gunnar. "Symbol and Allegory." *Journal of Aesthetics and Art Criticism* 28 (1969): 201–12.

Berger, Harry, Jr. *Revisionary Play: Studies in the Spenserian Dynamics*. Berkeley: University of California Press, 1988.

Bertelsen, Lance. "Jane Austen's Miniatures: Painting, Drawing, and the Novels." *Modern Language Quarterly* 45 (1984): 350–72.

"Journalism, Carnival, and *Jubilato Agno*." *ELH* 59 (1992): 357–84.

Bewell, Alan J. "The Political Implications of Keats's Classicist Aesthetics." *Studies in Romanticism* 25 (1986): 220–30.

Bialostosky, Don H., and Lawrence Needham, eds. *Rhetorical Traditions and British Romantic Literature*. Bloomington: Indiana University Press, 1995.

Blackmore, Richard. "An Essay upon Epick Poetry." In *Essays upon Several Subjects*. London: E. Curll, J. Pemberton, 1716. 1–185.

Prince Arthur. An Heroic Poem. In Ten Books. London: Awnsham and John Churchil, 1695.

Blair, Hugh. *Lectures on Rhetoric and Belles Lettres*. 2 vols. London: W. Strahan, 1783.

Blake, William. *The Complete Poetry and Prose of William Blake*. Ed. David V. Erdman. Rev. edn. Berkeley: University of California Press, 1982.

William Blake's Water-Colour Designs for the Poems of Thomas Gray. London: Trianon Press, 1971.

Blank, G. Kim, ed. *The New Shelley*. London: Macmillan, 1991.

Blessington, Lady Marguerite. "An Allegory." In *Sketches and Fragments*. London: Longman, Hurst, Rees, Orme, and Brown, 1822. 72–79.

Blood, Roger. "Allegory and Representation in *The Cenci*." *Studies in Romanticism* 33 (1994): 355–89.

Bloom, Harold, ed. *Iris Murdoch*. New York: Chelsea House, 1986.

Bloomfield, Morton W. "Allegory as Interpretation." *New Literary History* 3 (1972): 302–17.

Bloomfield, Morton W., ed. *Allegory, Myth, and Symbol*. Cambridge, Mass.: Harvard University Press, 1981.

Bohls, Elizabeth A. "Disinterestedness and Denial of the Particular: Locke, Adam Smith, and the Subject of Aesthetics." In *Eighteenth-Century Aesthetics and the Reconstruction of Art*. Ed. Paul Mattick, Jr. Cambridge University Press, 1993. 16–51.

Bond, Richmond P. *The Tatler: The Making of a Literary Journal*. Cambridge, Mass.: Harvard University Press, 1971.

Borris, Kenneth. "Allegory in *Paradise Lost*: Satan's Cosmic Journey." *Milton Studies* 26 (1990): 101–33.

Bourdieu, Pierre. *Outline of a Theory of Practice*. Tr. R. Nice. Cambridge University Press, 1977.

Bradley, A. M. *Napoleon in Caricature, 1795–1821*. 2 vols. New York: John Lane, 1911.

Braider, Christopher. *Refiguring the Real*. Princeton University Press, 1993.

Brilliant, Richard. *Visual Narratives*. Ithaca: Cornell University Press, 1984.

Bronson, Bertrand H. "Personification Reconsidered." In *New Light on Dr. Johnson*. Ed. Frederick W. Hilles. New Haven: Yale University Press, 1959. 189–231.

Brooks, Cleanth. "Keats's Sylvan Historian: History without Footnotes." In *The Well-Wrought Urn*. New York: Harcourt Brace, 1947. 139–52.

Brown, Marshall. "Contemplating the Theory of Literary History." *PMLA* 107 (1992): 13–25.

Preromanticism. Stanford University Press, 1991.

"Unheard Melodies: The Force of Form." *PMLA* 107 (1992): 465–81.

Browning, Robert. *The Plays of Robert Browning*. Ed. Thomas J. Collins and Richard J. Shroyer. New York: Garland, 1988.

The Ring and the Book. Ed. Richard D. Altick. New Haven: Yale University Press, 1971.

Robert Browning: The Poems. Ed. John Pettigrew. 2 vols. New Haven: Yale University Press, 1981.

Brownlow, Jeanne. "Epochal Allegory in Galdós's *Torquemada*: The Ur-Text and the Episteme." *PMLA* 108 (1993): 294–307.

Brunschwing, Jacques, ed. *Les Stoïciens et leur Logique*. Paris: Librairie Philosophique, 1978.

Bryson, Norman. "Centre and Margins in David." *Word and Image* 4 (1988): 43–50.

Word and Image. Cambridge University Press, 1980.

Buck-Morss, Susan. *The Dialectics of Seeing*. Cambridge, Mass.: MIT Press, 1990.

Burke, Edmund. *A Philosophical Enquiry into the Origin of Our Ideas of the Sublime and Beautiful*. Ed. J. T. Boulton. University of Notre Dame Press, 1958.

Burton, Robert. *Anatomy of Melancholy*. Ed. Holbrook Jackson. 3 vols. London: J. M. Dent, 1932.

Butlin, Martin, and Evelyn Joll. *The Paintings of J. M. W. Turner*. Rev. edn. 2 vols. New Haven: Yale University Press, 1984.

Butlin, Martin, and John Rothenstein. *Turner*. London: Heinemann, 1964.

Byron, George Gordon, Lord. *Childe Harold's Pilgrimage*. Vol. II of *Byron*. Ed. Jerome McGann. Oxford University Press, 1986.

Calvino, Italo. *The Castle of Crossed Destinies*. Trans. William Weaver. New York: Harcourt Brace Jovanovich, 1976.

Cosmicomics. Trans. William Weaver. New York: Harcourt Brace Jovanovich, 1968.

"Myth in the Narrative." In *Surfiction: Fiction Now and Tomorrow*. Ed. Raymond Federman. Chicago: Swallow Press, 1975. 75–81.

The Uses of Literature. Trans. Patrick Creagh. New York: Harcourt Brace Jovanovich, 1986.

Campbell, George. *The Philosophy of Rhetoric.* 2 vols. London: W. Strahan and T. Cadell, 1766.

Carlyle, Thomas. "On History." In vol. xxvii of *The Works of Thomas Carlyle.* Ed. H. D. Traill. London: Chapman and Hall, 1896–99. 83–95.

Carr, David. "Narrative and the Real World: An Argument for Continuity." *History and Theory* 25 (1986): 117–31.

Carr, Stephen L. "Illuminated Printing: Toward a Logic of Difference." Hilton and Vogler 177–96.

Carravetta, Peter. *Prefaces to the Diaspora: Rhetorics, Allegory, and the Interpretation of Postmodernity.* West Lafayette, Ind.: Purdue University Press, 1991.

Carroll, David, ed. *George Eliot: The Critical Heritage.* New York: Barnes and Noble, 1971.

Carter, Angela. *Nights at the Circus.* New York: Penguin, 1984.

Carter, Jennifer. "Laws, Courts and Constitution." In *The Restored Monarchy, 1660–1688.* Ed. J. R. Jones. Totowa, N.J.: Rowman and Littlefield, 1979. 71–93.

Caruth, Cathy. "The Claims of Reference." *Yale Journal of Criticism* 4 (1990): 193–205.

Castle, Terry. "Phantasmagoria: Spectral Technology and the Metamorphosis of Modern Reverie." *Critical Inquiry* 15 (1988): 26–61.

Chambers, Ephraim. *Cyclopedia.* 2 vols. London: W. Innys, 1751.

Chase, Cynthia. *Decomposing Figures.* Baltimore: Johns Hopkins University Press, 1986.

"The Witty Butcher's Wife: Freud, Lacan, and the Conversion of Resistance to Theory." *Modern Language Notes* 102 (1988): 989–1013.

Chaucer, Geoffrey. *Works.* Ed. F. N. Robinson. Boston: Houghton Mifflin, 1961.

Christensen, Francis. "John Wilkins and the Royal Society's Reform of Prose Style. Parts One and Two." *Modern Language Quarterly* 7 (1946): 179–87, 279–90.

Christensen, Jerome C. "The Romantic Movement at the End of History." *Critical Inquiry* 20 (1994): 457–76.

"The Symbol's Errant Allegory: Coleridge and His Critics." *ELH* 45 (1978): 640–59.

Chubb, William. "Minerva Medica and the Tall Tree." *Turner Studies* 1 (1981): 26–35.

Cicero, Marcus Tullius. *De Oratore.* Trans. and ed. H. Rackham. 2 vols. Cambridge, Mass.: Harvard University Press, 1970.

Rhetorica ad Herennium. Trans. Harry Caplan. Cambridge, Mass.: Harvard University Press, 1954.

Clare, John. *Autobiographical Writings.* Ed. Eric Robinson. New York: Oxford University Press, 1983.

John Clare. Ed. Eric Robinson and David Powell. New York: Oxford University Press, 1984.

Clark, David. " 'The Innocence of Becoming Restored': Blake, Nietzsche, and the Disclosure of Difference." *Studies in Romanticism* 29 (1990): 91–114.

Clark, Timothy. *Embodying Revolution: The Figure of the Poet in Shelley.* Oxford: Clarendon Press, 1989.

Clarke, Charles, and Mary Clarke. *Recollections of Writers.* New York: Charles Scribners, 1878.

Clej, Alina. "Walter Benjamin's Messianic Politics: Angelus Novus and the End of History." In Vol. xi of *Cross Currents.* New Haven: Yale University Press, 1992. 23–40.

Clifford, James. *The Predicament of Culture.* Cambridge, Mass.: Harvard University Press, 1988.

Cocking, J. M. *Imagination.* London: Routledge, 1991.

Cohen, Ralph. "Do Postmodern Genres Exist?" *Genre* 20 (1987): 241–58.

"Genre Theory, Literary History, and Historical Change." In *Theoretical Issues in Literary History.* Ed. David Perkins. Cambridge, Mass.: Harvard University Press, 1991. 85–113.

Cohen, Walter. "Marxist Criticism." In *Redrawing the Boundaries.* Ed. Stephen Greenblatt and Giles Gunn. New York: Modern Language Association, 1992. 320–48.

Coleridge, Samuel Taylor. *Biographia Literaria.* Ed. James Engell and W. Jackson Bate. 2 vols. in 1. Princeton University Press, 1983.

Coleridge: Poetical Works. Ed. Ernest H. Coleridge. 1912 rpt.; London: Oxford University Press, 1967.

Coleridge's Miscellaneous Criticism. Ed. Thomas M. Raysor. London: Constable and Co., 1936.

Lay Sermons. Ed. R. J. White. Princeton University Press, 1972.

Lectures 1808–19: On Literature. Ed. R. A. Foakes. 2 vols. Princeton University Press, 1987.

Logic. Ed. J. R. de J. Jackson. Princeton University Press, 1981.

Notebooks. Ed. Kathleen Coburn. 4 vols. New York: 1957– .

Sibylline Leaves. London: Rest Fenner, 1817.

Table-Talk. Ed. Carl Woodring. 2 vols. Princeton University Press, 1990.

Colie, Rosalie. *The Resources of Kind.* Ed. Barbara K. Lewalski. Berkeley: University of California Press, 1973.

Collins, David. "The Death of Allegory." *Poetry* 155 (January 1990): 276–77.

Collins, William. *The Works of William Collins.* Ed. Richard Wendorf and Charles Ryskamp. Oxford: Clarendon Press, 1979.

Cook, A. K. *A Commentary upon Browning's 'Ring and the Book.'* London: Oxford University Press, 1920.

Cope, Edward M. *An Introduction to Aristotle's Rhetoric.* London: Macmillan, 1867.

Cope, Edward M., ed. *Philosophy of Plato and Aristotle.* Rev. edn. John E. Sandys. New York: Arno Press, 1973.

Copeland, Rita. *Rhetoric, Hermeneutics, and Translation in the Middle Ages.* Cambridge University Press, 1991.

Copeland, Rita, and Stephen Melville. "Allegory and Allegoresis, Rhetoric and Hermeneutics." *Exemplaria* 3 (1991): 159–87.

Corns, Thomas N. *The Development of Milton's Style.* Oxford: Clarendon Press, 1982.

    Uncloistered Virtue: English Political Literature, 1640–1660. Oxford: Clarendon Press, 1992.

Cottom, Daniel. *Social Figures.* Minneapolis: University of Minnesota Press, 1987.

Coxe, William. *Travels in Switzerland, and in the Country of the Grisons.* 4th edn. 3 vols. London: T. Cadell and W. Davies, 1801.

Creuzer, Georg Friedrich. *Symbolik und Mythologie.* 4 vols. Leipzig: Leske, 1810–12.

Culler, Jonathan. "Apostrophe." *Diacritics* 7 (1977): 59–69.

Curle, Richard, ed. *Robert Browning and Julia Wedgewood, A Broken Friendship as Revealed by Their Letters.* London: J. Murray and I. Cope, 1937.

Curran, Stuart. *Poetic Form and British Romanticism.* New York: Oxford University Press, 1986.

    Shelley's Cenci: Scorpions Ringed with Fire. Princeton University Press, 1970.

Curran, Stuart, and Joseph A. Wittreich, Jr., eds. *Blake's Sublime Allegory.* Madison: University of Wisconsin Press, 1973.

Cvetkovich, Ann. *Mixed Feelings.* New Brunswick, N.J.: Rutgers University Press, 1992.

Dale, Peter Allan. "*Paracelsus* and *Sordello*: Trying the Stuff of Language." *Victorian Poetry* 18 (1980): 359–69.

Daly, Peter M. *Literature in Light of the Emblem.* University of Toronto Press, 1979.

Damon, S. Foster. *A Blake Dictionary.* New York: E. P. Dutton, 1965.

Damrosch, Leopold, Jr. *Symbol and Truth in Blake's Myth.* Princeton University Press, 1980.

Dante, Alighieri. *The Divine Comedy.* Trans. Allen Mandelbaum. Berkeley: University of California Press, 1980.

Darnton, Robert, and Daniel Roche, eds. *Revolution in Print.* Berkeley: University of California Press, 1989.

Davies, Tony. "The Ark in Flames." Benjamin, Cantor, and Christie 83–102.

Dawson, Paul M. S. *The Unacknowledged Legislator: Shelley and Politics.* Oxford: Clarendon Press, 1980.

De Baecque, Antoine. "The Allegorical Image of France, 1750–1800: A Political Crisis in Representation." *Representations* 47 (1994): 111–43.

Dees, Jerome S. "The Ship Conceit in *The Faerie Queene*: 'Conspicuous Allusion' and Poetic Structure." *Studies in Philology* 72 (1975): 209–25.

Defoe, Daniel. *The Life and Strange Surprizing Adventures of Robinson Crusoe.* London: W. Taylor, 1719.

De Luca, V. A. *Blake and the Poetics of the Sublime*. Princeton University Press, 1991.

De Man, Paul. *Allegories of Reading*. New Haven: Yale University Press, 1979.

Blindness and Insight. 2nd edn. rev. University of Minneapolis Press, 1983.

"The Epistemology of Metaphor." *Critical Inquiry* 5 (1978): 13–30.

"Introduction." *John Keats: Selected Poetry*. New York: Signet, 1966. ix–xxxvi.

"Phenomenality and Materiality in Kant." Shapiro and Sica 121–44.

Resistance to Theory. Minneapolis: University of Minnesota Press, 1986.

The Rhetoric of Romanticism. New York: Columbia University Press, 1984.

"Sign and Symbol in Hegel's *Aesthetics*." *Critical Inquiry* 8 (1982): 761–76.

Demetrius. *On Style*. Trans. W. Rhys Roberts. Rev. edn. Cambridge, Mass.: Harvard University Press, 1932.

Denham, John. *Coopers Hill*. London: H. Hills, 1709.

Derrida, Jacques. "The Law of Genre." In *Acts of Literature*. Ed. Derek Attridge. New York: Routledge, 1992. 223–52.

"The Pit and the Pyramid: Introduction to Hegel's Semiology." In *Margins of Philosophy*. Trans. Alan Bass. Chicago University Press, 1982. 69–108.

Diderot, Denis. *Encyclopédie ou Dictionnaire Raisonné des Sciences et des Métiers*. 35 vols. 1751–50 rpt.; Stuttgart: Friedrich Frommann, 1967.

Oeuvres Complètes, Vol. 1. Ed. J. Assézat. Paris: Garnier, 1875–77.

Salons. Ed. Jean Seznec and Jean Adhemar. 5 vols. Oxford: Clarendon Press, 1960.

Dillon, Steven C. "Browning and the Figure of Life." *Texas Studies in Language and Literature* 32 (1990):169–86.

Dipple, Elizabeth. *Iris Murdoch: Work for the Spirit*. Chicago University Press, 1982.

Dowd, David Lloyd. *Pageant-Master of the Republic*. Lincoln: University of Nebraska Press, 1948.

Drew, Philip. *The Poetry of Robert Browning*. London: Methuen, 1970.

Dubos, Abbé Jean-Baptiste. *Reflexions critiques sur la poésie et sur la peinture*. 3 vols. Utrecht: E. Neaulme, 1732–36.

Du Cange, Charles Du Fresne. *Glossarium mediae et infimae Latinitatis*. 10 vols. Graz: Akademische Druck, 1954.

Du Plessix Gray, Francine. "The Cult of the Cousin." *New York Times Book Review*. March 28, 1993. 13–14.

Easson, Roger R. "William Blake and His Reader in *Jerusalem*." Curran and Wittreich 309–28.

Eden, Kathy. "The Rhetorical Tradition and Augustinian Hermeneutics in *De doctrina christiana*." *Rhetorica* 8 (1990): 45–64.

Eggers, J. Phillip. "Memory in Mankind: Keats's Historical Imagination." *PMLA* 86 (1971): 990–98.

Eikon Basilike. 1662 rpt.; Ithaca, N.Y.: Folger Shakespeare Library, 1966.

Eliot, George. *Daniel Deronda*. Ed. Graham Handley. Oxford: Clarendon Press, 1984.

 Essays of George Eliot. Ed. Thomas Pinney. London: Routledge and Kegan Paul, 1965.

Elmes, James, ed. *Annals of the Fine Arts*. 5 vols. London: Elmes, 1816–20.

Encyclopaedia Britannica. 18 vols. Edinburgh: A. Bell and C. Macfarquhar, 1797.

"Une énigme iconographique: *L'Allégorie chrétienne*." Paris: Louvre Département des Peintures, 1996.

Essick, Robert N. "The Altering Eye: Blake's Vision in the *Tiriel* Designs." In *William Blake: Essays in Honour of Sir Geoffrey Keynes*. Ed. Morton D. Paley and Michael Phillips. Oxford: Clarendon Press, 1973. 50–65.

 "How Blake's Body Means." Hilton and Vogler 197–217.

Fallon, Stephen M. "The Metaphysics of Milton's Divorce Tracts." Loewenstein and Turner 69–84.

 Milton among the Philosophers. Ithaca: Cornell University Press, 1991.

 "Milton's Sin and Death: The Ontology of Allegory in *Paradise Lost*" *English Literary Renaissance* 17 (1987): 329–50.

Farington, Joseph. *The Farington Diary*. Ed. James Greig. 3rd edn. 8 vols. New York: George H. Doran, 1923.

Farmer, Norman K., Jr. "Illustrators." Hamilton 388–92.

 "'A Moniment Forever More': *The Faerie Queene* and British Art, 1770–1950." *Princeton University Library Chronicle* 62 (1990): 25–77.

Favret, Mary. *Romantic Correspondence*. Cambridge University Press, 1993.

Feinberg, Harvey. "The Four-Cornered Circle: Truth and Illusion in Browning's *The Ring and the Book*." *Studies in Browning and His Circle* 13 (1985): 70–96.

Ferguson, Frances. *Solitude and the Sublime*. New York: Routledge, 1992.

Ferry, Anne. *Milton's Epic Voice*. Cambridge, Mass.: Harvard University Press, 1963.

Finberg, A. J. *The History of Turner's Liber Studiorum*. London: Ernest Benn, 1924.

 The Life of J. M. W. Turner, R. A. 2nd edn. rev. Hilda F. Finberg. Oxford: Clarendon Press, 1961.

Findlay, Len. "Otherwise Engaged: Postmodernism and the Resistance to History." *English Studies in Canada* 14 (1988): 383–99.

Fineman, Joel. "Shakespeare's *Will*: The Temporality of Rape." *Representations* 20 (1987): 25–76.

 "The Structure of Allegorical Desire." In *Allegory and Representation*. Ed. Stephen J. Greenblatt. Baltimore: Johns Hopkins University Press, 1981. 26–60.

Finley, Gerald E. "J. M. W. Turner's *Rome from the Vatican*: A Palimpsest of History?" *Zeitschrift für Geschichte* 49 (1986): 55–72.

 Landscapes of Memory. Berkeley: California University Press, 1980.

Fletcher, Angus. *Allegory: The Theory of a Symbolic Mode.* Ithaca: Cornell University Press, 1964.

Foster, Hal, ed. *The Anti-Aesthetic: Essays on Postmodern Culture.* Port Townsend, Wash.: Bay Press, 1983.

Fowler, Alastair. *Kinds of Literature.* Cambridge, Mass.: Harvard University Press, 1982.

Fowler, Roger, ed. *A Dictionary of Critical Terms.* London: Routledge and Kegan Paul, 1973.

Fraistat, Neil. *The Poem and the Book.* Chapel Hill: University of North Carolina Press, 1985.

Francus, Marilyn. "The Monstrous Mother: Reproductive Anxiety in Swift and Pope." *ELH* 61 (1994): 829–51.

Freccero, John. *Dante: The Poetics of Conversion.* Cambridge, Mass.: Harvard University Press, 1986.

"The Fig Tree and the Laurel: Petrarch's Poetics." *Diacritics* 5 (1975): 34–40.

Frei, Hans W. *The Eclipse of Biblical Narrative.* New Haven: Yale University Press, 1974.

Freud, Sigmund. "Creative Writers and Day-Dreaming" ["Der Dichter und Das Phantasieren"]. In vol. IX of *The Complete Psychological Works.* Ed. James Strachey. London: Hogarth Press, 1959. 141–54.

The Interpretation of Dreams. Trans. James Strachey. New York: Avon, 1965.

Fried, Michael. *Absorption and Theatricality.* Berkeley: University of California Press, 1980.

Froula, Christine. "Browning's *Sordello* and the Parables of Modernist Poetics." *ELH* 52 (1986): 965–92.

Frye, Northrop. *Fearful Symmetry.* Princeton University Press, 1969.

Fuseli, Henri. *The Life and Writings of Henry Fuseli.* Ed. John Knowles. 3 vols. London: Henry Coburn, 1831.

Gadamer, Hans-Georg. *Truth and Method.* Trans. Garrett Barden and John Cumming. New York: Crossroad, 1984.

Gage, John. *Colour in Turner.* New York: Praeger, 1969.

J. M. W. Turner: "A Wonderful Range of Mind." New Haven: Yale University Press, 1987.

Gallagher, Catherine. "George Eliot and *Daniel Deronda*: The Prostitute and the Jewish Question." In *Sex, Politics, and Science in the Nineteenth-Century Novel.* Ed. Ruth Bernard Yeazell. Baltimore: Johns Hopkins University Press, 1986. 39–62.

Gallagher, Philip J. " 'Real or Allegoric': The Ontology of Sin and Death in *Paradise Lost.*" *English Literary Renaissance* 6 (1976): 317–35.

García Márquez, Gabriel. *The Autumn of the Patriarch.* Trans. Gregory Rabassa. New York: Harper and Row, 1976.

Gatta, John Jr. "Coleridge and Allegory." *Modern Language Quarterly* 38 (1977): 62–77.

Gayton, Edmund. *Pleasant Notes upon Don Quixote.* London: W. Hunt, 1654.

Gellrich, Jesse. "Deconstructing Allegory." *Genre* 18 (1985): 197–213.

Gentleman, David. *Design in Miniature.* New York: Watson-Guptill, 1972.

George, Mary Dorothy. *Catalogue of Political and Personal Satires.* 11 vols. London: Trustees of the British Museum, 1947.

    English Political Caricature to 1792. 2 vols. Oxford: Clarendon Press, 1959.

George Cruikshank, Karicaturist, 1792–1878. Stuttgart: Verlag Gerd Hatje, 1983.

Giddens, Anthony. "Structuration Theory." In *Giddens' Theory of Structuration.* Ed. C. Bryant and D. Jary. New York: Macmillan, 1991. 207–21.

Gilman, Ernest B. *Iconoclasm and Poetry in the English Reformation.* University of Chicago Press, 1986.

Girard, René. *Things Hidden since the Foundation of the World.* Trans. Stephen Bann and Michael Metteer. Stanford University Press, 1987.

Glanvill, Joseph. *The Vanity of Dogmatizing.* London: Henry Eversden, 1661.

Gleckner, Robert F. *Blake and Spenser.* Baltimore: Johns Hopkins University Press, 1985.

Godwin, William [Edward Baldwin]. *The Pantheon.* 1814 rpt.; New York: Garland, 1984.

Goethe, J. W. von. *Goethe on Art.* Ed. John Gage. Berkeley: University of California Press, 1980.

    "Observations on the Laocoon." *Monthly Magazine* 7 (1799): 349–52.

    "Symbolik." In vol. xvi of *Werke.* Ed. Ernst Beutler. Zurich: Artemis, 1971. 855–56.

    "Über Laokoon." In vol. xiii of *Werke.* Ed. Ernst Beutler. Zurich: Artemis, 161–74.

Goldberg, Jonathan. *Endlesse Worke: Spenser and the Structures of Discourse.* Baltimore: Johns Hopkins University Press, 1981.

Goldsmith, Steven. *Unbuilding Jerusalem.* Ithaca: Cornell University Press, 1993.

Gordon, D. J. "Ripa's Fate." In *The Renaissance Imagination.* Ed. Stephen Orgel. Berkeley: University of California Press, 1975. 51–74.

Goslee, David F. "Mr. Sludge The Medium – Mr. Browning The Possessed." *Studies in Browning and His Circle* 3 (1975): 40–58.

Goslee, Nancy. "Dispersoning Emily: Drafting as Plot in *Epipsychidion.*" *Keats–Shelley Journal* 42 (1993): 104–19.

    "Pursuing Revision in Shelley's 'Ode to Liberty'." *Texas Studies in Language and Literature* 36 (1994): 166–83.

    "Shelley at Play: A Study of Sketch and Text in his *Prometheus* Notebooks." *Huntington Library Quarterly* 48 (1985): 211–55.

Gossman, Lionel. *Between History and Literature.* Cambridge, Mass.: Harvard University Press, 1990.

Granville, George. *The Genuine Works in Poetry and Prose.* London: J. Tonson, 1732.

Gray, Thomas. *Poetical Works*. Ed. Austin Lane Poole. 3rd edn. London: Oxford University Press, 1937.

Greenblatt, Stephen J., ed. *Allegory and Representation*. Baltimore: Johns Hopkins University Press, 1981.

Gregerson, Linda. "Protestant Erotics: Idolatry and Interpretation in Spenser's *Faerie Queene*." *ELH* 58 (1991): 1–34.

Grimal, Pierre. *The Dictionary of Classical Mythology*. Trans. A. R. Maxwell-Hyslop. New York: Basil Blackwell, 1986.

Gross, Kenneth. *Spenserian Poetics: Idolatry, Iconoclasm, and Magic*. Ithaca: Cornell University Press, 1985.

Guillory, Jon. *Poetic Authority: Spenser, Milton, and Literary History*. New York: Columbia University Press, 1983.

Hagstrum, Jean H. *Eros and Vision: The Restoration to Romanticism*. Evanston, Ill.: Northwestern University Press, 1989.

The Sister Arts. University of Chicago Press, 1958.

William Blake: Poet and Painter. University of Chicago Press, 1964.

Hale, J. R, ed. *The Italian Journal of Samuel Rogers*. London: Faber and Faber, 1956.

Halmi, Nicholas. "How Christian Is the Coleridgean Symbol?" *The Wordsworth Circle* 26 (1995): 26–30.

Hamilton, A. C., ed. *The Spenser Encyclopedia*. University of Toronto Press, 1990.

Hamilton, William. *Memorandum on the Subject of the Earl of Elgin's Pursuits in Greece*. London: William Miller, 1811.

Hamlin, Cyrus. "The Temporality of Selfhood: Metaphor and Romantic Poetry." *New Literary History* 6 (1974): 169–93.

Harding, Anthony J. *Coleridge and the Inspired Word*. Kingston: McGill-Queens University Press, 1985.

Harpham, Geoffrey Galt. *Getting It Right*. University of Chicago Press, 1992.

Hartman, Geoffrey. *The Fate of Reading*. University of Chicago Press, 1975.

Haug, Walter, ed. *Formen und Funktionen der Allegorie*. Stuttgart: Metzler, 1979.

Hazlitt, William. *The Complete Works of William Hazlitt*. Ed. P. P. Howe. 21 vols. London: J. M. Dent, 1933.

Heffernan, James A. W. *The Re-Creation of Landscape*. Hanover: University Press of New England, 1985.

Hegel, G. W. F. *Aesthetics: Lectures on Fine Art*. Trans. T. M. Knox. 2 vols. Oxford: Clarendon, 1975.

Enzyklopädie der Philosophischen. Vols. VIII and X, *Werke*. Ed. Eva Moldenhauer and Karl Markus Michel. Frankfurt am Main: Suhrkamp, 1970.

Philosophy of History. Ed. C. J. Friedrich. Trans. J. Sibree. New York: Dover, 1956.

Science of Logic. Trans. A. V. Miller. London: George Allen and Unwin, 1969.

Henkel, Arthur, and Albrecht Schöne. *Emblemata: Handbuch sur Sinnbildkunst des XVI. und XVII. Jahrhunderts*. Stuttgart: J. B. Mezler, 1967.

Heppner, Christopher. *Reading Blake's Designs*. Cambridge University Press, 1995.

Hernadi, Paul. *Beyond Genre*. Ithaca: Cornell University Press, 1972.

Herson, Ellen Brown. "Oxymoron and Dante's Gates of Hell in Shelley's *Prometheus Unbound*." *Studies in Romanticism* 29 (1990): 371–93.

Hertz, Neil. "Lurid Figures." Bender and Wellbery 100–24.

Hesiod. *The Works and Days and Theogony*. In *Hesiod*. Trans. Richard Lattimore. Ann Arbor: University of Michigan Press, 1959.

Hiemstra, Anne. "Browning and History: Synecdoche and Symbolism in *The Ring and the Book*." *Studies in Browning and His Circle* 13 (1985): 47–58.

Hildebrand, William. "Self, Beauty and Horror: Shelley's Medusa Moment." Blank 150–65.

Hill, David. *Turner in the Alps*. London: George Philip, 1992.

Hilton, Nelson, and Thomas Vogler, eds. *Unnam'd Forms: Blake and Textuality*. Berkeley: University of California Press, 1986.

Hoban, Russell. *Riddley Walker*. New York: Simon and Schuster, 1980.

Hobbes, Thomas. *Answer to Davenant's Preface to 'Gondibert'*. Spingarn 54–67.

  Leviathan. London: J. Crooke, 1651.

Hobbes, Thomas, trans. *The Iliad*. Vol. x of *The English Works of Thomas Hobbes*. Ed. William Molesworth. London: Longman, Brown, Green, and Longmans, 1844.

Hobson, Marian. "History Traces." In *Post-Structuralism and the Question of History*. Ed. Derek Attridge, Geoff Bennington, and Robert Young. Cambridge University Press, 1987. 101–15.

Hodgson, John A. "Poems of the Imagination, Allegories of the Imagination: Wordsworth's Preface of 1815 and the Redundancy of Imaginative Poetry." *Studies in Romanticism* 27 (1988): 273–88.

Hoerner, Frederick C. "'Fire to Use': A Practice-Theory Approach to *Paradise Lost*." *Representations* 51 (1995): 94–117.

  "Nostalgia's Freight in Wordsworth's *Intimations Ode*." *ELH* 62 (1995): 631–61.

Hofkosh, Sonia. "The Writer's Ravishment: Women and the Romantic Author-The Example of Byron." Mellor 93–114.

Holcomb, Adele. "The Bridge in the Middle Distance: Symbolic Elements in Romantic Landscape." *Art Quarterly* 37 (1974): 31–58.

  "Turner and Rogers's *Italy* Revisited." *Studies in Romanticism* 27 (1988): 63–96.

Hollander, John. "The Gazer's Spirit: Romantic and Later Poetry on Painting and Sculpture." In *The Romantics and Us*. Ed. Gene W. Ruoff. New Brunswick, N.J.: Rutgers University Press, 1990. 130–67.

  Melodious Guile. New Haven: Yale University Press.

Homans, Margaret. "Keats Reading Women, Women Reading Keats." *Studies in Romanticism* 29 (1990): 341–71.

Homer. *The Iliad*. Trans. Robert Fagles. New York: Penguin, 1990.

  The Odyssey. Trans. Walter Shewring. Oxford University Press, 1980.

Houghton, Walter E. *The Victorian Frame of Mind*. New Haven, Conn.: Yale University Press, 1957.

Hughes, Felicity. "Imagination." A. C. Hamilton 392–93.

Hughes, John. "An Essay on Allegorical Poetry." In *Critical Essays of the Eighteenth Century*. Ed. Willard H. Durham. 1915 rpt.; New York: Russell and Russell, 1961. 86–110.

Hunt, John Dixon. "Wondrous Deep and Dark: Turner and the Sublime." *Georgia Review* 30 (1976): 139–64.

Hunt, Leigh. "Spenser." In *Imagination and Fancy*. 2nd edn. London: Smith, Elder, 1845. 49–53.

Hunt, Lynn. *The Family Romance of the French Revolution*. Berkeley: University of California Press, 1992.

    "History as Gesture; or, The Scandal of History." In *Consequences of Theory*. Ed. Jonathan Arac and Barbara Johnson. Baltimore: Johns Hopkins University Press, 1991. 91–107.

    Politics, Culture and Class in the French Revolution. Berkeley: University of California Press, 1984.

Hutcheon, Linda. *A Poetics of Postmodernism*. New York: Routledge, 1988.

    The Politics of Postmodernism. New York: Routledge, 1989.

Hyde, Virginia. "Robert Browning's Inverted Optic Glass in *A Death in the Desert*." *Victorian Poetry* 23 (1985): 93–96.

Imbert, Claude. "Stoic Logic and Alexandrian Poetics." In *Doubt and Dogmatism*. Ed. Malcolm Schofield, Myles Burnyeat, Jonathan Barnes. Oxford: Clarendon Press, 1980. 182–216.

    "Théorie de la représentation et doctrine logique." Brunschwing 223–50.

Jack, Ian. *Keats and the Mirror of Art*. Oxford: Clarendon Press, 1967.

Jacobs, Carol. *Uncontainable Romanticism*. Baltimore: Johns Hopkins University Press, 1989.

Jacobus, Mary. *Romanticism, Writing, and Sexual Difference*. Oxford: Clarendon Press, 1989.

Jameson, Fredric. *The Political Unconscious*. Ithaca: Cornell University Press, 1981.

    Postmodernism, or, The Cultural Logic of Late Capitalism. Durham: Duke University Press, 1991.

    "Third-World Literature in the Era of Multinational Capitalism." *Social Text* 15 (1986): 65–88.

JanMohamed, Abdul R. "The Economy of Manichean Allegory: The Function of Racial Difference in Colonialist Literature." *Critical Inquiry* 12 (1985): 59–87.

Jauss, Hans Robert. *Toward an Aesthetic of Reception*. Trans. Timothy Bahti. University of Minnesota Press, 1983.

Jewett, William. "Strange Flesh: Shelley and the Performance of Skepticism." *Texas Studies in Language and Literature* 38 (1966): 321–39.

Johnson, Samuel. *A Dictionary of the English Language*. 2 vols. London: W. Strahan, 1755.

The Lives of the Poets. Ed. George Birkbeck Hill. 3 vols. Oxford: Clarendon, 1905.

"The Vision of Theodore." In vol. xvi of *The Works of Samuel Johnson.* Ed. Gwin J. Kolb. New Haven: Yale University Press, 1990. 195–212.

Johnston, Kenneth, Gilbert Chaitin, Karen Hanson, and Herbert Marks, eds. *Romantic Revolutions.* Bloomington: Indiana University Press, 1990.

Johnstone, Robert. "The Impossible Genre: Reading Comprehensive Literary History." *PMLA* 107 (1992): 26–37.

Jonson, Ben. *Masque of Queens.* In *Masques and Entertainments.* Ed. Henry Morley. London: George Routledge, 1890.

Kames, Henry Home, Lord. *Elements of Criticism.* 3 vols. 1762 rpt.; New York: George Olms Verlag, 1970.

Kant, Immanuel. *Critique of Judgment.* Trans. J. H. Bernard. New York: Hafner, 1951.

Critique of Pure Reason. Trans. Norman Kemp Smith. New York: St. Martin's Press, 1965.

Karlin, Daniel. "Browning, Elizabeth Barrett, and 'Mesmerism'." *Victorian Poetry* 27 (1989): 65–77.

Keach, William. *Shelley's Style.* New York: Methuen, 1984.

Kearns, Sheila. *Coleridge, Wordsworth and Romantic Autobiography.* Madison, N.J.: Fairleigh Dickinson University Press, 1995.

Keats, John. *The Letters of John Keats: 1814–1821.* Ed. Hyder E. Rollins. 2 vols. Cambridge, Mass.: Harvard University Press, 1958.

The Poems of John Keats. Ed. Jack Stillinger. Cambridge, Mass.: Harvard University Press, 1978.

Keeble, N. H. *The Literary Culture of Nonconformity.* Leicester University Press, 1987.

Kelley, Theresa M. "J. M. W. Turner, Napoleonic Caricature, and Romantic Allegory." *ELH* 58 (1991): 351–82.

"Keats, Ekphrasis, and History." Roe 212–37.

"Poetics and the Politics of Reception: Keats's 'La Belle Dame sans Merci'." *ELH* 54 (1987): 333–62.

"Visual Suppressions, Emblems, and the 'Sister Arts'." *Eighteenth-Century Studies* 17 (1983): 28–60.

Kellner, Hans. "The Inflatable Trope as Narrative Theory: Structure or Allegory?" *Diacritics* 11 (1981): 14–28.

Kerferd, George B. "The Problem of Synkatathesis and Katalepsis." Brunschwing 251–72.

Kerrigan, William. "Atoms Again: The Deaths of Individualism." In *Taking Chances: Derrida, Psychoanalysis, and Literature.* Baltimore: Johns Hopkins University Press, 1984. 86–106.

Kibbey, Ann. *The Interpretation of Material Shapes in Puritanism.* Cambridge University Press, 1986.

King, John N. *Spenser's Poetry and the Reformation Tradition.* Princeton University Press, 1990.

Kisselgoff, Anna. "A Harsh yet Poetic Elegy on American Indian Life." *New York Times*. March 18, 1993. B3.

Kleist, Heinrich von. "On the Marionette Theatre." In *Essays on Dolls*. Trans. and ed. Idris Parry. London: Penguin, 1994. 1–12.

Knapp, Steven. *Personification and the Sublime*. Cambridge, Mass.: Harvard University Press, 1985.

Knoepflmacher, U. C. *Religious Humanism and the Victorian Novel*. Princeton University Press, 1965.

Korshin, Paul J. *Typologies in England 1650–1820*. Princeton University Press, 1982.

Korshin, Paul J., ed. *Studies in Change and Revolution*. Menston: Scolar Press, 1972.

Krieger, Murray. *Ekphrasis*. Baltimore: Johns Hopkins University Press, 1992.

"'A Waking Dream': The Symbolic Alternative to Allegory." Bloomfield 1– 22.

Kroeber, Karl. *British Romantic Art*. Berkeley: University of California Press, 1986.

"Experience as History: Shelley's Venice, Turner's Carthage." *ELH* 41 (1974): 321–39.

Kroll, Richard. *The Material Word*. Baltimore: Johns Hopkins University Press, 1991.

Kucich, Greg. *Keats, Shelley, and Romantic Spenserianism*. University Park: Pennsylvania State University Press, 1991.

Lacan, Jacques. *Ecrits*. Paris: Seuil, 1966.

Lamb, Jonathan. "The Job Controversy, Sterne, and the Question of Allegory." *Eighteenth-Century Studies* 24 (1990): 1–19.

Lanham, Richard. *A Handlist of Rhetorical Terms*. Berkeley: University of California Press, 1968.

"The Literal Britomart." *Modern Language Quarterly* 28 (1967): 426–45.

Lausberg, Heinrich. *Handbuch der Literarischen Rhetorik*. 2 vols. Munich: Max Hueber Verlag, 1960.

Lavie, Smadar. "'The One Who Writes Us': Political Allegory and the Experience of Occupation among the Mzeina Bedouin." In *Creativity/Anthropology*. Ed. Smadar Lavie, Kirin Narayan, and Renato Rosaldo. Ithaca: Cornell University Press, 1993. 153–83.

Leask, Nigel. *British Romantic Writers and the East*. Cambridge University Press, 1992.

Lemprière, J. A. *Classical Dictionary*. London: T. Cadell and W. Davies, 1804.

Lerner, Laurence. "*Daniel Deronda*: George Eliot's Struggle with Realism." Shalvi 89–112.

Lessing, Doris. *Marriages between Zones Three, Four, and Five*. New York: Knopf, 1980.

Lessing, Gotthold Ephraim. *Laocöon: An Essay on the Limits of Painting and*

Poetry. Trans. Edward A. McCormick. Baltimore: Johns Hopkins University Press, 1984.

Laokoon. Vol. VI of *Werke*. Ed. Albert von Schirnding. Munich: Carl Hanser Verlag, 1974.

Levin, Samuel R. "Allegorical Language." Bloomfield 23–38.

Levine, George. *The Realistic Imagination*. University of Chicago Press, 1981.

Levinson, Marjorie. *Keats's Life of Allegory*. Oxford: Basil Blackwell, 1988.

Lichtenstein, Jacqueline. "Making Up Representation: The Risks of Femininity." *Representations* 20 (1987): 77–87.

Liu, Alan. "The Power of Formalism." *ELH* 56 (1989): 721–71.

Wordsworth: A Sense of History. Stanford University Press, 1989.

Locke, John. *An Essay concerning Human Understanding*. Ed. Peter H. Nidditch. Oxford: Clarendon Press, 1975.

Loewenstein, David. *Milton and the Drama of History*. Cambridge University Press, 1990.

"Milton and the Poetics of Defense." Loewenstein and Turner 171–92.

Loewenstein, David, and James Grantham Turner, eds. *Politics, Poetics, and Hermeneutics in Milton's Prose*. Cambridge University Press, 1990.

Longinus. *On the Sublime*. Trans. W. Hamilton Fyfe. Rev. edn. Cambridge, Mass.: Harvard University Press, 1932.

Longxi, Zhang. "Historicizing the Postmodern Allegory." *Texas Studies in Language and Literature* 36 (1994): 212–31.

Lowth, Robert. *A Commentary upon the Larger and Lesser Prophets: Being a Continuation of Bishop Patrick*. London: R. Knaplock, 1727.

Lectures on the Sacred Poetry of the Hebrews. Trans. G. Gregory. Boston: Joseph Buckingham, 1815.

Luxon, Thomas H. "'Not I, but Christ': Allegory and the Puritan Self." *ELH* 60 (1993): 899–937.

McCobb, E. A. "*Daniel Deronda* as Will and Representation: George Eliot and Schopenhauer." *Modern Language Review* 80 (1985): 533–49.

McGann, Jerome. "The Aim of Blake's Prophecies and the Uses of Blake Criticism." Curran and Wittreich 3–22.

"Keats and the Historical Method." In *The Beauty of Inflections*. Oxford: Clarendon Press, 1985. 17–65.

"The Meaning of the Ancient Mariner." *Critical Inquiry* 8 (1981): 35–67.

The Romantic Ideology. University of Chicago Press, 1983.

McGowan, John. *Representation and Revelation*. Columbia: University of Missouri Press, 1986.

MacQueen, John. *Allegory*. London: Methuen, 1970.

Macrobius. *Commentarii in Somnium Scipionis*. Ed. Jacob Willis. Leipzig: Teubner, 1963.

Commentary on the Dream of Scipio. Trans. William Harris Stahl. New York: Columbia University Press, 1990.

McVaugh, Robert. "Turner and Rome, Raphael and the Fornarina." *Studies in Romanticism* 26 (1987): 365–98.

McWhir, Anne. "The Light and the Knife: Ab/Using Language in *The Cenci.*" *Keats-Shelley Journal* 38 (1989): 145–61.

Mâle, Emile. *L'art religieux après le concile de Trente.* Paris: Armand Colin, 1932.

Malouf, David. *Remembering Babylon.* New York: Pantheon, 1993.

Manning, Peter J. "Reading and Ravishing: The 'Ode on a Grecian Urn'." In *Approaches to Teaching Keats's Poetry.* Ed. Walter H. Evert and Jack W. Rhodes. New York: Modern Language Association, 1991. 131–36.

Reading Romantics. Oxford University Press, 1990.

Marx, Karl. *Capital.* Trans. Ben Fowkes. 2 vols. 1976 rpt. London: Penguin, 1990.

Kapital, in *Ökonomische Schriften.* Vols. v and vi of *Werke, Schriften, Briefe.* Ed. Hans-Joachim Liber and Benedikt Kautsky. Stuttgart: Cotta Verlag, 1963–64.

"On the Jewish Question." In *The Marx–Engels Reader.* Ed. Robert C. Tucker. 2nd edn. New York: Norton, 1978. 26–52.

Matteson, Lynn. "The Poetics and Politics of Alpine Passage: Turner's *Snowstorm: Hannibal and His Army Crossing the Alps.*" *Art Bulletin* 62 (1980): 385–95.

Matthews, G. M., ed. *Keats: The Critical Heritage.* New York: Barnes and Noble, 1971.

May, Georges. "Observations on an Allegory: The Frontispiece of the *Encyclopédie.*" *Diderot Studies* 16 (1973): 159–74.

Mee, John. *Dangerous Enthusiasms.* Oxford: Clarendon Press, 1992.

Meisel, Martin. *Realizations.* Princeton University Press, 1984.

Mellor, Anne, ed. *Romanticism and Feminism.* Bloomington: Indiana University Press, 1988.

Melville, Stephen. "Notes on the Reemergence of Allegory, the Forgetting of Modernism, the Necessity of Rhetoric, and the Condition of Publicity in Art and Criticism." *October* 19 (1981): 55–92.

Philosophy Beside Itself. Minneapolis: University of Minnesota Press, 1986.

Meyer, Susan. " 'Safely to Their Own Borders': Proto-Zionism, Feminism, and Nationalism in *Daniel Deronda.*" *ELH* 60 (1993): 733–58.

Michelet, Jules. *Histoire de la Révolution Française.* Rev. edn. 9 vols. Paris: Librairie Abel Pilou, 1847.

Millar, Oliver. *Rubens: The Whitehall Ceiling.* London: Oxford University Press, 1958.

Miller, Jacqueline T. "The Courtly Figure: Spenser's Anatomy of Allegory." *Studies in English Literature* 31 (1991): 52–68.

Miller, Robert P, ed. *Chaucer: Sources and Backgrounds.* New York: Oxford University Press, 1977.

Milton, John. *Complete Prose Works of John Milton.* Ed. Donald M. Wolfe. 8 vols. New Haven: Yale University Press, 1953.

Paradise Lost. Ed. Merritt Y. Hughes. Rev. edn. New York: Odyssey Press, 1962.

Paradise Regained, the Minor Poems, and Samson Agonistes. Ed. Merritt Y. Hughes. New York: Odyssey Press, 1937.

Mintz, Alan. "*Daniel Deronda* and the Messianic Vocation." Shalvi 137–56.

Mitchell, W. J. T. *Iconology.* University of Chicago Press, 1986.

"In the Wilderness." *London Review of Books* 15:7 (April 8, 1993): 11–12.

"Visible Language: Blake's Wondrous Art of Writing." In *Romanticism and Contemporary Criticism.* Ed. Morris Eaves and Michael Fischer. Ithaca: Cornell University Press, 1986. 46–95.

Montrose, Louis A. "'Shaping Fantasies': Figurations of Gender and Power in Elizabethan Culture." *Representations* 1 (1983): 61–94.

Moore, Thomas. *Irish Melodies and other Poems.* Dublin: William Power, 1815.

Moran, Richard. "Seeing and Believing: Metaphor, Image, and Force." *Critical Inquiry* 16 (1989): 87–112.

More, Hannah. *Parley the Porter: An Allegory.* Dublin: W. Watson, 1796.

Sunday Reading. The Pilgrims: An Allegory. London: J. Marshall, 1797.

Morgan, David. "The Rise and Fall of Abstraction in Eighteenth-Century Art Theory." *Eighteenth-Century Studies* 27 (1994): 449–78.

Morier, Henri. *Dictionnaire de poétique et de rhétorique.* Paris: Presses Universitaires de France, 1961.

Murdoch, Iris. *Acastos.* New York: Penguin, 1986.

The Sea, the Sea. New York: Penguin, 1978.

Murray, John. *A Handbook for Travellers in Switzerland, and the Alps of Savoy and Piedmont.* London: J. Murray, 1838.

Murrin, Michael. *The Veil of Allegory.* University of Chicago Press, 1969.

Neuse, Richard. "Book VI as Conclusion to *The Faerie Queene.*" *ELH* 35 (1968): 329–53.

Newbery, John. *The Art of Poetry on a New Plan.* 2 vols. London: J. Newbery, 1762.

Nicholson, Kathleen. *Turner's Classical Landscapes.* Princeton University Press, 1990.

Niclaes, Hendrik. *Terra Pacis.* London: Samuel Sutterthwaite, 1649.

Nicoll, Allardyce. *Stuart Masques and the Renaissance Stage.* New York: Benjamin Blom, 1968.

Nicolson, Marjorie H. *The Microscope and English Imagination.* Northampton, Mass.: Smith College, 1935.

Niermeyer, Jan Fredrik. *Mediae Latinitatus Lexicon Minus.* Leiden: Brill, 1954.

Nietzsche, Friedrich. *On the Advantage and Disadvantage of History for Life.* Trans. Peter Preuss. Indianapolis: Hackett, 1980.

Nochlin, Linda. *Realism.* New York: Penguin, 1971.

Nohrnberg, James. *The Analogy of the Faerie Queene.* Princeton University Press, 1976.

Norbrook, David. *Poetry and Politics in the English Renaissance.* London: Routledge and Kegan Paul, 1984.

Norris, Christopher. *What's Wrong with Postmodernism.* Baltimore: Johns Hopkins University Press, 1990.

Nussbaum, Martha C. *The Fragility of Goodness.* Cambridge University Press, 1986.

Ogilvie, John. *Poems.* Vol. II. London: George Pearch, 1769.

O Hehir, Brendan. *Expans'd Hieroglyphicks.* Berkeley: University of California Press, 1969.

Ovid, P. Naso. *The Metamorphoses.* Trans. Horace Gregory. New York: Penguin, 1960.

Owens, Craig. "The Allegorical Impulse: Toward a Theory of Postmodernism, Part 2." *October* 13 (1980): 59–80.

"The Discourse of Others: Feminists and Postmodernism." Foster 57–82.

Ozouf, Mona. *Festivals and the French Revolution.* Trans. Alan Sheridan. Cambridge, Mass.: Harvard University Press, 1988.

Parker, Patricia. *Inescapable Romance.* Princeton University Press, 1979.

Literary Fat Ladies. London: Methuen, 1987.

"Metaphor and Catechresis." Bender and Wellbery 60–73.

Patterson, Annabel. "No Meer Amatorious Novel?" Loewenstein and Turner 85–102.

Paulson, Ronald. *Emblem and Expression.* Cambridge, Mass.: Harvard University Press, 1975.

The Fictions of Satire. Baltimore: Johns Hopkins University Press, 1967.

Literary Landscape: Turner and Constable. New Haven: Yale University Press, 1982.

Representations of Revolution 1789–1820. New Haven: Yale University Press, 1983.

Peacock, Thomas L. *Rhododaphne.* London: T. Hookham, 1818.

Pépin, Jean. *Mythe et Allégorie.* Aubier: Edition Montaigne, 1958.

Perkins, David. *Is Literary History Possible?* Baltimore: Johns Hopkins University Press, 1992.

"Some Prospects for Literary History." *Modern Language Quarterly* 54 (1993): 133–39.

Peterfreund, Stuart. "Seduced by Metonymy: Figuration and Authority in *The Cenci.*" Blank 184–203.

Philostratus. *The Life of Apollonius.* Trans. Edward Berwick. London: T. Payne, 1809.

Phinney, A. W. "Keats in the Museum: Between Aesthetics and History." *JEGP* 90 (1991): 208–29.

Plato. *The Republic.* Trans. Paul Shorey. 2 vols. Cambridge, Mass.: Harvard University Press, 1937.

Pocock, J. G. A. *The Machiavellian Moment.* Princeton University Press, 1975.

The Poems of Gray, Collins, and Goldsmith. Ed. Roger Lonsdale. London: Longman, 1969.

Pooley, Roger. "Anglicans, Puritans and Plain Style." In *1642: Literature and Power in the Seventeenth Century.* Ed. Francis Barker. University of Essex Press, 1981. 187–200.

"Language and Loyalty: Plain Style at the Restoration." *Literature and History* 6 (1980): 2–18.

Pope, Alexander, trans. *The Iliad*. Vols. VII and VIII of *The Poems of Alexander Pope*. Ed. Maynard Mack. New Haven: Yale University Press, 1967.

The Odyssey, Books I-XII. Vol. IX of *The Poems of Alexander Pope*. Ed. Maynard Mack. New Haven: Yale University Press, 1967.

Popkin, Jeremy D. "Pictures in a Revolution: Recent Publications on Graphic Art in France, 1789–99." *Eighteenth-Century Studies* 24 (1990–91): 252–59.

Porter, Jeffrey. "'Three Quarks for Mister Mark': Quantum Wordplay and Nuclear Discourse in Russell Hoban's *Riddley Walker*." *Contemporary Literature* 31 (1990): 448–69.

Potter, Lois. *Secret Rites and Secret Writing*. Cambridge University Press, 1989.

Prins, Yopie. "'Violence bridling speech': Browning's Translation of Aeschylus' *Agamemnon*." *Victorian Poetry* 27 (1989): 151–70.

Putnam, Hilary. *Realism and Reason*. Cambridge University Press, 1983.

Puttenham, George. *The Arte of English Poesie*. Ed. Gladys D. Willcock and Alice Walker. Cambridge University Press, 1936.

Pyne, W. H. *The History of the Royal Residences*. Vol. I, London: A. Dry, 1819.

Quilligan, Maureen. *The Language of Allegory*. Ithaca: Cornell University Press, 1979.

Milton's Spenser. Ithaca: Cornell University Press, 1983.

Quintilian. *Institutio oratoria*. Trans. H. E. Butler. 4 vols. Cambridge, Mass.: Harvard University Press, 1921.

Radzinowicz, Mary Ann. "The Politics of *Paradise Lost*." In *Politics of Discourse*. Ed. Kevin Sharpe and Steven N. Zwicker. Berkeley: University of California Press, 1987. 204–29.

Rahn, B. J. "*A Ra-ree Show – A Rare Cartoon*: Revolutionary Propaganda in the Treason Trial of Stephen College." Korshin 77–98.

Rajan, Tilottama. *Dark Interpreter*. Ithaca: Cornell University Press, 1980.

The Supplement of Reading. Ithaca: Cornell University Press, 1990.

Reed, Arden, ed. *Romanticism and Language*. Ithaca: Cornell University Press, 1984.

Reed, Joel. "Restoration and Repression: The Language Projects of the Royal Society." *Studies in Eighteenth-Century Culture* 19 (1989): 399–411.

Reed, Thomas A. "Keats and the Gregarious Advance of Intellect in *Hyperion*." *ELH* 55 (1988): 195–232.

Reedy, Gerard. "Mystical Politics: The Imagery of Charles II's Coronation." Korshin 19–41.

Reiman, Donald H. *Shelley's Triumph of Life*. Urbana: University of Illinois Press, 1965.

Reiss, Timothy J. *Discourse of Modernism*. Ithaca: Cornell University Press, 1982.

Reynolds, Graham. *Turner*. London: Thames and Hudson, 1969.

Reynolds, Joshua. *Discourses on Art*. Ed. Robert Wark. New Haven: Yale University Press, 1975.

Rhymer, Thomas. "Preface of the Translation." Spingarn 163–81.

Richter, Jean Paul. *Vorschule der Aesthetik*. Munich: C. Hauser, 1963.

Richter, Simon. *Laocoon's Body and the Aesthetics of Pain*. Detroit: Wayne State University Press, 1992.

Ricks, Christopher. *Keats and Embarrassment*. Oxford University Press, 1974.

Milton's Grand Style. New York: Oxford University Press, 1963.

Rickward, Edgell. *Radical Squibs and Royal Ripostes*. London: Adam Dart, 1971.

Ricoeur, Paul. "Image and Language in Psychoanalysis." Vol. III of *Psychiatry and the Humanities*. Ed. Joseph H. Smith. New Haven: Yale University Press, 1978. 293–324.

Rieger, James. "'The Hem of Their Garments': The Bard's Song in *Milton*." Curran and Wittreich 259–80.

Ripa, Cesare. *Iconologia*. Padua: Tozzi, 1618.

Roe, Nicholas, ed. *Keats and History*. Cambridge University Press, 1995.

Rogers, Neville. *Shelley at Work*. 2nd edn. Oxford: Clarendon Press, 1967.

Rogers, Samuel. *Italy, a Poem*. London: T. Cadell, 1838.

Rose, Edward J. "Los, Pilgrim of Eternity." Curran and Wittreich 83–100.

Rosen, Charles, and Henri Zerner. *Romanticism and Realism*. New York: Viking Press, 1984.

Rosmarin, Adena. *The Power of Genre*. Minneapolis: University of Minnesota Press, 1985.

Rubin, James H. "Allegory versus Narrative in Quatremère de Quincy." *Journal of Aesthetics and Art Criticism* 44 (1986): 383–92.

Rumrich, John P. "Uninventing Milton." *Modern Philology* 87 (1990): 249–65.

Ruskin, John. *Modern Painters*. 5 vols. New York: Merrill and Baker, 1897.

Ryals, Clyde de. *Browning's Later Poetry 1871–89*. Ithaca: Cornell University Press, 1975.

Sage, Lorna. "The Pursuit of Imperfection: *Henry and Cato*." Bloom 111–20.

Saisselin, Rémy G. "Ut Pictura Poesis: DuBos to Diderot." *Journal of Aesthetics and Art Criticism* 20 (1961–62): 144–56.

Sallis, John. "Mimesis and the End of Art." In *Intersections*. Ed. Tilottama Rajan and David L. Clark. Albany: State University of New York Press, 1995. 60–78.

Sayce, R. A. *The French Biblical Epic in the Seventeenth Century*. Oxford: Clarendon Press, 1955.

Schama, Simon. *Citizens*. New York: Knopf, 1989.

Schelling, F. W. J. von. *Philosophie der Kunst, Part II*. Vol. v of *Sämtliche Werke*. Stuttgart: J. G. Cottascher Verlag, 1859.

The Philosophy of Art. Trans. and ed. Douglas W. Scott. Minneapolis: University of Minnesota Press, 1989.

Schlegel, Friedrich. *Gespräch über die Poesie*. In *Charakteristiken und Kritiken I*, vol. II of *Kritische Ausgabe*. Ed. Hans Eichner. Munich: Ferdinand Schoningh, 1967.

Schor, Naomi. "Triste Amérique: Atala and the Postrevolutionary Construction of Woman." In *Rebel Daughters: Women and the French Revolution*. Ed. Sara E. Melzer and Leslie W. Rabine. New York: Oxford University Press, 1992. 139–56.

Schulze, Earl. "Allegory against Allegory: 'The Triumph of Life'." *Studies in Romanticism* 27 (1988): 31–62.

Schwartz, Regina. "From Shadowy Types to Shadowy Types: The Unendings of *Paradise Lost*." *Milton Studies* 24 (1988): 123–39.

Scott, Grant F. *The Sculpted Word: Keats, Ekphrasis, and the Visual Arts*. Hanover, N.H.: University Press of New England, 1994.

Scrivener, Michael. *Radical Shelley*. Princeton University Press, 1982.

Seidel, Michael. *Robinson Crusoe: Island Myths and the Novel*. Boston: Twayne, 1991.

Semmel, Bernard. *George Eliot and the Politics of National Inheritance*. Oxford University Press, 1994.

Shaffer, Elinor S. *"Kubla Khan" and the Fall of Jerusalem*. Cambridge University Press, 1975.

Shaftesbury, Lord. *Second Characteristicks, or The Language of Forms*. Ed. Benjamin Rand. 1713 rpt.; Cambridge University Press, 1914.

Shakespeare, William. *Complete Plays*. Ed. W. A. Neilson and C. J. Hill. New York: Houghton Mifflin, 1942.

Shalvi, Alice, ed. *Daniel Deronda*. Jerusalem Academic Press, 1976.

Shapiro, Gary, and Alan Sica, eds. *Hermeneutics: Questions and Prospects*. University of Amherst Press, 1984.

Shaw, W. D. "Browning's Murder Mystery: *The Ring and the Book* and Modern Theory." *Victorian Poetry* 27 (1989): 79–98.

Shelley, Mary. *Frankenstein*. Ed. James Rieger. University of Chicago Press, 1974.

The Last Man. Ed. Hugh J. Luke, Jr. Lincoln: University of Nebraska Press, 1965.

Shelley, Percy B. *The Complete Poetical Works of Percy Bysshe Shelley*. Ed. Thomas Hutchinson. New York: Oxford University Press, 1933.

The Complete Works of Percy Bysshe Shelley. Ed. Roger Ingpen and Walter E. Peck. 10 vols. New York: Charles Scribner's Sons, 1929.

Drafts for Laon and Cythna. Ed. Tatsuo Tokoo. Vol. XIII of *The Bodleian Shelley Manuscripts*. New York: Garland, 1992.

Drafts for Laon and Cythna, Cantos V-VII. Ed. Steven E. Jones. Vol. XVII of *The Bodleian Shelley Manuscripts*. New York: Garland, 1994.

Posthumous Poems of Shelley. Ed. Irving Massey. Montreal: McGill-Queen's University Press, 1969.

The Prometheus Unbound Notebooks. Ed. Neil Fraistat. Vol. IX of *The Bodleian Shelley Manuscripts*. New York: Garland, 1991.

Shelley's Selected Poetry and Prose. Ed. Donald H. Reiman and Sharon B. Powers. New York: W. W. Norton, 1977.

The Triumph of Life. Ed. Donald H. Reiman. Vol. 1 of *The Bodleian Shelley Manuscripts.* New York: Garland, 1986.

Sheridan, Richard. *Plays.* New York: W. W. Norton, 1930.

Sheriff, Mary D. *Fragonard.* University of Chicago Press, 1990.

Sherman, Sandra. "Servants and Semiotics: Reversible Signs, Capital Instability, and Defoe's Logic of the Market." *ELH* 62 (Fall 1995): 551–74.

Shugar, Debora. *Sacred Rhetoric.* Princeton University Press, 1988.

Siebers, Tobin. *The Ethics of Criticism.* Ithaca: Cornell University Press, 1988.

Siegchrist, Mark. *Rough in Brutal Print: The Legal Sources of Browning's Red Cotton Night-Cap Country.* Columbus: Ohio State University Press, 1981.

Simpson, David. *Romanticism, Nationalism, and the Revolt against Theory.* University of Chicago Press, 1993.

Siskin, Clifford. *The Historicity of Romantic Discourse.* New York: Oxford University Press, 1988.

Slemon, Stephen. "Monuments of Empire: Allegory/Counter-Discourse/Post- Colonial Writing." *Kunapipi* 9 (1987): 1–16.

"Post-Colonial Allegory and the Transformation of History." *Journal of Commonwealth Literature* 23 (1988): 157–68.

"Revisioning Allegory: Wilson Harris's *Carnival.*" *Kunapipi* 8 (1987): 45–55.

Slinn, E. Warwick. "Language and Truth in *The Ring and the Book.*" *Victorian Poetry* 27 (1989): 115–33.

Smart, Christopher. *The Poetical Works of Christopher Smart.* Vol II, ed. Marcus Walsh and Karina Williamson; vol. IV, ed. Karen Williamson. Oxford: Clarendon Press, 1983 and 1987.

Smith, Nigel. *Perfection Proclaimed: Language and Literature in English Radical Religion 1640–1660.* Oxford: Clarendon Press, 1989.

Smith, Sheila. "Contemporary Politics and 'The Eternal World' in Turner's *Undine and the Angel Standing in the Sun.*" *Turner Studies* 6 (1986): 40–50.

Solger, Karl. *Erwin. Vier Gespräche über das Schöne und die Kunst.* Ed. Wolfhart Henckmann. Munich: W. Fink, 1971.

Spacks, Patricia. *The Insistence of Horror.* Cambridge, Mass.: Harvard University Press, 1962.

Spector, Sheila A. "*Tiriel* as Spenserian Allegory *Manqué.*" *Philological Quarterly* 71 (1992): 313–35.

Spence, Joseph. *Polymetis.* London: R. Dodsley, 1747.

Spencer, Lloyd. "Allegory in the World of the Commodity: The Importance of 'Central Park'." *New German Critique* 34 (1985): 59–77.

Spencer, T. J. B, ed. *A Book of Masques.* Cambridge University Press, 1967.

Spenser, Edmund. *The Faerie Queene.* London: J. Bindley, 1751.

The Faerie Queene. Ed. Ralph Church. 4 vols. London: William Faden, 1758.

The Faerie Queene. Ed. Thomas P. Roche, Jr. New York: Penguin, 1978.

The Poetical Works of Edmund Spenser. 8 vols. In *Bell's Edition. The Poets of Great Britain.* Edinburgh: Apollo Press, 1778.

Spenser's Faerie Queene. Ed. John Upton. London: J. and R. Tonson, 1758.

The Works of Edmund Spenser. Ed. John Hughes. 6 vols. London: Jacob Tonson, 1715.

The Works of Edmund Spenser. Ed. John Hughes. 6 vols. London: J. and R. Tonson, 1750.

The Works of that Famous English Poet, Mr. Edmund Spenser. London: Henry Hill, 1679.

Spingarn, J. E, ed. *Critical Essays of the Seventeenth Century.* Vol. II. Bloomington: Indiana University Press, 1957.

Spitzer, Leo. "The 'Ode on a Grecian Urn', or Content vs. Metagrammar." In *Essays on English and American Literature.* Princeton University Press, 1962. 67–97.

Sprat, Thomas. *History of the Royal Society.* London: J. Martyn and J. Allestry, 1667.

St. Clair, William L. *Lord Elgin and the Marbles.* London: Oxford University Press, 1967.

Stafford, Barbara. *Body Criticism.* Cambridge, Mass.: MIT Press, 1993.

Stein, Richard. *Victoria's Year.* New York: Oxford University Press, 1987.

Steiner, George. *After Babel.* New York: Oxford University Press, 1975.

Stewart, Garrett. *Reading Voices.* Berkeley: University of California Press, 1990.

Stewart, Susan. *On Longing.* Baltimore: Johns Hopkins University Press, 1984.

Stillinger, Jack. "Who Does What to Whom at the End of 'Ode on a Grecian Urn'?" In *The Hoodwinking of Madeline.* University of Chicago Press, 1971. 167–73.

Stonum, Gary. "Surviving Figures." Shapiro and Sica 199–211.

Stuckey, Charles. "Turner, Masaniello, and the Angel." *Jahrbuch der Berliner Museen* 18 (1976): 155–75.

Swann, Karen. "Harassing the Muse." In *Romanticism and Feminism.* Ed. Anne K. Mellor. Bloomington: Indiana University Press, 1988. 81–92.

Swift, Jonathan. *Gulliver's Travels.* Ed. Peter Dixon and John Chalker. New York: Penguin, 1967.

Tacitus, Cornelius. *The Annals of Tacitus.* Vol. 1. Trans. George G. Ramsey. London: John Murray, 1914.

Tayler, Irene. *Blake's Illustrations to the Poems of Gray.* Princeton University Press, 1971.

Taylor, Anya. "Coleridge on Persons and Things." *European Romantic Review* 1 (1991): 163–80.

Teskey, Gordon. "Allegory." A. C. Hamilton 16–22.

"From Allegory to Dialectic: Imagining Error in Spenser and Milton." *PMLA* 101 (1986): 9–23.

"Irony, Allegory, and Metaphysical Decay." *PMLA* 109 (1994): 397–408.

"Mutability, Genealogy, and the Authority of Forms." *Representations* 41 (1993): 104–22.

Thesaurus Linguae Latinae. 10 vols. Lipsiae: B. G. Teubneri, 1900–58.

Thomson, James. *Castle of Indolence.* In *Poetical Works.* Ed. J. Logie Robertson. London: Oxford University Press, 1908.

Thornbury, Walter. *The Life of J. M. W. Turner, R. A.* 2 vols. London: Hurst and Blackett, 1862.

Tiedemann, Rolf. "Historical Materialism or Political Messianism? An Interpretation of the Theses 'On the Concept of History'." *Philosophical Forum* 15 (1983–84): 71–104.

Titzmann, Michael. "Allegorie und Symbol im Denksystem der Goethe-zeit." Haug 642–65.

Todorov, Tzvetan. *Theories of the Symbol.* Trans. Catherine Porter. Ithaca: Cornell University Press, 1982.

Tomlinson, Janis A. "Landscape into Allegory: J. M. W. Turner's *Frosty Morning* and James Thomson's *The Seasons.*" *Studies in Romanticism* 29 (1990): 181–96.

Trickett, Rachel. "The Augustan Pantheon: Mythology and Personification in Eighteenth-Century Poetry." *Essays and Studies* n.s. 6 (1953): 71–86.

Trilling, Lionel. "Why We Read Jane Austen." *TLS* (March 5, 1976): 252.

Tucker, Herbert C. *Browning's Beginnings.* Minneapolis: University of Minnesota Press, 1980.

"The Dramatic Monologue and the Overhearing of Lyric." In *Lyric Poetry: Beyond New Criticism.* Ed. Chaviva Hošek and Patricia Parker. Ithaca: Cornell University Press, 1985. 226–43.

"Epiphany and Browning: Character Made Manifest." *PMLA* 107 (1992): 1208–21.

"Memorabilia: Mnemonic Imagination in Shelley and Browning." *Studies in Romanticism* 19 (1980): 285–325.

Tuve, Rosamond. *Allegorical Imagery.* Princeton University Press, 1966.

Tyndale, William. *The Obedience of a Christian Man.* 1528 rpt.; Amsterdam, Theatrum Orbis Terrarum, 1977.

Ulmer, Gregory L. "The Object of Post-Criticism." Foster 83–110.

Ulmer, William A. *Shelleyan Eros.* Princeton University Press, 1990.

Venning, Barry. "Turner's Annotated Books: Opie's *Lectures on Painting* and Shee's *Elements of Art* (III)." *Turner Studies* 3 (1983): 33–44.

Vickers, Brian. "The Royal Society and English Prose Style: A Reassessment." In *Rhetoric and the Pursuit of Truth.* Los Angeles: William Andrews Clark Library, 1985. 3–76.

Viscomi, Joseph. *Blake and the Idea of the Book.* Princeton University Press, 1993.

Walker, Stephen C. "The Dynamic Imagery of *The Ring and the Book*." *Studies in Browning and His Circle* 4 (1986): 7–29.

Wallace, Marcia Briggs. "J. M. W. Turner's Circular, Octagonal, and Square Paintings 1840–1846." *Arts Magazine* 55 (April 1979): 107–17.

Wasserman, Earl. *Shelley: A Critical Reading*. Baltimore: Johns Hopkins University Press, 1971.

The Subtler Language. Baltimore: Johns Hopkins University Press, 1959.

Watkins, Daniel. "Historical Amnesia and Patriarchal Morality in Keats's *Ode on a Grecian Urn*." In *Spirits of Fire*. Ed. G. A. Rosso and Daniel Watkins. London: Associated University Press, 1990. 240–59.

Watkins, W. B. C. *An Anatomy of Milton's Verse*. Baton Rouge: Louisiana State University Press, 1955.

Weber, Samuel. "Walter Benjamin's Romantic Concept of Criticism." Johnston 302–19.

Webster, T. B. L. "Personification as a Mode of Greek Thought." *Journal of the Warburg and Courtauld Institute* 17 (1954): 10–21.

Weinbrot, Howard D. *Britannia's Issue*. Cambridge University Press, 1993.

Weiskel, Thomas. *The Romantic Sublime*. Baltimore: Johns Hopkins University Press, 1976.

Wellbery, David. *Lessing's Laocoon: Semiotics and Aesthetics in the Age of Reason*. Cambridge University Press, 1984.

Whately, Richard. *Elements of Rhetoric*. London: John W. Parker, 1846.

Wheeler, Kathleen, ed. *German Aesthetic and Literary Criticism: The Romantic Ironists and Goethe*. Cambridge University Press, 1984.

White, Hayden. *Metahistory*. Baltimore: Johns Hopkins University Press, 1973.

Whitley, William T. *Art in England*. Vol. ii. New York: Hacker Art Books, 1973.

Whitman, Jon. *Allegory: The Dynamics of an Ancient and Medieval Technique*. Cambridge, Mass.: Harvard University Press, 1987.

Wilding, Michael. "Milton's *Areopagitica*: Liberty for the Sects." *Prose Studies* 9 (1986): 7–38.

Wilkinson, Gerald. *Turner on Landscape: Liber Studiorum*. London: Barrie and Jenkins, 1982.

Williams, Helen Maria. *Letters Written in France, in the Summer of 1790*. Vol. i of *Letters from France*. Ed. Janet Todd. 1796 rpt.; Delmar, N.Y.: Scholars' Facsimiles, 1975.

Williams, William Carlos. *Paterson*. Ed. Christopher MacGowan. Rev. edn. New York: New Directions, 1992.

Williamson, George. *Seventeenth-Century Contexts*. Rev. edn. University of Chicago Press, 1969.

Wilton, Andrew. *J. M. W. Turner: His Life and Art*. New York: Rizzoli, 1979.

Turner in the British Museum: Drawings and Watercolours. London: Trustees of the British Museum, 1975.

Turner in Switzerland. Zurich: De Clivo Press, 1976.

William Pars: Journey through the Alps. Zurich: De Clivo Press, 1979.

Wimsatt, James I. *Allegory and Mirror.* New York: Pegasus, 1970.

Wofford, Susanne L. "Britomart's Petrarchan Lament: Allegory and Narrative in *The Faerie Queene* III, iv." *Comparative Literature* 39 (1987): 28–57.

"Gendering Allegory: Spenser's Bold Reader and the Emergence of Character in *The Faerie Queene* III." *Criticism* 30 (1988): 1–21.

Wolfson, Susan. " 'Comparing Power': Coleridge and Simile." In *Coleridge's Theory of Imagination Today.* Ed. Christine Gallant. New York: AMS Press, 1989. 167–95.

"Feminizing Keats." In *Critical Essays on John Keats.* Ed. Hermione de Almeida. Boston: G. K. Hall and Co., 1990. 317–56.

The Questioning Presence. Ithaca: Cornell University Press, 1986.

" 'Something must be done': The Dilemma of Feminine Violence in Shelley and Hemans." Paper presented at Modern Language Association Convention. San Diego, California, 1994.

Wolin, Richard. *Walter Benjamin: An Aesthetic of Redemption.* New York: Columbia University Press, 1982.

Wollstonecraft, Mary. *A Vindication of the Rights of Woman.* Ed. Carol H. Poston. 2nd edn. New York: Norton, 1975.

Wood, James. "Bewitchment." *London Review of Books* 16:3 (December 8, 1994): 20– 21.

Woodman, Ross. "Metaphor and Allegory in *Prometheus Unbound.*" Blank 166–83.

Woodring, Carl. "Road Building: Turner's *Hannibal.*" *Studies in Romanticism* 30 (1991): 19–36.

Woolford, John. *Browning the Revisionary.* London: Macmillan, 1988.

Worden, Blair. "Despairing Radicals." *London Review of Books* 14 (June 25, 1993): 16–17.

Wordsworth, Dorothy. *Journals.* Ed. Mary Moorman. 2 vols. 1941 rpt.; Hampden, Conn.: Archon, 1970.

Wordsworth, William. *Home at Grasmere.* Ed. Beth Darlington. Ithaca: Cornell University Press, 1977.

The Prelude 1799, 1805, 1850. Ed. Jonathan Wordsworth, M. H. Abrams, and Stephen Gill. New York: Norton, 1979.

The Prose Works of William Wordsworth. Ed. W. J. B. Owen and Jane W. Smyser. 3 vols. Oxford: Clarendon Press, 1974.

The Thirteen-Book Prelude. Ed. Mark L. Reed. Ithaca: Cornell University Press, 1991.

Zwicker, Steven N. *Lines of Authority: Politics and English Literary Culture, 1649–1689.* Ithaca: Cornell University Press, 1993.

Index

340

CAMBRIDGE STUDIES IN ROMANTICISM

GENERAL EDITORS
MARILYN BUTLER, *University of Oxford*
JAMES CHANDLER, *University of Chicago*